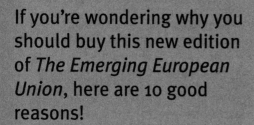

If you're wondering why you should buy this new edition of *The Emerging European Union*, here are 10 good reasons!

1. A new chapter on **public opinion** provides the most up-to-date data on the perspectives of Europeans throughout the union.

2. This text covers the **eastern enlargement** of the European Union with information on new member countries like Romania and Bulgaria, as well as accession talks with Turkey and Croatia.

3. The authors explore the **Treaty of Lisbon** and the effects it will have on institutions and citizen participation in the European Union.

4. Especially in today's world, understanding **economic systems** is important. This book gives you the latest European Union budget and analyzes the allocation of its resources.

5. In addition to giving you insight into the global economy, this European Union with countries like India and China.

6. Critical thinking questions added at the end of each chapter will help you **apply different theoretical perspectives** on what you have read about the European Union.

7. This book addresses the current state of **transatlantic relations** and considers the war on terrorism and the war in Iraq.

8. The authors frame the book as a study of the European Union as an experiment; their introductory, concluding, and end-of-chapter questions will help you understand the current state of the experiment.

9. The authors provide ample **current examples to highlight key developments** and include figures and tables with the latest data.

10. This book also includes expanded discussion of the European Union's **environmental policies** to address greenhouse gas emissions and the Kyoto target.

PEARSON

Europe

© European Communities, 1995–2009

Source: http://europa.eu/abc/european_countries/index_en.htm or http://europa.eu/abc/maps/print_index_en.htm

FIFTH EDITION

The Emerging European Union

Birol A. Yeşilada
Portland State University

David M. Wood
University of Missouri–Columbia

Longman
Boston   Columbus   Indianapolis   New York   San Francisco
Upper Saddle River   Amsterdam   Cape Town   Dubai   London
Madrid   Milan   Munich   Paris   Montreal   Toronto   Delhi   Mexico City
Sao Paulo   Sydney   Hong Kong   Seoul   Singapore   Taipei   Tokyo

For Susan and Mary

Acquisitions Editor: Vikram Mukhija
Editorial Assistant: Toni Magyar
Marketing Manager: Lindsey Prudhomme
Production Manager: Kathy Sleys
Creative Director: Jayne Conte
Cover Designer: Bruce Kenselaar
Cover Art: Gregor Schuster/Photographer's Choice/Getty Images

Full-Service Project Management:
 Sadagoban Balaji/
 Integra Software Services
Composition: Integra Software Services
Printer/Binder/Cover Printer:
 R. R. Donnelley & Sons
Text Font: Times

Map facing title page adapted from (http://europa.eu/abc/european_countries/index_en.htm or http://europa.eu/abc/maps/print_index_en.htm). Copyright of the map is owned by the European Communities, 1995–2009 but reproduction is authorized.

Library of Congress Cataloging-in-Publication Data
Yesilada, Birol A.
 Emerging European union/Birol A. Yesilada, David M. Wood.—5th ed.
 p. cm.
Wood's name appears first on earlier editions.
Includes bibliographical references and index.
ISBN-13: 978-0-205-72380-5 (alk. paper)
ISBN-10: 0-205-72380-2 (alk. paper)
1. European Union. 2. European federation. 3. European Union countries—Economic policy.
 4. European Union countries—Foreign relations.
I. Wood, David Michael, 1934- II. Title.
JN30.W66 2010
341.242'2—dc22
                                                                    2009008685

10 9 8 7 6 5 4 3 2

Longman
is an imprint of

www.pearsonhighered.com

ISBN-13: 978-0-205-72380-5
ISBN-10: 0-205-72380-2

Brief Contents

Contents

Preface

When we look at world events, it is quite evident that the European Union (EU) plans to become an influential and powerful global actor. From the Maastricht Treaty to the Lisbon Treaty, the EU's recent enlargement and the further deepening of integration among member states underline this goal. Yet, the road ahead is not an easy one. The decision of the EU to expand its membership to the Central and East European countries represents the largest and perhaps the most difficult expansion proposal in the EU's history. The implications of this enlargement are significant for the EU in terms of political, economic, and security interests and for the future stability of Europe. As the EU positions itself to become a global actor in the international sphere, its leaders and citizens contemplate future enlargement and the implications of such enlargement, for example, the inclusion of Croatia, Macedonia, Serbia, and Turkey. Recent developments in France and the Netherlands where voters rejected the proposed EU constitution cast doubt over further deepening of economic and political integration. Is this a sign of a growing gap between EU's political elites and citizens? Eurobarometer surveys suggest that there might be some truth behind this gap and that it might affect future plans of European leaders. However, a series of reports from the Commission (Agenda 2000) and the signing of the Lisbon Treaty in December 2007 suggest that the EU leaders are quite determined to push forward with further deepening of regional economic and political integration among member states. Without further integration, the EU will not attain the full benefits of economic and monetary union (EMU), nor will it maximize improvement of quality of life for its citizens. Enlargement, on the other hand, assures peace and stability in volatile areas of Europe and paves the road ahead for better understanding between peoples of member states. Together, this dual goal of European leaders aims at making the EU a powerful and influential global actor on the world scene. So, the future of the EU promises to be as lively and exiting to EU watchers as it has been for the last five decades.

We first began to look at European integration in 1988 when very few academics or policymakers in the United States were paying attention to events across the Atlantic. The economic crisis of the 1970s and the slowing down of regional integration in the European Community (EC) had dramatically reduced academic interest in this topic. Ernst Haas's *The Obsolescence of Regional Integration Theories* was a good example of the state of affairs in the field of European integration. At that time, most pioneers of EC integration had given up hope for future of the Community as a world economic crisis took its toll on everyone concerned. One after another, member states' governments opted for nationally secure policies in dealing with economic recession at the expense of what might have been necessary to hold EC together. The failure of the snake-in-a-tunnel regional monetary policy is perhaps the best example of this state of affairs. Yet, there were a few scholars like Ronald Inglehart and Roy Pierce who kept probing and looking for answers to this sudden surge of integration that got jump-started with the Single European Act and Project 1992. Initially, we were not among these few EC followers—at least, not until we got together following my 11-month research leave in Europe in 1987. During that time, I witnessed events that made me a total believer in the future of the European experiment. One of these events was a conference in Istanbul where academics and officials from the EC, NATO, and European states discussed the future of Europe. I could not help but notice that "Europe" meant different things to different people. When NATO officials talked about it, they referred to the Western Alliance. When EC officials talked about it, they referred to something much bigger. When academics talked about it, they fell somewhere in between. As I continued my research, I began to realize that something was indeed becoming a reality in the form of a new economic and political power in Europe that would shape the future of global power transition.

When I returned to the University of Missouri at Columbia, I got together with David Wood and proposed that we should combine our knowledge of the comparative politics of Western Europe and international political economy to examine the EC and consider its implications for the United States and global economies. One of our early papers addressed how one might approach teaching the EU holistically rather than including it as the last unit in a course on Western European politics. Soon afterwards, the first edition of *The Emerging European Union* came out in 1996 and attempted to address how and why this modest experiment of regional economic cooperation in energy policy in Western Europe evolved into a giant experiment that captured most of Europe and brought peace and prosperity to its citizens. The title captures the evolutionary process of this European experiment and remains appropriate. Even though the EU became a legal entity in 1992, it still represents a dynamic process of economic and political integration that shapes social and political values of its citizens. It is by no means complete, as exemplified by the ongoing reforms of its institutional governance, economic and monetary union, and enlargement.

FEATURES

The Emerging European Union is designed for use in numerous courses where the EU is a subject of interest, including comparative European politics, international political economy, and international organizations. For comparative European politics courses, the book draws the attention of students to how membership in the EU and its predecessor, the EC, has affected and has been affected by the domestic politics of the member countries. For international political economy courses, the book treats the EU as the product of fundamental systemic and regional changes that had profound impact on member states. For international organizations courses, the EU serves as the unique case of a regional organization that has moved beyond the strictly intergovernmental format of the typical international organization. In every chapter of the book, we examine the ways in which the EU has pushed the concept of an international organization to the limit by combining intergovernmental and supranational features.

The book is organized to give the students a comprehensive understanding of this European experiment, its aspirations and goals, historical evolution, and policies that have shaped the lives of its citizens. However, we do not want to simply present a mere historical overview and policy description of the EU experience. That approach would not give students an understanding of how and why the EU has been so successful in getting to where it is today while other experiments of integration in other parts of the world have been less fortunate in their efforts. Therefore, we start this book with a comprehensive overview of regional integration theories that range from the early paradigms of functionalism and neofuntionalism to more recent models of interdependence, liberal intergovernmentalism, historical institutionalism, and constructivism. In the subsequent chapters, we provide relevant study questions that enable students to address topics covered from different theoretical perspectives. The theoretical overview is followed by three chapters that provide a historical development of the EU from the Schumann Plan to Lisbon Treaty. In each chapter, we highlight how political developments at the state, regional, and international systemic levels interacted and shaped the EU process. Furthermore, we explain how individual leaders like Robert Schumann, Charles de Gaulle, Helmut Schmidt, Giscard d'Estaing, Margaret Thatcher, and Jacques Delors shaped the future of the EU. Chapter 6 focuses on EU enlargement—past and future. It includes an analysis of how different future enlargement scenarios are likely to affect EU's position as a global actor as the world undergoes a new power transition, with China overtaking the United States as the world's largest economy in mid-twenty-first century. In contrast, the relative share of the EU in world economy is declining and will continue to slide until large countries like Turkey and Ukraine become EU's members. However, as we show in our analysis of public opinion and preferences of important political leaders of some member states, this is not a forgone conclusion. Chapter 7 follows with a comprehensive study of EU's institutions and decision-making processes. It also explains how the EU public is taking shape and influencing European policies. Special attention is given to how these institutions will change when the Lisbon Treaty takes effect. This is followed by a new addition, Chapter 8, on electoral politics and public opinion in the EU.

The remaining chapters, Chapters 9–13, provide a detailed overview and analysis of EU's domestic and external policies with special attention to how EU agenda changed as the Union moved from a simple intergovernmental organization to a complex economic and political union. Most of these policies fall within Pillar I (the EC pillar) of the EU. Chapter 9 is a comprehensive analysis of how EMU became a reality. Yet, students who may not have a prior exposure to monetary literature will find the discussion quite easy to follow. Chapter 10 introduces the politics of the EU budget, allocation of funds for Common Agricultural Policy (CAP), and various cohesion policies. Historical overview familiarizes students to these issues while discussion of current challenges and policy alternatives provides complexities of policy-making in the EU. Chapter 11 follows with EU's external economic relations with emphasis on how the Union acts with one voice rather than many of its member states. It includes analysis of EU's trade and investment relations with the United States, China, India, Japan, EFTA, Mediterranean neighbors, and former European colonies. Chapter 12 shifts focus to EU's second pillar of Common Foreign and Security Policy. It explains how policies in this area are the most intergovernmental in nature compared to supranational policies of Pillar I. It includes evolution of EU's security and defense institutions and policies and their implementation in different geographical areas during the last two decades. The final policy chapter (Chapter 13) analyzes Justice and Home Affairs policies of Pillar III. In this chapter, we introduce students to the fundamentals of EU law, citizenship issues, challenges of common asylum and immigration policies, border controls, and cooperation in judicial and police matters between EU institutions and member states.

NEW TO THIS EDITION

Substantial revisions in the fifth edition include recent theoretical advances in the study of EU institutions, the rejection of the proposed constitution by Dutch and French citizens and the subsequent signing of the Lisbon Treaty and its ratification pains, eastern enlargement and its implications, future enlargement of the EU and global power transition, electoral politics and public opinion in the EU, the state of transatlantic relations following the war on terrorism and Iraq, and thorough discussion of major developments in the growing policy agenda of the EU that include evolution of EU Law. In each chapter, we provide ample current examples to highlight key developments, and include figures and tables representing the latest data. We have also included study questions at the end of each chapter to challenge students to link theory and substance by analyzing developments from different theoretical perspectives of regional integration.

Specifically, Chapter 5 now includes discussion of the Lisbon Treaty and how it is likely to affect the future of the Union. Chapter 6 includes new material on accession talks with Croatia and Turkey, as well as future prospects for talks with Macedonia. We also assess how eastern enlargement affected the EU's domestic and external policies. Finally, a new section on public opinion draws on Eurobarometer data to show the degree of support among EU citizens for future EU expansion. In Chapter 7, new materials include how the Lisbon Treaty reforms EU's institutional arrangement in areas such as qualified majority voting, seats in the European Parliament, reform of the Commission, the Court of Justice, and other issues pertaining to citizens' role in governance.

Chapter 8 is a new addition to the book as we became aware of the quite vast differences among citizens of member states in their familiarity with and expectations from the EU. We believe that public opinion is often ignored in textbooks on the EU, and given growing citizen interest in European affairs, it is imperative that this topic be given proper attention. We use data from the Eurobarometer to formulate charts and figures to show citizens' concerns about being heard in the EU decision making, what citizens appreciate about the EU, their perceptions on benefits of EU membership, their trust in EU institutions versus their trust in national institutions and governments, and their expectations form the EU.

We have made extensive revisions to the policy chapters to include latest developments in each area. Chapter 9 on the EMU includes new discussion on the euro as a global reserve currency and its implications for the U.S. dollar. We also address the future of EMU as member states ponder their future place in the Eurozone. Chapter 10 includes the new budget of the EU, allocation of resources between CAP and various cohesion policies, and political competition between members for these funds. We expanded our discussion of the EU's environmental policies to address greenhouse gas emissions and the Kyoto target. In Chapter 11, we added new discussion on EU's external economic relations with China and India. We also added new materials on trade conflict between the EU and the United States. Chapter 12 not only updates developments in the European Security and Defense Policy but also includes new material on areas where the EU is tested for common security policy in the Balkans, Afghanistan, and Iraq. Chapter 13 includes new material on EU law and expanded analysis of the Schengen area.

Finally, the conclusion reevaluates original questions set in the introduction to provide an overview of what a complex experiment EU has been for Europeans. With this overview and study questions at the end of each chapter, students might be better equipped to answer whether or not the EU is indeed *sui generis*.

SUPPLEMENTS

Longman is pleased to offer several resources to qualified adopters of *The Emerging European Union* and their students who will make teaching and learning from this book even more effective and enjoyable.

MyPoliSciKit Video Case Studies Featuring video from major news sources and providing reporting and insight on recent world affairs, this DVD series helps instructors integrate current events into their courses by letting them use the clips as lecture launchers or discussion starters.

Longman Atlas of World Issues (0-321-22465-5) Introduced and selected by Robert J. Art of Brandeis University and excerpted from the acclaimed Penguin Atlas Series, the *Longman Atlas of World Issues* is designed to help students understand the geography and major issues facing the world today, such as terrorism, debt, and HIV/AIDS. These thematic, full-color maps examine forces shaping politics today at a global level. Explanatory information accompanies each map to help students better grasp the concepts being shown and how they affect our world today. Available at no additional charge when packaged with this book.

New Signet World Atlas (0-451-19732-1) From Penguin Putnam, this pocket-sized yet detailed reference features 96 pages of full-color maps plus statistics, key data, and much more. Available at a discount when packaged with this book.

Careers in Political Science (0-321-11337-3) Offering insider advice and practical tips on how to make the most of a political science degree, this booklet by Joel Clark of George Mason University shows students the tremendous potential such a degree offers and guides them through deciding whether political science is right for them; the different career options available; job requirements and skill sets; how to apply for interview and compete for jobs after graduation; and much more. Available at a discount when packaged with this book.

ACKNOWLEDGMENTS

We would like to thank the following individuals who reviewed the current and previous editions of the manuscript and provided helpful suggestions:

Philip P. Baumann, Moorhead State University
Laura Brunell, Gonzaga University
Britt Cartrite, University of Pennsylvania
Patrick Conge, University of Arkansas
Louise K. Davidson-Schmich, University of Miami
Desmond Dinan, George Mason University
William M. Downs, Georgia State University
Robert Evans, Bologna Center, Johns Hopkins University
Richard B. Finnegan, Stonehill College
Gary P. Freeman, University of Texas
Norman Furniss, Indiana University
Arthur B. Gunlicks, University of Richmond
Louis D. Hayes, University of Montana
Gunther Hega, Western Michigan University
James F. Hollifield, Southern Methodist University
Juan Fernandez Iglesias, Winona State University
Steven Lewis, University of Wisconsin
Peter Loedel, West Chester University
Anthony M. Messina, Tufts University
Anthony Mughan, Ohio State University
Jorgen Rasmussen, Iowa State University
Leonard Ray, Louisiana State University
Martin Slann, Clemson University
Konstantin Vossing, Ohio State University
Guy Whitten, Texas A&M University
David S. Wilson, University of Toledo
Stephen Wright, Northern Arizona University

BIROL A. YEŞILADA
DAVID M. WOOD

Abbreviations

ACP	African, Caribbean, and Pacific countries (Lomé states)
ACP–EC PA	ACP–EC Partnership Agreement
AMS	Aggregate measure of support
ASEAN	Association of South East Asian Nations
Benelux	Belgium, the Netherlands, and Luxembourg Customs
BSE	Bovine spongiform encephalopathy
CAP	Common Agricultural Policy
CCP	Common Commercial Policy
CDU/CSU	Christian Democrats (Germany)
CEDEFOP	European Center for the Development of Vocational Training
CEEC	Central and Eastern European Countries
CFSP	Common Foreign and Security Policy
CMO	Common Market Organization
COR	Committee of the Regions
COREPER	Committee of Permanent Representatives
CSCE	Conference on Security and Cooperation in Europe
CU	Customs Union
DG	Directorate General
DGXIV	Directorate General XIV of the European Commission
DM	Deutsche mark (Germany)
EAGGF	European Agricultural Guidance and Guarantee Fund
EAP	Environmental Action Program
EBRD	European Bank for Reconstruction and Development
EC	European Community
ECB	European Central Bank
ECJ	European Court of Justice
ECOFIN	Council of Economic and Finance Ministers
ECSC	European Coal and Steel Community
ecu	European currency unit
EDC	European Defense Community
EDF	European Development Fund
EEA	European Economic Area
EEAS	European External Action Service
EEC	European Economic Community
EES	European Economic Space
EFTA	European Free Trade Association
EIB	European Investment Bank
ELDR	European Liberal Democrats and Republicans (EP group)
EMI	European Monetary Institute
EMS	European Monetary System
EMU	Economic and Monetary Union
EP	European Parliament
EPC	European Political Cooperation
EPP	European People's Party (Christian Democratic EP group)

ERM	Exchange rate mechanism
ERRF	European Rapid Reaction Force
ESC	Economic and Social Committee
ESCB	European System of Central Banks
ESDI	European Security and Defense Identity
ESDP	European Security and Defense Policy
ESF	European Social Fund
ESPRIT	European Strategic Program for Research and Development in Information Technologies
EU	European Union
EUA	European Unit of Account (currency)
Euratom	European Atomic Energy Community
euro	EMU single currency
EUT	European Union Treaty
FDP	Free Democratic Party (Germany)
FIFG	Financial Instrument for Fisheries Guidance
GATT	General Agreement on Tariffs and Trade
GDP	Gross domestic product
GDR	German Democratic Republic (former East Germany)
GMP	Global Mediterranean Policy
GNP	Gross national product
GSP	EU's General System of Preferences
IEPG	Independent European Program Group
IFOR	Multinational military implementation force (in Bosnia-Herzegovina)
IGC	Intergovernmental conference
IGO	Intergovernmental organization
IMF	International Monetary Fund
ISPA	Instrument for Structural Policies for Pre-accession
JHA	Justice and Home Affairs
JRC	Joint Research Center
KFOR	International security forces in Kosovo
KLA	Kosovo Liberation Army
MCA	Mandatory compensatory account
MEDA	Financial instrument for the Euro-Mediterranean partnership
MEP	Member of the European Parliament
MFN	Most favored nation
MITI	Ministry of International Trade and Industry (Japan)
MP	Member of Parliament (Britain)
MRP	Popular Republican Movement (French Christian Democrats)
MTR	Midterm review
NAFTA	North American Free Trade Agreement
NATO	North Atlantic Treaty Organization
NCB	National Central Bank
NMBC	Nonmember (of EU) Mediterranean Basin countries
NTA	New Transatlantic Agenda
OCT	Overseas Countries and Territories
OECD	Organization for Economic Cooperation and Development
OSCE	Organization for Security and Cooperation in Europe
PCF	French Communist Party
PES	European Socialist Party (Socialist EP group)

PHARE	Technical Assistance for Central and Eastern Europe
QMV	Qualified majority voting
R&D	Research and development
RPR	Rally for the Republic (French Neo-Gaullists)
SAPARAD	Special Accession Program for Agricultural and Rural Development
SCVPH	Scientific Committee of Veterinary Measures Relating to Public Health
SDR	Special drawing rights (of the IMF)
SEA	Single European Act
SPD	Social Democratic Party (Germany)
STABEX	Commodity Export Earnings Stabilization Scheme (of Lomé)
SYSMIN	Mineral Accident Insurance System (of Lomé)
TACIS	Technical Assistance in Confederation of Independent States
TEU	Treaty on European Union (Maastricht Treaty)
TRNC	Turkish Republic of Northern Cyprus
TSE	Total support estimate
UDF	Union for French Democracy
UK	United Kingdom
UN	United Nations
UNMIK	United Nations Mission in Kosovo
UNPROFOR	United Nations Peacekeeping Forces in the former Yugoslavia
UNSCR	United Nations Security Council Resolution
USSR	Union of Soviet Socialist Republics
VAT	Value-added tax
VER	Voluntary export restraint
WEAG	Western European Armaments Group
WEU	Western European Union
WTO	World Trade Organization

About the Authors

Birol A. Yeşilada is professor of Political Science and International Studies and holder of the Contemporary Turkish Studies Chair at Portland State University. He received his doctorate from the University of Michigan in 1984. Among his publications are one edited book, *Comparative Political Parties and Party Elites: Essays in Honor of Samuel J. Eldersveld*; two coedited books, *The Political and Socioeconomic Transformation of Turkey* and *Agrarian Reform in Reverse: The Food Crisis in the Third World*; and articles and chapters in scholarly journals and research books. He specializes in the EU policies of integration and enlargement, power transition theory, international political economy, decision making and conflict resolution, and Turkish politics.

David M. Wood is professor emeritus of Political Science at the University of Missouri–Columbia. He received his doctorate from the University of Illinois in 1960. Among his publications are two coauthored books, *Comparing Political Systems: Power and Politics in Three Worlds*, Fourth Edition, and *Back from Westminster: British Members of Parliament and Their Constituents*; and numerous articles in scholarly journals. He specializes in the study of European political systems, including the EU, and comparative legislative behavior.

Chapter 1

Introduction

The subject of this book is the European Union (EU), which came into being in 1993, when the Maastricht Treaty (Treaty on European Union) went into effect. Each significant development in the evolution of the EU has involved the pooling of some governmental functions and powers by the Western European member states. During the 1950s, three regional European organizations were formed: the European Coal and Steel Community (ECSC), the European Economic Community (EEC), and the European Atomic Energy Community (Euratom). Initially, six states were involved in the formation of these organizations: Belgium, France, Italy, Luxembourg, the Netherlands, and West Germany (the German Federal Republic). Today there are 27 members, 10 of whom became members together in May 2004 and another two joined the Union in January 2007. The members are listed alphabetically in Table 1.1.

In this introductory chapter, we provide a brief overview of the EU from two points of view: (1) how the EU governing institutions collectively make policies designed to be implemented by the 27 member states and (2) how the domestic politics of the member states are related to the politics of the EU.

THE FRAMEWORK OF THE EUROPEAN UNION

The EU has emerged as something more than an organization of regional economic cooperation. It is both an Economic and Monetary Union (EMU) and a political union. EMU has opened the way for common fiscal and monetary policies jointly developed by and for all member states. A common central banking system, akin to the U.S. Federal Reserve System, now exists for member states, and on January 1, 1999, 11 of the then 15 EU members adopted the euro as their common currency, replacing the separate currencies of those states. Coins and bills in euro denominations were introduced into circulation at the beginning of 2002. At the time EMU came into being, three of the 15 member states—Britain, Denmark, and Sweden—did not join it, while Greece, one of the newest members at the time, joined at the beginning of 2001, after satisfying the economic criteria for membership. So far, the 10 newest members of the EU remain outside EMU, while their economic policies reflect varying degrees of progress toward fulfilling the criteria for EMU membership.

The meaning of political union is a combination of what the EU is at present after approximately 50 years of evolution and the aspirations for future political integration leading

Table 1.1 ■ EU Member Countries

Country	Year Joined	Country	Year Joined
Austria	1995	Latvia	2004
Belgium	1958	Lithuania	2004
Bulgaria	2007	Luxembourg	1958
Cyprus	2004	Malta	2004
Czech Republic	2004	Netherlands	1958
Denmark	1973	Poland	2004
Estonia	2004	Portugal	1986
Finland	1995	Romania	2007
France	1958	Slovakia	2004
Germany	1958	Slovenia	2004
Greece	1981	Spain	1986
Hungary	2004	Sweden	1995
Ireland	1973	United Kingdom	1973
Italy	1958		

to the creation of a European federated state. Currently, political union takes the form of specific institutions that are either intergovernmental or supranational in character. This distinction is similar to that between a confederation and a federation. A *confederation* makes decisions through a process of intergovernmental bargaining, whereas a *federation* has decision-making bodies that are independent of the member states. For example, one of the legislative bodies of the EU is the Council of Ministers, which consists of ministers of the governments of the 27 EU countries. But the other legislative body, the European Parliament, consists of members elected by the voters in the member states in much the same way as the U.S. Congress is elected. The Council of Ministers is an intergovernmental body, whereas the Parliament is a supranational one. Decision making is a balancing act in the EU, which operates sometimes as a confederation and sometimes as a federation. Supranational bodies can act independently of individual national governments, but their acts can be overridden by intergovernmental bodies, which generally have the upper hand. However, overriding supranational decisions is not necessarily easy and, even if accomplished, may give rise to new supranational decisions with intended effects similar to those earlier rejected.

Intergovernmental bodies bring together political leaders or delegates of the 27 member governments. The principal intergovernmental body is the *Council of Ministers*: a group of 27 ministers who meet to adopt policy measures applicable to all member states. At its apex is the *European Council*, which consists of heads of state and government. This body meets four times a year to make the EU's most important decisions, setting the agenda for other legislative bodies to implement. When new institutional arrangements, the admission of new members, or major departures in EU policy are under consideration, the European Council will find the unanimous consensus to give direction to the Council of Ministers, or the new steps will not be taken. Leadership of the Council of Ministers (called the presidency) is rotated from member to member every six months. While the presidency has some agenda-setting powers, decisions are made by the Council as a collective body. Intergovernmental conferences are held from time to time, functioning somewhat like constitutional conventions to consider revisions to the treaties on which the EU is based. Intergovernmental conferences preceded the four major revisions of the Rome Treaty, in 1985, 1991, 1996–1997, and 2000. Then, in 2003, such a body—drawn more broadly from portions of all EU members' polities, not only from the governments—wrote a "constitutional treaty," which required ratification by all 25 members before it could take effect. In fact, rejection in 2005 by voters in two of the original member states, France and the Netherlands, was enough to bury the treaty and its innovations, at least temporarily, only to be revised under a new document called the Lisbon Treaty in December 2007. (See Chapter 5.)

Supranational bodies bring together nationals of the member states that are not accountable to their governments, but deliberate in the name of the European citizenry as a whole. The principal supranational institutions follow the threefold separation of powers familiar to students of U.S. government. The European *Commission* is the executive body. It consists of 27 commissioners, one of whom is separately chosen the president by agreement among the 27 member governments, while the other 26 are chosen individually by governments of each of the other 26 countries and then formally chosen by the Council of Ministers. The separately chosen president assigns responsibilities to the other commissioners. The European Parliament can reject the proposed Commission as a whole, but cannot stop the appointment of individual commissioners.

The other two supranational bodies are the *European Parliament* (EP) and the *European Court of Justice* (ECJ). The 732 members of the EP are directly elected by voters in "Euro elections" every five years. The formal powers of the EP have been growing since the 1970s, but it still shares its legislative power with the Council of Ministers. The ECJ has 27 judges, who, like the commissioners, are nominated by their member governments and formally chosen by the Council of Ministers. The ECJ interprets the treaties of the European Union and has established its authority to declare actions of EU bodies and member states to be in violation of EU law. Its power is akin to the judicial review exercised by the U.S. Supreme Court.

While the European Council and the Council of Ministers act as 27-member intergovernmental bodies that try to find common ground among all member states before making decisions, in the 1980s and 1990s the practice grew, with the encouragement of three treaty revisions, to decide matters in the Council of Ministers by *qualified majority vote* (QMV).[1] Historically, as QMV advanced, the sovereign independence of the member states, especially the smaller ones, receded, making the EU increasingly, but not exclusively, a supranational arrangement of institutions. The Commission, the ECJ, and the EP are supranational bodies, but they remain dependent on the intergovernmental bodies to register the consensus among member states necessary to move the EU ahead. Clearly, the member states, individually as well as collectively, are major actors in the EU political process. But some are more "major" than others, and there are important differences between them that are relevant to the ways they act at the European level.

This, then, is a brief outline of the EU's institutional framework. In Chapter 7, we will examine in more depth the respective powers of these institutions and the degree to which they collectively meet the criteria for a democratic system of governance. We will also consider the degree to which the EU is departing from a confederal (i.e., intergovernmental) mode of power sharing and moving toward a federal (i.e., supranational) pooling of sovereignty.

THE MEMBER STATES

Each of the 27 member states (see the list in Table 1.1) encompasses a political system with its own set of laws, governing institutions, political parties, elections, interest groups, and subnational levels of government. Increasingly, developments within the EU have affected these domestic political systems. For example, with the evolution of the European Council as the EU's principal agenda-setting body, the influence of heads of state and government in their own national political systems has grown at the expense of other elected officials. Summit meetings generate a great amount of media attention, and national-level political actors are dependent on the president or prime minister to negotiate effectively with other heads on behalf of the member country's interests. Successful negotiations of European Community (EC) package agreements in the 1980s added to the stature of German Chancellor Helmut Kohl, French President François Mitterrand, and British Prime Minister Margaret Thatcher, all of whom cultivated an image of toughness combined with tactical adroitness in knowing when to make concessions, while retaining the principal advantage. Such image management at the EU level undoubtedly contributed to the exceptional longevity in office of all three of these national leaders. However, as we will see in Chapter 5, the more difficult decisions on the EU agenda in the opening years of the twenty-first century have made it harder for current leaders to elevate their prestige through the bargains struck in high-level intergovernmental negotiations.

In most of the 27 member states, the domestic government operates within a parliamentary, or semi-parliamentary, system. In such a system, the head of government and the ministers (department heads or cabinet) chosen by the head of government are responsible to a majority in the legislative body, or Parliament. If the government in power loses a vote of confidence in Parliament, it means that its members no longer have the support of the majority, and they must resign in order to allow the Parliament to choose a new government. In some parliamentary systems, as in Britain, they may instead call new elections in order to get the support of the electorate for a new Parliament with a favorable majority.

Britain is usually cited as the classic example of a parliamentary system. British voters choose between candidates of political parties in single-member districts. The winner of the most votes (*plurality*) in each district gains a seat in the House of Commons. The leader of the party that gains a majority of House of Commons seats becomes the prime minister. He or she then chooses a cabinet from among the elected members to govern the country with the support of the House of Commons majority. The party that wins the election stays in power until defeated in a subsequent election or in a vote of no confidence.

With some specific differences, the other EU members that have parliamentary systems operate under similar rules. The main distinguishing feature of the British system is that one or the other of its two main parties is strong enough to win a majority in its own right. In this, the main parties are helped by the single-member district plurality electoral system, which encourages voters not to waste their votes on smaller parties, but instead to vote for the candidates of parties with a chance of winning a majority of seats, enabling them to form a government. British voters know that the parties that do not get a majority of the seats in Parliament will be on the outside looking in as far as policy making is concerned. In other European parliamentary systems, coalition governments are usually formed because it is rare for one party to have a majority. In all of the parliamentary EU countries other than Britain, the electoral system is one or another variant of proportional representation, which gives parties a share of seats in parliament roughly proportional to their share of the popular vote. Such electoral systems do not penalize voters for voting for smaller parties, although there are thresholds to keep out very small parties, such as the 5 percent barrier in Germany. Most of the members who joined in 2004 have mixed systems, similar to those of France or others discussed below.

Britain is one of a minority of member countries in which issues relating to the EU have been sufficiently divisive that they can affect political contests at the national level. In Chapters 3–5, we discuss some of the British debates over Europe that have occurred over the past 40 years. From the mid-1950s to the mid-1970s, the fights were over the question of whether or not Britain should join or, later, stay in the EC. Since the late 1980s, debate has centered on the main elements of the Maastricht Treaty of 1992 and the Constitutional Treaty of 2004. Most British politicians prefer that the EU remain essentially an intergovernmental union, and they oppose any further extension of the powers of supranational bodies. EMU has meant a substantial transfer of economic-policy-making capability from the member states to a supranational institution, the European Central Bank (ECB). The Labour government of Tony Blair, when elected in 1997, put off until after the next election the decision on whether Britain would give up the pound for the euro, while most Conservatives strongly opposed British membership in the EMU. Two reelections later (in 2001 and 2005), Blair appeared to be no more interested in joining the EMU than he was in 1997, and it is safe to say that it is no longer on the British agenda.

By contrast, in another parliamentary member country, Germany, EU politics has not produced many serious domestic political divisions. Unlike Britain, Germany has more than two political parties with a reasonable chance of sharing governmental power. Also unlike Britain, it is very rare for one party to have a majority of seats in the Bundestag, the body comparable to the British House of Commons. This is because Germany uses a system of proportional representation in translating votes into seats. There are two large parties, the Christian Democrats (CDU/CSU) on the right and the Social Democrats (SPD) on the left. The smaller Free Democratic Party (FDP) joined the CDU/CSU to form a coalition government under Chancellor Helmut Kohl (the CDU leader) from 1982 to 1998. Then a new coalition of Social Democrats and Greens came to power with Social Democratic leader Gerhard Schröder as chancellor. Issues that distinguish the two coalitions have not included German policy toward the EU. In the federal election of September 2005, Schröder's Social Democrats were defeated by the narrowest of margins, and, after lengthy negotiations, in November 2005, CDU leader Angela Merkel became chancellor of a coalition government of her own party and the SPD. With the possible exception of the issue of Turkey's eventual EU membership, which Merkel has opposed, the two leading parties appear unlikely to be at odds over EU issues.

Among the other member countries with parliamentary systems, Denmark and Sweden have shown the greatest interparty and public disagreement over the question of EU powers. As in Britain, the Maastricht Treaty proved particularly divisive in Denmark; the voters failed to ratify the treaty in a 1992 referendum. But a year later, when the Social Democrats, who had opposed Danish ratification in 1992, were back in power, they supported ratification; the voters were again consulted, and the treaty was ratified. It was uncertain whether voters would ratify Swedish accession to EU membership in 1994, but as in Denmark, when the Social Democrats returned to power shortly before the referendum, they supported Swedish entry, and their voters provided the necessary votes for ratification. However, Denmark, Sweden, and Britain chose to remain outside of the EMU.

Five of the pre-2004 EU member countries—Austria, Finland, France, Ireland, and Portugal—do not have pure parliamentary systems of government, nor are they presidential systems like the United States. They have elements of both presidential and parliamentary systems—what Matthew Shugart and John Carey have called "premier–presidential" systems.[2] All of them have directly elected presidents, like the U.S. president. They also have premiers who, like the British prime minister, rely on the support of majorities in directly elected legislative bodies. In the four smaller premier-presidential countries, the president plays a relatively passive role, allowing executive authority to be wielded by the premier and cabinet. At times of political deadlock, the president is available to step in and resolve conflicts, but parties in Austria, Finland, Ireland, and Portugal prefer to work out their differences in the parliament rather than letting the president play a stronger role. This mixed system prevails as well in four of the ten members who joined in 2004: Poland, Estonia, Lithuania, and the Czech Republic.

The formal institutional arrangements in France are unique among EU members. France has had the mixed premier-presidential form since the formation of the Fifth Republic in 1958. The first president of the Fifth Republic, General Charles de Gaulle (1958–1969), played a strong role in ending the Algerian War, which had brought on the fall of the Fourth Republic; he also took upon himself as president the formulation of French foreign policy, as well as its policy as a member of the original EEC. He determined who would be his prime minister, a practice followed by his successors until the mid-1980s. This meant that the president was ultimately in control of domestic as well as foreign policy. If he allowed his premier to make decisions, they had to be decisions that followed the president's general policy lines. When conflicts occurred between president and premier, the latter would have to yield or be replaced by someone more compliant with the president's wishes.

De Gaulle wanted France to control the development of the EC; otherwise, he would not cooperate with the other member governments.[3] He approved of the economic benefits France gained from membership, but he did not want the EC to infringe on French sovereignty in more politically sensitive areas. After de Gaulle left office in 1969, his successors gradually became more cooperative with EC partners, while continuing to exercise leadership, usually in tandem with Germany. By the mid-1980s, the EC had virtually ceased to be a major issue among French politicians. Public opinion polls showed that the initially skeptical French populace had become comfortable with France's role in the EC.

However, an inherent contradiction within the premier–presidential system surfaced in 1986. Prior to the parliamentary elections in March of that year, the Socialist Party of President François Mitterrand, the leading left-of-center party, had a solid majority in the National Assembly, the popularly elected lower house of Parliament. The election proved to be a serious setback for Mitterrand's Socialists. The two principal opposition right-of-center parties, the Union for French Democracy (UDF) and the Rally for the Republic (RPR), gained a bare majority of seats, enough to make it impossible for Mitterrand to appoint his own person as premier. He was forced to choose the leader of the "neo-Gaullist" RPR, Jacques Chirac, who then formed his own right-of-center government. Mitterrand and Chirac therefore found themselves locked in what was quickly termed "cohabitation," meaning that a president of the left and a premier of the right were required to live together. This happened because the president is elected for a seven-year term, but Parliament's term is only five years, so the elections do not usually coincide. It also happened because the Constitution of the Fifth Republic contains the normal parliamentary provision that a majority of the National Assembly can vote the premier out of office: If the president named one of his own supporters premier, he would be inviting repudiation of his choice by the National Assembly.

Two other cohabitation periods have occurred, one in Mitterrand's second term, when he shared power with Gaullist Edouard Balladur from 1993 to 1995, and the other from 1997 to 2002, when President Jacques Chirac was forced to give up much of his power to Premier Lionel Jospin, a Socialist. During cohabitation periods, the consensus across left and right over European policy matters has prevented deadlocks between president and premier. Both attend meetings of the European Council, but the president has been generally recognized by the other leaders around the table as the legitimate spokesperson for France.

When there is cohabitation in France, presidential powers recede, but when a president is elected along with a parliamentary majority of his supporters, he becomes the preeminent leader. This was true of President Chirac, who took a firmer hold on French foreign and EU policy, as well as domestic policy, after his election in June 2002. His successor, Nicolas Sarkozy, has also pursued a similar position. It has not been the case in Austria, Finland, Ireland, or Portugal. In these countries, the premier is the chief policy maker, but the president's role as a sort of "conscience" of the government is important. In their first 15 years since the collapse of Communism, the members from East Central Europe that entered the EU in 2004 have been trying out their new institutions. In most, mixed presidential and parliamentary features have developed. Strong presidents have been avoided, as prime ministers responsible to parliaments have, in most cases, played the head of government role, successfully making these new polities work.

Only one of the 12 members joining in 2004, Hungary, has a clear-cut parliamentary system of government, and Cyprus is the only new member with a clear-cut presidential system. The other eight have varieties of presidential and premier-presidential systems, although none of them, except perhaps Cyprus, has as strong a president as does France. The rest have power balanced between an elected president with significant policy-making leverage and a parliament that has a voice in the appointment of government members.

This brief discussion of the political institutions of the EU and its member states has been designed to demonstrate that the politics of the EU goes on simultaneously at two levels. What happens on one level has an important effect on the other. But, contrary to the formal definition of a federal system, the transfer of powers from the national level to the institutions of the EU has not meant that the national governments have ceased to be involved in deciding how they will be used.[4]

In Chapter 2, we will review the leading theories of European integration, presenting them in their historical context. Chapters 3, 4, and 5 provide a historical overview of the development of the EU from its origins in the Schuman Plan of 1950 to the failed ratification of the Constitutional Treaty in 2005. Chapter 3 outlines the growing political coordination between the member states in the 25-year period up to the mid-1970s, when the European Council was established, a development that represented a turning point in the process of political integration. Chapter 4 traces the steps leading to the agreement at Maastricht in December 1991, as well as the struggle to ratify the treaty in 1992–1993. Chapter 5 begins with the follow-up Treaty of Amsterdam and the two principal projects that have followed it in the early years of the new century: the Nice Treaty and the ill-fated Constitutional Treaty. Chapter 6 traces the politics of EU enlargement and looks at potential challenges facing the Union in future expansion of membership. Chapter 7 outlines the roles played by the principal agenda-setting and decision-making institutions of the EU: the European Council, the Council of Ministers, the European Commission, the European Parliament, and the European Court of Justice. It also considers the extent to which an EU "public" is taking shape, capable of influencing the course of European integration independent of the wishes of political leaders. Chapter 8 looks at democratic governance and electoral politics in the EU, with special focus on public opinion polls from the Eurobarometer.

Chapter 9 examines the developing macro-level economic policy coordination that took place in the European Monetary System, including the exchange rate mechanism that controlled monetary fluctuations among member country currencies, and that has been strengthened under the EMU with its single currency, the euro.

In Chapter 10, we examine the politics of the EU budget, the Common Agricultural Policy (CAP), and cohesion policies, all of which aim to promote economic and social cohesion by reducing disparities between different regions of the EU. Chapter 11 looks at the EU's external economic relations, with special emphasis on the United States and Japan, the Mediterranean Basin, and the Lomé (African, Caribbean, and Pacific, or ACP) states. We maintain that the policy packages adopted toward these states are crucial to understanding the EU's competition with the United States and other major economies as an emerging world economic power.

Chapter 12 examines Pillar II policies and the EU's attempts to formulate a Common Foreign and Security Policy (CFSP) and assesses how the member states cope with security as borders disappear between them. This is a fundamental challenge for the member states, as CFSP represents a major step beyond European political cooperation (EPC) in merging political and security matters.

In Chapter 13, we introduce policies pertaining to Justice and Home Affairs (JHA) that make up policies of Pillar III. Four areas of citizens' rights and internal security fall under the third pillar: the free movement of persons between member states; citizenship rights across the EU (e.g., equal opportunities, individual political, and civil rights); immigration policy; and judicial and police cooperation.

The overall purpose of the fifth edition is not only to update developments in the EU but to provide answers to important questions of theoretical and policywise importance, such as, what is the EU experiment and where is it going? Is this experiment feasible for other regions? In March 2007, the EU celebrated its 50th birthday with a big fanfare in Berlin and the members renewed their vows to the Union. They highlighted EU's accomplishments in achieving peace and prosperity in Europe as well as advances made in human rights. Yet, these are not the first items that come to the minds of the Europeans when asked about the EU. A Financial Times/ Harris poll found that a majority of the Europeans polled identified the single market and large bureaucracy as the two features they most associated with the 50-year-old project.[5] Despite their negative opinion of Brussels's red tape, most EU citizens showed considerable support for the EU to do more in such policy areas as the environment and climate change, fighting crime, and social policy. Given these results, it is quite obvious that while they may not be ready for further centralization of bureaucratic authority at the EU level, citizens of the EU expect tangible results from policies that directly affect themselves and their milieu. In view of this picture, it is then important to consider this question: *What does the EU mean for its citizens after 51 years?* We will try to provide answers to these questions throughout the book with analysis of events, policies, and outcomes, and examination of public opinion polls.

ENDNOTES

1. Votes of the member states in the Council of Ministers are weighted roughly according to the relative sizes of the members' populations. Passing a motion by qualified majority requires combining slightly more than 71 percent of the weighted votes.

2. Matthew Soberg Shugart and John M. Carey, *Presidents and Assemblies: Constitutional Design and Electoral Dynamics* (Cambridge: Cambridge University Press, 1992), p. 41.

3. Andrew Moravcsik, *The Choice for Europe: Social Purpose and State Power from Messina to Maastricht* (London: UCL Press, 1999), chap. 3.

4. Robert D. Putnam, "Diplomacy and Domestic Politics: The Logic of Two-Level Games," *International Organization* 42 (1988): 427–460; Emil Joseph Kirchner, *Decision-Making in the European Community: The Council Presidency and European Integration* (Manchester, England, and New York: Manchester University Press, 1992).

5. George Parker, "EU Citizens Voice Concern at Meddling Eurocrats," *Financial Times*, March 18, 2007.

Theories of European Integration

In this chapter, we review the major theories of regional integration that have been formulated during the half-century since European integration became more than just a gleam in the eyes of European visionaries. However, we do need to give two warnings before we begin. First, theories of international integration, like all political theories, are produced in order to better understand ongoing political events and solve distressing problems that preoccupy political leaders. Thus, they follow the times, and they compete with one another to set the trend. Those theories that get the most attention are "fashionable"; they are not necessarily the ones that will continue to provide inspiration for political thinkers a half-century, or even a decade, later. In this chapter, several theories with varying degrees of staying power will be reviewed. None of them is sufficient to fully understand where the European Union (EU) is today or how it got that way. But we will draw on those that are general enough and strong enough to give us part of the explanation.

Second, political theorists attempt to do three things: explain, predict, and prescribe. All the theories we will discuss in this chapter have done a better job of explaining what has happened than predicting what will happen. If they had been better at predicting, they might have stayed in fashion longer. As for prescribing, it is safe to say that they often prefer outcomes that are the same as those they predict. For example, if the theorist wants to see a European federal state created, then the theory will be constructed so as to show how that outcome will be achieved, both by highlighting recent trends that have already moved Europe in the right direction and by showing how a continuation of those trends will lead to the predicted outcome. In this chapter and the next three, we will concentrate on the explanatory and predictive elements of most of the theories, but there will be hints of the prescribed outcomes as well. We will also compare theory with practice over time.

The chapter has a third purpose, which is to describe briefly the major events in the early years of European integration, roughly from 1950 to 1957.

REALISM AND IDEALISM

Why would a nation-state like France or Germany give up any of its sovereign powers to a regional collectivity? To do so would be to do away with flexibility in dealing with unforeseen problems; it would also make the nation-state subject to collective decisions and actions that might not be in the best interests of its own citizens. Adherents of the *realist school* of international relations insist that the governments of nation-states usually act rationally on behalf of their citizens, carefully weighing the likely consequences of their decisions for the societies they govern. From this perspective, national governments will not generally do things that run counter to the national interest. Hans Morgenthau, the founder of this post–World War II school of international relations, defined national interest as the power that governments must protect in order to achieve their objectives. Nation-states, according to Morgenthau, are the most powerful actors on the international scene.[1]

How do we know that nation-states act rationally? Because they constantly seek to maintain and enhance their power, say the realists. But how do we know that states will always act this way? What if they make mistakes or their leaders get swept up in some "irrational" sentiment, like the urge to help others (altruism) or to find the Holy Grail (idealism)? The realists' answer tends to be that "governments don't do such things." Even though some of their decisions may turn out to have been ill-advised, the leaders have calculated that they are in the nation's best interest—that is, they will enhance the power of the nation-state. Marshall Plan aid after World War II may have looked to some Americans like incredible generosity emanating from Washington, with the flow of benefits going entirely in the direction of Europe. But realists insist that the United States obtained political benefits far in excess of the economic costs and that, in fact, within a decade, the economic benefits to the United States outweighed the original economic costs as well.[2] On the other hand, the series of decisions made in the 1960s as the United States became more embroiled in the Vietnam War was seen at the time by many critics, and later by historians, as being misguided, but they, too, were based on the government leaders' assessments of the "best interests" of the United States. "Realistic" calculations superseded whatever other premises might have prevailed.

The *idealist school* of international relations, more recently labeled *neoliberal internationalism*, acknowledges that nation-states sometimes seek to protect or expand their relative power positions. This tendency is what leads them to commit acts of aggression and to attempt to strengthen themselves in ways that are likely to provoke countermeasures on the part of other nation-states. This school both hopes and predicts that nation-states will give up such uncivilized habits and learn to live with one another peaceably without arming to the teeth, arguing that there is a higher rationality than the egoistic quest for power. Nation-states can improve the welfare of their citizens more certainly by burying their short-term differences and reaching accords with one another designed to promote their *mutual* well-being over the longer run. Idealists ask if it is rational for states to distort the economic division of labor within their societies by building up stores of arms and conscripting young citizens out of the domestic workforce. War will disrupt international trade, adversely affecting the economies of many countries. Finally, they believe that institutions of national governments and international organizations can be improved, through democratization and the spread of the rule of law, in such a way that the temptation to go to war will be held in check.[3]

FEDERALISM, FUNCTIONALISM, AND "MONNETISM"

Two plans that were gaining support in the late 1940s were federalism and functionalism. The former attracted the support of nongovernmental organizations and movements led by prominent public figures; the latter was pursued more quietly by governmental officials.

Federalists believed that the vulnerable states of Western Europe should join together in a political union in which they could exercise mutual self-help in the face of threats to their common security. By forming a federation of once-sovereign states, they could pool their individual capacities to organize their defenses, mobilize their resources and industrial strengths, and guide their economies in the direction of modernization and economic growth. The basic thrust was political. The purpose of federation would be to concentrate the power of the federating states in a central authority. That authority would be given control over certain economic levers in order to better accomplish its overriding objective of providing for the collective security of the member states. The states would retain control over those aspects of their domestic affairs that were not seen to be vital for the common effort. But the pooling of sovereignty in the "federal government" would be substantial, and once having given up this sovereignty, each state would be bound to abide by common decisions.[4] As idealists, they believed that political leaders would simultaneously recognize that wars could be prevented only if nations pooled their military resources in a political union dedicated to resolving conflicts among them peaceably.

The closest Western Europe came to attaining such a political union was the European Defense Community (EDC), which was agreed on in 1952 and was to include the six original members of the future EU: France, West Germany, Italy, Belgium, the Netherlands, and Luxembourg. The EDC would bring the armed forces of the six countries under a single multinational command structure. A political community was also envisioned at that time, to provide institutions for democratic political control over the multinational defense structure.[5] But these plans fell by the wayside in 1954 when the EDC treaty was rejected by the French National Assembly. Further concrete steps toward European integration did not follow the federalist blueprint.

Unlike the federalists, the *functionalists* did not outline plans for an elaborate division of political responsibilities. They were pragmatists, concentrating on the immediate economic needs of the survivors of World War II.[6] The leading functionalist theorist was David Mitrany, who produced the main writings on the subject during and immediately after the war.[7] He was interested not in the functional integration of European nations per se, but in the creation of international organizations to fulfill certain specific needs. These might include organizing relief efforts for war refugees, regulating air traffic, formulating and enforcing international health and safety standards, or promoting more efficient agricultural methods. According to Mitrany's vision, several such organizations might come into being for different purposes and comprise different sets of member states, sometimes including members from different continents and subregions around the globe. They would not all involve a given set of members found in a particular region. That is, they would not gradually become a collective statelike territorial entity in their own right. Mitrany rejected federalism on the grounds that it would replace the old states with a new, larger one without necessarily reducing human misery.[8]

Yet Mitrany is generally regarded as a forerunner of a movement for *European* functional integration, which actually did go on to achieve the first real success in that direction: the European Coal and Steel Community (ECSC). This was the brainchild of a Frenchman, Jean Monnet, who had served in the League of Nations before its collapse on the eve of World War II; as a liaison among France, Britain, and the United States during the war; and as the head of the French economic planning commission after the war. Monnet had always concentrated on finding very practical solutions to immediate problems, usually problems of an economic nature. Like Mitrany, Monnet believed that, when faced with their own inability to solve problems that could be solved only by international cooperation, states would, even though reluctantly, relinquish limited elements of their sovereignty and pool their efforts in international organizations.

Monnet was optimistic about nation-states and their leaders. He believed that government leaders could be persuaded to move from a narrow, short-run definition of the national interest to one that acknowledged the long-term benefits of joining forces. And Monnet was a very persuasive individual. Throughout his career, he had accumulated a rich network of contacts in many countries—people who shared elements of his ideas and were willing to support his goals.[9] He drew these contacts—many of whom occupied positions of governmental authority in Western

Europe in the 1950s—into his Action Committee for a United States of Europe. The group successfully mobilized elite support in Western Europe for the creation of the European Economic Community (EEC), the forerunner of today's EU.[10] In the final analysis, Monnet was committed to a regionally specific set of countries joining together in what would eventually become a European federation. But his method of attaining it was indirect. Federalism was essentially a political goal for Monnet, ultimately involving a common foreign and security policy, which is sometimes called "high politics."[11] But Monnet preferred to begin by attaining consensus among a limited number of states to cooperate in "low politics," essentially policies for regulating production and trade.

The concrete problem with which Monnet began was that of overproduction in the European coal and steel industries. This situation made it necessary for production to be publicly regulated in order to avoid the likelihood of a severe depression in these sectors, which would drive producers out of business and threaten the security of the region by diminishing reserve productive capacity. If governments of the affected countries could come together to regulate production—a common goal that was limited in scope, but strategically crucial—market failure could be avoided. Monnet's plan was popularly known as the Schuman plan, after Robert Schuman, the French foreign minister who publicly initiated it in 1950. The "European six"— France, West Germany, Italy, Belgium, the Netherlands, and Luxembourg—agreed to form the ECSC with surprising rapidity, and it came into being less than two years later. The six nations invited Britain to join, but the Labour government was suspicious of what looked like longer-run federalist objectives, and Britain stayed out.[12]

Monnet was a pragmatist. While he envisioned a United States of Europe along federal lines, after the defeat of the EDC in 1954, he refocused his attention on more immediately achievable goals. These were economic goals rather than political objectives.[13] The EDC was a spectacular initiative that was proposed by French and German leaders less than a decade after the defeat of Germany in World War II, ending the German occupation of France and the Benelux countries. Concentration on building an economic community turned out to be a much more realistic goal, and a more necessary one, given the roles of the United States and North Atlantic Treaty Organization during the Cold War. By the end of the Cold War more than three decades later, political integration was back on the agenda, but its military side was limited to pinpoint assistance to governments in post-Communist East Central Europe. (See Chapter 12.)

Government leaders of the Monnetist persuasion formulated a new agenda for the European six in the mid-1950s. The result was the creation, in 1958, of the European Atomic Energy Community (Euratom) and the EEC. Euratom achieved only modest results, largely because of the unwillingness of governments, especially that of France, to give up their sovereign control of what was considered a vital element of national strength. In contrast, the EEC achieved remarkable success as a customs union[14] during the first decade of its life. Yet by the end of that decade, its chances of achieving a full-fledged *political* union still appeared to be visionary. (See Chapter 3 for a fuller discussion of these developments.)

THE RISE AND DECLINE OF NEOFUNCTIONALISM

The attainment of economic goals through political means lies at the heart of the scholarly revision of functionalism that came to be called *neofunctionalism*. Its founder was Ernst B. Haas, an American political scientist who had witnessed at first hand the emergence of a new European agenda in the 1950s. Haas was sufficiently impressed by Monnet's strategy and tactics to put them into a theoretical framework that was more elaborate and academic in nature.[15] Haas argued that functional integration would most likely occur if influential and powerful elites were motivated to take decisive steps toward it. These must include members of governments and other political leaders, but the politicians could not be expected to take action unless pressure was exerted by opinion leaders and special interest groups, especially those in the economic sector: business, labor, and agricultural leaders. He was more skeptical about the potential impact of the European federalists. He did not disagree with their goal, at least as an ideal, but he believed that mass opinion was likely to be too passive to be moved directly by groups promoting idealistic causes and that political elites were too hardheaded to risk their careers by single-mindedly supporting objectives that were not high on the national agenda.[16]

Haas's first major work, *The Uniting of Europe* (1958), was an examination of the experience of the ECSC. He introduced a number of neofunctionalist concepts to help explain the steps toward regional integration that had already occurred, as well as elucidating any further steps that might occur. Two central concepts were *spillover* and *supranationalism*.[17] By spillover, Haas meant that if the tasks of a regional organization were to expand, it would occur as a result of experiences with the tasks the organization was already performing. The ECSC had positive achievements that invited emulation in other spheres; it also had some unintended consequences that had to be addressed. Hence, the EEC, which came on its heels, was an attempt both to produce the same advantages in other sectors and to deal with some of the ECSC's side effects. In Haas's view, the motivating forces for integration could be found essentially within the organization itself and its members.

But Haas emphasized that there was nothing automatic in spillover. Task expansion by the regional organization would require political initiative. "Cross-national networks" were becoming more frequent and broader. This process of communication made it possible for elites to address common problems in concrete terms and to discover an "upgraded common interest." The communications net corresponded to neither a federal nor a confederal framework; instead, it was supranational.[18] Although the principal actors were nationally based, they came together predisposed to find common solutions to their mutual problems, and their method of arriving at decisions was by unanimous consent, avoiding votes, vetoes, and subsequent expressions of antagonism. The bias, Haas found, was in favor of reaching agreements.[19] This was the spirit in which Monnet had operated.

It was also the spirit that guided Walter Hallstein, the West German politician and administrator who became the first president of the EEC Commission. Under Hallstein's leadership, the EEC developed a method of decision making that refused to acknowledge the absence of consensus. In the early 1960s, midnight deadlines were imposed on meetings of the Council of Ministers, and the clock was stopped at a minute before, with the meetings continuing on into the next day or days until agreement could be reached.[20]

With the publication of his later study of the International Labor Organization,[21] Haas gave greater attention to the importance of leadership as a part of his conception of supranationalism. The executive leaders of international organizations can play an important role in "upgrading the common interest" if they use their skills to (1) define an organizational ideology, (2) build a bureaucracy committed to that ideology, and (3) build coalitions of national actors supporting the leadership and its ideology.[22] Haas saw these attributes as necessary for the organization to be able to expand its functions. Without them, the organization's method of decision making would not be supranational because an essential element would be lacking for bringing member states together to upgrade the common interest.

In 1965, Commission President Hallstein attempted to force spillover from the economic to the political realm by presenting the Council of Ministers with a plan that would provide for a greater transfer of revenues from the national governments to the EEC. This would have strengthened the organization's economic impact. President Charles de Gaulle of France objected to Hallstein's plan and pulled his ministers out of the Council for what turned out to be a period of six months, from July 1965 to January 1966. Ultimately, Hallstein and the governments of the other five countries had to withdraw the budget expansion proposal and concede to France informally, and counter to the spirit of supranationalism, that when a member government considered very important interests of its country to be at odds with a given proposal to be voted on in the Council, it could insist on the unanimity rule and thereby exercise a veto.[23]

The earlier supranational assumption that consensus would be reached and action would be taken whenever the Council met to decide an issue began to wither away with this French-imposed "empty-chair" crisis. (See Chapter 3.) Although further items on the original Rome Treaty agenda were adopted and implemented later in the 1960s, spillover was no longer taking place; new agenda items were not being taken on board in response to the effects of policies already adopted. Efforts were made to move from the concrete commitments of the Rome Treaty to more ambitious and far-reaching objectives such as the Economic and Monetary Union (EMU), but the Council of Ministers never got down to the bargaining stage on such projects because governments were reluctant to make further concessions of sovereignty.

By the early 1970s, neofunctionalists were no longer as optimistic as they had been a decade earlier. Leon Lindberg and Stuart Scheingold conceded that the nation-state had reoccupied the political high ground and that the progress toward regional integration made in the 1950s and early 1960s had been confined to the low politics realm of economic, especially trade and agricultural, policy.[24] In the mid-1970s, Ernst Haas observed that "global turbulence" was destroying the coherence of the EC and other regional economic organizations.[25]

A PAINFUL LEARNING EXPERIENCE

Global Economic Interdependence

As Chapter 3 will show in greater depth, the 1970s were difficult years for regional integration in Europe. Important economic changes were taking place that would be better understood in the following decade. Advanced industrial countries in the 1970s experienced a slowing down of economic growth, which had been unusually rapid for most of them in the preceding 20 years. Along with slower growth came greater monetary instability. The U.S. dollar ceased to be a reliable anchor for other currencies, which gained substantially in value relative to the dollar during the 1970s, requiring adjustments in the world monetary order. EC economic growth was more sluggish than that of Japan and other East Asian economies. The Pacific Rim countries were competing in product areas where Western Europeans had held a comparative advantage before the 1970s. EC member countries were finding it more difficult to control unemployment, inflation, adverse trade balances, and monetary instability. Then came the oil crisis of 1973–1974. Domestic economies were being hit by a multitude of international shocks.

Because he was writing about an organization in the early years of its development, Ernst Haas had focused on the dynamic elements of the process of integration. When this dynamic process appeared to be slowing down, the possibility of spillover to new purposes and new organizational structures appeared less likely to occur. More recent students of European integration have pointed to the continuity of an organizational complex that, today, is more than a half-century old. What was more noticeable in the intervening years was the ability of existing European institutions to maintain the momentum of this complex of organizations by adapting to changing circumstances through continual modification of the institutions' agendas for decision and implementation. The changing circumstances have included the influx of ten new members in 2004. (See Chapter 5.) EU policy making proceeds along many paths at different speeds, without any necessary spillover. When, as in mid-2005, efforts to reach agreement on far-reaching institutional changes were found to be irrelevant to voters' preoccupations, the developments immediately in focus were stymied, but other business of the EU institutions went on without interruption. Member states continue to play a vital role. Heads of government, foreign ministers,

ministers of finance and economic affairs, and other governmental officials set the numerous agendas and move them along. "Supranational" actors play major roles as well. Any analysis of these processes has to take into account the institutional complexity, which is described at greater length in Chapter 6.

Intergovernmentalism

By the early 1980s, many analysts felt that the European Community (EC) had become, at bottom, an intergovernmental organization. In this period, the Commission was no longer looked to for leadership. Most major policy issues were decided in the European Council in negotiations between governmental leaders. Even obligatory decisions, like the EC annual budget or farm prices under the Common Agricultural Policy (CAP), could be held up without decision in the Council of Ministers by an intransigent government (most notably the British government under Margaret Thatcher). Such deadlocks had to await resolution at the next meeting of the European Council, where the heads of state and government could make commitments to one another that their ministers could not. It was the prevailing academic view that the EC worked through intergovernmentalism, which pointed to the fact that the nation-state was not dead in Western Europe. Member states had come to dominate the EC and had reduced the supranational Commission to a subordinate role.[26]

On the other hand, realists of an earlier day might have been surprised at the extent to which, even at the height of the economic turbulence in the mid-1970s, the governments of the EC member countries had come to regard themselves as partners in a community in which armed conflict between them could no longer be imagined. This had freed them to concentrate on the economic problems that separated them and to cooperate in seeking solutions. Though major decisions were reached with great difficulty, they were made collectively through consultation and bargaining. When disagreements could not be resolved, decisions were postponed.

At the June 1985 Milan summit meeting, the European Council accepted a White Paper that called for making the EC institutions more efficient in order to facilitate completion of the Common Market through adoption of a Single European Act (SEA). The SEA was ratified two years later. At this point, it should be noted that earlier theories of regional integration were unable to predict that the members of the EC would conclude that a more thoroughgoing removal of trade barriers among themselves would be needed in order to cope with competition from more efficient and technologically up-to-date competitors. This was not a neofunctionalist spillover from one policy domain to another. Instead, it involved returning to an already existing policy domain and improving EC performance in line with the original Rome Treaty objectives. It was prompted by changes in the world in which the EC found itself rather than by processes internal to the EC, as neofunctionalists would have anticipated.

Theorists sought to explain the SEA in terms of some of the various formulations we have thus far discussed in this chapter, or combinations of them. Neofunctionalist arguments were used in part, especially in placing emphasis on the leadership of the EC Commission. But the argument was also made that economic interdependence had superseded the efforts of EC nations or the EC itself to exercise effective economic regulation.[27] Nevertheless, theorists were generally in agreement that member states, pursuing their own interests, had to reach some convergence of interest in order for the major departure to take place.[28] The latter point of view was highlighted by the study of the SEA by Andrew Moravcsik, who argued that it was achieved through an intergovernmental process of bargaining, in which the Commission and even the Commission's president played roles that were secondary to those of the governments of the leading states, France, Britain, and West Germany. Changes in the domestic political configurations of these countries, especially of France, had cleared the ground for the SEA, according to Moravcsik.[29]

By the early 1980s, an institutional pattern was emerging in which the member governments, as well as the Commission and other supranational actors, shared in both setting the EC's agenda and choosing between alternative policies.[30] This institutional pattern has continued through to the first decade of the new millennium. To a considerable extent, analysis of institutional processes and adaptations has replaced the broader theoretical perspectives of the debate between neofunctionalists and neorealists. Today analytical tools developed in the field of comparative politics have become important alongside those of international relations in the study of the institutional framework and dynamics of the EU.[31]

In 1988, the president of the EC Commission, Jacques Delors, resurrected plans originally outlined in 1970 for an EMU. In 1990, two intergovernmental conferences were instituted that developed separate parts of a Treaty on European Union that was adopted at the Maastricht summit of December 1991. The two parts were (1) the EMU, which entailed a European central bank, closer economic and monetary policy coordination, and a common EC currency; and (2) the political union, which extended the principle of qualified majority voting to new policy realms and added further to the powers of the directly elected European Parliament. Symbolically, Delors also succeeded in changing the name of the organization from "European Community" to "European Union."

These steps, taken in the early 1990s, moved well beyond what neofunctionalism might have predicted as realizable in such a short period of time. They were much more than an incremental accretion of low-politics functions. That they sought EU before allowing time to absorb the single market or even to begin the stages envisaged for EMU was due primarily to the events in Eastern Europe, which dramatically altered the stable security equation of the Cold War and, in particular, presented them in 1990 with the imminent achievement of German unification. Global political change served as a stimulus to integration. This "great leap forward" to EU seemed to resemble the blueprints of the old discarded European federalism: Seize the opportunity when it arrives because it may not come again soon! Yet in the early years of the new century, questions are being raised among theorists and practitioners about the EU's longer-term directions and next steps.

REGIONAL INTEGRATION THEORY TODAY

Most students of European integration today, including the authors of this text, have concluded that no single theoretical framework can hope to account for the phenomena they study. This is the case for two reasons.

First, major economic and political events that are beyond the control of the EU as an organization, or any of its members acting singly or jointly, continue to occur in defiance of any EU efforts to pursue a stable course of action. Not only are the member states dependent on one another, but also, if they are to plan ahead for their mutual security and economic well-being, they are dependent on the rest of the world to "stay still" long enough for them to agree on and carry out coherent courses of action. Broad theories of international interdependence help us to understand the dilemmas the EU faces,[32] but they do not provide answers as to what will occur when and with what effects.

Second, as was demonstrated by voters in France and the Netherlands in the ill-fated effort in 2005 to ratify the Constitutional Treaty, EU decision makers, both supranational and intergovernmental, can lose touch with their constituencies at the national level. Although such setbacks are frequent experiences for national politicians and do not, as a rule, leave them without positive alternatives, the loss of common understanding between national leaders and their domestic constituencies poses very important questions about the future of European integration. (See Chapter 5.)

As a decision-making mechanism, the EU has become much too complex to be captured by any simplifying framework that draws on familiar ideas that political scientists commonly accept. The EU is a multilevel and polycentric set of institutions.[33] Different theories discussed above, including federalism, functionalism, neofunctionalism, and neorealism, can all find levels or niches within this organizational complexity that "work" the way the theories tell us they should. Given its complexity, the EU permits a variety of equally coherent definitions of existing relationships, explanations of how they got that way, and predictions of where they are going, every one of which is plausible if one accepts the beginning assumptions.

A process of intergovernmental decision making is not incompatible with a willingness to concede sovereignty on important matters if mutual benefits can be perceived by all member governments and what is given up does not offend the deeply held values and norms of member states' citizens. Thus, outcomes may be supranational in the neofunctionalist sense, even though decision processes are not. To understand how these decisions are made, we can still find theories of international relations useful. But once the decisions are made, there follows a process that involves supranational decision-making institutions within domains about which there is already longer-standing agreement and where affected interest groups may be brought into agreement. This suggests a two-step process: (1) Intergovernmental bargaining produces the transfer of new powers to supranational institutions, which, in turn, (2) make decisions in ways similar to how their counterparts at national levels make them. There is a legislative process in the EU that bears some similarity to legislative processes nationally; likewise, there is an executive wielding executive powers and a judiciary exercising judicial powers.

Today, writers employing the intergovernmental perspective in the study of the EU place emphasis on the trading that takes place between member states, each pursuing its own interests, but recognizing that it cannot prevail without making concessions on issues where it has less to lose than what it will gain if the agreement is reached. Andrew Moravcsik has developed a "liberal intergovernmental" view of the process,[34] according to which the member states are motivated primarily by economic interests when they decide to propose, accept, or reject compromises on EU policy issues. These interests, as well as the institutional constraints, must be examined in order to understand policy outcomes.

Governments, according to Moravcsik, are not the billiard balls of international relations theory; they act "on the basis of goals that are defined domestically," with foreign policies "varying in response to shifting pressure from domestic social groups, whose preferences are aggregated through political institutions."[35] These are national political institutions headed by national political leaders: "Whereas neo-functionalism stresses the autonomy of supranational officials, liberal intergovernmentalism stresses the autonomy of governmental leaders."[36] Yet both neofunctionalism and Moravcsik's liberal intergovernmentalism have made economic issues central to their analyses of EU decision making. For Haas, initial integration of economic decision making gives supranational agencies the leverage to induce governments to support further integration. For Moravcsik, governments can be persuaded to pursue cooperation within the EU framework for economic objectives, but this is because they cannot attain their objectives unilaterally, not because they have been maneuvered into giving up their best interests by supranational policy entrepreneurs. There is no automatic spillover from fulfilling one policy commitment to reaching agreement on another. The process is controlled by the member governments coordinating their own agendas, with very limited help from the Commission.

Moravcsik's view of how EU decisions are made could, without too much trouble, be converted into a version of what is called "rational-choice institutionalism."[37] It posits that national governments act rationally on behalf of their preferences, but Moravcsik downplays the significance of the EU's supranational institutions, whether the Commission, the European Parliament, or the European Court of Justice. He is not even very explicit about the institutional characteristics of the intergovernmental bodies—the Council of Ministers and the European Council. These are arenas in which national players contest for advantage and reach compromise solutions. Simon Hix and other proponents of rational-choice institutionalism[38] argue that national and supranational actors have preferences that they promote in the bargaining that goes on under the rules of the EU institutional framework. Some may have economic preferences, some more strictly political ones, and others various combinations of both. The contests between actors' priorities are more highly regulated by institutional rules and norms than Moravcsik suggests, as he concentrates on the more informal bargaining that goes on between heads of state and government over the larger architectural decisions, which, in fact, often determine what the institutional rules will be that guide decision making in other bodies.

Challenging Moravcsik's liberal intergovernmentalism is another theoretical perspective that puts more emphasis on the supranational decision-making processes of the EU. This is the theoretical framework known as "historical institutionalism."[39] It, too, is better at explaining the past than at predicting the future, but it may be better than the earlier theories at predicting what *won't* happen. It does appear to have a better grasp of the EU as it has evolved in the more recent past than either Haas's neofunctionalist framework or Moravcsik's liberal intergovernmentalism. Neofunctionalism applied best for the earliest years of European integration, while versions of intergovernmentalism better explained the years from the empty-chair crisis of the mid-1960s until the Fontainebleau and Milan summit of the mid-1980s. Moravcsik's theory best explains the bargains struck between heads of state and government that resulted in the SEA and its largely successful implementation. But the more highly charged political atmosphere surrounding the fundamental issues that were dealt with over 15 years in the Maastricht, Amsterdam, and Nice treaties (1990–2000), the ill-fated Constitutional Treaty (2005), and the Lisbon Treaty (2007) extended beyond the capacity of a single-value economic motivation to explain. (See Chapter 5.)

Historical institutionalism as advanced by Paul Pierson[40] does not offer a superior explanation for the historical bargains, but it insists that such bargains are only part of the story of European integration—indeed, only the tip of the iceberg. The bargains have to be implemented, and the supranational institutions play an important role in their implementation, as do the member governments themselves. But once the bargains have been made and the structures and processes have been developed or redirected to implement them, they take on a life of their own. Although the architectural decisions of the leaders have fashioned them in the first place, the institutions of implementation (which include national as well as EU institutions) cannot easily be redirected or dismantled because this would require that new bargains be struck. These may be more difficult to achieve than was the original bargain that set up and empowered the implementive institutional framework in the first place. At the core of historical institutionalism is the premise that institutions are "path-dependent," which means that what happened at time 0 (the original authorization) will have a substantial influence on what happens at time 1 (the up and-running implementive structure) and that what exists at time 1 will have a substantial effect on what we will discover at time 2. By the later stages, whatever persists from time 0 can be undone by the original decision makers only with great difficulty and in the face of considerable bureaucratic resistance.

Pierson gives an example of this logic in the case of the Maastricht Treaty negotiations, when British Prime Minister John Major negotiated an "opt-out" from the social-policy innovations that the other 11 members had agreed to. Major calculated that he could not get the treaty ratified by the British House of Commons if he committed to the social policy. The others went ahead with a Social Protocol that was placed in the treaty's appendix, which they pledged to implement by further action. According to Pierson, the catch for Major was that, once the social policy was in place in the form of institutions for implementing it in the 11 countries, there would be nothing to stop a future British government from "opting in" to it, which indeed is what the Labour government of Tony Blair did, shortly after the Labour Party won the May 1997 British general election. The Social Protocol then became a full-fledged part of what can be considered the EU's constitutionally sanctioned agenda. But it had already been accepted by the 11 members, and any effort to reverse what had been done would have been futile. Opt-outs by individual countries may be tolerated, but retrospective opt-outs by all the member governments—unanimous agreement to undo what had been done—have become flatly impossible.[41]

Pierson presents historical institutionalism as a successor to neofunctionalism in its emphasis on supranational institutions as key promoters of further European integration. But historical institutionalism does not provide much guidance as to how new departures, such as the Social Protocol, are initiated. It seems evident that intergovernmentalist approaches, as demonstrated by Moravcsik in his major study (1999), are better at accounting for the broad treaty revision agreements, such as the SEA and the Maastricht Treaty. They have involved trade-off bargains made between heads of state and government, but it does not appear that a strictly economic interpretation of the motivations behind the bargains, such as that which Moravcsik offers, is justified. In recounting the major decisions that created and modified the institutions and policy commitments of the EU (Chapters 3–5), we will emphasize the roles played by heads, as well as key supranational actors, most notably the president of the Commission. But the motivations behind the agreements will be shown to have varied from instance to instance depending on the substance of the issues.

When we turn from the broad agreements reached between governments to the process of implementing them, the focus on supranational institutions and processes becomes more appropriate. Rational-choice institutionalism will be used in Chapter 6 in addition to straight institutional description to analyze the ways in which decisions are made by the "Rome Treaty institutions" of the EU: the Council of Ministers, the Commission, the European Parliament, and the European Court of Justice. Historical institutionalism will come into play in tracing the evolution of policies over time and in showing why some choices prevailed over others because of the need to build on existing commitments that could not be reversed.

Historical institutionalism is a theoretical framework whose major applications have been in the field of comparative politics. This is likewise true of rational-choice institutionalism. Borrowing from Hinich and Munger, Hix presents the following equation to summarize a wide variety of complex processes that can be interpreted via rational-choice institutionalism:

$$\text{Preferences} \times \text{Institutions} = \text{Outcomes}$$

According to Hix, "if *preferences change*, outcomes will change, even if *institutions remain constant*, and if *institutions change*, outcomes will change, even if *preferences remain constant.*"[42] Thus, both preferences and institutions are important for analysis of what happens in any decision-making process. The example of the unanimity rule suggests that outcomes would change if the preferences of the last holdout changed to become more compatible with those of the rest of the members. But if the institutional rule were to change so that a qualified majority on the issue would suffice to adopt a proposed action, then the holdout can be ignored and concessions would not have to be made. Examples of this have occurred in the history of European integration. The ratification of the SEA (1987), which replaced the unanimity requirement for the adoption of single-market legislation, allowed a large shopping list of legislative measures to make their way through the EC legislative process before the target date of December 31, 1992. Fewer of these measures would have passed before the target date if, as was often the rule before that time, a single member had been able to veto their adoption.

Rational-choice institutionalism has contributed "middle-range" propositions to the study of European integration. To the extent that scholarly attention has been routed in this direction, it has been at the expense of broader historical explanations. Some would argue that the latter have usually failed to *predict* actual developments that have occurred in the immediate aftermath of their publication. They have been much better at *explaining* what has already occurred. Thus, neofunctionalists could explain much of the process of integration that occurred before the mid-1960s. But Moravcsik's extensive revision of this history[43] demonstrates that a different system of explanation can interpret the same set of events quite differently, leaving one to imagine that the truth lies somewhere in between.

A more recent response to the rationalist and institutionalist approach to regional integration has come from the constructivist reinterpretation of neofunctionalism.[44] As Ben Rosamond explains, "constructivism [social constructivism] has become difficult to ignore in contemporary International Relations scholarship . . . although a number of writers have been exploring constructivist themes, without using the heading, for many years."[45] Constructivists' explanation of EU integration argues that deepening of integration is a consequence of interaction of members' interests and that social norms, in which actors are embedded, regulate their behavior and constitute their identities, interests, and preferences.[46] This is consistent with the constructivist argument that structures of world politics are social rather than material in character.[47] When applied to EU integration, constructivists view EU policy making as "grounded in the accumulation of positive experiences of cooperation, which seep into the preference pattern of participating states and open the way to future integration. Cooperation among members develops into trust and a habit of coordination, which other actors are able to exploit and turn into specific instances of policy making."[48] That is, constructivists focus on how European identities, with common norms, emerge and how such norms, in turn, affect the behavior of the players. These writers argue that this perspective captures intergovernmental bargaining much better than its realist or liberal intergovernmentalist alternatives.

It is possible that theories attuned to particular areas of EU activity will be developed when overarching theories are deemed inappropriate. A case in point is the study of EU enlargements. What motivates the existing member countries to accept new members into the Union? The question may have been a manageable one to answer prior to the enlargement of 2004, when ten countries joined the EU. (See Chapter 5.) Most of the ten were former Communist bloc states that turned to democratic forms of government after the collapse of the Soviet Union. Anticipation of economic and institution-building assistance from the EU, as well as a belief in democracy, would, it was thought, be assured with EU membership. As for the 15 member states prior to the enlargement, their motivations in joining the EC varied with the conditions prevailing at the times they joined, but only two or three joined at each enlargement, and their joining was less likely to have a major impact on the way the EC operated.

The study of the EU has become a highly specialized activity since the days when Jean Monnet helped to shape its original form and Ernst Haas theorized about the process of "community formation" that appeared to be following Monnet's blueprint. Today there are many middle-range theories of European integration, each focusing on a range of activity that the theory explores and explains. The broad terms—*neofunctionalism, supranationalism,* and *liberal intergovernmentalism*—superseded *idealism* and *realism* decades ago. But each term highlights a different part of the EU's institutional arrangements. In Chapter 6, we will discuss how these and more recently developed theoretical perspectives have been applied to particular parts of the institutional framework: neofunctionalism to the Commission and the European Court of Justice, intergovernmentalism to the European Council and the Council of Ministers, and democratic theory to the European Parliament. But first we will show in the next three chapters how these institutions evolved from the relative simplicity of 50 years ago to the complexity we find today.

STUDY QUESTIONS

1. What are the main tenets of neofunctionalism?
2. Compare and contrast the realist and idealist arguments on regional integration.
3. What are the constructivist criticisms of the rational intergovernmentalist model of regional integration?
4. How does historical institutionalism differ from liberal intergovernmentalism?

5. Some would argue that no one theory of regional integration provides a satisfactory explanation of the causal relationships behind EU integration. Do you agree or disagree with this notion? Explain in detail.

ENDNOTES

1. Hans J. Morgenthau, *Politics Among Nations: The Struggle for Power and Peace*, 3d ed. (New York: Knopf, 1962), pp. 507–509.

2. Robert O. Keohane, *After Hegemony: Cooperation and Discord in the World Political Economy* (Princeton, N.J.: Princeton University Press, 1984), pp. 136–141.

3. Charles W. Kegley, Jr., and Eugene R. Wittkopf, *World Politics: Trend and Transformation*, 3d ed. (New York: St. Martin's Press, 1989), pp. 12–15.

4. Charles Pentland, *International Theory and European Integration* (London: Faber and Faber, 1973), chap. 5.

5. F. Roy Willis, *France, Germany and the New Europe 1945–1967*, rev. ed. (London: Oxford University Press, 1968), chaps. 6 and 7.

6. Stephen George, *An Awkward Partner: Britain in the European Community* (Oxford: Oxford University Press, 1990), pp. 16–22.

7. David Mitrany, *A Working Peace System* (Chicago: Quadrangle Books, 1966).

8. Ibid., pp. 64–65. In a sense, Mitrany foreshadowed the insistence of British Prime Minister John Major in 1991–1992 on his country's right to opt out of some functions to be performed by the emerging EU, such as a common defense and a common monetary policy.

9. See the essays on Monnet in Douglas Brinkley and Clifford Hackett, eds., *Jean Monnet: The Path to European Unity* (New York: St. Martin's Press, 1991).

10. Leon N. Lindberg and Stuart A. Scheingold, *Europe's Would-Be Polity: Patterns of Change in the European Community* (Englewood Cliffs, N.J.: Prentice-Hall, 1970), pp. 33–34.

11. Pentland, *International Theory*, p. 109. Although the boundary between high politics and low politics fluctuates depending on who is using the terms and in what context, foreign and defense policy matters are commonly considered high politics and policies limited to particular economic sectors are considered low politics. The gray area in between is occupied by macroeconomic policy, especially monetary policy, which, given its widespread implications today for countries' international standing, probably ought to be considered within the realm of high politics. In other words, it is an area, along with foreign and defense policy, over which nation-states are least willing to give up control.

12. George, *An Awkward Partner*, p. 21.

13. George W. Ball, "Introduction," in Brinkley and Hackett, eds., *Jean Monnet*, p. xix; Derek W. Urwin, *The Community of Europe: A History of European Integration Since 1945* (London and New York: Longman, 1991), p. 61.

14. A customs union is a regime established between states in which all tariffs and quotas restricting trade between the participating countries have been removed, while common tariffs and quotas are established vis-à-vis other countries. A common market goes further in removing all obstacles to trade between the countries, including such impediments as border controls and government regulations, state purchasing policies, and taxes that discriminate between the producers of one member country and those of another. The SEA of 1987, which provided for the removal of all such obstacles to trade among EC members by the end of 1992, popularly labeled "Project 1992," represents an effort to approximate the conditions of a true common market among the EC members.

15. Ernst B. Haas, *The Uniting of Europe: Political, Social, and Economic Forces, 1950–1957* (Stanford, Calif.: Stanford University Press, 1958); and Ernst B. Haas, *Beyond the Nation-State* (Stanford, Calif.: Stanford University Press, 1964).

16. Haas, *The Uniting of Europe*, chap. 1.

17. Ibid., chaps. 8 and 13.

18. Robert O. Keohane and Stanley Hoffmann, "Institutional Change in Europe in the 1980s," in Robert O. Keohane and Stanley Hoffmann, eds., *The New European Community: Decision Making and Institutional Change* (Boulder, Colo.: Westview Press, 1991), p. 15.

19. Haas, *The Uniting of Europe*, p. 523.

20. Lindberg and Scheingold, *Europe's Would-Be Polity*, pp. 96–97.

21. Haas, *Beyond the Nation-State*, chap. 3.

22. Leon N. Lindberg, "Political Integration as a Multidimensional Phenomenon Requiring Multivariate Measurement," in Leon N. Lindberg and Stuart A. Scheingold, eds., *Regional Integration: Theory and Research* (Cambridge: Harvard University Press, 1971), pp. 94–95.

23. See John Newhouse, *Collision in Brussels: The Common Market Crisis of 30 June 1965* (New York: Norton, 1967).

24. Lindberg and Scheingold, *Europe's Would-Be Polity*, pp. 70–75.

25. Dale L. Smith and James Lee Ray, "European Integration: Gloomy Theory Versus Rosy Reality," in Dale L. Smith and James Lee Ray, eds., *The 1992 Project and the Future of Integration in Europe* (Armonk, N.Y., and London: Sharpe, 1993), pp. 32–33; Ernst B. Haas, *The Obsolescence*

of Regional Integration Theory, Research Series no. 25 (Berkeley, Calif.: Institute for International Studies, 1975).

26. Paul Taylor, *The Limits of European Integration* (New York: Columbia University Press, 1983).

27. Wayne Sandholtz and John Zysman, "1992: Recasting the European Bargain," *World Politics* 42 (October 1989): 95–128.

28. Ibid., 111–113; Keohane and Hoffmann, "Institutional Change," pp. 23–24.

29. Andrew Moravcsik, "Negotiating the Single European Act," in Keohane and Hoffmann, eds., *The New European Community*, pp. 41–84.

30. The distinction between setting the agenda and choosing between alternatives is that of John W. Kingdom, *Agendas, Alternatives, and Public Policies* (Glenview, Ill., and London: Scott, Foresman, 1984), pp. 3–4.

31. Simon Hix, *The Political System of the European Union* (New York: St. Martin's Press, 1999), chap. 1.

32. Keohane, *After Hegemony*; Robert O. Keohane and Joseph S. Nye, *Power and Interdependence*, 2nd ed. (Glenview, Ill., and London: Scott, Foresman, 1984), pp. 3–4.

33. Dale L. Smith and James Lee Ray, "The 1992 Project," in Smith and Ray, eds., *The 1992 Project*, pp. 6–10; John Peterson and Elizabeth Bomberg, "The EU After the 1990s: Explaining Continuity and Change," in Maria Green Cowles and Michael Smith, eds., *The State of the European Union: Risks, Reform, Resistance, and Revival*, vol. 5 of European Community Studies Association series (Oxford and New York: Oxford University Press, 2000), pp. 19–41.

34. Andrew Moravcsik, "Preferences and Power in the European Community: A Liberal Intergovernmentalist Approach," *Journal of Common Market Studies* 31 (December 1993): 473–524; Andrew Moravcsik, *The Choice for Europe: Social Purpose and State Power from Messina to Maastricht* (Ithaca, N.Y.: Cornell University Press, 1998).

35. Moravcsik, *Choice for Europe*, p. 481.

36. Ibid., p. 491.

37. See the debate between Moravcsik and Jeffrey Checkel, a "rationalist" versus a "constructivist" and an updated version of intergovernmentalism versus supranationalism, in Jeffrey T. Checkel and Andrew Moravcsik, "A Constructivist Research Program in EU Studies?" *European Union Politics* 2 (June 2001): 219–249.

38. Simon Hix, "The Study of the European Community: The Challenge to Comparative Politics,"

West European Politics 17 (January 1994): 1–30; George Tsebelis, "The Power of the European Parliament as a Conditional Agenda-Setter," *American Political Science Review* 88 (1994): 128–142; Mark A. Pollack, "Delegation, Agency and Agenda Setting in the European Community," *International Organization* 51 (1997): 99–134.

39. Sven Steinmo, Kathleen Thelen, and Frank Longstreth, eds., *Structuring Politics: Historical Institutionalism in Comparative Analysis* (Cambridge: Cambridge University Press, 1992).

40. Paul Pierson, "The Path to European Integration: A Historical Institutionalist Analysis," *Comparative Political Studies* 29 (1996): 123–163; later version (same title) by Pierson in Wayne Sandholtz and Alec Stone Sweet, eds., *European Integration and Supranational Governance* (Oxford and New York: Oxford University Press, 1998), pp. 27–58.

41. Pierson, "The Path" (1996), pp. 154–155; Laura Cram, *Policy-Making in the EU: Conceptual Lenses and the Integration Process* (London: Routledge, 1997).

42. Hix, *Political System*, p. 13 (Hix's emphasis); H. J. Hinich and M. C. Munger, *Analytical Politics* (Cambridge: Cambridge University Press, 1997), p. 17.

43. Moravcsik, *Choice for Europe*, chaps. 2–3.

44. Wayne Sandhltz and Alec Stone Sweet, *European Integration and Supranational Governance* (Oxford: Oxford University Press, 1998) and Thomas Risse, "Social Constructivism and European Integration," in Antje Wiener and Thomas Diez, eds., *European Integration Theory* (Oxford: Oxford University Press, 2004).

45. Ben Rosamond, *Theories of European Integration* (New York: St. Martin's Press, 2000), p. 171.

46. Risse, "Social Constructivism and European Integration," p. 163. For a detailed discussion of constructivist approach to EU integration also see Jeffrey T. Checkel, "Social Construction and Integration," *Journal of European Public Policy* 6 (1999): 545–560 and Jeffrey T. Checkel, "Constructing European Institutions," in Mark Aspinwall and Gerald Schneider, eds., *The Rules of Integration: Institutionalist Approaches to the Study of Europe* (Manchester: Manchester University Press, 2001).

47. Rosamond, *Theories of European*, p. 172 and Jeffrey T. Checkel, "Norms, Institutions, and National Identity in Contemporary Europe," *International Studies Quarterly* 43 (March 1999): 83–115.

48. Federica Bicchi, *European Foreign Policy Making toward the Mediterranean* (New York: Palgrave Macmillan, 2007), p. 13.

Chapter 3

The Rome Treaty and Its Original Agenda: 1957–1975

In this chapter, and in the two that follow, we will be reviewing the history of the European Union (EU) from the adoption of the Treaty of Rome to the present. The current chapter takes the story up to the mid-1970s, Chapter 4 carries it to the mid-1990s, and Chapter 5 brings it into 2006. Box 3.1 lists governments in France, Germany, and Britain from the beginning of the European Economic Community (EEC) until mid-2008. French governments are listed by presidents of the Republic (although there was more than one premier for each president), and German and British governments are listed by chancellor and by prime minister, respectively. In all three chapters, we relate political developments within the major member states and the European institutions to policy decisions made in implementing the original agenda of the European Community (EC) and in bringing new items onto the agenda. Relevant changes in the larger world are taken into account as well. We begin in the mid-1950s with the decision by the European six to create a customs union. Pre-1957 developments that led up to the formation of the EEC were outlined in Chapter 2.

When the original six member states of the EC agreed in 1957 to the Treaty of Rome, establishing the EEC, they set an agenda for themselves and the new EEC institutions that was expected to preoccupy them for at least a decade. The principal items on this agenda were the first steps toward economic integration, involving the freeing of trade among the six economies and the establishment of a common trading policy with respect to the rest of the world. The principal areas of trade that they had in mind were manufactured goods and agricultural products, although eventually there were to be, among other things, free movement of persons and capital, a common transportation policy, a common monetary regime, and a common social policy.[1] Ultimately, the six countries envisaged an evolution from an economic community to a political union. But while these goals above and beyond the new trade and commercial regime were mentioned in the Treaty of Rome or, in the case of political goals, hinted at in the treaty's preamble, they were not considered priority items by the drafters of the treaty. The *ordinary agenda* was the new trading bloc, which was to be created by 1970, before most other steps were to be taken.[2]

Box 3.1   Successive Governments in France, Germany, and Britain, 1958–2009

French Presidents and Supportive Parties and Coalitions

Charles de Gaulle, 1958–1969: Gaullists, assorted center and right support

Georges Pompidou, 1969–1974: Gaullists, assorted center and right support

Valéry Giscard d'Estaing, 1974–1981: Giscardist center-right, Gaullist RPR

François Mitterrand, 1981–1986: Socialists, Communists until 1984

François Mitterrand, 1986–1988: Cohabitation with Jacques Chirac's RPR–UDF coalition

François Mitterrand, 1988–1993: Socialists, center-left

François Mitterrand, 1993–1995: Cohabitation with Edouard Balladur's RPR–UDF coalition

Jacques Chirac, 1995–1997: Gaullists, assorted center and right support

Jacques Chirac, 1997–2002: Cohabitation with Lionel Jospin's Socialist–Green–Communist coalition

Jacques Chirac, 2002–2007: Gaullists, assorted center and right support

Nicolas Sarkozy, 2007–present: Gaullists, assorted center and right support

German Chancellors and Supportive Parties and Coalitions (Chancellor's Party Listed First)

Konrad Adenauer, 1949–1963: CDU/CSU, FDP

Ludwig Erhard, 1963–1966: CDU/CSU, FDP

Kurt-Georg Kiesinger, 1966–1969: CDU/CSU, SPD

Willy Brandt, 1969–1974: SPD, FDP

Helmut Schmidt, 1974–1982: SPD, FDP

Helmut Kohl, 1982–1998: CDU/CSU, FDP

Gerhard Schröder, 1998–2005: SPD, Greens

Angela Merkel, 2005–present: CDU/CSU, SPD

British Prime Ministers and Their Parties

Harold Macmillan, 1957–1963: Conservative

Sir Alec Douglas-Home, 1963–1964: Conservative

Harold Wilson, 1964–1970: Labour

Edward Heath, 1970–1974: Conservative

Harold Wilson, 1974–1976: Labour

James Callaghan, 1976–1979: Labour

Margaret Thatcher, 1979–1990: Conservative

John Major, 1990–1997: Conservative

Tony Blair, 1997–2007: Labour

Gordon Brown, 2007–present: Labour

When we refer to the *agenda* of the EU, we have in mind the issues that are being actively addressed by its decision-making organs. Under the Treaty of Rome, the timing of proposed legislative measures envisaged by the treaty is within the job definition of the Commission. In the early years, the steps to be taken to create the customs union and the Common Agricultural Policy (CAP; see Chapter 8) were developed by the Commission as proposals and sent to the Council of Ministers for action, that is, placed on the Council's agenda. These were what we call the *ordinary agenda* because, in putting them on the Council's agenda, the Commission was simply fulfilling its responsibilities under the Rome Treaty. However, during the first decade, there were occasions when items that had not been authorized by the treaty or items for which member governments disputed the right of the Commission to make proposals were placed on the *extraordinary agenda*. An example that will be given prominent attention in this chapter is the 1965 set of proposals by Commission President Walter Hallstein, which touched off what was called the "empty-chair crisis."

A BRIEF PERIOD OF CONSENSUS

The Six in 1957

In 1957, the commitment to the original agenda was shared by political leaders and ruling political parties in all six of the original EEC countries. For the most part, the leaders were centrists in the party politics of their countries: Christian Democrats of the center-right, Social Democrats of the center-left, or Liberals variously located between center-left and center-right. In France and Italy, these political parties of the broad center coexisted with strong Communist parties on the extreme left and nationalist parties on the far right that did not share the centrists' agenda. In West Germany and the three Benelux countries, any existing extreme parties were weak; in the case of West Germany, communist and "neo-Nazi" parties were outlawed.

The pro-European centrists in the six countries shared an acceptance of the Europe of the 1950s as it was and sought to make the best of it. What they had accepted in particular was the existence of the Cold War and the dominant role played by a "hegemon" on either side of the politically divided continent: the USSR to the east and the United States to the west. They were motivated to organize their part of Europe in such a way as to make their economic, and ultimately their political, development less dependent on "their" hegemon, the United States. For the time being at least, little could be done about the Soviet hegemony by the six acting apart from Washington. The creation of the EEC and the priority it gave to reorganizing trade relationships were a realistic way of putting Europe in a more self-sufficient position economically, if not politically.[3]

Table 3.1 shows that support for and opposition to the EEC among parties ranged from left to right for four countries: France, West Germany (FRG), Italy, and Britain. Among the six member countries, support for the new EEC and its agenda was weakest in France in 1957. The extreme parties of both left and right in France were more strident in their opposition to European integration than were their counterparts in Italy. Communists in all West European countries accepted the leadership of the Soviet Communist Party in officially opposing integration as a means by which the United States maintained its hold on its allies and capitalists enriched themselves at the expense of the working class.[4] For the French Communist Party (PCF), European integration had special significance as an American-backed means by which German capitalists would gain control over the French economy. Throughout the 1950s, the PCF was unalterably opposed to each new initiative in the process of European integration.[5]

On the French right, the principal opposition to French membership in these various communities was provided by General Charles de Gaulle and the movement that supported him.

Table 3.1 ■ Positions of Parties in Four Countries on EEC Issues in the 1950s

Country	Left/Anti	Left/Pro	Center/Pro	Right/Pro	Right/Anti
France	Communists	Socialists	MRP, Radicals	Independents	Gaullists
FRG	Social Democrats		FDP	CDU/CSU	
Italy	Communists		Christian Democrats	Liberals	Neo-fascists
	Socialists		Socialists, Democrats, Republicans		
Britain	Labour		Liberals		Conservatives

"Pro" and "anti" refer to position on EEC. FRG–Federal Republic of Germany, MRP–Popular Republican Movement (French Christian Democrats), FDP–Free Democratic Party (German Liberals), CDU/CSU–Christian Democratic Union (national)/Christian Social Union (Bavaria only).

The Gaullists were weaker at the time of the Rome Treaty than they had been during the debates over Europe earlier in the decade. De Gaulle himself was in semiretirement. Nevertheless, his views concerning France's role in Europe were well known and echoed by political figures and writers both inside and outside the Gaullist movement. De Gaulle had his own agenda for Europe, which he was to put into play after he returned to power in mid-1958.[6] He rejected the notion that the division of Europe between East and West was necessarily frozen, especially if this meant that France must subordinate its own interests to the wishes of the United States. De Gaulle saw the EEC as potentially destructive of the France that he knew and loved, and especially of the leading role in Europe that France could claim as U.S. influence declined.[7]

In West Germany by 1957, the political party system, at least as represented in the Bundestag, consisted almost exclusively of parties of the center-left and center-right, all officially committed to the EEC and its agenda, although the Social Democrats (SPD) on the center-left had only recently endorsed the new community. Earlier in the 1950s, the SPD had opposed the European Coal and Steel Community (ECSC) and the European Defense Community (EDC) as helping to solidify the division between East and West Germany, making reunification impossible in the foreseeable future. By contrast, Christian Democratic Chancellor Konrad Adenauer had pursued a policy of acceptance of the division of Europe and the consequent division of Germany as unalterable for the time being. Through membership in the Western European and Atlantic organizations, Adenauer sought to strengthen West Germany's economy, political structure, and national security while options in the East were closed off by Soviet power and policy. During the mid-1950s, the opposition SPD came around to a positive position on European integration.[8]

The British Problem

While the established centrists of the six gave solid support to the EEC and its original agenda, there was no clear "Eurocenter" in the British political party system in the 1950s. The British had not joined the ECSC in the early 1950s, but they were invited in 1955 to the Messina conference, where plans were laid for the Rome Treaty. They arrived as skeptical observers, assuming that little would come out of the talks in view of the EDC debacle. When it became clear that the six were indeed going to create a customs union, Britain sought to entice them over to a broader plan for a European free-trade area that would be looser and without the pretensions to political integration that the six had in mind. The British were set against anything that resembled European federalism, even in the distant future. But while there was sympathy among some of the six for the British plan, the desire to move ahead with a stronger form of market integration prevailed in each country, and the Treaty of Rome was duly signed and ratified. The EEC came into being in 1957. Britain then took the free-trade idea to smaller countries outside the six—Denmark, Sweden, Norway, Austria, Switzerland, and Portugal—and the European Free Trade Association (EFTA) was formed in 1960.[9]

A *free-trade area* differs from a *customs union*. The former allows each member state to choose its own tariff schedule to impose on goods from nonmember countries, while agreeing to a uniform set of tariff levels for trade between members. All members in a customs union impose the same tariff levels on goods from outside the union. Without a common barrier to goods from outside, the markets of countries wanting to restrict such trade would be open to goods entering first through their low-tariff partners.[10] Opposition to the proposed customs union was widely shared by leaders of both major British political parties—Conservative and Labour. The weak center Liberal Party was the only one taking a positive position. The prevailing British view in 1957–1960 was that membership in the EEC would interfere with the economic and political links Britain enjoyed with the United States and Commonwealth countries. Britain had a world role; membership in the EEC would narrow its focus to one region, albeit an important one. There was also a deeply ingrained suspicion of French motives, as well as a belief that the British system of parliamentary sovereignty was unique and superior to institutional frameworks found on the continent of Europe.[11]

These attitudes on the part of the British government meant that the EEC and its agenda had a "British problem." The six could move ahead with their agenda, but if they were to go much beyond the initial priorities—that is, if they began to develop a new extraordinary agenda—it would become even more difficult to make an accommodation that could bring Britain into the community. If the six indeed saw the EEC as a step in the direction of a stronger, more independent Europe, able to operate on a plane of equality with the major world players, then it was reasonable that they would want Britain, which was still regarded as a major power in the world, to join them. This was the dilemma facing the Eurocentrists.

THE STRUGGLE OVER THE EXTRAORDINARY AGENDA

For Charles de Gaulle, the British problem was quite different. In May 1958, the French Fourth Republic was embroiled militarily in a colonial war against the Algerian independence movement. Weak centrist governments in Paris vacillated in their policies toward the war, as they had done earlier in the 1950s in the process of losing French control over Indochina. On May 13, a revolt broke out in Algiers and other cities led by civilians, but taken over by French Army generals in what was essentially a military coup directed against the government in Paris. After a few days of uncertainty, the leaders of the revolt called on the politicians in Paris to hand over the power to General de Gaulle.[12] When President René Coty called on the General to become premier, de Gaulle expressed his willingness to do so, but on the condition that he would oversee the writing of a new constitution, which would be presented to the French voters for their approval. On September 16, 1958, the constitutional referendum was overwhelmingly supported by the voters, and the Fifth Republic came into being. In December, de Gaulle was elected the first president of the Fifth Republic.

From 1958 to 1962, when he brought the war to a conclusion by granting Algeria its independence, de Gaulle was a dominant leader willing to take extraordinary measures in order to defeat threats to his government and to his policy of gradually yielding independence to Algeria. But although Algeria was a continuing concern during this period, de Gaulle also began his efforts to change the agenda of the EEC to suit his purposes.

The Clash of Grand Designs

In the summer of 1961, two events occurred that were to reveal what de Gaulle's agenda for the EEC would be.[13] The first was his success in getting his fellow EEC government leaders, meeting in Bonn in July, to put on their own agenda a proposal for greater political cooperation that he had been advancing in one form or another since 1959. The heads of state and government agreed at Bonn to ask an ad hoc committee chaired by a close associate of de Gaulle, Christian Fouchet, to draft proposals for a treaty to establish a "union of states." The proposals were presented to the six governments in November 1961. By then, the second event had occurred, the August 1961 application of the Conservative British government headed by Prime Minister Harold Macmillan for membership in the EEC, which was followed by similar applications by two of Britain's EFTA associates—Denmark and Norway—and by the Republic of Ireland.

The French proposals considered by the Fouchet committee envisaged that major political decisions on foreign and defense policy matters, as well as on cultural and scientific matters, were to be taken *unanimously* by the heads of state and government meeting at the summit. In essence, the proposals anticipated amendment of the Treaty of Rome to create a "political union," with a new agenda and agenda-setting mechanism. There would be a separate "European Political Commission," comprising officials of the six foreign ministries who would reside in Paris and coordinate agendas for meetings of foreign ministers and heads, leaving the EEC Commission in Brussels with the ordinary economic agenda-setting role assigned it by the Treaty of Rome.[14]

There was a potential link between these proposals and British entry in that this more forthrightly intergovernmental mode of decision making was much more congenial to the British government than the mode envisaged in the Rome Treaty. Already some decisions of the EEC Council of Ministers were officially being taken by qualified majority vote (QMV; see Chapter 1) rather than unanimously, and the treaty indicated that this would be true of many more Council decisions by 1966. If Britain and the others were to enter the EEC, they would have to accept majority decisions taken on the ordinary agenda. But the Fouchet plan for political union would ensure that any extraordinary agenda items, especially those involving matters of political significance that would threaten British autonomy, could be vetoed by Britain, even if supported by all of the other members. At least on this narrow basis, de Gaulle and the British shared an intergovernmentalist view of the community's future. But the Fouchet proposals were too intergovernmentalist to suit the Eurocentrists in other EEC countries, especially in the Netherlands and Belgium, and negotiations were broken off in 1962.[15]

In January 1963, de Gaulle vetoed British entry, which canceled the entry bids of Denmark, Norway, and Ireland as well. The standard interpretation of the French veto of British entry is that de Gaulle's vision for Europe differed from that of the British in a fundamental sense. The Macmillan government did not want to be drawn into political obligations in Europe that would interfere with Britain's ties with the United States and the Commonwealth. Britain was showing slower economic growth than the European six, which is what had moved the Macmillan government to reverse direction and seek EEC membership. The British recognized that the customs union had produced more dynamic economic results in the first years of the EEC than had their own free-trade area, but they certainly did not want economic integration to spill over into political integration. As F. S. Northedge has observed:

> For continental Europeans who had looked forward to the opportunity to build a united Europe during the long years of Nazi occupation, bodies like the Council of Europe, the Coal and Steel Community, the Economic Community, were the fulfillment of a dream. For Britain, joining organizations such as these represented the disappointment of expectations, of hopes of better things. In their inmost thoughts the British were never really convinced about the merits of European unity: unity was all right as a slogan, . . . but it was not a programme for practical action.[16]

De Gaulle wanted his proposed system of political cooperation to extend far enough to bind member countries to commonly agreed projects, so long as these were projects of French inspiration, following de Gaulle's own vision of Europe's political future. He believed that he had brought Chancellor Adenauer in agreement with him in this objective through the personal relationship they had established in 1959, which was to lead to a Treaty of Friendship and Reconciliation between the two countries in January 1963. With France and Germany coordinating their foreign policies in line with de Gaulle's vision, it would be a simple matter to bring the smaller and weaker members of the six along with them. If Britain, and perhaps three others likely to follow the British lead, were to join the EEC, there would be another grand design competing with de Gaulle's—a design he believed to be of American inspiration.[17] Accordingly, he vetoed British entry in January 1963; this canceled the entry bids of the other three as well. Ironically, his veto of British entry helped to undermine the position of Chancellor Adenauer in West Germany. Before the year was out, there was a new chancellor in Bonn, Ludwig Erhard, an "Atlanticist" who did not wish to play games in world politics according to French rules.[18]

A very different interpretation of de Gaulle's motives in vetoing British entry has been presented by political scientist Andrew Moravcsik.[19] Based on economic rather than political motivation, it suggests that the very economic benefits Britain wished to achieve through EEC membership were threatening to those de Gaulle anticipated for France. Moravcsik identifies the basis of de Gaulle's veto as follows:

> The preponderance of evidence, including most of de Gaulle's own statements, supports instead an economic interpretation. De Gaulle decided against British membership early on, despite common geopolitical interests on many issues—not least shared opposition to supranational institutions and concern about Germany—because Britain was certain to block generous financing for the CAP [the EEC's Common Agricultural Policy]. This would have negated the principal advantage for France from a customs union.[20]

To the British, an EEC trading regime that benefited French farmers and small, vulnerable French industries would be too costly for British consumers and taxpayers. In 1963, this regime was still being negotiated. The entry of Britain into the organization before the deal was solidified would clearly reduce the gains de Gaulle expected to achieve from the agreement for French farmers and taxpayers. Moravcsik's point is a solid one and needs to be taken into account in explaining the French veto. But it cannot substitute for the geopolitical motivation. De Gaulle's strength lay in the fact that his political design coincided with what he saw as the way to protect and strengthen the French economy.

The Empty-Chair Crisis and the Luxembourg Compromise

The refusal by France to allow Britain to enter the EEC left France in a smaller organization, most of whose members continued to harbor preferences for an EEC that would eventually move beyond the Rome Treaty in a supranational direction. For the first seven years of the EEC's life, most important decisions were taken either by unanimous consent or by QMV, the latter according to a formula that was designed to protect smaller countries from being swamped by an alliance of bigger countries. Commission President Walter Hallstein had followed a pattern of encouraging the Council to continue its deliberations without voting until it was possible to register unanimous consent. A useful method was to combine measures into package deals so that on different issues countries would make concessions to each other. The package would then be accepted in its entirety, sometimes after days of negotiation among the ministers. Even after QMV came to be applicable in formal terms across a wider array of decisions, this same style of consensus building ensured that there would be no big winners or big losers.[21]

Much of the bargaining activity in the first half of the 1960s had involved a three-way struggle among France, West Germany, and Italy over the establishment of the customs union and the CAP. The crisis that began on June 30, 1965, revolved around France's desire for an agricultural policy that would benefit farmers, to the detriment of consumers and taxpayers in all six countries, through higher farm prices and subsidies. As a strong exporter of manufactured goods, West Germany needed to establish a customs union for manufactured goods—one that would give German industries assured markets for their products and protection from imports from non-EEC countries. Italy, which was experiencing a rapid shift from farming to manufacturing, expected to have to pay for the CAP out of the uncertain proceeds from the sale of its manufactures, so the Italian government wanted "side payments" in the form of regional assistance and a lessened share of budget contributions. A package that put both the customs union and the CAP into place, while providing side payments to Italy, seemed to the Commission to be an obvious way of moving the EC ahead toward economic integration. The French government, which rested on the farmers' electoral support, appeared to have a high stake in achieving just that. Therefore, Commission President Hallstein believed he could up the ante with proposals that would enhance political, as well as economic, integration. In this, he reckoned without President de Gaulle's commitment to his own plans and his seemingly invulnerable domestic political position.[22]

Hallstein presented his proposals to the Council of Ministers in March 1965. Those relating to CAP financing involved the collection of levies on farm goods imported from non-EEC countries and their disbursement to farmers in the member countries to compensate for the lower prices they were getting worldwide for their products. The CAP was to take full effect by July 1, 1967, but the customs union for manufactured goods was not to reach its completion until 1970. In an effort to gain the support of West Germany and other members, Hallstein proposed accelerating the customs union so that its completion would coincide with that of the CAP. This was linked to a proposal to route the proceeds of agricultural levies and customs duties to the Commission for it to administer as the EEC's "own resources." The Commission would remit to the six governments a portion of this amount, but it would keep a part for itself to be spent according to the provisions of the annual budget adopted by the Council of Ministers.[23] Although no amendment to the Rome Treaty was required by these proposals they would mean a very substantial increase in the funds available to the Commission, above what had been expected by the member states.

But the third of Hallstein's proposals for the Commission's funding departed substantially from the Rome Treaty, requiring amendments to two treaty articles.[24] Because the six governments could join forces against the Commission and interfere with its planned uses of its newfound largesse, it was proposed that the European Parliament be allowed to make amendments to the Commission's annual draft budget by simple majority vote.[25] If the Commission approved such an amendment, the Council of Ministers could turn it down only if five of the six members voted to do so. Although this appeared to increase the Parliament's budgetary powers, it would also enhance the ability of the Commission to control the whole process because it was also proposed that the Commission be allowed to offer amendments to the Parliament's amendments, which could be accepted by a two-thirds majority of the Council.[26] If accepted, the proposed procedures would mean that France and West Germany could be outvoted in the Council by the less powerful member states, and the will of the supranational bodies would then prevail over that of the two strongest states.

For de Gaulle, the assertion by the Commission president of the authority to impose extraordinary agenda items on the Council of Ministers was unacceptable. His earlier proposals for regular political cooperation among the governments of the six member countries had rested on the assumption that the Rome Treaty was *a restrictive document that authorized only those powers and functions explicitly stated in it* and that any extension of EEC powers beyond those authorized by the treaty could be made only if all six governments decided to amend the treaty or reach a new contract. The problem for de Gaulle was that, with the imminent arrival of majority voting, the Commission could make proposals that would go beyond the French interpretation of the treaty and France could be outvoted.

Just before the June 30 deadline, the French foreign minister called for an end to the Council of Ministers meeting that was deliberating over the Hallstein package.[27] This signified a French veto of the package. Six months still remained until the installation of more generalized majority voting—a rules change that was mandated by the treaty and would presumably be placed automatically on the Council's agenda. It soon became clear that, by refusing to send his ministers to Council meetings, de Gaulle was forcing at least a postponement in the ordinary agenda of the Rome Treaty, attempting to make the others accept a continuation of the unanimity rule in defiance of the intent of the framers of the Rome Treaty.[28]

In January 1966, the French ministers returned to their seat on the Council of Ministers. De Gaulle had been unexpectedly taken to a second ballot in the French presidential election of December 1965, failing to gain a majority on the first ballot as a result of unexpectedly strong showings by François Mitterrand, the candidate of the left, and a relatively unknown centrist candidate, Jean Lecanuet. The latter benefited from the votes of many farmers, who punished de Gaulle on the first ballot for producing the EEC crisis, thus jeopardizing the CAP and its expected benefits to French agriculture. While de Gaulle won the second ballot runoff against Mitterrand, a dent had been made in his image of invulnerability.[29]

For their part, the five other member governments were more willing to compromise by early 1966. While the question of who won and who lost in the crisis has long been disputed, it seems clear that on the most fundamental point at issue—whether the EEC would remain basically an intergovernmental organization or take a significant step toward supranationalism—what was called the "Luxembourg compromise" sustained intergovernmentalism. First, the original Rome Treaty budget procedure remained intact, with the European Parliament having no more than an advisory role. EC budgets would continue to be controlled by the Council of Ministers, which would make the final determination about the distribution of the EEC's "own resources." Second, the ability of the Commission to put items on the agenda of the Council of Ministers was restricted by the requirement that they first be shown to the representatives of the six governments permanently residing in Brussels (see "Completing the Original Agenda," below). Regarding voting in the Council of Ministers, a vague formula was mutually accepted that permitted the change from unanimity to majority voting to take place as scheduled in the treaty; however, it stated that, where "issues very important to one or more member countries are at stake," ministers will seek to reach solutions with which all can be comfortable.[30] From the standpoint of the Eurocentrists in the various governments, this simply formulated what had been the practice up to mid-1965; from de Gaulle's standpoint, it legitimized the continued right of a state to veto unacceptable EEC initiatives.

ACCOMPLISHMENTS IN THE MIDST OF DIMINISHING EXPECTATIONS

Completing the Original Agenda

Out of the Luxembourg compromise, there arose a procedure whereby the Committee of Permanent Representatives (COREPER) would work closely with the Commission in examining and modifying Commission proposals to be sent to the Council. (COREPER members are ambassadors of the member governments residing in Brussels.) This has had two effects: By removing obstacles of lesser importance, it smoothed the way for proposals once they reached the Council. It also kept items off the Council's agenda that were likely to be rejected at the Council level by one or more governments. The COREPER thus became the gatekeeper for the EC's ordinary agenda, playing a key role, along with the Commission, both in setting the agenda and in defining alternatives to be addressed by their political superiors in the Council of Ministers.[31]

During the remainder of the 1960s, the EEC completed a number of the tasks on its ordinary agenda with relatively little controversy.[32] In 1967, the executives of the ECSC, the European Atomic Energy Community, and the EEC were merged into one, thus establishing a single Commission.[33] The Commission assumed responsibility for negotiating on behalf of all six members in the Kennedy Round of the General Agreement on Tariffs and Trade (GATT) negotiations. The customs union for manufactured products was completed in 1968, 18 months early and with all six members, including France, having lowered their tariffs according to the accelerated schedule. Between 1967 and 1973, all six countries adopted a common value-added tax (VAT), a step that was designed to reduce disparities among the six markets in the prices ultimately charged consumers for the same goods.

After de Gaulle

In May 1968, the presidency of Charles de Gaulle was dealt a severe blow by the outbreak of a student revolt, which started in Paris, spread to other French cities, and was followed by a general strike of French workers. With the considerable help of his premier, Georges Pompidou, de Gaulle managed to weather the storm, and order was restored in June 1968. But de Gaulle's personal authority had been seriously weakened, as was confirmed in April 1969, when a referendum he presented to the voters was defeated, partly because a segment of his majority, led by former Finance Minister Valéry Giscard d'Estaing, opposed it. In response, de Gaulle resigned as president and returned to his country home to write his memoirs, until his death the following year. A new presidential election was held in June 1969, which Georges Pompidou won handily over a severely divided opposition. He appointed fellow Gaullist Jacques Chaban-Delmas as premier. Giscard d'Estaing, who led his own smaller and moderately pro-EC party, returned to his previous post as finance minister.

As a Gaullist, Pompidou had no sympathy for a supranationalist EC, but he was willing to take steps to remove the animosities between France and its EC partners that had accumulated during the de Gaulle years.[34] He made it clear that he would not automatically turn his back on a renewal of the British application for membership in the EC.[35] Pompidou called for an EC summit meeting at the Hague in December 1969.

The Hague summit set in motion the first concrete actions that successfully went beyond the Rome Treaty. Pompidou decided to take these steps in part because of the growing significance of

West Germany in the affairs of Europe. Between 1966 and 1969, the Christian Democratic (CDU) monopoly of power in West Germany had given way to a "Grand Coalition" of the CDU/CSU and the opposition SPD, now led by Willy Brandt.[36] On EC matters, the SPD under Brandt had become Eurocentrist, verbally in favor of steps toward European integration, but usually preferring to wait for France to take the initiative. As foreign minister in the Grand Coalition government, Brandt had begun to fashion a new *Ostpolitik*, designed to reopen contact with Eastern European bloc countries, especially with East Germany.[37]

In the parliamentary elections of September 1969, an emerging center-left coalition of the SPD and the smaller Free Democratic Party (FDP) defeated the CDU/CSU, and Willy Brandt became the new chancellor. From the point of view of his EC partners, this change augured a change in the direction of West Germany's principal foreign policy preoccupations. At a time when West Germany was emerging as one of the strongest and most dynamic world economies, Pompidou feared that it would turn its back on the EC and fashion a separate foreign policy toward Eastern Europe. Bonn might be tempted to use its considerable economic power to lessen the opposition of the Soviet Union to closer relations between East and West Germany. This could be a step in the direction of German reunification. It was still too close to World War II for Pompidou to look favorably on such a prospect, which was a consideration that influenced him to promote the Hague summit.

The Hague summit produced a declaration of support for negotiations with Britain over the terms of entry. Conditions soon ripened in Britain for a new effort. In June 1970, the Conservatives returned to power, unexpectedly defeating Harold Wilson's Labour Party. The new prime minister was Edward Heath, who was unambiguously Eurocentrist.[38] Heath, in fact, had been the chief British negotiator during the first bid to enter the EC in 1961–1963. His Conservative Party had come a long way from the Macmillan days; there was now only a small fringe on the party right-wing that opposed entry in 1970, whereas the Labour Party was sharply divided on the issue.[39] Negotiations for the British entry went fairly smoothly. The main issues involved Britain's budget contribution—a problem exacerbated by the fact that the benefits going to Britain's small, but efficient farm sector would be outweighed by the cost to the British consumer of higher-priced food. But the issues involving the CAP and the British contribution to the EC budget were fudged in the formula established for gradually phasing in the new member's obligations.[40] Heath was able to get the Treaty of Accession through the House of Commons, and Britain joined the EC in 1973, along with Denmark and Ireland, both of which ratified the treaty after comfortable yes votes in popular referenda. The fourth applicant, Norway, failed to ratify the treaty after a negative referendum vote, with farmers and fishing communities voting heavily against accession.[41]

In addition to paving the way for enlargement of the EC, the Hague summit approved the financial provisions for the CAP through establishment of the EC's own resources by national contributions from the agricultural levies and industrial customs duties collected.[42] The European Parliament obtained a say in the use of these funds. France had opposed such an arrangement since the empty-chair crisis, but now Pompidou stepped back from de Gaulle's negative position. At the summit, it was also agreed that Economic and Monetary Union (EMU) would be achieved by 1980.[43] In 1970, the Council of Ministers appointed a committee headed by Luxembourg Prime Minister Pierre Werner to sort out the competing proposals for EMU. The Werner plan presented to the Council later in the year included proposals for coordination of economic and monetary policies and for an eventual common currency. But when the global monetary crisis began in 1971, the plan was shelved indefinitely.

So long as France's partners were willing to take an intergovernmental approach to achieving cooperation in the foreign policy realm, the French were all for it, as were the British. Following the Hague meeting, the six foreign ministers commissioned a report by a committee headed by Belgian diplomat Etienne Davignon. The Davignon report on European "political cooperation," which came to be known as EPC, recommended regular meetings of the six foreign ministers wearing their hats as guardians of national interests rather than as members of the EC Council of Ministers deliberating on general EC policy matters. The idea was to develop habits of regular contact and collaboration among the member countries to allow "Europe" to speak with a single voice in diplomatic questions; this raised the potential of France, Germany, and the others to influence matters normally controlled by the superpowers. In fact, although confined to the member states, EPC would not be an integral part of the EC or its institutions. The early steps toward EPC paved the way for more significant moves toward political cooperation taken in the mid-1970s after the EC was enlarged to nine members.[44]

In general, the Hague summit represented the opening of a new extraordinary agenda for the EC. But it was an agenda that bore little evidence of the sort of Commission initiative taking and power aggrandizement that had been attempted under President Hallstein. Heads of government, foreign ministers, and career diplomats were in the forefront of the new steps being taken. In two cases, the consequent steps were essentially intergovernmental. The entry of Britain into the EC strengthened the hand of intergovernmentalist France in the Council meetings. Pompidou and Heath formed a new, if temporary, axis of power within the EC. And the new procedures for EPC were decidedly intergovernmentalist, with the Commission having no more than the right to express its views on agenda items initiated by the governments.[45] However, the completion of the CAP and the new budget provisions strengthened the supranational elements of the EC.

The Rise of the European Council

The Hague summit of 1969 can be regarded as a prototype of the agenda-setting summit meetings that began to be held in the 1970s. The next major package deal was reached at the Paris summit of December 1974, at which the practice was established of holding thrice-yearly summit meetings of the heads of state and government. This was the inauguration of the European Council, whose presidency rotates among the member countries every six months, following the existing practice in the Council of Ministers.[46] It was at the initiative of the new French president, Valéry Giscard d'Estaing, who was not a Gaullist, but was a center-right Gaullist ally. Giscard d'Estaing was elected president in May 1974, succeeding the deceased Georges Pompidou. The European Council idea had the support of the new German chancellor, Helmut Schmidt, who had replaced his fellow SPD leader, Willy Brandt, in March 1974.

Giscard d'Estaing and Schmidt had already established a good working relationship in prior years. Both had served as finance ministers under their predecessors at a time when intense efforts were being made to cope with the monetary chaos of the 1971–1973 period (see Chapters 4 and 9). Both were of a practical bent, with little sympathy for the European visionaries found in the Commission, the European Parliament, and some of the governments of the other member countries.[47] Both recognized that France and West Germany working together held the key to increasing the influence of the EC in Europe and in the larger world, and neither was looking for an edge over the other.[48]

Shortly before Schmidt and Giscard d'Estaing took the controls of their governments, in the general election of February 1974 power shifted back in Britain from the Conservatives under Edward Heath to the Labour Party headed by Harold Wilson. Whereas Heath had fit the pragmatic Europe-first mode of the new French and German leaders, Wilson, with an uncertain majority in Parliament and an economy in shambles, was necessarily more preoccupied with Britain than with Europe, and he tended to view European issues in the light of their significance for British domestic politics and economics.[49]

Wilson's strategy in domestic politics was to use the EC as a means of strengthening the moderate, or "social democratic," wing of the Labour Party against the party's left wing.

The Labour left, led by Industry Minister Tony Benn, was calling for Britain to leave the EC and threatening to use the issue to siphon off some of Wilson's support base elsewhere in the party. To counter this danger, Wilson promised in the election campaign of February 1974 to renegotiate the Treaty of Accession under which Britain had entered the EC. After winning the election, Wilson signaled to the other EC members that he wished to renegotiate the terms of British membership; failing this, Britain would leave the EC. The partners reluctantly agreed in principle, but while Wilson managed to gain some minor advantages for Britain out of the negotiations, he claimed for purposes of home consumption that he had gained more for Britain than the facts justified. Although Chancellor Schmidt lent the British considerable assistance in the negotiations, he had little patience with Wilson's tactics.[50]

The heads of state and government agreed at the Paris summit to pursue an EC regional policy, giving economic assistance to the poorer regions of the member countries. This agreement represented side payments that France and West Germany made to Italy and Ireland in particular, although it was also a policy that the British Labour government supported in the hope that British regions would benefit as well. It represented a step beyond the Rome Treaty, as did the decision to hold regular European Council meetings. Simon Bulmer and Wolfgang Wessels point out that "a key difference from earlier summits was that the commitments were not just pious hopes but had been based on the details of policy as well. . . . The EC's position had been stabilized; its relevance to the 1970s was confirmed."[51]

The decision at the Paris summit to put direct elections of the European Parliament on the agenda of the Council of Ministers was not so much a departure from the original Rome Treaty agenda as it was a long-delayed removal of French resistance to direct elections, which had stood in the way of fulfillment of the treaty for the 15 years of Gaullist rule. It was one of the specific elements of the intergovernmentalism versus supranationalism debate between the Gaullists and the Eurocentrists in France where Giscard d'Estaing sided with the latter. Beginning in 1978, there would be regular elections for all seats in the European Parliament every five years. Giscard d'Estaing was able to put together an ad hoc Eurocentrist majority in the French National Assembly against the combined opposition of the Communists and Gaullists to enable direct elections to be held in France. With French resistance to direct elections removed, the British became the footdraggers. The British Parliament was slow to adopt the electoral law because of left-wing Labour and right-wing Conservative opposition; as a result, the first Euro-elections were delayed in all nine countries until June 1979.[52]

The European Community in the Mid-1970s

The principal innovations in the EC during the first half of the 1970s were set in motion in one fashion or another by the Hague summit of December 1969 and were rounded off by the Paris and Dublin summits five years later. They confirmed the significance of the empty-chair crisis and the Luxembourg compromise of the mid-1960s. It was now clear that additions to and alterations of the original Rome Treaty agenda could be undertaken only on the initiative of the heads of state and government. With the establishment of the European Council, a regular procedure became available for agenda items to be introduced by the heads.[53]

In the mid-1970s, EPC was becoming a vehicle by which the EC nine could take foreign policy positions that were at least gently at odds with the priorities of the United States. Through EPC, the heads of state and government probed alternatives to the American pro-Israel position in Middle East questions. More concretely, EPC followed along the lines of reducing tensions between Eastern and Western Europe that de Gaulle had pioneered in the second half of the 1960s with his policy of *détente* and that Brandt had dramatically achieved in the 1970s with his *Ostpolitik*. In 1975, the Conference on Security and Cooperation in Europe (CSCE) was held at

Helsinki, which brought together the states of Western and Eastern Europe, including the Soviet Union, and the United States and Canada. A declaration was produced that outlined steps for reducing tensions and accelerating human contacts between East and West. The nine EPC states acted essentially as one under the leadership of the government currently holding the presidency of the Council. The process was strictly intergovernmental because EPC existed outside the Rome Treaty framework. Major initiatives to be taken in CSCE negotiations were decided on in meetings of the nine foreign ministers under general guidelines given at summit meetings.[54]

With respect to the ordinary agenda, beyond finalizing the customs union and the CAP, the Rome Treaty provided only very general guidelines as to what should happen next. The budget was often the object of intense conflict between the Commission and the Council, between the European Parliament and the Council, and between individual member states within the Council, but somehow budgets were produced, and the ability of the European Parliament to influence parts of them increased. In 1975, a treaty amending the Rome Treaty was adopted. This treaty, which came into force in June 1977, for the first time gave the European Parliament the ability to reject the budget outright, and it created a Court of Auditors to monitor the EC's use of its revenues. Furthermore, appointment of members of the European Court of Justice (ECJ) was now subject to review and endorsement by the European Parliament.[55]

But the EC in this period was better known for its abortive ordinary agenda items, many of which were proposals by the Commission for harmonizing the separate technical standards that acted as barriers to inter-EC trade, preventing the customs union from having its full economic effect. Although some of these, including some with environmental significance, were adopted by the Council of Ministers in the 1970s, many were buried by the COREPER or delayed in the Council of Ministers when individual governments, under pressure from economic interest groups that might be adversely affected by harmonization, implicitly exercised a veto.[56] Movement on these blocked agenda items would await the achievement of the package deal in the mid-1980s that brought about the Single European Act with its Project 1992 measures for liberalization of trade and harmonization of regulatory regimes affecting trade between the member economies.[57]

On the other hand, below the surface of public attention, a process was going on in the 1960s and 1970s by which the interpretation of the Rome Treaty's ordinary agenda was being expanded. The ECJ was in the process of establishing a body of EC constitutional law in a case-by-case fashion, much as the U.S. Supreme Court had done in the early nineteenth century under John Marshall. Without challenging the member governments directly, in the 1960s the ECJ asserted the principle that the Rome Treaty has the status of a constitution and therefore its provisions are superior to the laws of the member states. It also granted to "individuals" (usually companies registered in the member states) the right to challenge actions of the member states by bringing cases to the ECJ for interpretation, which might result in a finding that the member state was in violation of the Treaty of Rome. This led in the 1970s to the declaration that, when actions of the member states are in conflict with lawmaking actions of the EC taken in pursuit of the Rome Treaty, EC law would prevail.[58] These assertions would have had little effect if the courts of the member states had refused to accept them, simply regarding the treaty as an international agreement among sovereign states that were competent individually to interpret its meaning for themselves. But gradually in the 1960s and 1970s, national courts did cite decisions of the ECJ as authority for upholding EC law in the face of resistance by national governments and parliaments.[59]

The opinions of the ECJ did not, in and of themselves, have the effect of expanding the ordinary agenda unless the more politically oriented EC bodies were willing to use them for that purpose. The ECJ could not by itself force new EC legislation. The 1970s were years of Commission caution and serious disagreement among the member governments on many policy issues. Nevertheless, the eventual reopening of both the ordinary and the extraordinary agendas in the 1980s was to benefit from the less restrictive interpretation of the treaty that had emerged in the previous decade. The ECJ's work had helped to create the new atmosphere.[60]

By the end of 1975, much of the primary work that the six original EEC members had agreed on in the Treaty of Rome had been accomplished. The customs union and the CAP were in place. Differences in conception of how the institutions were to function, which had come to a head in the mid-1960s crisis, had been smoothed over in practice. At least for the time being, intergovernmentalism had come to prevail over supranationalism, not least of all because of the entry of intergovernmentalist Britain, the major holdout of the 1950s. To be sure, direct elections to the European Parliament had been agreed on, and the European Parliament had gained a greater role in the budgetary process, but these supranational (and democratic) advances were counterbalanced by intergovernmentalist gains in the institutionalization of summit meetings and the forms established for EPC. Meanwhile, the arrival of EMU, heralded in 1969, had been delayed indefinitely.

STUDY QUESTIONS

1. What were the economic and political factors that drove European leaders to establish the institutions of the EEC?

2. How did the European leaders overcome traditional rivalries to build supranational institutions of the EEC?

3. What is the "empty-chair" crisis and what key lessons were learned from this experience?

4. Write a critical assessment of the rise of European Council from neofunctionalist and liberal intergovernmentalist perspectives.

5. How does historical institutionalism explain developments in EU integration during the 1960s and early 1970s?

6. How does constructivism explain developments in the EU integration during the 1960s and early 1970s?

ENDNOTES

1. "Preamble and Selected Articles of the Treaty Establishing the European Economic Community, March 25, 1957," in Howard Bliss, ed., *The Political Development of the European Community: A Documentary Collection* (Waltham, Mass.: Blaisdell, 1970), pp. 47–66.

2. Lindberg and Scheingold rank decision-making functions of the EEC as of 1968 according to the mix of EC-level and national-level decisions involved. The highest rank received was for functions wherein there was policy making at both levels, but wherein "Community activity predominates." The two functions in this category were "agricultural protection" and "movement of goods, services, and other factors of production within the customs union." For the 20 other functions listed, decision making was either exclusively or predominantly at the national level. Leon N. Lindberg and Stuart A. Scheingold, *Europe's Would-Be Polity: Patterns of Change in the European Community* (Englewood Cliffs, N.J.: Prentice-Hall, 1970), p. 71.

3. Derek W. Urwin, *Western Europe Since 1945: A Political History*, 4th ed. (London and New York: Longman, 1989), pp. 131–134.

4. Roy Godson and Stephen Haseler, *"Eurocommunism": Implications for East and West* (New York: St. Martin's Press, 1978), pp. 97–99.

5. F. Roy Willis, *France, Germany and the New Europe, 1945–1967*, rev. ed. (London: Oxford University Press, 1968), pp. 98–99, 140–141, 262–264.

6. Extensive analyses of de Gaulle's strategy in Europe within the context of his general worldview are found in Philip G. Cerny, *The Politics of Grandeur: Ideological Aspects of de Gaulle's Foreign Policy* (Cambridge: Cambridge University Press, 1980); Alfred Grosser, *The Western Alliance: European-American Relations Since 1945* (New York: Vintage Books, 1982); Stanley Hoffmann, *Decline or Renewal? France Since the 1930s* (New York: Viking Press, 1974); and Edward Kolodziej, *French International Policy Under de Gaulle and*

Pompidou: The Politics of Grandeur (Ithaca, N.Y.: Cornell University Press, 1974).

7. Hoffmann, *Decline or Renewal?* pp. 301–302; Charles de Gaulle, *Memoirs of Hope: Renewal and Endeavor*, trans. Terence Kil-martin (New York: Simon and Schuster, 1971), pp. 163–170.

8. William E. Paterson, *The SPD and European Integration* (Lexington, Mass.: Lexington Books, 1974), chaps. 3–5.

9. Stephen George, *An Awkward Partner: Britain in the European Community* (Oxford: Oxford University Press, 1990), pp. 26–28.

10. John Pinder, *European Community: The Building of Union* (Oxford and New York: Oxford University Press, 1991), pp. 45–46; Dennis Swann, *The Economics of the Common Market*, 5th ed. (Hammondsworth, England: Penguin Books, 1984), p. 22.

11. F. S. Northedge, "Britain and the EEC Past and Present," in Roy Jenkins, ed., *Britain and the EEC* (London and Basingstoke, England: Macmillan, 1983), pp. 15–37.

12. For accounts of the Algerian War and the transformation of the Fourth Republic into the Fifth Republic, see Edgar S. Furniss, Jr., *France, Troubled Ally: De Gaulle's Heritage and Prospects* (New York: Praeger, 1960); and Roy C. Macridis and Bernard Brown, *The De Gaulle Republic: Quest for Unity* (Homewood, Ill.: Dorsey Press, 1960).

13. Derek W. Urwin, *The Community of Europe: A History of European Integration Since 1945* (London and New York: Longman, 1991), pp. 103–107.

14. Suzanne J. Bodenheimer, *Political Union: A Microcosm of European Politics, 1960–1966* (Leiden, Netherlands. A. W. Sijthoff, 1967), pp. 59–60.

15. Ibid., pp. 92–99. The West German government sought unsuccessfully to reach a compromise between the French position and that of the others. Jan Werts, *The European Council* (Amsterdam: North Holland, 1992), pp. 23–25.

16. Northedge, "Britain and the EEC," p. 26.

17. This is the idea of Britain as a "Trojan horse" supporting U.S. interests within the EEC. Miriam Camps, *European Unification in the Sixties: From the Veto to the Crisis* (New York: McGraw-Hill, 1966), p. 3.

18. Werner J. Feld, *West Germany and the European Community: Changing Interests and Competing Policy Objectives* (New York: Praeger, 1981), pp. 50–51.

19. Andrew Moravcsik, *The Choice for Europe: Social Purpose and State Power from Messina to Maastricht* (London: UCL Press, 1999), pp. 176–193.

20. Ibid., p. 189.

21. Urwin, *The Community of Europe*, pp. 110–111.

22. John Newhouse, *Collision in Brussels: The Common Market Crisis of 30 June 1965* (New York: Norton, 1967), pp. 67–71.

23. Camps, *European Unification in the Sixties*, pp. 38–43.

24. Ibid., p. 43.

25. According to the Treaty of Rome, what we are consistently calling the European Parliament was officially named the "Assembly." The members of the Assembly themselves called it a Parliament from an early stage, although its powers were very weak under the treaty. It could propose budget amendments to the Council of Ministers, but the Council was "under no obligation to accept any amendments" and could adopt its original version of the budget by qualified majority. Ibid., p. 44.

26. Camps, *European Unification in the Sixties*, pp. 43–45.

27. Urwin, *The Community of Europe*, p. 111.

28. Werts, *The European Council*, p. 28.

29. Camps, *European Unification in the Sixties*, pp. 95–101.

30. Ibid., p. 112.

31. John W. Kingdon, *Agendas, Alternatives and Public Policies* (Glenview, Ill., and London: Scott, Foresman, 1984), p. 4; Newhouse, *Collision in Brussels*, pp. 161–165.

32. Urwin, *The Community of Europe*, pp. 130–132.

33. Willis, *France, Germany and the New Europe*, p. 361.

34. F. Roy Willis, *The French Paradox: Understanding Contemporary France* (Stanford, Calif.: Hoover Institution, 1982), pp. 10, 105.

35. In 1967, the government of Prime Minister Harold Wilson made a second effort to bring Britain into the community. For a second time, the bid was turned down by de Gaulle. George, *An Awkward Partner*, pp. 37–38.

36. Urwin, *The Community of Europe*, pp. 137–138.

37. Wolfram Hanrieder, *Germany, America, Europe: Forty Years of German Foreign Policy* (New Haven, Conn., and London: Yale University Press, 1989), pp. 196–198.

38. George, *An Awkward Partner*, p. 49.

39. David Butler and Uwe Kitzinger, *The 1975 Referendum* (New York: St. Martin's Press, 1976), pp. 17–20.

40. George, *An Awkward Partner*, p. 56.

41. Urwin, *The Community of Europe*, pp. 140–145.

42. For discussions of the Hague summit, see Simon Bulmer and Wolfgang Wessels, *The European Council: Decision-Making in European Politics* (Basingstoke, England, and London: MacMillan, 1987), pp. 28–30; Urwin, *The Community of Europe*, chaps. 9 and 10.

43. Rainer Hellman, *Gold, the Dollar, and the European Currency Systems: The Seven-Year Monetary War* (New York: Praeger, 1979), pp. 20–22.

44. *European Political Cooperation (EPC)*, 5th ed. (Bonn: Press and Information Office of the Federal Government, 1988); Wolfgang Wessels, "New Forms of Foreign Policy Formulation in Western Europe," in Werner J. Feld, ed., *Western Europe's Global Reach: Regional Cooperation and Worldwide Aspirations* (New York: Pergamon, 1980), pp. 12–29.

45. *European Political Cooperation (EPC)*, p. 28.

46. Bulmer and Wessels, *The European Council*, pp. 11–13.

47. Urwin, *The Community of Europe*, p. 173.

48. Bulmer and Wessels, *The European Council*, pp. 41–42.

49. George, *An Awkward Partner*, pp. 74–78.

50. Ibid., pp. 82–87.

51. Bulmer and Wessels, *The European Council*, p. 46.

52. Urwin, *The Community of Europe*, pp. 167–168; Dominique Remy with Karl-Hermann Buck, "France: The Impossible Compromise or the End of Majority Parliamentarism?" pp. 99–125; Mark Hagger, "The United Kingdom: The Reluctant Europeans," in Valentino Herman and Mark Hagger, eds., *The Legislation of Direct Elections to the European Parliament* (Westmead, England: Gower, 1980), pp. 204–238; David M. Wood, "Comparing Parliamentary Voting on European Issues in France and Britain," *Legislative Studies Quarterly* 7 (February 1982): 101–117.

53. Bulmer and Wessels, *The European Council*, p. 46.

54. *European Political Cooperation (EPC)*, pp. 95–97; William Wallace, "Political Cooperation: Integration Through Intergovernmentalism," in Helen Wallace et al., eds., *Policymaking in the European Community*, 3rd ed. (Chichester, England: Wiley, 1983), pp. 378–380. See Chapter 12 for the evolution from EPC to the CFSP of today's EU.

55. Helen Wallace, *Budgetary Politics: The Finances of the European Communities* (London: Allen & Unwin, 1980), pp. 77–91, 102.

56. Alan Dashwood, "Hastening Slowly: The Community's Path Towards Harmonization," in Wallace et al., eds., *Policymaking in the European Community*, pp. 184–187; Bulmer and Wessels, *The European Council*, p. 5.

57. Alberta M. Sbragia, "Asymmetrical Integration in the European Community: The Single European Act and Institutional Developments," in Dale L. Smith and James Lee Ray, eds., *The 1992 Project and the Future of Integration in Europe* (Armonk, N.Y., and London: Sharpe, 1993), pp. 101–104; Helen Wallace, "The Council and the Commission After the Single European Act," in Leon Hurwitz and Christian Lequesne, eds., *The State of the European Community: Policies, Institutions and Debates in the Transition Years* (Boulder, Colo.: Lynne Reinner, 1991), pp. 24–25.

58. Anne-Marie Burley and Walter Mattli, "Europe Before the Court: A Political Theory of Legal Integration," *International Organization* 47 (Winter 1993): 41–76; Karen J. Alter, "The European Union's Legal System and Domestic Policy: Spillover or Backlash?" *International Organization* 54 (Summer 2000): 489–518.

59. Martin Shapiro, "The European Court of Justice," in Alberta M. Sbragia, ed., *Euro-Politics: Institutions and Policymaking in the New European Community* (Washington, D.C.: Brookings Institution, 1992), p. 127.

60. David R. Cameron, "The 1992 Initiative: Causes and Consequences," in Sbragia, ed., *Euro-Politics*, pp. 52–53.

The Single European Act and the Maastricht Treaty (1975–1993)

This chapter will concentrate on two significant extensions of European Union (EU) competence: the Single European Act (SEA) and the Treaty on European Union (TEU), better known as the Maastricht Treaty. Both of these accomplishments were achieved in spite of considerable resistance by the United Kingdom and Denmark, especially by British Prime Minister Margaret Thatcher.

PRIME MINISTER THATCHER AND THE BUDGET ISSUE

In the late 1970s, the general reluctance of the British to take new steps toward integration continued. Memories of past British glory, long-standing rivalry, and, at times, brutal experiences with France and Germany were not easily erased in Britons' minds. Because of their special relationship with the United States and with other areas of the world colonized by British subjects and still linked in the Commonwealth of Nations—Canada, New Zealand, and Australia—the British could not completely identify with their neighbors across the Channel.

The government of James Callaghan was at odds with its European Community (EC) partners over another issue that reached down to the roots of the British "difference." From the British point of view, the Common Agricultural Policy (CAP) was simply *unfair*. It was seen, first of all, as a mechanism by which taxpayers in EC countries like Britain that were net food importers were subsidizing not only the farmers of other EC countries, but also the governments of those countries, which were thus relieved by the CAP of part of their responsibility for protecting farmers' incomes. Second, the CAP was seen as a factor adding to both external dislocations (high oil prices) and internal strains (budgetary deficits, high labor costs) that had produced runaway British inflation in the mid-1970s.[1]

British consumers found themselves paying higher prices than they were used to for food, much of which came into their grocery stores in very visible form from France, Holland, and Denmark. Yearly negotiations with EC partners over CAP prices and budgetary contributions provided the Callaghan government with constant reminders that its political problems at home were made more difficult by policies of an organization that many Labour supporters felt should not have been joined in the first place. In the May 1979 general election, Callaghan's Labour Party was defeated by the Conservatives, whose leader, Margaret Thatcher, then became the new prime minister.

The rise of Margaret Thatcher marked a new era in British politics. While Callaghan had ruffled feathers in EC circles from time to time, Thatcher adopted the politics of confrontation as a personal style. Like de Gaulle, she appeared intractable in negotiation, but she was not at all aloof and inscrutable. She jumped right into the middle of the fray, and her adversaries knew where she stood. But they were no happier with the positions she took than de Gaulle's opponents had been in the 1960s.[2] On the CAP budget issue, she made it very clear that the existing arrangements were unfair and that Britain would not countenance further progress toward EU so long as the unfairness remained.

From the standpoint of the Commission in Brussels and the original six members, Britain had never accepted true "European" goals and norms. Britain resisted the goals of economic, monetary, and political union, and the others recognized that any moves they might make in these directions would elicit a British veto or refusal to take part, as in the case of the European Monetary System (EMS). But Thatcher's claim of unfairness in the CAP budget discussions was seen by her fellow heads of state and government as a repudiation of norms of the EC. The term *community* reflected the belief of political elites in France, West Germany, Italy, and the Benelux countries that members had joined in the desire to engage in a cooperative effort to solve problems they could not solve individually. Policies that the six had put in place prior to Britain's entry constituted what was called in French the *acquis communautaire*, that body of established laws and practices that made them a true *community*. This body had been accumulated through long and painful negotiations, involving the give-and-take of members who were not disposed to reexamine them at such a late date. When Britain joined the EC, it had accepted the *acquis communautaire* and its consequences, including its budgetary consequences. None of the member countries would insist that the CAP was perfect and should not be reformed. But until agreement could be reached on CAP reform, the budgetary arrangements would have to continue.[3]

It was not lost on Thatcher that France, which was one of the members most resistant to an accommodation with Britain over the budget, had always fought for its own corner fiercely, even when the rest of the EC membership was aligned on the other side. But while Helmut Schmidt was still Germany's chancellor, he sought to find ways to bring the British and the French together on the issue. According to Thatcher, he pointed out that "the CAP was a price which had to be paid, however high, to persuade members like France and Italy to come into the Community from the beginning."[4] In October 1982, a coalition of Helmut Kohl's CDU/CSU and the centrist FDP replaced the coalition of Schmidt's SPD and the FDP, with the Free Democrats having changed sides.

New Chancellor Kohl had to deal with Margaret Thatcher's demand for a fairer mechanism involving the British budget contribution. On the one hand, he could sympathize with her argument that British taxpayers should not be subsidizing the French and other governments because Germany was itself the largest net contributor to the EC budget. Thus, Kohl joined Thatcher in resisting a lifting of the budget ceiling within which the EC had to operate. But he also knew that an important component of his electoral support came from West German farmers. So he resisted Thatcher's call for CAP reforms that would reduce payments to inefficient farmers, as well as her call for reform of the budget structure, because any substantial reduction in the British contribution would have to be picked up mainly by his own government.[5]

On the French side of the triangle, a major change in government occurred in May 1981, when François Mitterrand was elected president, defeating the incumbent Valéry Giscard d'Estaing. Mitterrand's government included four Communist ministers and some Socialist ministers drawn from the left wing of the Socialist Party. Traditional French left-wing hostility to European integration now had a voice in the French cabinet. In the first two years of his presidency, Mitterrand and his ministers were preoccupied with an ambitious and radical program of domestic socioeconomic reforms that included nationalization of leading multinational industrial firms and banks and a reflationary strategy to reduce unemployment. By 1983, it was clear that this program was too expensive and was threatening France's capacity to maintain its position in the EMS. Continual pressure was being put on the franc, which could only with great difficulty maintain its value vis-à-vis the strong deutsche mark (DM). Left-wing members of Mitterrand's government were calling for France to pull out of the exchange rate mechanism (ERM) of the EMS, but in March 1983, Mitterrand decided to stay in, although the consequence would be a reversal of the socioeconomic reforms in favor of a serious austerity program to defend the franc within the ERM.[6]

With his majority in disarray and his own popularity in decline, Mitterrand needed a success on the international scene to divert attention from the failure of his government's economic policies. The main opportunity appeared in early 1984 when France assumed the EC Council presidency, affording Mitterrand a chance to play a leadership role.[7] To bring about a policy success at the European level, Mitterrand had to find a way to mollify the British prime minister. The obvious way was to make concessions to her regarding the British budget contribution.

This meant an approximately two-thirds reduction in the British CAP-mandated contribution. Mitterrand's commitment to resolving the issue was manifested in his willingness to assume a major part of the financial burden that Germany was refusing, enabling Kohl to accept part of it as well.[8] Agreement on the British budgetary contribution received the headlines, while significant steps that were taken at the Fontainebleau summit toward what was to become the Single European Act (SEA) went largely unnoticed.

THE SINGLE EUROPEAN ACT

The Fontainebleau summit illustrates the value of regular summit meetings. They had become a means by which progress could be made in economic and political integration whenever favorable national and international circumstances coincided with the turn of the right member in the Council presidency. At Fontainebleau, the heads of government and state made the single market their first priority in the quest for economic union. This meant a commitment to removing barriers to the exchange of goods and services and to the movement of labor and capital among the member countries. These were barriers that had continued to exist after creation of the customs union or that had been erected more recently, preventing the customs union from becoming a true single market.

Kohl, Mitterrand, and Thatcher were the three principal leaders whose policy commitments converged initially in order to set the agenda for the SEA at Fontainebleau. Once the budget issue was successfully managed, the heads of state and government gave the Commission the task of working out the details of the single market. The Commission had already prepared substantial parts of it for presentation to the Council of Ministers. Now, instead of the glacial progress of piecemeal trade liberalization legislation, the inclusion of many items in one omnibus package of reforms appealed to the free-trade "neoliberalism" of Margaret Thatcher and her government and to important leaders of the German governing coalition.

The single market was more attractive to the heads of state and government because of increased Japanese and American competition in both international markets and the EC market itself.[9] European business leaders had come to focus on their disadvantageous position with respect to economies of scale. It is also important to recognize that by the mid-1980s some degree of monetary stability had been achieved through the EMS, as member governments, including the French, acknowledged the value of monetary discipline imposed by their ties to the DM.[10] The strong push by the Commission to promote single-market legislation after Mitterrand's finance minister, Jacques Delors, became Commission president in January 1985 can also be cited as a crucial step in the eventual achievement of the SEA.

Delors assigned Lord Cockfield, the commissioner for the Internal Market, the task of preparing a white paper that included a list of 300 measures needed for achieving a true common market. Delors also laid out a timetable to be followed by the EC members to complete adoption of these measures by December 31, 1992—hence, the name Project 1992. Most of the white paper measures were eventually agreed on and mandated by the SEA. Scheduled to be removed was a wide array of laws and government practices of the member countries that served as barriers to intra-EC trade. These included, among others, bureaucratic procedures imposing delays in the movement of goods and persons at borders between member countries, differences in standards for manufacturing products that made illegal the sale in one member country of goods produced in another, government procurement policies discriminating against products from other member countries, conflicting taxes and levels of taxation making for differences in price of the same goods produced in different countries, and differences in the price of services involved in moving goods and persons from one country to another.[11]

Institutional reforms were a part of the SEA package. The European Parliament had continually urged that steps be taken toward political union, modest versions of which found their way into the SEA. A cross-party group of Members of the European Parliament (MEP), known as the "Crocodile Club," became the driving force behind the Parliament's demands for institutional reform in order to make the EC more democratic and politically accountable. The club's proposals were brought together as a draft European Union Treaty (EUT) to amend the Rome Treaty. The resolution supporting the EUT was adopted by the European Parliament on February 14, 1984, four months before the Fontainebleau summit.[12] As support for the single-market idea began to build, it was argued in the European Parliament that institutional reform should be attached to it. The most central provision of the EUT was the abolition of the veto in the Council of Ministers. But another important proposal that saw the light of day in the SEA was that of a "cooperation" procedure between the European Parliament and the Council of Ministers that would make it more difficult for the Council to ignore amendments proposed by the former (See Chapter 7).

The EUT was one of two influential initiatives that preceded the SEA and contributed elements of institutional reform to it. The other was the Solemn Declaration on European Union, which was adopted by the European Council at its Stuttgart summit in June 1983. This step, taken at the initiative of German Foreign Minister Hans Dietrich Genscher and Italian Foreign Minister Emilio Columbo, may be seen as presenting an alternative to the direction the European Parliament was promoting.

The Parliament's EUT initiative included an effort to curtail the agenda-setting role of the European Council, whereas the Solemn Declaration explicitly stated that the European Council "initiates cooperation in new areas of activity" and gives "general political guidelines for the European Communities and European Political Co-operation."[13] It was an intergovernmental statement, downplaying the role of the Commission, especially in calling for greater intergovernmental cooperation in foreign policy making. But it also envisioned a modest increase in the role of the European Parliament in decision making, a step that had the enthusiastic support of both the German and the Italian governments, if not the French and British. Instead of the abolition of the veto advocated by the European Parliament, it suggested a voluntary discontinuation of its use in the Council of Ministers. This could be accomplished if governments abstained instead of voting negatively, a practice that was already occurring in Council of Ministers meetings.[14]

At Fontainebleau, at the same time the single market reached the extraordinary agenda, the European Council added to it institutional reforms that were to become part of the SEA at the urging of President Mitterrand. Earlier in the year, Mitterrand had held discussions with Altiero Spinelli, who evidently influenced the French president to add his weight to the increase in European Parliament powers.[15] Mitterrand induced the heads of state and government at Fontainebleau to appoint a committee of governmental representatives to take both the EUT and the Solemn Declaration and work out a version of the EUT that would be acceptable to the ten governments. This committee, headed by Senator James Dooge of Ireland, reported to the Milan summit a year later, recommending that an intergovernmental committee be formed to draft what the Dooge report called a Treaty on European Unity. After several stages of approval, it acquired as its title the Single European Act.[16]

At Milan in June 1985, Italian Prime Minister Bettino Craxi, presiding over the European Council, proposed that an intergovernmental conference (IGC) be convened to propose a set of amendments to the Rome Treaty that would incorporate changes in the institutions along some of the lines proposed in the EUT and the Solemn Declaration. Margaret Thatcher objected strenuously to this proposal, as she believed that the present rules would allow the single market to be legislated, given the substantial consensus she believed to be behind it. But Craxi, implicitly supported by the other eight heads of state and government, ruled that under the Rome Treaty the IGC could be called by simple majority vote in the Council of Ministers. Thatcher objected, but she was overruled. At this point, she might have repeated de Gaulle's empty-chair ploy. She also had the option of staying in the meeting, but refusing to send a representative of the British government to meetings of the IGC, implicitly vetoing any proposed amendments to the Rome Treaty that might emerge. She did neither of these, staying at the summit meeting and later sending her representative to the IGC meeting, which was held in Luxembourg during the second half of 1985. Unlike de Gaulle, her first priority was achieving her desired policy change: the trade-liberalizing features of the SEA. Acceptance of more qualified majority voting (QMV) could help achieve this end through legislation to achieve the single market.

In response to the desires of the new members, the SEA specifically targeted regional issues, recognizing that redistribution of economic resources from richer to poorer areas of the EC was essential in order to achieve harmonious economic integration. In line with the SEA mandate, members reached an agreement in 1988 to double the size of the structural funds directed to the poorer regions before the completion of Project 1992.

THE DELORS INITIATIVES OF 1987–1989

The late 1980s witnessed the zenith of the Commission's influence within EC policy-making circles, as the prestige of its president reached heights never achieved by his predecessors.[17] In February 1987, President Delors presented what became known as his "package," a combination of measures designed to reduce the complex of issues among member states over the CAP and the budget. The Delors package included three components: (1) creation of new budgetary resources by additions to member contributions from sources other than their CAP obligations, (2) reform of the CAP to reduce spending obligations and the CAP share of the EC budget, and (3) enhancement of the system of redistribution favoring poorer states and regions.[18] This represented an effort by Delors to bring Margaret Thatcher into the consensual center of the EC because it answered her call for greater control over CAP spending and a shifting of revenue obligations from those based on food imports to those reflecting the relative strength of members' economies. The package made little headway at summits held in 1987, but when Germany took over the Council presidency in January 1988, the Kohl government was willing to lend its weight to support the Delors package. The Delors package was adopted in February 1988 at an extraordinary Brussels summit called by Kohl to clear the ground for progress on single-market legislation and for a new effort to achieve economic and monetary union.[19]

In the late 1980s, the surge of optimism that accompanied the early days of the SEA was further sustained by the solid performance of the EMS. By 1987, exchange rates within the ERM had become remarkably stable, and inflation rates had dropped from double digits in most EC countries in 1982 to less than 5 percent for all ERM members, while three of the four EC members not in the ERM were above that figure.[20] To the Delors Commission and the Mitterrand government, the time seemed ripe to broach the issue of the Economic and Monetary Union (EMU) again. EMU was put on the extraordinary agenda at the June 1988 meeting of the European Council at Hanover, with Chancellor Kohl presiding. The agenda-setting decision was to establish a committee headed by Delors to produce a document that could serve as a basis for revision of the Rome Treaty.[21]

The Delors report on the EMU, officially presented to the member governments in April 1989, proposed a gradual process of economic and monetary unification.[22] The plan stated that stage 1 would begin on July 1, 1990, and include liberalization of capital markets, enlarged ERM membership, and coordination of monetary policies by the EC Committee of Central Bank Governors. Stage 2, which would require revision of the Treaty of Rome, would include creation of the European System of Central Banks (ESCB), similar to the U.S. Federal Reserve system. This institution would set monetary policy, but would leave its execution to the national central banks. Furthermore, currency realignments would be allowed only under exceptional circumstances. Finally, in stage 3, exchange rates would irrevocably be fixed and national central banks would be replaced by the ESCB. The plan left open whether the process would culminate in the adoption of a single European currency.[23] (See Chapter 9.)

Of the major member states, France was the most enthusiastic about moving ahead to EMU. From the French standpoint, the dominant position of the Bundesbank in aligning ERM currencies around a strong DM meant that severe restrictions were placed on French economic policy making, especially limiting the ability of the French government to counteract recession and unemployment. The EMU would make monetary policy subject to the collective decision making of the ESCB, thus reducing Bundesbank control and giving the Bank of France, and therefore the French government, more influence.[24] To Kohl, the idea of moving ahead to EMU was acceptable, although he had to set aside Bundesbank objections in giving the Delors report his government's approval.[25] To Margaret Thatcher, whose irritation with Delors had been stimulated the year before by the statements he had made envisaging substantial transfers of sovereignty to the Community, EMU was far from acceptable. Delors's own enthusiasm for the EMU was based on his expectation of precisely such a transfer of sovereignty to EC institutions. But the Delors report effectively put the EMU on the extraordinary agenda for the early 1990s.

THE MAASTRICHT STRUGGLE

The new EU that came into being in late 1993 resulted from two main strands of activity by its principal architects. Between 1989 and 1992, they produced the blueprints for both the Economic and Monetary Union (EMU) and Political Union. Plans for EMU were agreed on in general terms at the Madrid summit of June 1989; then, with the overturn of Communist regimes in Eastern Europe and the unification of Germany, it was agreed that important steps toward Political Union would be undertaken. Both EMU and Political Union were further developed and agreed on in the Maastricht Treaty.

Economic and Monetary Union on the Agenda

The first steps on the road to Maastricht, in the years from 1988 to 1990, brought to the extraordinary agenda Economic and Monetary Union (EMU) and the Community Charter of Fundamental

Social Rights for Workers (the Social Charter), both of which were conceived as extensions of EC powers that would be necessitated by the opening of the single market. The EMU involved three stages leading to the creation of a central banking system and, potentially, a single currency. Both EMU and the Social Charter, which was designed to achieve uniformity in social provisions, conditions of employment, and industrial relations, were put on the extraordinary agenda on the initiative of Delors, Kohl, and Mitterrand at the Hanover summit of June 1988. After being reelected in March 1988, President Mitterrand joined Delors in giving strong support to the EMU, after succeeding in bringing along Chancellor Kohl, who overrode the objections of the Bundesbank. At the June 1989 Madrid summit, pressed hard by her foreign secretary and finance minister not to leave Britain in an isolated position, Prime Minister Thatcher conceded the creation of an IGC to draft treaty amendments that would provide for an EMU.[26] At the Strasburg summit in December 1989, it was agreed to convene the IGC at the end of 1990.

Prime Minister Thatcher's opposition to the EMU was based on an unwillingness to see an EC central bank and single currency that would take away Britain's capacity to conduct its own monetary policy. She was even opposed to the idea of Britain's pound sterling being brought within the Exchange Rate Mechanism (ERM) of the European Monetary System (EMS), which her finance minister, Nigel Lawson, had been advocating since the mid-1980s. Margaret Thatcher's governments since 1979 had followed the monetarist premise that inflation is caused by an increase in the national money supply and that it can therefore be controlled by controlling the money supply. Lawson had come to the conclusion that money supply could not be effectively controlled and that a more effective means of achieving monetary stability would be to anchor sterling to the strong DM through membership in the ERM. Since the Bundesbank pursued an effective counterinflationary policy by controlling interest rate levels, Britain could do likewise by following the German lead, as France, the Netherlands, and Ireland were doing. Thatcher disliked tying Britain's hands in this way. If the Bundesbank raised or lowered German interest rates, Britain would have to do likewise in order to keep the pound–DM exchange rates within ERM limits, regardless of the effects on the British economy. Given her strong aversion to a loss of British sovereignty, Thatcher inevitably resisted this step, as well as the proposed EMU, as she believed that a "Euro-version" of the Bundesbank would be controlling British macroeconomic policy. In October 1990, a year after Lawson's resignation, Thatcher finally allowed his successor, John Major, to take the pound into the ERM, but she did so with great reluctance.[27]

Growing inflation and unemployment since the 1987 British election had led to a loss of public support for the Conservatives, and especially for Thatcher. Conservative members of the British Parliament (MPs) were made uneasy about their reelection prospects with Thatcher still at the helm. When she made it clear in a speech to the House of Commons that Britain would hold out alone against the version of EMU that was emerging from intergovernmental deliberations, her deputy prime minister, former Foreign Minister Geoffrey Howe, resigned from the cabinet and gave a speech of his own that undoubtedly swung some Conservative backbenchers against her. These defectors combined with others willing to find a more electable prime minister to deny her a majority in a vote of the parliamentary party on November 22, 1990. She resigned six days later, and John Major became prime minister following a vote of the Conservative MPs.[28] While it was generally expected that Major would follow the broad outlines of Thatcher's policies, it was also clear that an important obstacle to the achievement of a treaty on European union had been removed.

Political Union on the Agenda

The other institutional innovations of the three pillars of the eventual Maastricht Treaty were of a more political nature, if the term is taken to include internal and external security concerns, as well as institutional changes. They did not reach the extraordinary agenda until after the upheavals in

Central and Eastern Europe and the October 1990 unification of Germany. The desire of the Federal Republic of Germany and its EC partners to anchor the new Germany solidly in the EC framework propelled the EC 12 to join monetary and political union into a single project that reached its fruition in the agreements at the Maastricht summit of December 1991.

When the Berlin Wall came down in November 1989, there was general rejoicing throughout the EC because it represented a victory for Western democracy and market economies. But when Chancellor Kohl began in late November to openly advocate early unification of the two Germanies, doubts began to be raised privately and hinted at publicly by both Prime Minister Thatcher and President Mitterrand. In meetings with Mitterrand in December 1989 and January 1990, Prime Minister Thatcher expressed her opposition to unification on the grounds that a larger, more powerful Germany would upset the balance within Europe by gaining excessive influence over the newly emerging East European states. While agreeing with Thatcher in principle, Mitterrand was pessimistic about the chances of preventing unification and thought it best to exercise damage control by strengthening the EC, thus locking the new Germany into a cooperative mode. Thatcher opposed this view, believing that it was precisely within the EC that Germany's "hegemony" would assert itself and that it was important for Britain and France to develop links with the post-Communist Eastern European countries, looking toward a "widening" of the EC before attempting to "deepen" it through further political integration.[29]

This position of the British prime minister was, in fact, the opposite of the view Jacques Delors was then taking, which was that the EC should strengthen itself internally, especially by achieving EMU, before expanding to include either the Alpine and Scandinavian countries of the European Free Trade Association (EFTA) or Poland, Hungary, and Czechoslovakia, which were being widely mentioned as potential candidates for EC membership. Mitterrand decided that, to keep the Franco-German coalition together and to keep Germany from going off in adventuresome directions to the east, it was best to continue supporting Delors's strategy. Chancellor Kohl enthusiastically endorsed it as well, and Thatcher found herself again facing a bloc of the other three principal EC actors solidly arrayed against her.[30]

Political Union was placed on the EC agenda in the first half of 1990. The most important initiative was taken in March by Mitterrand and Kohl, who jointly sent a letter to the Irish prime minister, Charles Haughey, asking him to convene a special meeting of the European Council in April 1990 to consider ways to strengthen political cooperation among EC members. Before the April summit, Mitterrand and Kohl sent a letter to the other heads of state and government calling for the European Council to set up a second IGC to examine Political Union. At the June 1990 Dublin summit, the decision was reached to commission an IGC for Political Union, which would begin its work in December in parallel with the IGC for Economic and Monetary Union. Britain, still under Margaret Thatcher's leadership, again resigned itself to working within the IGC framework to try to minimize the federalizing features of the treaty that would emerge.

Negotiation of the treaty in the two IGCs went on during 1991, under the Council presidencies of Luxembourg and the Netherlands. Central issues that were eventually hedged in the treaty were as follows:

1. Whether to fulfill the European Parliament's maximalist objective of achieving coequal status with the Council of Ministers as one of the two "chambers" of a bicameral legislative body.
2. Whether the EC institutions would acquire competence in the defense policy sphere, rivaling the North Atlantic Treaty Organization (NATO), to which all of the EC members at that time, except neutral Ireland, belonged.
3. Whether all member states should be committed to reaching the third stage of EMU.
4. Whether all member states should be committed to the Social Charter that Delors had broached in 1988.

On all of these issues, Britain took a negative stance. It was joined on the powers of the European Parliament by France; on the defense issue by Ireland, Denmark, and Greece; and on the third stage of EMU by Denmark, the Bundesbank, and a growing percentage of the German public, though not by the Kohl government. On the Social Charter, Britain was isolated even from its usual ally, Denmark, as upward harmonization of EC social policy was a strong Danish commitment.

At the Maastricht summit in December 1991, the treaty was agreed on by all 12 heads of state and government. Thatcher's successor as prime minister, John Major, successfully held out for weak language regarding an EC defense policy, for Britain's right to opt out of a single currency, and for separation of the Social Charter from the main body of the treaty, thus making it applicable to the other 11 countries, but not to Britain. On the issue of legislative powers, Italy and Germany were able to get more for the European Parliament than Britain and France wanted, but less than "maximalists" in the Parliament itself were seeking.[31]

Ratification

The Maastricht Treaty was signed by the 12 foreign ministers on February 7, 1992.[32] It was expected that ratification could be completed by the end of the year, so the EU would come into being at the same time as Project 1992 was concluded. Getting all 12 member states to ratify the treaty in time turned out to be a great deal more difficult than was originally anticipated. The governments that approved the treaties had all made concessions to one another. Still, the general public had little idea of what was emerging and certainly lacked an understanding of the intricacies.

In 9 of the 12 member countries, this isolation of the decision makers from the general public did not pose a serious difficulty for the ratification process. Eight parliaments succeeded in ratifying the treaty by large majorities before the end of 1992: the parliaments of Belgium, Germany, Greece, Italy, Luxembourg, the Netherlands, Portugal, and Spain. In Ireland, a referendum was held in June, and the treaty was ratified with a 69 percent "yes" vote. But the treaty received a severe referendum setback in Denmark earlier the same month when 50.7 percent of those voting judged the treaty unacceptable. This put the later ratifications under a cloud of uncertainty, although the 12 foreign ministers met a few days later and agreed that the process should go on, assuming that the Danes would reconsider. Meanwhile, in order to demonstrate strong support for the treaty, François Mitterrand declared that ratification in France, which would normally have been accomplished simply by a parliamentary vote, would likewise be subject to a referendum.

Mitterrand's decision proved to be a miscalculation. Left-wing and right-wing opponents of the treaty, although weak in the French National Assembly, were able to stir up hostility to the treaty among the public. The issue of loss of sovereignty was played up by the Communists on the left and the National Front on the right, which also played to fears of an opening of French borders to additional immigrants with the creation of an EC citizenship superseding French citizenship. Mitterrand could not claim that the barely positive outcome—a 51 percent "yes" vote—represented a resounding endorsement of the treaty. But in any event, France had ratified the treaty.

With the referendum surprises in Denmark and France, Euro-skepticism came out of retirement. The optimism of the late 1980s and early 1990s now seemed to have been misplaced. Important sectors of opinion in all three of the major countries were expressing disagreement with the treaty. Polls in Germany were revealing that 70 percent opposed giving up the DM in favor of a single EC currency.[33] In the British House of Commons, which had provided a 336-to-92 majority for the treaty in its preliminary reading in May, Conservative Party backbenchers were expressing growing opposition, while from the House of Lords Margaret Thatcher, now Baroness Thatcher, was lobbying for an antiratification vote in an attempt to force the Major government to reverse its position in support of the treaty.

Coincidentally, on July 1, 1992, Britain assumed the presidency of the Council for the latter half of the year. Britain's term of office had not passed its halfway point before the European monetary system experienced a crisis in September 1992. This had been brought on by the Bundesbank's effort to keep the DM strong by raising interest rates. Other central banks and governments were forced to follow suit in order not to have to devalue their currencies. Speculation that Britain would devalue the pound drove its value downward vis-à-vis the DM. Reluctant to slow British economic growth by raising interest rates, the Major government was forced to take the pound out of the ERM. Opposition to the treaty was given further stimulus by these events, since arguments the government had made on behalf of joining in the first two stages were seriously undermined by this evidence of the inability of the member states to coordinate their macroeconomic policies, a capacity that would have to be developed anew if EMU was to succeed.

By October, it was clear that the treaty could not be ratified before the end of 1992. A special summit called by Major to deal with the monetary crisis was held in Birmingham, England, in mid-October. Addressing the problem of ratifying the treaty, the heads of state and government issued a statement designed to assure Britain and Denmark that the treaty would be interpreted in practice so as not to trample on the sovereign rights of the member states. Major took this assurance to the House of Commons and on November 4 gained a majority of three on a vote supporting Maastricht, although not formally ratifying the treaty.[34] He promised that British ratification would await the outcome of the Danish process.

In December, the regular summit under the British presidency was held in Edinburgh, and there a series of assurances was made to help the Danish government get a successful result from a second ratification referendum. Among the concessions made were commitments (1) to increase the transparency of decision making, especially in the Council of Ministers; (2) to give real meaning to the principle of "subsidiarity," that is, to make sure that the EC would not take on new policy-making functions in areas that were best left to the national, or even subnational, governments; and (3) immediately after ratification, to begin the process of negotiation leading to the membership in the EU of Denmark's Nordic neighbors, Sweden, Finland, and Norway. These concessions to Denmark were likely to make Prime Minister Major's task easier as well.

Also during December 1992, both houses of the German Parliament voted overwhelmingly to ratify the treaty, but a challenge to the treaty's constitutionality was lodged in Germany's Federal Constitutional Court, which did not rule favorably until late October the next year. This made Germany the last member to ratify the treaty. Denmark held a second referendum in May 1993, with a favorable vote of 56.8 percent. This helped John Major in steering the treaty through the House of Commons, which he did with some shaky moments. Although Maastricht was now fully ratified, how it would work in practice would be influenced considerably by the "minimalist" interpretation on which the British and Danish governments insisted in return for their efforts to bring about ratification. Their successors continue this insistence more than a decade later.

THE INSTITUTIONAL FRAMEWORK ESTABLISHED BY THE TREATY ON EUROPEAN UNION

The Maastricht Treaty, formally the Treaty on European Union (TEU), rewrote the Rome Treaty (as amended by the SEA) in order to create the new European *Union*. It indicates what the 12 member states agreed to abide by in the future, including former commitments, going back to those that the original six had agreed to in Rome. The 12 members expected any new entrants to the European Union to commit themselves to these old and new undertakings as well. The name was changed to "European Union" because the first "pillar"—the EC—was joined by two others: the Common Foreign and Security Policy (CFSP) pillar, which brought the former European

Political Cooperation (EPC) into the Rome Treaty framework, and the Justice and Home Affairs (JHA) pillar, which added new functions in the realm of internal security to the functions specified in the Rome Treaty and the SEA. Compared to the EC pillar, the CFSP and JHA pillars have a more intergovernmental structure of decision making and implementation, wherein the Commission and the European Parliament play more limited roles. Figure 4.1 provides the layout of the three pillars of the EU.

Citizens of the member countries now became, in a limited sense at least, citizens of the EU. They had the right to live and work in any of the 12 countries without restrictions that did not apply to citizens of those countries. They also had certain political rights. In any of the member countries where an EU citizen of another member country resided, he or she could vote in local elections or become a candidate for the European Parliament. Regarding the EC pillar, the principle of "subsidiarity" was stated and reinforced by the declaration emerging from the December 1992 Edinburgh summit in a new article inserted into the Rome Treaty:

ARTICLE 3B

In areas which do not fall within its exclusive competence, the Community shall take action, in accordance with the principle of subsidiarity, only if and in so far as the objectives of the proposed action cannot be sufficiently achieved by the Member States and can therefore, by reason of the scale or effects of the proposed action, be better achieved by the Community. Any action by the Community shall not go beyond what is necessary to achieve the objectives of this Treaty.[35]

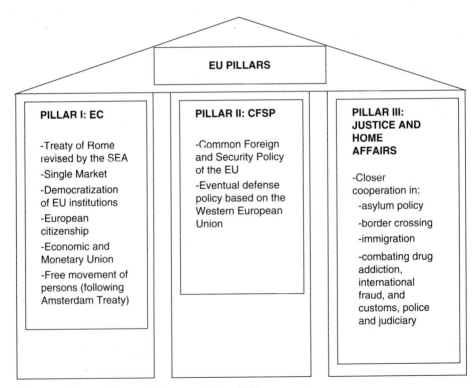

EU PILLARS

PILLAR I: EC

-Treaty of Rome revised by the SEA
-Single Market
-Democratization of EU institutions
-European citizenship
-Economic and Monetary Union
-Free movement of persons (following Amsterdam Treaty)

PILLAR II: CFSP

-Common Foreign and Security Policy of the EU
-Eventual defense policy based on the Western European Union

PILLAR III: JUSTICE AND HOME AFFAIRS

-Closer cooperation in:
-asylum policy
-border crossing
-immigration
-combating drug addiction, international fraud, and customs, police and judiciary

Figure 4.1 ■ Three Pillars of the EU

Although subsidiarity was regarded by intergovernmentalists like Britain's John Major as reinforcing the prerogatives of the member states, it could as plausibly become the means by which regional and local governments in hitherto centralized states (e.g., Britain and France) would gain in power.

The European Parliament gained power in certain policy areas by virtue of a new procedure called *codecision*. Under this procedure, if a legislative act adopted by Council of Ministers is amended by the European Parliament, the Council may adopt any such amendments by QMV, except in the case of amendments on which the Commission has rendered a negative opinion, in which case the Council may pass them only if unanimity is obtained. If the Council should fail to adopt a Parliament amendment or if the Parliament should reject the Council's "common position," a conciliation committee would be established, consisting of members of both the Council and the European Parliament. This committee would then attempt to arrive at a version of the bill that was acceptable to both the Parliament and the Council. If that happened, the Parliament could adopt it by simple majority (a majority of the votes cast) and the Council by QMV. If either body failed to do so, the bill would fail.[36] If no joint text emerged from the conciliation committee, the Council could pass its own version (common position) by QMV, so long as the European Parliament did not reject the common position by an absolute majority. Note that the Commission will be left out of the process, at least formally, once the Council has forced the establishment of a conciliation committee.

Thus, the European Parliament was given the power to reject legislation the Council of Ministers had adopted, while an opportunity existed for the Parliament and the Council to work out a mutually acceptable legislative measure. But the kinds of legislation to which the codecision procedure applies are restricted. Included are "measures on the single market, education, culture, health and consumer protection, as well as programs for the environment, research and trans-European networks."[37] The Parliament's legislative powers remained restricted in politically sensitive domains such as agricultural and industrial policies. However, the parliamentary body gained further powers: the power to approve international agreements reached by the EU if they touched on budgetary matters or areas where the Parliament had a legislative veto; the power to approve the membership of the Commission, including its président, at the beginning of its new term; and the power to deny admission of new countries to EU membership.[38] (See Chapter 7 for further discussion.)

The powers of the European Court of Justice (ECJ) to interpret EC legislation expanded as the legislative powers expanded. But the ECJ was not explicitly given a role to play concerning the third pillar, Justice and Home Affairs. Concerning first-pillar matters, in which the ECJ did have jurisdiction, if the Commission found that a member state had failed to comply with a prior judgment of the ECJ, it could recommend that a fine be paid, and the ECJ could impose it if it chose to do so. Another new institutional development was the creation of a Committee of the Regions, consisting of members appointed by the Council on the proposal of member governments. The Committee's powers were advisory only, but its creation gave recognition to the growing voice of regions, especially the German states (Lander).[39]

The EC pillar[40] that was outlined in the treaty represented a considerable expansion of the domains of EU power beyond those found in the Rome Treaty and the SEA. They included education, research, culture, public health, consumer protection, trans-European infrastructure, networks, labor market policy, and industrial policy. In three additional areas, regional development, social assistance, and environmental policies, EU functions that had existed prior to the treaty's ratification were considerably expanded. One of the policy areas that was left protected by individual member states' veto option was taxation, seen by some governments as a non-negotiable element of national sovereignty.

Social policy was an area in which EU powers were at least potentially expanded. As defined in EU parlance, this referred primarily to conditions of work, remuneration, and rights of employment, including equal entitlements for employees of both genders and processes of labor–management relations. The Social Protocol to the treaty registered the fact that 11 of the member states, with the exclusion of the United Kingdom, separately contracted to coordinate their social policies through legislation that would follow the original Rome Treaty procedures, with some measures subject to QMV in the Council of Ministers and others requiring unanimity. In actual practice, subsequent progress on the legislation of social policy measures was slow, while the other members awaited the results of the next British election. When the Labour Party came back to power in the May 1997 election, after 18 years of Conservative rule, Britain opted in to the Social Protocol, and it became a part of the regular EU treaties.[41]

The most important policy development of the EU pillar was the inclusion of the EMU, which is discussed at greater length in Chapter 9. The principal institutional developments involved in the EMU were to be the creation of the European Central Bank (ECB) and a single currency. In another special protocol to the treaty, Britain was conceded the right to opt out of these developments if it so wished.

The coordination for the second pillar, the CFSP, would be the province of the foreign ministers meeting as the Council of Ministers between summit meetings, where the heads of state and government made foreign policy decisions together, with the assistance of their foreign ministers. General foreign policy decisions required unanimous approval, but more detailed implemental decisions by the foreign ministers could be taken by QMV. On defense matters, the Western European Union (WEU) could implement CFSP decisions. Linked to the North Atlantic Treaty Organization (NATO), as well as to the EU, the WEU comprised of ten EU members, while two EU members, Denmark and Ireland, were not members of WEU.[42] (See Chapter 12.)

Justice and Home Affairs—the third pillar—involved efforts of interior ministers to join forces in dealing with problems of asylum, immigration, and other cross-border law enforcement matters, such as those involving fugitive criminals, terrorism, and drugs. In all of these areas, national laws were enforced within national borders, and it would be up to the interior ministers to reach agreement on conventions that defined new rules and procedures.[43] (See Chapter 13.) Both CFSP and JHA were partially modified in a supranational direction by the Amsterdam Treaty of 1997. (See Chapter 5.)

THE AFTERMATH OF MAASTRICHT

In the months that followed ratification of the Maastricht Treaty in October 1993, the EU members were preoccupied with the enlargement of the EU to include three new member countries: Austria, Finland, and Sweden, bringing the number of EU's members up from 12 to 15. The addition of these four relatively small and relatively rich "northern" members meant a change in the Council voting balance between small and large members and between richer northern and poorer southern members. As both a larger and a poorer southern member, Spain was reluctant to see an enlargement that would take away the ability of two larger members and one smaller member (e.g., Britain, Spain, and Portugal) to block qualified majorities because the enlargement would increase the number of votes necessary for blocking from 23 to 25. This would mean that, if three members opposed, all three had to be larger members to have enough votes to block action in the face of a solid majority of the other members. Spain sought to keep the blocking minority at 23, which would mean raising the necessary votes for a qualified majority from 71 percent to 75 percent of the total votes. With the three additions, membership of the EU rose to 15. This meant that the total number of votes in the Council of Ministers would rise from 76 to 87. The Ionnina compromise would not, however, either rise or decline in significance because a negative coalition of two larger members and one smaller member would still not be quite enough to block a qualified majority. As the members headed into still another round of treaty revision, it was clear that the compromise could be only a temporary one.

STUDY QUESTIONS

1. The SEA is one of the most critical turning points in EU integration. Write a comparative assessment of reasons behind the passing and implementation of this Act from a realist perspective.
2. Write a similar essay to question 1 from a liberal intergovernmentalist perspective.

3. What are the Delors initiatives of 1987–1989?
4. Explain the main points of the Maastricht Treaty.
5. How did the TEU alter the future direction of regional integration in Europe?

ENDNOTES

1. Stephen George, *An Awkward Partner: Britain in the European Community* (Oxford: Oxford University Press, 1990), pp. 132–133.

2. David M. Wood, *Old Thinking and the New Europe: The Persisting Influence of de Gaulle and Thatcher*. Occasional Paper no. 9211 (St. Louis, Mo.: Center for International Studies, University of Missouri, December 1992).

3. George, *An Awkward Partner*, p. 134.

4. Margaret Thatcher, *The Downing Street Years* (New York: HarperCollins, 1993), p. 257.

5. Ibid., pp. 538–541.

6. Peter A. Hall, *Governing the Economy: The Politics of State Intervention in Britain and France* (Oxford: Oxford University Press, 1986), pp. 198–202.

7. Andrew Moravcsik, "Negotiating the Single European Act," in Robert O. Keohane and Stanley Hoffmann, eds., *The New European Community: Decisionmaking and Institutional Change* (Boulder, Colo.: Westview Press, 1991), pp. 51–52.

8. Moravcsik, "Negotiating the Single European Act," pp. 56–57; George, *An Awkward Partner*, pp. 155–159.

9. There is a considerable amount of work devoted to the process by which the single market came into being. See especially Paul Taylor, "The New Dynamics of EC Integration in the 1980s," in Juliet Lodge, ed., *The European Community and the Challenge of the Future* (New York: St. Martin's Press, 1989), pp. 3–25; Moravcsik, "Negotiating the Single European Act"; David Cameron, "The 1992 Initiative: Causes and Consequences," in Alberta M. Sbragia, ed., *Euro-politics: Institutions and Policymaking in the "New" European Community* (Washington, D.C.: Brookings Institution, 1992), pp. 23–74.

10. John T. Woolley, "Policy Credibility and the European Monetary System," in Sbragia, ed., *Euro-politics*, pp. 157–190.

11. Paolo Cecchini, *The European Challenge 1992: The Benefits of a Single Market* (Aldershot, U.K.: Wildwood House, for the Commission of the European Communities, 1989), pp. 1–7.

12. Juliet Lodge, "European Union and the First Elected European Parliament: The Spinelli Initiative," *Journal of Common Market Studies* 22 (June 1984): 378.

13. Quoted in Simon Bulmer and Wolfgang Wessels, *The European Council: Decision-Making in European Politics* (Basingstoke, England, and London: Macmillan, 1987), p. 77.

14. Cameron, "The 1992 Initiative," pp. 54–55.

15. Lodge, "Ten Years of an Elected European Parliament," p. 15.

16. Cameron, "The 1992 Initiative," pp. 23–24.

17. Peter Ludlow, "The European Commission," in Keohane and Hoffmann, eds., *The New European Community*, pp. 116–121.

18. Loukas Tsoukalis, *The New European Economy: The Politics and Economics of Integration* (Oxford: Oxford University Press, 1991), p. 62.

19. Emil Joseph Kirchner, *Decision-Making in the European Community: The Council Presidency and European Integration* (Manchester, England: Manchester University Press, 1992), p. 99.

20. Cameron, "The 1992 Initiative," p. 48.

21. Kirchner, *Decision-Making in the European Community*, p. 102.

22. Peter Ludlow, "Introduction: The Politics and Policies of the EC in 1989," in Center for European Policy Studies, *The Annual Review of European Community Affairs 1990* (London: Brassey's, 1991), p. xli.

23. "How to Hatch an EMU," *Economist*, April 22, 1989, p. 45.

24. David R. Cameron, "British Exit, German Voice, French Loyalty: Defection, Domination and Cooperation in the 1992–93 ERM Crisis." Paper presented at the Third International Conference of the European Studies Association, Washington, D.C., May 27–29, 1993, p. 13.

25. Ludlow, "Introduction," p. xlii.

26. Margaret Thatcher, *The Downing Street Years* (New York: HarperCollins, 1993), p. 752.

27. Ibid., pp. 688–726.

28. Philip Norton, "The Conservative Party from Thatcher to Major," in Anthony King et al.,

eds., Britain at the Polls (Chatham, N.J.: Chatham House, 1993), pp. 29–59.

29. Thatcher, *The Downing Street Years*, pp. 796–798.

30. For a discussion of the issues and government positions in the making of the TEU, see Andrew Moravcsik, *The Choice for Europe: Social Purpose and State Power from Messina to Maastricht* (Ithaca, N.Y.: Cornell University Press, 1998), chap. 6.

31. Desmond Dinan, *Ever Closer Union: An Introduction to European Integration*, 2nd ed. (Boulder, Colo.: Lynne Rienner, 1999), pp. 175, 428.

32. For detailed discussion see Richard Corbett, "Governance and Institutional Developments," *Journal of Common Market Studies* 31 (August 1993): 27–50.

33. Walter Goldstein, "Europe After Maastricht," *Foreign Affairs* 71 (Winter 1992/93): 117–132.

34. David Baker, Andrew Gamble, and Steve Ludlam, "Whips or Scorpions? The Maastricht Vote and the Conservative Party," *Parliamentary Affairs* 46 (April 1993): 151–166.

35. Council and Commission of the European Communities, *Treaty on European Union*, pp. 13–14.

36. Ibid., pp. 76–78.

37. *The Economist*, October 17, 1992, p. 60. "Trans-European networks" refers to "transport, telecommunications and energy infrastructures." Council and Commission of the European Communities, *Treaty on European Union*, p. 51.

38. Juliet Lodge, "EC Policymaking: Institutional Dynamics," in Juliet Lodge, ed., *The European Community and the Challenge of the Future* (New York: St. Martin's Press, 1993), p. 32.

39. Council and Commission of the European Communities, *Treaty on European Union*, p. 69.

40. Although the discussion in this paragraph refers to the provisions of the treaty applying to the EC pillar, the acronym EU is used so that it will be clear we are referring to the *post-Maastricht* powers of the *European Union.*

41. Dinan, *Ever Closer Union*, 2nd ed., pp. 175, 428.

42. Council and Commission of the European Communities, *Treaty on European Union*, pp. 123–129.

43. Ibid., pp. 131–135.

5

Efforts to Reach the Next Level (1994–2008)

At the beginning of the twenty-first century, the European Union (EU) embarked on two major projects that transcended all of its other preoccupations: (1) the incorporation of states to its east and south and (2) the revision of its institutional design to accommodate a potentially much larger membership and to bring the EU closer to being a democratic state. Here the focus will be on the most important developments that occurred in these two realms during the period from 1994 to 2008. Also included in the chapter are four attempts at treaty revision, all of which were designed to make the larger and more complex EU better able to discharge its growing responsibilities. The four attempts were the Amsterdam Treaty (1997), the Nice Treaty (2001), the ill-fated Constitutional Treaty, signed in 2004, but rejected in 2005 by French and Dutch voters, and the Lisbon Treaty, signed in 2007.

THE AMSTERDAM TREATY AND FURTHER EU ENLARGEMENT

At the December 1994 summit in Essen, steps were taken that would lead to enlargement of the EU into Central and Eastern Europe. Six countries already had agreements with the EU: Poland, the Czech Republic, Slovakia, Hungary, Bulgaria, and Romania. The prospect of absorbing these poorer countries and others in the region into the EU was a daunting one. It would dominate discussions in the 1996 intergovernmental conference (IGC) to reexamine the Maastricht Treaty. The issues the conference would face included how to alter the institutional framework to give more expression to the values of democracy, subsidiarity, openness, and decisional efficiency. There would be serious debates over whether to extend further the powers of the European Parliament (urged by Germany to reduce the democratic deficit), whether to transfer more power from the national to the supranational level by moving second- and third-pillar decisions to the first pillar and/or by extending qualified majority voting (QMV) in the Council of Ministers to more first-pillar areas of legislation, and whether to reduce the number of commissioners and the number of countries taking a regular turn at the Council presidency. And, of course, the vexing issue of the method of calculating a qualified majority would have to be dealt with once again. These were all likely to be contentious issues, dividing governments in different ways, but also raising the possibility of bargaining trade-offs.

Added to the complexities was the uncertainty as to whether enough member countries would meet the standards listed in the Maastricht Treaty for membership in the Economic and Monetary Union (EMU). High public deficits in the Mediterranean countries—Italy, Spain, Portugal, and Greece—made their eligibility for EMU problematic. Public skepticism about a single currency was running high in Britain and Germany, given the conservatism of most people about what they carry in their wallets and pocketbooks.[1] The prospect of enlargement to include newly democratized and newly capitalist Eastern European countries made an already complicated set of questions a virtual nightmare.[2] Eastward enlargement in its own right made many people in regions of the existing EU fearful that their Common Agricultural Policy (CAP) subsidies and cohesion funding would have to be cut back in order to provide equal benefits to new members. Governments of the Mediterranean countries resisted the idea of an enlargement that would bring in even poorer and less industrialized countries.

In the late summer of 1994, Prime Minister Edouard Balladur of France tentatively broached the need for varying degrees of EU membership: an inner core of countries that could meet the EMU criteria by the late 1990s, presumably Germany, France, and the smaller northern countries; a middle rank that would include Britain and the Mediterranean countries, which could not or would not fully join the EMU, but would take part in most of the domestic and foreign policies of the EU; and an outer circle, made up of the East European countries. Similar ideas were put forward by the Christian Democratic Union, German Chancellor Kohl's party. Because of the way they were advanced, the proposals got a hostile reception from the countries not included in the "inner core," especially the larger ones, Britain, Italy, and Spain. But, in fact, the idea was not so far-fetched, considering that EU programs like the exchange rate mechanism (ERM), the Social Charter, and the Western European Union already had varying memberships, with more variation anticipated when Austria and the Scandinavian countries joined.[3] Though France and Germany withdrew their suggestions in the face of criticism, they had managed to focus attention on some of the dilemmas facing the EU in the years ahead—dilemmas that would still be there in the new century.

While avoiding mention of "inner cores" or "outer circles," Chancellor Kohl made sure the question of eastward enlargement headed the agenda for the Essen summit of December 1994.[4] Although no firm commitments were made at Essen, the Commission was charged with helping the potential members adapt to the requirements of the single market and other joint programs for cooperation among EU members.[5] It was clear that any of the East European countries that could meet the economic standards would be seriously considered, leading to speculation that Hungary and the Czech Republic, at least, might gain entry to the EU by 2000. To satisfy the objections of the Mediterranean members, whose chief spokesman was the French prime minister, in June 1994 the European Council placed two Mediterranean applicants for membership, Cyprus and Malta, in the same category as Hungary, the Czech Republic, Poland, Slovakia, Bulgaria, and Romania—countries that were "next in line" after 1996.[6]

But at the same time the EU was holding out the prospect of membership, it was also specifying the conditions that would have to be satisfied in order for new members to be admitted to the Western European "club." These had previously been outlined by the European Council in its June 1993 Copenhagen summit. In order for the newly emerging democracies to be eligible for membership, they had to meet the following criteria:

1. *Europeanness:* The applicant country has to be a member of the European family of states.
2. *Political:* The political system must be characterized by democracy and the rule of law, respect for human rights, and protection of minorities.

3. *Economic:* The country must have a strong market economy that encompasses the free movement of goods, capital, services, and people.
4. *Other:* The country must
   a. support the aims of political, economic, and monetary union; and
   b. adopt the *acquis communautaire* (i.e., the rights and obligations derived from EU treaties, laws, and regulations over the years).

Since then, these requirements came to be known as the Copenhagen criteria for membership. Clearly, if the EU insisted on all of this, the length of time before even the first new members could be admitted would be greater than they were initially anticipating, and in point of fact, the 1995 intake of Austria, Finland, and Sweden was not to be followed quickly with new admissions.

The Amsterdam summit in June 1997 reviewed the recommendations of the intergovernmental conference, which had been working during the previous year, but had reached many of its final recommendations only after the British government changed hands in the May general elections.[7] The Labour government of Tony Blair opted in to the Social Protocol, but it pledged to wait until after the next election, at the earliest in 2001, before making a decision on EMU membership. Apart from these issues, Blair did not appear any more enthusiastic about European "federalism" than his predecessor had been. True to British traditions, he was comfortable with the EU as an organization with primarily intergovernmental decision making for the most important issues, including foreign and security policy issues, where he wanted Britain to play a more positive role than it had previously.[8]

What emerged as the Amsterdam Treaty, amending the previous treaties (Rome, Single European Act [SEA], and Treaty of European Union [TEU]), involved a very modest tinkering with the supranational institutions and the European Community (EC) pillar and a more innovative approach to the intergovernmental second and third pillars. With enlargement firmly in mind, the IGC attempted to work out institutional changes that would make decision making less unwieldy. Proposals were made to reduce the number of commissioners to one from each country. The five largest members were naturally opposed, as they would each lose the right to name one of the two commissioners to which they had been entitled. Germany sought a change in voting weights in the Council of Ministers to reflect its larger population since unification, but other members were not yet ready for this change. Modifications in QMV rules along the lines of the informal Ionnina compromise were suggested by larger and richer members concerned with the possible influx of many smaller and poorer members. The outlines of a package deal were there, but the incentive to realize it was not, perhaps because many of the member governments were not yet ready to focus seriously on the addition of a large set of new members. So the necessary institutional adjustments were postponed until another IGC could be commissioned to reach agreement on these issues. The likelihood of new entrants very early in the next decade was starting to appear unrealistic.

Progress was made on other dimensions by the IGC and at the Amsterdam summit. The European Parliament's membership was capped at 700, not a huge increase from its 626 members following the 1995 enlargement. Clearly, if there was to be a redistribution when the future enlargement occurred, then some or all of the existing members' delegations would have to be reduced. The complicated procedural rules governing the legislative process for the European Parliament, the Commission, and the Council were simplified somewhat by the near elimination of the cooperation procedure (introduced by the SEA) and modification of the codecision procedure (introduced by the TEU) to make the European Parliament more of a coequal of the Council. Essentially, three procedures remained: consultation (the Rome Treaty procedure, which gives the Parliament only a very weak role); codecision, which puts the Parliament in a good position to bargain with the Council over changes in legislative proposals; and the assent procedure, which gives the Parliament an up-or-down veto. (See Chapter 7.)

Significant increments of EU capability were achieved under the Amsterdam Treaty in the areas of second- and third-pillar functions—Common Foreign and Security Policy (CFSP) and Justice and Home Affairs (JHA). In the case of CFSP, decision-making rules changed to allow the Council of Ministers to vote by qualified majority in adopting common strategies that could be implemented by taking common EU positions or joint actions, so long as there were no military or defense implications in the proposed measures. Unanimity would continue to apply for decisions with military or defense implications. Where unanimity applies, the Council may act without expressed approval by some members, so long as they abstain from voting against the proposal. This process, labeled "constructive abstention," allows some members to take actions with the tacit acceptance of other members that do not join in the action.[9]

A very serious concern of the negotiators of the Amsterdam Treaty was the absence of a single EU voice in foreign and security policy. This was especially evident in the failure of the EU to reach a common approach to the war in Bosnia in the mid-1990s. Achieving a reasonably effective cease-fire and negotiation of terms in this multisided crisis eventually required the intervention of the North Atlantic Treaty Organization (NATO), led by the United States. Accordingly, one of the most significant Amsterdam Treaty steps was the creation of a new role for the Council's secretary general, that of high representative for common foreign and security policy. It was intended to be a high-profile role that would be filled by a prominent European public figure who could serve as a spokesperson for CFSP and recommend initiatives to the Council, as well as taking charge of their implementation if so directed. The first occupant of the role, former Spanish Foreign Minister and NATO Secretary General Javier Solana, appointed in 1999, closely fit the job description (see Chapter 12).[10]

Finally, JHA was divided in two: Some politically sensitive policy areas were transferred to the EC pillar, while the remainder continued to be subject to strictly intergovernmental decisions and actions. The first group included movement of persons over external borders into the EU for purposes of asylum or immigration; combating drug addiction; combating fraud on an international scale; and judicial cooperation on civil matters (e.g., white-collar crimes). Conversion of these areas of jurisdiction to the first pillar meant that the Commission and the European Parliament would participate along with the Council in formulating and adopting EU laws and the European Court of Justice (ECJ) could rule on the validity of acts of the EU institutions and the member governments in these areas. The set of matters remaining within the third pillar was deemed by the governments to touch too closely on sovereignty to give up exclusive control. These include judicial cooperation on criminal matters, customs cooperation to combat crimes involving cross-border traffic, and police cooperation to prevent terrorism and other serious international crimes (see Chapter 13).[11]

During the remaining years of the decade, the principal preoccupation of the EU and its members was the formation of the EMU, whose third stage was set to begin on January 1, 1999 (see Chapter 9). The Maastricht Treaty had set forth the timetable and the criteria for conversion of member countries' national currency to the single currency (subsequently called the "euro") and for the creation of the European Central Bank (ECB). Public attention during the two years between the Amsterdam summit and the mid-1998 decision focused on the criteria used to judge eligibility and the progress of the candidates toward meeting them. Of the various criteria, the most important "acid test" for membership was the requirement that an EU member country's annual government deficit for the year 1997 not exceed 3 percent of its gross domestic product (GDP).

In fact, by the beginning of 1998, only Greece, among the members applying for the EMU, was clearly too far above the 3-percent mark to be considered a realistic candidate. Other applicants for EMU membership had brought their deficits down to the 3-percent level or below. Three countries—Denmark, Sweden, and the United Kingdom—had made it clear that they would not join in the single currency, whether or not they met the criteria. Eleven of the remaining countries were deemed eligible, even though most of them did not satisfy the second criterion, that the cumulative government debt not exceed 60 percent of GDP. Not even Germany, Belgium, or the Netherlands met this criterion at the beginning of 1998, even though all three were leaders of the "fast-track" set, which had the economic stability necessary to back up a strong euro.[12] But by another measure, all of the EU members poised to enter the EMU were maintaining low rates of inflation.[13] The third stage of the EMU began on schedule on January 1, 1999. During the first two years, the value of the new euro against the U.S. dollar dropped 30 percent.[14] While explanations for the disappointing start were complex and the seriousness of the situation was debatable, the loss of value of the euro vis-à-vis the U.S. dollar was undoubtedly a factor in the defeat of a Danish referendum over joining the EMU in September 2000. On January 1, 2001, bills and coins of the individual EMU members were replaced with the new currency, the euro. (See Chapter 9.) By this time, the euro had returned roughly to a parity value with the dollar. In January 2001, Greece became the twelfth member of the EMU.

Another major set of uncertainties concerning the future involved the 12 Central and Eastern European countries waiting to join the EU. All of these applicants were assessed according to economic and political criteria such as those applied (although less thoroughly) to Greece, Spain, and Portugal in the 1980s. As in the 1980s, candidates for entry were poor countries relative to existing members and were in most cases only recently democratized. Unlike earlier enlargements, the magnitude of the anticipated enlargement was daunting. During the 1990s, the projected dates for the first entrants moved to the next decade.

An associated problem, which has continued to grow in importance, involves the movement of persons from east to west and from south to north in Europe. The applicant countries of Eastern Europe have themselves experienced an influx of immigrants from the former Soviet Union, many of whom continue westward into the EU countries, while additional flows come from countries on the Mediterranean and Adriatic shores to the south and east of the EU members. This has produced considerable strife within senior member countries that are the first to receive the immigrant wave, especially Germany and Austria, close to the EU's eastern flank, and France, Spain, and Italy on its southern side. The domestic politics of these countries have been affected, with normal voting patterns altered and existing political coalitions threatened by rising parties of the extreme right.

By 2000, divisions among the governments of the member states became more evident as considerations of institutional change followed closely on tensions over EMU eligibility and prospects for enlargement. A certain amount of solidarity could be discerned among the original six members, which constituted a sort of inner core of members intent on developing their own pattern of "closer cooperation," whatever exceptions might have to be made for later arrivals wishing to preserve what they considered vital sovereign rights.[15] Further treaty revision would have to address the question of how much more integration could be achieved without the emergence of a multispeed Union, with original members achieving integration in varying ranges of functions and new entrants sharing only those functions that would not overburden any members, old or new.

THE TREATY OF NICE

During the second week in December 2000, the EU heads of state and government met as the European Council in the city of Nice, France. Although the summit had several matters on its agenda, the largest amount of its time was taken up with the attempt to pick up where the Amsterdam Treaty had stopped and make the EU institutions more "efficient"—that is, to change the institutional decision-making process before the countries of Central, Eastern, and Southern Europe joined the EU. The summit lasted more than four days, a record length, and produced a package of institutional changes that would require ratification by all 15 member states.[16] Not entirely satisfied with their efforts, the heads agreed to convene another treaty-amending meeting of the European Council in 2004 that would include the heads of the applicant countries, which would by that time be on the threshold of entering the EU. In fact, admission of the first ten applicant countries occurred in 2004, while Romania and Bulgaria were deemed not yet ripe for admission (see Chapter 6).[17]

Among the most important institutional changes of the Nice Treaty, which came into effect in January 2005, are those that concentrate on the decision-making powers of the Council of Ministers. The most obvious way of making the Council's decisions more efficient would be to do away with the unanimity rule for decisions where it applied and replace it with QMV, so that no single member, old or new, would be in a position to block decisions desired by all the other members. With the addition of ten new members, the chances of such vetoes being wielded would increase. At the time, approximately 80 percent of treaty articles involved Council decisions by QMV, but the remaining 20 percent, including some of the most important decisions, required unanimity. The summit managed to reduce this percentage to about 10 percent.[18] QMV now would apply for the approval of trade negotiations on services and on some immigration and asylum issues, but France insisted on continuing the veto for culture and education, and Britain wanted the veto for taxation and social security issues.[19] Outside of the legislative field, QMV replaced unanimity in the election by member governments of the Commission president and the secretary general of the Council Secretariat, who under the Amsterdam Treaty had become the high representative for common foreign and security policy.

Voting weights in the Council of Ministers were altered to give the larger current members a greater weight relative to smaller members (see Table 5.1). For the larger member countries, these increases in seats better reflected the size differential vis-à-vis the smaller member countries. For example, Luxembourg's increase was from 2 to 4 seats (a 100 percent increase), while Britain's was from 10 to 29 seats (an increase of 190 percent). However, because of French resistance, Germany's total remained equal to that of each of the other three larger countries, even though its population had become considerably larger with reunification.[20] The total voting weights of the Netherlands, Belgium, and Luxembourg were arranged to equal 29, the same as that of each of the larger members, France, Germany, Italy, and Britain.

In order to compensate Germany for its concession, it was agreed that any of the larger countries could question a decision made by QMV, which would then not be adopted unless countries totaling 62 percent of the total EU population supported it; thus, Germany plus two of the next three largest states could together block it. To compensate the small states for their lesser share in decision making, a decision also had to have the support of a majority of countries, regardless of their populations. This meant that the application of QMV became more difficult than it had been, although not as difficult as in cases where unanimity still applied. As further compensation to the smaller members, the number of commissioners assigned to each of the five largest current members would be reduced from two to one with the beginning of the next Commission on January 1, 2005. Whenever the total membership reached 27, the Commission size would be fixed at an unspecified figure, but one lower than 27, necessitating a rotation system of some sort.[21] The capacity of the Commission president to coordinate Commission action was strengthened by being given a freer hand in appointing enough Commission vice presidents to allow effective coordination of a larger number of member states.[22]

The idea of "closer" or "enhanced" cooperation, which had come up in the Amsterdam Treaty negotiations, was accepted in order to give the enlarged EU more flexibility without setting up sharply separate tiers of members. It was agreed that any group of eight or more member countries could move ahead more rapidly with integration in certain policy areas—for example, environmental policy, justice and home affairs, or taxation. One subset of members might move ahead without the participation of some other members, while another subset might develop "enhanced cooperation" in another policy area. Such arrangements could be authorized by QMV, since a unanimity rule would make its adoption highly unlikely.[23] Whereas the Conservative British government of John Major

Table 5.1 ■ Voting Weights in the Council of Ministers, Treaty of Nice and Treaty of Lisbon

Country	Population (in millions)	Weights under the Treaty of Nice	Weights under the Lisbon Treaty
Germany	82.0	29	29
Britain	59.2	29	29
France	59.0	29	29
Italy	57.6	29	29
Spain	39.4	27	27
Poland	38.7	27	27
Romania*	22.5	14	14
Netherlands	15.8	13	13
Greece	10.5	12	12
Czech Republic	10.3	12	12
Belgium	10.2	12	12
Hungary	10.1	12	12
Portugal	10.0	12	12
Sweden	8.9	10	10
Bulgaria*	8.2	10	10
Austria	8.1	10	10
Slovakia	5.4	7	7
Denmark	5.3	7	7
Finland	5.2	7	7
Ireland	3.7	7	7
Lithuania	3.7	7	7
Latvia	2.4	4	4
Slovenia	2.0	4	4
Estonia	1.4	4	4
Cyprus	0.8	4	4
Luxembourg	0.4	4	4
Malta	0.4	3	3

*Members in January 2007.

had opposed the idea at the time of the Amsterdam negotiations, it was accepted in principle by Tony Blair, whose vision of EU foreign policy included a leading role for Britain, while more neutralist members might opt out of future foreign policy coordination. However, the concept of enhanced cooperation remains vague and ill-defined. Like other features of the Nice Treaty, it was adopted in anticipation of the coming accession to EU membership of countries that were experiencing afresh the opportunities and pitfalls of the rule of law and of democratic political institutions and market economies. Would the second-class status of these new entrants last for only a brief interim period, or would it become fixed and permanent as longer-standing members set themselves up as participants in an enhanced and restrictive higher order of membership?[24]

On June 7, 2001, Irish voters rejected ratification of the Nice Treaty in a referendum vote for which only 35 percent of the electorate turned out (as opposed to 62 percent in the Irish ratification of the Amsterdam Treaty). In spite of the substantial economic benefits Ireland had received from the EU, of which Irish voters were fully aware, 54 percent of those voting voted "no." Uncertainty about when the treaty would come into effect ended with a 63 percent favorable vote in a second Irish referendum on October 19, 2002. Other member states ratified the Treaty without any objection. As for the new members of the EU, all ten new members had ratified their accession treaties by late September 2000. In Latvia, the tenth, ratification was by popular vote, as it had been earlier in seven of the other nine inductees. A turnout of 35 percent in Latvia was required for the vote to be a valid indication of support. The actual turnout was 72.5 percent, of which 67 percent voted for ratification. Only Cyprus and Malta had ratified without consulting the electorate. Malta, but not Cyprus, had a closely fought campaign before the vote. But there was no indication at the time that the scope of the enlargement was seen as a source of future problems.

THE CONSTITUTIONAL TREATY

Annexed to the Nice Treaty when it was signed by the 15 foreign ministers in February 2001 was a "Declaration on the Future of the European Union." The language of the Declaration was vague, but since 1999, the member governments had been committed to agreement on an EU Charter of Fundamental Rights, a document that might well accompany a "Constitution for the European Union." It was speculated that at least some of the heads of state and government at Nice had such a constitution in mind. Opinion leaders of more advanced integrationist views took it as a strong signal in the right direction, encouraged by statements made by German leaders, especially Foreign Minister Joschka Fischer.[25] A year later, at the Laeken summit of December 2001, it was decided that a Convention for the Future of Europe would be set up to recommend a "Constitutional Treaty for Europe." It was agreed that former French President Valéry Giscard d'Estaing would chair the convention, in recognition of the contributions he had made both to European integration generally and to the development of the intergovernmental features of the EU in particular. The convention would comprise representatives of the 15 member states and 13 applicants, for a total of 104 convention delegates. Its task would be to draft a treaty that would be closer to a definitive constitution of the EU, more federalist than the original Rome Treaty or its amending treaties.

The convention's agenda included direct election of a European Commission president and extension of QMV to more sensitive areas. But the British government made it clear that relations between the EU and its member states should be altered not by adding to the EU's powers, but rather by restoring tasks to member states that they can handle as well or better—that is, a reiteration of the principle of subsidiarity.

Some likened the convention to the one held at Philadelphia in 1787 that wrote the U.S. Constitution. The largest number of delegates were members of legislative bodies, the European Parliament (16 delegates) and the national parliaments (56 delegates), while the 28 member and candidate governments had 28. Two former prime ministers, Jean-Luc Dehaene of Belgium and Giuliano Amato of Italy, assisted Giscard d'Estaing in chairing the convention.

The convention brought together members of the national parliaments and the European Parliament and government representatives, including subnational government representatives. More enthusiastic Europeanists in delegations other than the British and French succeeded in putting some ideas of Jacques Delors on the agenda, including linking the composition of the Commission to the outcome of European Parliament elections, in order to bring the European Parliament closer to the role of a national parliament, and "reinforced cooperation" among member states identifiable as "a willing subgroup." At the same time, France and Britain joined in expressing the belief that "the European Council should take the lead more resolutely in setting the EU's agenda."[26]

An issue of considerable significance was whether the existing rotating presidency of the Council should be maintained or replaced, either (1) with a single president, who might be expected, however chosen, to transcend the influence of the individual governments, or (2) with a collective presidency composed of a mixture of large and small state members, changing every two-and-a-half years (a Swedish proposal). Either might make for greater continuity in Council policies, including the European Council, than had been true of the existing six-month rotation system. But it would leave coordination of an expected 27 or more members in the future just as difficult. The proposal of a single president was supported by three of the larger current members' leaders, French President Jacques Chirac, British Prime Minister Tony Blair, and Spanish Prime Minister Jose Maria Aznar, all considered EU heavyweights. It was the alternative adopted.

Most basically, the convention was to decide whether the existing treaties of the European Union should give way to a constitution, which might be federal in spirit, if not in name.[27] Another IGC, called by a later European Council meeting, was to follow the convention to work out a final draft for agreement by the European Council, the procedure employed in earlier treaty revisions. Its final approval, requiring ratification in 25 member countries, was not expected to follow closely on the heels of the convention. As it turned out, the convention was able to agree on only part of the changes on its agenda, notably the replacement of the rotated Council presidency with a full-time president with a five-year term; an EU foreign minister; an extension of the European Parliament's powers, along with a role for national parliaments in scrutinizing proposed EU legislation; and a mechanism for a member state to leave the EU. Voting powers in the Council of Ministers and a limitation of the number of members of the European Commission were left on the agenda for further consideration, as was the question of a system for rotation of the presidencies of the sectoral ministerial councils (e.g., the economic, environmental, and transport councils). But it was hoped that last-minute stitching of the holes in the constitution would produce a draft Constitutional Treaty that would be sent through the ratification processes of 25 states.[28] There were misgivings regarding the capacity of the draft Constitutional Treaty to ease the way for the new members. The issue of voting weights in the Council of Ministers produced deadlock at the December 2003 summit. Agreement on the treaty had to be postponed until a later summit. The big countries called for a dual standard for votes to pass; that is, they must be carried by at least 50 percent of the member states representing 60 percent of the EU population, a formula assuring that a coalition of the three largest states—Germany, France, and Britain—would be able to block any proposal for constitutional reform even with all of the other members arrayed against them. Needless to say, the other members disliked this formula. The two largest of the remaining members, Poland and Spain, actively opposed it.

Ireland's Prime Minister Bertie Ahern, holding the presidency for the first half of 2004, proposed that a measure could be adopted by a majority of member states voting in favor of it, representing at least a majority of EU citizens. This was agreed to by all but Spain and Poland, whose joint holdout continued until the arrival of a new Spanish prime minister changed the Spanish position and left Poland by itself in blocking agreement. The determination of the Polish government to hold its position was matched by French President Chirac's determination not to let Poland have its way.

Chirac saw that satisfying Poland would reduce the capacity of the three largest members to use their blocking ability to steer EU decision making. This they could do as long as they remained in threefold agreement and could garner the support of some smaller members, which they usually could.[29] Another issue, this time dividing small states from both medium-sized and large states, was how to limit the Commission to 18 members, which would necessitate devising an equal rotation system in and out of the Commission only for smaller members.

The treaty was designed to strengthen the EU's capacity to deal with pressing issues such as economic reform and terrorism. By late March 2004, work had progressed to the point that the signing of the treaty could be expected as early as June 2004, still during the Irish presidency.

A principal feature was to be the creation of the EU offices of president and foreign minister, which would strengthen the EU's capacity to act in the realms of countering terrorism and stimulating economic reform. Another was the greater involvement of national parliaments, which had previously been left out of the EU decision-making process.[30]

Members began to exhibit a sense of urgency as the final stages in the preparation of the Constitutional Treaty were reached. Opinion polls were providing evidence that the EU was losing public support, which had dropped below 50 percent for the first time. It stood at 48 percent overall and only at 28 percent in the United Kingdom.[31] Ratification of the treaty by referendum was seriously being considered by French and British leaders Chirac and Blair. But slowing down the process was ruled out because of the danger of losing momentum. Indeed, momentum appeared already to have receded in the hands of the powerful European Council, after its failure in December 2003 to approve the constitution. The richest and most powerful member state, Germany, was arguing for freezing of the EU budget at 1 percent of GDP at the very moment that ten, mostly poorer, new members were coming on board, hoping to reproduce the economic success Ireland had experienced after joining.[32] The "big three" were dominating the Council of Ministers, having converged on a level of Euro-skepticism closer to where Britain had been than to accustomed French and German levels.

The commitments by both the French and the British governments to hold referenda on the Constitutional Treaty were made in April 2004, despite the signs the polls were displaying. Prime Minister Blair was making it clear that a treaty referendum would wait until after the next British general election in 2005.[33] For their part, the opposition Conservatives had promised to oppose the treaty whenever it came to a vote. As for France, the British decision put pressure on President Chirac to hold a referendum on the constitution in spite of his memories of the narrow 51 percent French ratification of the Maastricht Treaty in 1992.[34]

The rhetoric for and against the Constitutional Treaty continued to escalate in the spring of 2004. Critics of the treaty complained that it did not give sufficient attention to national parliaments, which would remain as they had been, outsiders. The British Conservatives held the view that the treaty should include a provision that, if five national parliaments objected to a new or existing EU law on the ground that it was a matter for member state deliberation, it should be withdrawn or, if already adopted, repealed. On the other side, French President Chirac was proposing that members failing to ratify the treaty should be obliged to leave the European Union,[35] a stance that was to appear ironic a year later.

The European Council would remain the locus of power in the EU of Giscard d'Estaing's constitution. Enlargement to 27 or more members would reinforce this reality because heads of state and government could make EU decisions when meeting together much more quickly and certainly than could an enlarged parliamentary body with divisions along both national and political party lines. But what role should be played by the 27 or more national parliaments? Here national political forces were likely to come into their own.[36]

British Prime Minister Tony Blair, while promising he would not be another Margaret Thatcher regarding EU treaty changes, nevertheless was insisting that decisions regarding taxation, social security, judicial cooperation, and EU financing should continue to require unanimity, while France and Germany, as well as many of the smaller members, believed this to be a prescription for deadlock. And Blair was alone in demanding continuation of the British rebate, which was a compensation for the net agricultural bill shouldered by EU members with small farm sectors.[37] Members fed up with the rebate argued that reforms had reduced the magnitude of farmers' subsidies to the point that the British rebate should no longer apply.

Although success of the treaty would depend on a wide array of ratification procedures, the French and German governments exhibited confidence that the treaty would make it through, as had previous treaties, with only a few minor surprises. To the extent that they recognized an absence of consensus, the alternative seemed to be that there would be different combinations of members involved in different EU policies and functions, while the EU as a whole would deal with only a limited range of issues.[38] There would be a hard core of members participating in the full range of EU activities, but its size remained unclear. Thus, France and Germany were trying to lead the organization in directions of their choosing. But the other three of the five largest—Britain, Spain, and Poland—were pulling in other directions.

During the first months of 2004, Irish Prime Minister Ahern showed himself to be astute and inventive, successfully reaching compromises regarding the voting system in the Council of Ministers and the allocation of seats in the European Parliament, satisfying Spain and Poland regarding the former and the smallest states regarding the latter. But British insistence on a veto for tax, social security, and foreign policy issues remained a seemingly insurmountable barrier to final agreement on the Constitutional Treaty.[39]

The voting formula finally agreed on was an elaborate form of QMV, in which a minimum of 15 member states had to support a proposed policy decision, representing a minimum of 65 percent of the EU population. A coalition of the three largest members—France, Germany, and the United Kingdom—would not suffice as a blocking minority without at least a fourth country voting with them.[40] With this issue resolved, the treaty was approved by the 25 governments, moving it on to the stage of ratification at the national level.

THE RATIFICATION BATTLES

It was recognized that the treaty would have to run the test of voter approval, at least in those countries where support for the EU was not automatic. In some countries, it was not considered necessary for a referendum to be held; in others, it was controversial enough that ratification without referendum might make the constitution illegitimate in the eyes of voters. France was one of the latter, while Germany was actually prevented by its Basic Law from using referenda to settle policy issues. Ratification by national parliament was a surer method, given that governments were supported by parliamentary majorities in almost all of the member countries. In the French case, President Chirac had a great deal at stake in ratification of a treaty that seriously divided his country. Ratification by parliament, as in Germany and other original member countries, would have been a safer method, but after a long hesitation, he decided to send French citizens to the polling booth in 2005. Tony Blair, even though he had even more serious misgivings, likewise made the decision to consult the electorate. But the British referendum was not to be until 2006.[41]

Gradually, the objections of the governments of Britain, Spain, and Poland were overcome, attesting to Prime Minister Ahern's moderating skills.[42] But lasting animosities had surfaced during the constitution-making process. Neither Britain nor France was fully satisfied with the results, the Blair government finding the French to blame and President Chirac reciprocating. The former complained of Franco-German arm twisting, while the latter regarded the British as insufficiently socialized into the EU way of doing things (i.e., that of following Franco-German leadership), and British leaders were well aware of the French view. Chirac's French critics castigated him for not holding out against Britain's insistence on keeping the veto for tax and welfare issues. But France had successfully promoted the idea of "enhanced cooperation" among willing member states, which allowed circumvention of the veto. If Britain and other more skeptical members refused to join in certain cooperative programs, others could move forward.[43]

The Constitutional Treaty provided that, if 80 percent of the member countries have ratified the treaty, but others have encountered difficulties, the European Council will consider what action to take. Implicit in this provision was the expectation that the hard-core original six members of the EC would be in the forefront of those voting positively and that, if later comers (most likely the United Kingdom and maybe Poland) were to vote against the treaty, this would accelerate the development of "variable geometry" (i.e., different subsets of members involved in different EU programs), but it would not defeat the Constitutional Treaty. However, the strategy ignored three problems that had surfaced in the otherwise successful effort to create the treaty and gain the unanimous support of member governments for it. First, the treaty had the support of alliances in each country, some of which were solid, while others were conditional and vulnerable to new complications that might arise. Second, the treaty held different meanings for different members, as governments varied in emphasis and interpretation in reporting back to their respective publics. And, third, leaders in some countries were taking their voters' support for granted.[44]

Governments of some member countries had little to fear from ratification, as their voters were positively inclined. Such governments appeared to include most of the new members. Most of these did not hold referenda, choosing instead to ratify by parliamentary vote. In these cases, the ratification process held little danger. Even Poland could not be considered Euro-skeptic, as there was not a public desire to kill the Constitutional Treaty. Along with Spain, Poland sought parity with the "big three" members, achieving some satisfaction of its claims from the fact that, under the treaty, the three largest members would need the support of a fourth member to have the requisite voting majority. More crucial were the questions of which countries would hold referenda and what would happen if there were negative votes in any of the countries holding them, especially Britain and France. Prime Minister Blair did not want Britain to be the one to kill the treaty, so he decided not only to wait until after British general elections were held (early in 2005), but also to delay treaty ratification until the following year. More unexpected was the decision of Jacques Chirac to hold a referendum in France, and an early one at that. It was a gamble that, if won, might well reverse the decline of his own and his government's popularity, with time left for his party to win the next presidential election, when he was expected to name his party's candidate for the succession.[45]

By this time, President Chirac was facing the rising popularity of a member of his own party, Nicholas Sarkozy, a strong supporter of the Constitutional Treaty, as was Chirac, but, unlike Chirac, not a supporter of Turkey's membership in the EU. Opposition to Turkey's entry was growing in the member countries, even though it was an event that could occur only after a waiting period that would stretch beyond 2010. (See Chapter 6.) This rising sentiment in France put Chirac's referendum at risk.[46]

A similar phenomenon was occurring in the Netherlands, where Dutch voters would follow French voters in a Constitutional Treaty referendum. Since both countries were charter members of the European Union, a "no" vote was not expected by their leaders, whatever the polls were saying. There was an expectation that majorities of some of the more Euro-skeptic countries would vote "no." But such a result would fit the growing sentiment among leaders of the original members that latecomers could move on a slower track without slowing the integration process among the more advanced members. Polls in early 2005 were showing comfortable majorities in favor of the treaty. Only the United Kingdom had a negative plurality: 30 percent opposed to the treaty versus 20 percent in favor. But the undecided percentages were high. Along with growing disenchantment with President Chirac and his government, French voters were drifting to the "no" side in polls by March. Socialist voters were switching as divisions among their leaders surfaced. In April, the "father" of the treaty, Giscard d'Estaing, acknowledged that the Constitutional Treaty could not go forward if the French were to vote against it.[47]

By this time, polls were indicating that 56 percent of French voters were opposed to ratification, while the Dutch "no" sentiment was running close behind the French at 53 percent. Meanwhile, other members (Hungary, Italy, Lithuania, and Slovenia) had ratified, not by referendum, but by parliamentary votes with support distributed comfortably across the left-right spectrum. A similar result was expected from the German Parliament, despite an unemployment level, like that of France, at 10 percent. Ratification by parliament could be kept under control; ratification by voters could not.[48]

As failure of ratification in France emerged from the unthinkable stage in January 2005 to that of looming disaster by May, former Commission President Jacques Delors weighed in with the suggestion that a "Plan B" treaty might be produced to replace the Plan A version if the latter was defeated in the referendum.

Given the poll evidence in the last weeks before the first referendum, the outcome should not have been very surprising. At the end of May 2005, the French voters defeated the treaty by a 55 percent to 45 percent margin, followed by the Dutch voters, whose vote against the treaty was even more decisive: 62 percent to 38 percent. In both countries, the strongest percentage of "no" votes came from those of the hard left and hard right, but many voters from all across that political spectrum voted "no" as well. The positions of both governments on the Constitutional Treaty were repudiated by many of their usual supporters, as well as by their opponents. Unlike many votes in EU countries on EU issues, these were not general antigovernment votes; they were antitreaty. And they suggest that, in at least some of the countries where ratification proceeded smoothly through parliaments, the outcomes would have been quite different if the issue had been presented to the voters to decide.[49]

LISBON TREATY

During the remaining months of 2005, it could be observed that the goal of a federal Europe, in which member governments would operate within a common framework of objectives and constraints, could be no more than a distant goal that could be reached only if the 27 or eventually more member states gradually reached consensus on its necessity.

Meanwhile, as the dust settled from the referendum disasters, the question of further enlargement returned to the center of attention. In the case of Romania and Bulgaria, waiting in the wings, it was a matter of keeping to their scheduled entry or postponing it until the implications of the Constitutional Treaty's demise were sorted out. In the cases of Turkey and the Balkan states, it was a question of whether or not to satisfy expectations of eventual membership. (See Chapter 6.)

By the end of 2005, it was clear that it would take time for the EU15 to digest the 2004 influx of 12 member states. In mid-December, *Financial Times* analyst Quentin Peel summarized the year: "It has been a dreadful year in the European Union, and the mood in Brussels has seldom been so gloomy."[50] Peel acknowledged that the most spectacular setbacks were the "no" votes by French and Dutch voters, who had essentially killed the Constitutional Treaty. Two other problems were intensifying as he wrote: (1) The Doha round of global trade talks was stalled, in large part because of the French refusal to reduce EU farm subsidies. (2) An opinion was growing among some leaders of established EU member governments that the recent enlargement had been too ambitious, as it was seen as threatening jobs and public finance in the older member states. Older, richer member governments were beginning to ask whether the enlargement had been worth a sacrifice of economic benefits they perceived to have been the principal advantage EU membership afforded them, while the new, poorer members were seeking from older members the investment needed to catch up.

Attempting to make headway at the December summit, British Prime Minister Tony Blair found he could not get the French government to budge on agricultural subsidies without having to give up Britain's rebate that Margaret Thatcher had won from François Mitterrand two decades earlier. An agreement to adjust both the CAP and the British rebate was brokered by the new German chancellor, Angela Merkel. It involved a reduction of payments to French farmers, an increase in payments to Polish farmers, and a reduction of the British rebate, all of which pointed in the right direction as far as the economic health of all 25 members was concerned, without requiring any of the principal contenders to suffer serious financial disappointment. Merkel received the lion's share of the credit for brokering the agreement, especially as it invoked memories of the constructive role Germany had played in earlier times.[51] But the magnitude of the changes was not impressive, especially as the prospect of further enlargement loomed ahead.

Following these difficult bargaining processes, the EU25 pushed ahead, with Bulgaria and Romania joining in January 2007, to find the alternative Plan B solution for the constitutional debacle. The outcome was the Reform Treaty, known as the Lisbon Treaty, which leaders signed on December 13, 2007, at the Lisbon summit meeting. All members states are expected to ratify the treaty, which will enter into force in 2009. However, failure of ratification by any member state would kill the treaty.

The new treaty contains many of the changes the proposed constitution attempted to introduce: (1) a politician chosen to be president of the European Council for two-and-a-half years, replacing the current system where countries take turns at being president for six months; (2) a new post combining the jobs of the existing foreign affairs supremo, Javier Solana, and the external affairs commissioner, Benita Ferrero-Waldner, to give the EU more clout on the world stage; (3) a smaller European Commission, with fewer commissioners than there are member states, from 2014; (4) a redistribution of voting weights between the member states, phased in between 2014 and 2017; (5) new powers for the European Commission, European Parliament, and European Court of Justice, for example, in the field of justice and home affairs; and (6) removal of national vetoes in a number of areas.[52] The Commission established an educational Web site for interested individuals to search for answers regarding what the new treaty brings to the EU (see http://europa.eu/lisbon_treaty/faq/index_en.htm). The new treaty calls for substantial revisions of the governance structure of the EU. While the details of these reforms are discussed in Chapter 7, it is important to highlight some key developments.

For the first time in EU's history, national parliaments receive recognition as part of the democratic framework of the European Union. It provides for special arrangements to help national parliaments become more closely involved in the work of the Union. Specifically, national parliaments will act as "watchdogs" of the principle of *subsidiarity*, which has been an issue of contention between member states and the Brussels institution.[53] This principle is intended to ensure that decisions are taken as closely as possible to the citizen and that constant checks are made as to whether action at Community level is justified in light of the possibilities available at the national, regional, or local level. Under the new treaty, national parliaments will have the power to have a say at a very early stage of a draft legislation emerging from the Commission, before the proposal goes to the European Parliament and the Council of Ministers. In an attempt to improve participatory democracy by citizens at the EU level, the treaty introduces the European Citizens' Initiative.[54] Accordingly, one million citizens coming from yet to be determined number of member states could start an initiative.

The new treaty also addresses reform of the QMV in the Council of Ministers (see Chapter 7). The new system that will become effective in 2014 calls for a double majority system where passsage of decisions will require the consent of 55 percent of member states (currently 15 out of 27) and that it represent at least 65 percent of the EU population. Table 5.1 provides data on the distribution of votes among member states under the new treaty.[55] Moreover, to prevent a small number of large states from blocking a decision, the blocking minority must include at least four member states. Failure to achieve this minimum requirement would mean that the qualified majority has been reached even if the population criterion was not met. The treaty also stipulates that during the first three years of the new system, until 2017, any member country may request that an act be adopted in accordance with the QMV system defined in the Nice Treaty.[56]

The treaty reforms the number of Commissioners and the Parliament as of 2014 and creates permanent posts of the President of the European Council and the High Representative of the Union for Foreign Affairs and Security Policy. The latter will also become Vice-President of the Commission and chair the External Relations Council.

On the issue of EU citizens' fundamental rights, which caused a lot of controversy during the consitution debates, the new treaty makes a reference to it without specifically outlining the detials of the Charter. The treaty makes it legally binding, but the full text does not appear, even in an annex. The six chapters of the Charter cover individual rights related to dignity, freedoms, equality, solidarity, rights linked to citizenship status, and justice. These rights are drawn from other international instruments, like the European Convention on Human Rights, giving them legal presence in the Union. The European Court of Justice has the power to ensure its application. However, the UK has secured a written guarantee that the Charter cannot be used by the European Court to alter British labour law, or other laws that deal with social rights. Other cases of opting out include Ireland and the UK from policies concerning asylum, visas, and immigration, Poland seeking the same assurances as the UK on labor issues, and Denmark continuing with its current opt-out from justice and home affairs policies, with the right under the new treaty to opt for the pick-and-chose system any time in the future.

STUDY QUESTIONS

1. How did the Amsterdam Treaty modify the Maastricht Treaty?

2. What are the key reform points outlined in the Nice Treaty? Why were these reforms necessary for the future of the EU?

3. What were the key tenets of the draft constitution? Why did it fail?

4. What is the Lisbon Treaty and how does it differ from the failed draft constitution?

5. Provide a critical analysis of the post-Maastricht treaties of the EU from two theoretical perspectives (realist, neofunctionalist, liberal intergovernmentalist, historical institutionalism, and constructivism) of your choice.

ENDNOTES

1. *Financial Times*, September 27, 1994, p. 3.

2. Ibid., September 3, 1994, p. 3; September 5, 1994, p. 3.

3. Ibid., December 12, 1994, pp. 1–2.

4. Graham Avery and Fraser Cameron, *The Enlargement of the European Union* (Sheffield, England: Sheffield Academic Press, 1999), pp. 17–18.

5. Ibid., p. 96.

6. Ibid., chap. 1.

7. Andrew Moravcsik and Kalypso Nicolaidis, "Explaining the Treaty of Amsterdam: Interests, Influence, Institutions," *Journal of Common Market Studies* 37 (March 1999): 59–85.

8. Ibid., p. 68.

9. Desmond Dinan, *Encyclopedia of the European Union*, updated ed. (Boulder, Colo.: Lynne Rienner, 2000), pp. 84–85.

10. Anthony Forster and William Wallace, "Common Foreign and Security Policy: From Shadow to Substance?" in Helen Wallace and William Wallace, eds., *Policy-Making in the European Union*, 4th ed. (Oxford: Oxford University Press, 2000), p. 484.

11. Monica den Boer and William Wallace, "Justice and Home Affairs: Integration Through Intergovernmentalism?" in Wallace and Wallace, eds., *Policy-Making in the European Union*, pp. 513–514.

12. Desmond Dinan, *Ever Closer Union: An Introduction to European Integration*, 2nd ed. (Boulder, Colo.: Lynne Rienner, 1999), p. 475.

13. Loukas Tsoukalis, "Economic and Monetary Union: Political Conviction and Economic Uncertainty," in Wallace and Wallace, eds., *Policy-Making in the European Union*, pp. 155, 168.

14. *Financial Times*, November 3, 2000, p. 2.

15. Desmond Dinan and Sophie Vanhoonacker, "IGC 2000 Watch (Part 2): The Opening Round," *ECSA Review* 13 (Summer 2000): 8.

16. *The Economist*, December 16, 2000, pp. 25–28.

17. David Galloway, *The Treaty of Nice and Beyond: Realities and Illusions of Power in the EU* (Sheffield, England: Sheffield Academic Press, 2001), p. 8.

18. *Financial Times*, December 12, 2000, p. 2.

19. *The Economist*, December 16, 2000, p. 2.

20. Desmond Dinan and Sophie Vanhoonacker, "IGC 2000 Watch (Part 3): Pre- and Post-Nice," *ECSA Review* 13 (Fall 2000): 1.

21. Galloway, *The Treaty of Nice*, pp. 80–81.

22. Ibid., p. 50.

23. Eric Philippart, "The New Provisions for 'Closer Cooperation'? A Call for Prudent Politics," *ECSA Review* 14 (Spring 2001): 6–7.

24. George A. Bermann, "Law in an Enlarged European Union," *EUSA Review* 14 (Summer 2001): 1–6.

25. Bruno de Witte, "Apres Nice: Time for a European Constitution?" *ECSA Review* 14 (Spring 2001): 10–11.

26. *Financial Times*, February 25, 2002, p. 14; June 10, 2002, p. 13.

27. Ibid., June 10, 2002, p. 13.

28. Ibid., December 10, 2003, p. 2.

29. Ibid., March 17, 2004.

30. Ibid., March 27, 2004.

31. Ibid., March 25, 2004.

32. Ibid., March 27, 2004.

33. Ibid., April 19, 2004.

34. Ibid., April 22, 2004.

35. Ibid., April 30, 2004.

36. Ibid., May 6, 2004.

37. Ibid., May 20, 2004.

38. Ibid., May 17, 2004.

39. Ibid., March 9, 2004; May 18, 2004.

40. Ibid., June 21, 2004.

41. Ibid., June 15, 2004.

42. Ibid., June 14, 2004.

43. Ibid., May 14, 2004.

44. Vernon Bogdanor, "Europe Needs to Connect with Its Voters," *Financial Times*, June 16, 2004.

45. Wolfgang Munchau, "In or Out: Europe's Ditherers Must Now Decide," *Financial Times*, June 21, 2004.

46. Ibid., December 10, 2004.

47. Ibid., April 4, 2005.

48. Ibid., April 19, 2005.

49. Ibid., June 3, 2005.

50. Quentin Peel, "Europe's Leaders Must Shake Off Their Gloom," *Financial Times*, December 15, 2005.

51. Wolfgang Munchau, "Merkel Finds Hope in Europe's Gloom," *Financial Times*, December 19, 2005.

52. From BBC NEWS: http://news.bbc.co.uk/go/pr/fr/-/2/hi/europe/6901353.stm. For complete reading of the treaty see Commission of the European Union, *Treaty of Lisbon amending the Treaty on European Union and the Treaty establishing the European Community, signed at Lisbon, 13 December 2007* (Brussels: EU Publications Office, 2007).

53. *Treaty of Lisbon,* Article 6, p. 16.

54. Ibid., Article 8B, p. 20.

55. Ibid., "Title II: Provisions Concerning the Qualified Majority, Article 3" p. 199.

56. Ibid.

Chapter 6

Enlargement of the European Union

The recent enlargement of the European Union (EU) to admit 12 Central and East European countries (CEECs) was the largest expansion in the EU's history. This enlargement took place against a background of complex political and economic changes in Europe and the international system. In Europe, the collapse of the Soviet Union created a power vacuum and a threat of regional instability, as demonstrated by the civil war in the former Yugoslavian states. The international system also saw changes in power distribution in terms of both the economic and the security regimes. The EU reacted to these challenges by further deepening integration and expanding its membership to newly democratic CEECs in an attempt to position itself as a global actor. Eastern enlargement, however, is by no means over. The EU indicated that other potential members include Albania, Bosnia-Herzegovina, Former Yugoslav Republic of Macedonia (FYROM), Kosovo, Montenegro, Serbia, and Turkey. At present, Croatia, FYROM, and Turkey are candidate countries for membership, and talks with Croatia and Turkey are underway. The implications of eastern enlargement are significant both for the EU's and the CEECs' respective political, economic, and security interests and for the future stability of Europe.

REASONS BEHIND ENLARGEMENT

Each enlargement focused on two major goals of the EU—peace and security in Europe and economic growth and improved quality of life for the Union's citizens. In this regard, progress made in the single market did not go unnoticed by the other countries around the EU. Particularly noteworthy were the European Free Trade Association (EFTA) countries that applied to the European Community (EC) for membership in the late 1980s and early 1990s: Austria (1988), Finland (1992), Norway (1992), and Sweden (1991). With the exception of Norway, citizens of these countries voted to join the EU as of January 1, 1995. Furthermore, many of the Eastern European and Mediterranean countries applied for full membership in the EU soon after they obtained their freedoms following the collapse of the Eastern Bloc.

EU members were also interested in enlargement because it would enhance their influence in Europe and in the world. Peripheral countries wanted to join because of the expected economic benefits of integration. EU officials expressed their view of enlargement in the joint declaration of the heads of state and government at the Edinburgh summit in December 1992. They stated that the EU intended to extend membership to the Central and Eastern European countries sometime in the future. At the Copenhagen summit in June 1993, it was announced that the EFTA countries would be included in the next enlargement and that the EU intended to improve economic and political relations with the other European countries that would apply for membership.

The EU strategic view of enlargement was also reflected in an opinion paper prepared by the Economic and Social Council on January 25, 1989.[1] The efforts of the EU in providing economic assistance and leadership to the new democracies of the Central and Eastern European countries through the establishment of the European Bank for Reconstruction and Development (EBRD), revisions of the EU's Global Mediterranean Policy (GMP), and participation in peace negotiations in the former Yugoslavia in partnership with the United Nations were all made with views such as those expressed by the Economic and Social Council in mind. While improvement of economic and political relations between the EU and its periphery was in the interest of both sides, the eventual membership in the EU for any candidate state depended on two factors: how well the candidate fared with regard to the conditions for membership and whether there existed a consensus among the EU members to grant membership to the applicant.

As explained in the previous chapter, the *acquis communautaire* is one of the main requirements for membership in the EU. The requirements are quite specific about what conditions the candidate countries must meet prior to accession. Furthermore, the EU leaders are clearly committed to preparing these countries for membership.

In its relations with peripheral countries, the EU also tries to improve ties by establishing association agreements. These agreements provide for greater economic and political cooperation between the EU and recipient countries. There are two types of association agreements extended to nonmember countries. The first type provides for economic and technical assistance and for improvement of trade relations in specified commodity categories. Countries in this category—the African, Caribbean, and Pacific (ACP) countries and most of the Mediterranean Basin countries—are not targeted for eventual accession to full membership. The second type of association prepares nonmembers for eventual membership in the EU or calls for the creation of a customs union between the nonmember state and the EU. Agreements with EFTA countries; with Cyprus, Malta, and Turkey; and with the CEECs all fall into this second category.[2]

THE EASTERN ENLARGEMENT

Democratization in Central and Eastern Europe served as a catalyst to refashion EU policies toward this region. Soon after the collapse of the Communist regimes, the EU initiated an economic reconstruction program for the newly emerging democratic states. This initiative resulted, in part, from a call in July 1989 by the G7 countries to the Commission to coordinate the Western countries' support for political and economic reforms in the CEECs.[3] The initial program, known as PHARE, called for assistance to Hungary and Poland. Later, the program expanded to include other CEECs as they abandoned communism. The scope of the program also expanded from development credit to cooperation and reconstruction. Finally, the EU went a step further and proposed a "global policy," similar in nature to the GMP, which emphasized the importance of establishing mutual association relationships with the CEECs. The prerequisites for establishing such relationships, on the part of the former Communist states, were political democratization and economic reforms toward a market system. According to Françoise de la Serre, "more than anything else, the experience the [EU] has accumulated in terms of trade and cooperation policy with third countries or in the field of operations (e.g., food aid) has allowed it to become the privileged interlocutor for eastern Europe."[4] The program developed by the EU Commission to help the CEECs had four major points:

1. Trade liberalization to establish a free trade area with Eastern Europe;
2. Industrial, technical, and scientific cooperation;
3. A program of financial assistance; and
4. The creation of a system of political dialogue.[5]

One year after the negotiations began with the new democracies, the EU initiated "Europe agreements" with Czechoslovakia, Hungary, and Poland; these were known as the "Visegrad countries" because on February 15, 1991, a Hungarian–Polish–Czechoslovak summit was held in Visegrad, a small town at the Danube bend in northern Hungary. At this summit, Hungarian Prime Minister Jozsef Antall, President Lech Walesa of Poland, and Czech President Václav Havel signed a comprehensive agreement to cooperate in their efforts to attain EU membership for their countries by the end of the twentieth century. While these agreements were similar in scope to the association agreements that helped Greece, Portugal, and Spain to join the EU, they had one important difference in that there was no timetable set for membership in the EU. After Czechoslovakia split, the EU renegotiated the Europe agreements with the Czech Republic and Slovakia. The EU then signed two more Europe agreements, with Bulgaria (1992) and Romania (1992).

At the Essen meeting of the European Council during December 9–10, 1994, the EU leaders agreed to prepare six CEECs (Poland, Hungary, the Czech Republic, Slovakia, Bulgaria, and Romania) for accession to full membership.[6] While the EU made this commitment, it also stated that accession negotiations with these countries would not start until after the 1996 Intergovernmental Conference to review the state of the Maastricht Treaty. Since then, the EU has been proceeding with a complex set of assistance policies aimed at preparing 11, and later 13, CEECs for membership.

The first 12 countries were the ones identified at the Luxembourg 1998 summit of the European Council in a two-phase enlargement plan. The first phase was to include Cyprus, the Czech Republic, Estonia, Hungary, Malta, Poland, and Slovenia. In the second phase Bulgaria, Latvia, Lithuania, Romania, and Slovakia were to be included. After briefly withdrawing its candidacy, Malta reentered the picture in February 1999, and at the Helsinki summit in December 1999, the European Council invited Turkey to be a candidate, but without committing to accession talks until the Turks could meet the Copenhagen criteria for membership.

Complex sets of state interests drove these events. As stated earlier, when we assess the reasons behind this ambitious enlargement plan, it becomes clear that, with the end of the Cold War, the EU and the CEECs had no real alternative but to reach out to each other. The CEECs needed to achieve market reforms, integrate their economies with global financial markets, and build democratic institutions. EU membership provided the easiest possible way to achieve these objectives. On the other hand, the CEECs represented new market opportunities that would increase the EU's collective power in the new international economic order by making it the largest economic bloc. Agenda 2000 further elaborated on these issues by identifying three challenges that faced the EU at the end of the century:

1. How to strengthen and reform the EU's policies so that they could deal with enlargement and deliver sustainable growth, higher employment, and improved living conditions for Europe's citizens;
2. How to negotiate enlargement, while at the same time vigorously preparing all applicant countries for the moment of accession; and
3. How to finance enlargement, the advance preparations, and the development of the EU's internal policies.[7]

The EU citizens gave mixed support to these plans. According to the Eurobarometer Survey 56 of 2002, 51 percent of EU citizens supported enlargement. The highest level of support was in Greece with 74 percent, followed by Denmark and Sweden with 69 percent each. In five countries, the level of support for enlargement was below the EU average: Belgium—49 percent; Germany—47 percent; Austria—46 percent; Britain—41 percent; and France—39 percent.[8] However, 68 percent overall believed that enlargement would make the EU a more important actor in world affairs, and 64 percent viewed enlargement as contributing to the cultural richness of the EU and to greater peace and security in Europe.[9]

With public support generally behind enlargement plans, the EU leaders took up the issue at the EU summit in Nice (December 4–6, 2000), reaffirmed their commitment to enlargement, and outlined institutional changes that would take place after enlargement, such as changing voting weights in the Council and number of seats in the European Parliament.[10] The Nice Treaty initially ran into a problem in Ireland when the Irish voters rejected it in a national referendum in 2001. After a yearlong intense campaign by the Irish government, the voters revisited the Nice Treaty in a new referendum on October 19, 2002, and gave it a 63 percent thumbs up.[11] Finally, at the Copenhagen summit on December 12, 2002, the EU invited ten candidates to become members on May 1, 2004.[12] Bulgaria and Romania joined in January 2007.

The final stretch to accession was not without problems. One of the candidate countries, Cyprus, represented a serious problem for the EU. As a politically and territorially divided country, with foreign Greek and Turkish troops present to protect their respective kin on the island, Cyprus had been an insurmountable challenge to the United Nations (UN) and the Western alliance for more than 40 years. Admitting Cyprus into the EU prior to solving the political problem between the Greek and Turkish Cypriots meant that the EU would take on an immense responsibility, as well as a serious threat to cohesion among the members.

After this major enlargement, speculation continued over which countries might be next, in addition to Bulgaria and Romania, which were already in the process of meeting eligibility requirements. Two very large countries, Turkey and Ukraine, were high on some lists. But Turkey is the only one of these two that has started accession talks with the EU. Italian Prime Minister Silvio Berlusconi supported Ukraine President Leonid Kuchma's bid for his country's admission, and Commission President Romano Prodi led the support for Turkey. The latter received candidacy status in December 2004, while Ukraine remains on hold. Speculation about Balkan countries centered on Serbia, Albania, Croatia, and Bosnia. Warfare and evidence of genocide made the chances of the admission of Serbia and Croatia questionable. The EU wanted assurance that the 1991–1992 war between these two parts of the former Yugoslavia was truly over. Eventually, the EU decided that all of these Western Balkan countries are prospective candidates for membership as long as they meet the Copenhagen criteria.

IMPLICATIONS OF ENLARGEMENT

Enlargement presents several internal complications for the EU. As discussed earlier, necessary reforms were made in the institutions and policies of the EU to address the issues faced because of the enlargement process. These issues covered such items as the determination of the number of parliamentarians from the new members and the number of commissioners, judges, and auditors; and revision of the qualified majority voting (QMV) system in the Council of Ministers. At the same time, the CAP, the cohesion policies, and the budget of the EU require reforms to make it possible for the new countries to be integrated into the EU. While the institutional reforms took place, there was setback in the EU as the French and Danish voters rejected the proposed constitution and as disagreements arose over the 2007–2013 budget. Finally, Eastern enlargement brought the Cyprus problem into the EU with all its multifaceted implications (e.g., EU's relations with Turkey, regional stability, and the protracted conflict between the Greek and Turkish Cypriot communities).

Despite these mixed results of the recent enlargement, there are clear indications that, if the EU wants to be a global player, future expansion of its membership is necessary. A series of reports from the Commission (e.g., Agenda 2000) and analyses by EU scholars argue that future enlargement is needed if the EU wants to be able to compete economically and politically with other global actors.[13] If this is the case for the EU, do European leaders realize that their future global challenger might be someone other than the United States? According to the Lisbon Strategy of 2000—a call for economic reforms aimed at making the EU the world's most competitive knowledge-based economy by 2010—the EU leaders are determined to make the EU a highly competitive player in the world economy. Yet, the accompanying research from the European Commission focused on the United States and did not pay much attention to China. This oversight on the part of European leaders and Commission technocrats has become a serious embarrassment for all concerned, as they now realize the impact of China's economic development plans and trade policies on the EU's economy.[14] A recent study by Birol Yesilada, Brian Efird, and Peter Noordijk analyzed the regional and global implications of the potential entry of Turkey, Ukraine, and Byelorussia into the EU, using power transition theory.[15] Figures 6.1 and 6.2 show their findings, where the y axis represents "Share of System Productivity for Major Contenders" and the size of each bubble represents "Productivity per capita" based on data standardized in terms of purchasing power parity. Their findings show that, if the EU maintains its present composition of 27 member states, it will continue to lose ground against the United States and China, and to a lesser extent India, in the global economy, while its per capita productivity will remain fairly constant (Figure 6.1). In the scenario where Turkey joins the EU, its contribution

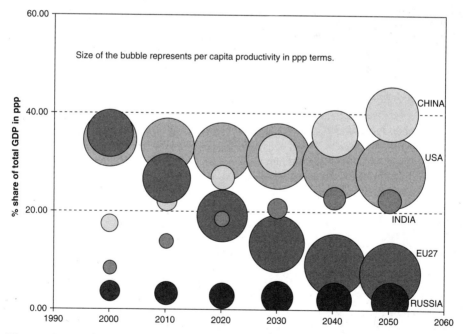

Figure 6.1 ■ Forecasting GDP and Per Capita Productivity Shares: EU27 and Global Partners, 2000–2050

Source: Birol Yesilada, Brian Efird, and Peter Noordijk "Competition among Giants: A Look at How Future Enlargement of the European Union Could Affect Global Power Transition," *International Studies Review* Vol. 8, no. 4 (December 2006): 607–622.

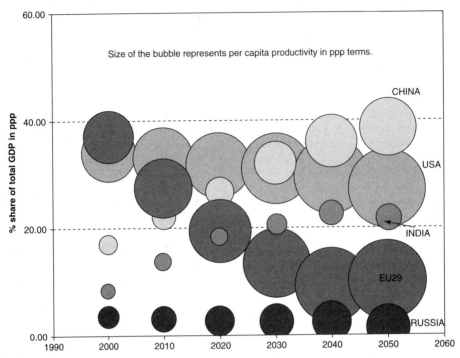

Figure 6.2 ■ Forecasting GDP and Per Capita Productivity Shares: EU29 (including Turkey and Ukraine) and Global Competitors, 2000–2050

Source: Birol Yesilada, Brian Efird, and Peter Noordijk "Competition among Giants: A Look at How Future Enlargement of the European Union Could Affect Global Power Transition," *International Studies Review* Vol. 8, no. 4 (December 2006): 607–622.

becomes apparent by 2040, and the decline in the EU's share of global gross domestic product (GDP) levels off at around 10 percent and begins to show a slow increase (Figure 6.2). Implications of these results for integration, future enlargement, and policy making are clear. The EU needs to include Turkey, and preferably Ukraine as well, among its ranks for future competitiveness with China, India, and the United States.

Cohesion

Enlargement presents three major challenges for cohesion policy. First, regional disparities in economic development in the EU will become more apparent (Table 6.1). Whereas enlargement increased the EU's population by one-third, it added only 5 percent to the overall GDP. Second, the focus of cohesion policy shifted to Eastern Europe, where 98 million live in regions whose current GDP is below 75 percent of the average of the enlarged EU. And, third, the existing inequalities among the EU15 regions remained, adding to the complicated picture. In order to address these problems, the Commission proposed a strengthening of the existing preaccession assistance programs with an action plan for the EU's regions bordering candidate countries,[16] which complements the Second Report on Economic and Social Commission, adopted in January 2001. Under the program, the Instrument for Structural Policies for Pre-accession (ISPA) provided assistance to candidate countries with environment and

Table 6.1 ■ Key Statistics: EU15 and the CEEC Countries

Country	Population (millions)	Area (000 km)	GDP (€ billion)	GDP (€ per head)	GDP Change (%)	Inflation (%)
Bulgaria	8.2	111	44.3	5,400	5.8	10.3
Cyprus	0.8	9	12.4	18,500	4.8	4.9
Czech Republic	10.3	79	135.1	13,500	2.9	3.9
Estonia	1.4	45	12.1	8,500	6.9	3.9
Hungary	10.0	93	117.0	11,700	5.2	10.0
Latvia	2.4	65	15.6	6,600	6.6	2.6
Lithuania	3.7	65	24.3	6,600	3.3	0.9
Malta	0.4	0.3	4.6	11,900	5.0	2.4
Poland	38.6	313	337.9	8,700	4.0	10.1
Romania	22.4	238	135.4	6,000	1.6	45.7
Slovak Republic	5.4	49	58.3	10,800	2.2	12.1
Slovenia	2.0	20	32.0	16,100	4.6	8.9
Turkey	65.3	775	433.3	6,400	7.2	54.9
EU15	378.3	3,191	8,499	22,500	3.4	2.1

Source: Eurostat, from national sources year 2000, http://europa.eu.int/comm/enlargement/faq/faq2.htm# statistics

transport projects and had a budget of 1,040 million per year during 2000–2006. Also, under the INTERREG III program, cooperation projects were possible between regions in the EU15 and the candidate countries. The net impact of these efforts on harmonization was limited. As the EU moved into a new budget, challenges presented by the recent enlargement strained relations between the old and newer members of the EU.

Eastern Borders

With Poland and the Baltic states joining the EU, the tiny Russian enclave of Kaliningrad (population 900,000) presents a serious problem for EU–Russian relations (Map 6.1). Kaliningrad is bordered on two sides by the new EU member states and by the Baltic Sea on the other. Eastern enlargement created a serious travel problem for the residents of this Russian Baltic enclave. When Lithuania and Poland joined the EU, visa-free travel for Russians crossing their territories came to an end. This also complicated travel for Russians between Kaliningrad and Russia. When confronted with this problem, the Brussels Commission stated that the EU would not relax its policy of requiring visas for Russians traveling to and from Kaliningrad through Lithuania or Poland.

In response to these developments, the Russian government warned that such a policy would damage EU–Russia relations. President Vladimir Putin went as far as calling this dilemma a matter of national principle and vowed to defend the right of the Russians to free travel between Kaliningrad and Russia.[17] As a counterproposal, the Commission proposed a special passport for Kaliningrad

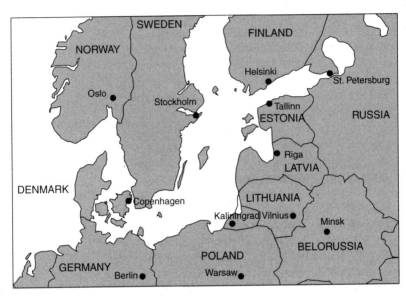

Map 6.1 ■ The EU and Kaliningrad

Source: European Commission, http://www.europa.eu.int/comm/external_relations/north_ dim/kalin/index.htm

residents for travel across EU territory. Russia again rejected this proposal in September. Finally, in November 2002, the EU and Russia reached a tentative agreement on travel between Kaliningrad and mainland Russia for residents of the enclave. According to this accord, residents of Kaliningrad need only a cheap, multientry obtainable "facilitated transit document."[18] In addition, the Russian airline Aeroflot doubled its direct flights to Kaliningrad to ease the burden of land travel for residents of the enclave. However, the EU–Russia accord is not without problems. Lithuania's tough border controls continue to draw criticism from Russian officials, who claim that Lithuania deliberately attempts to hinder the transit of Russian passengers and cargos between Kaliningrad and mainland Russia.[19]

Challenges Presented by Cyprus

The membership of Cyprus presents a sensitive problem for the EU because of the protracted conflict that exists between the Greek and Turkish Cypriots of the island. European officials had hoped that the Cyprus problem would be resolved prior to this country joining the Union in May 2004. Yet, the failure of the UN-sponsored peace plan resulted in the Greek part of the island entering the EU while the Turkish-controlled north remained separate. As such, Cyprus is the only politically divided member of the EU and presents a difficult challenge for the Union.

Initially, Cyprus' case did not present economic obstacles for its accession; rather, the issue was the unresolved political tension between the island's Greek and Turkish populations. This problem has troubled the Western alliance since 1963, when civil war broke out between the two communities. Since July 1974, when Turkey intervened to protect the Turkish Cypriot minority and prevent the union of Cyprus and Greece, the island has been divided into the Turkish Republic of Northern Cyprus (TRNC) and the internationally recognized Cyprus Republic in the south. The TRNC is recognized only by Turkey. In addition, the island is one of the most militarized pieces of real estate in the world.

Unfortunately, accession talks between Cyprus and the EU did not progress as was hoped. On March 12, 1998, President Glafkos Clerides attended the European Conference in London and presented a timetable to the EU outlining the Cypriot strategy for accession talks. The proposal included an invitation to the Turkish Cypriots to take part in the Cyprus negotiating team. The Turkish Cypriots rejected this invitation on grounds that the Greek Cypriot government did not represent all of Cyprus and that the Turkish Cypriot side had been excluded in prior EU–Cyprus relations. Additional objections raised by the Turkish Cypriots included controversies surrounding the Cyprus Republic's constitution. The first problem concerned the legality of the Cypriot application for membership. The Constitution of Cyprus requires that both communities support the decision to apply for membership in the EU. The Turkish Cypriots were clearly excluded in this process. The second complicating legal factor pertained to the Turks' objection to Greek Cypriot application on the basis of international treaties signed in 1960. The Turkish side maintained that the Greek Cypriots' application for EU membership on behalf of the whole island was simply illegal based on Articles I and II of the 1960 Treaty of Guarantee, Annex F of the Treaty of Establishment, and Article 50 Par. 1(a) and Article 185 No. 2 of the 1960 Constitution of Cyprus. The 1959 Zurich and London Agreements stipulate that Cyprus cannot join international organizations or pacts of alliance of which both Turkey and Greece are not members, and the 1960 Treaty of Guarantee contains the provision that Cyprus cannot participate, in whole or in part, in any political or economic union with any state whatsoever.[20]

There is a lot of speculation about whether the EU is an intergovernmental organization (IGO) or a state. It is clear that the EU is an IGO that has statelike aspirations. Nevertheless, this is not the key problem with "union with another state." The EU is a union—an economic and monetary union and, to a lesser extent, a political union. To verify this point, one must start with the Maastricht Treaty and end with the Nice Treaty of the EU. When a country joins the EU, it gives up part of its national sovereignty, whether it be to adhere to monetary policy or to EU regulations and guidelines. Moreover, the new member enters into a full economic and monetary union and a partial political union with the current members of the EU.

The Greek Cypriot government, Greece, and the EU rejected or ignored these legal issues as real problems. They maintained that in the current state of affairs in Cyprus, where Turkey was viewed as an occupying power and where the Turkish Cypriots had established their own "illegal" state in the north, the Turks were in no position to argue the legitimacy of the very treaties they had violated. Article II Part 2 of the Cyprus Constitution clearly prohibits any action that could result in the partitioning of Cyprus. Furthermore, Turkey's military presence in northern Cyprus and its recognition of TRNC independence contradicted the guarantor powers' commitment to Cyprus's unity under that treaty. Faced with such problems, the Bush administration pursued shuttle diplomacy between the parties concerned, in an effort to find a compromise before the Copenhagen summit in December 2002. The UN and the EU joined this effort and pushed for a settlement under a new comprehensive plan, known as the Annan Plan, that envisioned a new united Cyprus constructed as a cross between a federal and a confederal state, made up of two politically equal entities (a Greek Cypriot state and a Turkish Cypriot state). The plan also called for a limited migration between the two states for settlement and addressed the future of peace building on the island. The new state would then join the EU as a single country. Despite the serious efforts of the international community, the Turkish Cypriot leadership rejected the Annan Plan. With this rejection, the talks failed, and the Greek Cypriots proceeded to sign the accession treaty without Turkish Cypriot participation.

Despite this failure, the international community did not give up on efforts to find a solution for Cyprus. The Annan Plan underwent five revisions. The new reformist government in Ankara, led by the Islamist AK Party of Recep Tayyip Erdogan, consolidated its power and withdrew support from the hardline Turkish Cypriot leader Rauf Denktas. With the loss of such support, Denktas's followers lost ground in the national elections in the TRNC in December 2003. The new Turkish Cypriot leadership, led by Prime Minister Mehmet Ali Talat, signaled its willingness to support the Annan Plan. These developments, however, coincided with national elections in the

Greek part of Cyprus in which ultranationalist, former EOKA leader Tassos Papadopoulos succeeded reformist and prounification President Clerides. To make matters worse, the progressive government of Simitis and Papandreau in Greece lost the national elections and was replaced by center-rightist Constantine Karamanlis, who did not show any sign of pressuring Papadopoulos to accept the Annan Plan. Against this backdrop, the parties met in New York under the auspices of the Secretary General and agreed to try to work out their differences and present a peace plan to their respective citizens in separate referenda prior to the May 1, 2004, accession date. They further agreed that, if the leaders of the two Cypriot communities failed to reach a compromise, the Secretary General would simply "fill in" the blanks and present the parties a final peace document. The final plan did not reflect a compromise the leaders jointly endorsed. The Turkish side was more inclined to accept it, whereas the Greek side saw it as being unacceptable. The final outcome was an overwhelming acceptance by the Turkish Cypriots (65.4 percent "Yes" and 35.1 percent "No"), with 84.35 percent participation, and a resounding rejection in the south (75.8 percent "No" and 24.2 percent "Yes"), with 96.53 percent participation.[21] With that, the Greek side joined the EU, while the Turkish Cypriots remained in an "uncertain" place—technically, in the EU with *acquis* being suspended in North Cyprus and its political status unclear.

Enlargement Commissioner Gunter Verheugen presented a scathing criticism of President Papadopoulos for hijacking the EU process and for wanting to use EU membership to pressure the Turkish side to cave in to Greek Cypriot wishes. A similar statement followed from the president of the European Parliament. In an attempt to reward the Turkish side for its endorsement of the Annan Plan, the Commission prepared a policy package that would have established direct trade between North Cyprus and EU markets and also provided for €249 million in direct aid. Verheugen argued that "I am making a serious call on our member states to make a decision to stick to their promises [to the Turkish Cypriots]," adding that the European Commission had done, and was willing to do, everything it could to back the Turkish Cypriots.[22] Despite such goodwill, the efforts of the Commission failed in both tasks, as the Council of Ministers ruled that the plans violated existing EU regulations, since North Cyprus (TRNC) could not be viewed as separate from member state Cyprus. Therefore, all EU linkages to the Turkish side of the island had to go through the official government of Cyprus—which the Turkish Cypriots refused in turn.

The failure of the EU to deliver its promise to Turkish Cypriots and the Greek Cypriots' determination to use their new EU membership to punish both Turkish Cypriots and Turkey during accession talks further soured relations between north Cyprus and Brussels. Official contacts between the two Cypriot communities came to a halt, and Turkey refused to extend its Customs Union agreement to Cyprus in direct retaliation to EU's inaction in rewarding the Turkish Cypriots. In turn, the EU suspended eight accession chapters with Turkey (see below). The Turks countered by using their membership in NATO to block Cypriot participation in alliance operations that included EU partnership.[23] Turkey also continues to block Cyprus's accession to the OECD and even the European Center for Medium-Range Weather Forecasts.[24] This spiral worsening of relations threatened to permanently divide Cyprus unless something was done.

In an attempt to reach out to the Turkish part of Cyprus, the EU designated a €259 million aid program to Turkish Cypriots that cover the following aspects: "(1) developing and restructuring of infrastructure; (2) promoting social and social development; (3) fostering reconciliation, confidence building measures, and support to civil society; (4) bringing the Turkish Cypriot community closer to the European Union; (5) Preparing the Turkish Cypriot community to introduce and implement the *acquis communautaire*; (6) sectoral programme for upgrading the quality and management of water supply and sanitation services; (7) support to the Turkish Cypriot community as regards management and protection of potential Natura 2000 sites in the northern part of Cyprus; (8) development and restructuring of the energy infrastructure; (9) traffic safety improvement program; and (10) development and restructuring of telecommunications infrastructure, Rural Development Sector Programme."[25] However, this program is stumbling over

Greek Cypriots' refusal to acknowledge Turkish Cypriot institutions created after the 1974 invasion and adds to Turkish Cypriots' distrust of the EU and its ability to resolve the impasse.

Recent presidential elections in Cyprus resulted in the replacement of the nationalist Papadopoulos with a communist leader of AKEL, Demetris Christofias. With this change in government, the international community called upon the leaders of the two communities to restart bicommunal negotiations under UN auspices to resolve the Cyprus problem. The EU has given its full support for these talks with the hope that it would result in a fair and just settlement of the problem.

ASSESSING THE CANDIDATES

There are three countries currently on the candidate list of the EU, with other western Balkan states identified as potential candidates. Enlargement represents the project parallel to deepening of regional integration in Europe and is considered an essential component of achieving peace and prosperity.

Croatia

At the Brussels summit of the European Council during December 13–14, 2004, the heads of state and government invited the Commission to present to the Council a proposal for a framework for negotiations with Croatia.[26] The Council asked that this framework take full account of the experience of the recent enlargement of the EU and that plans be made to start accession talks on March 17, 2005, provided that the Croatian government fully cooperated with the UN war crimes tribunal (ICTY) in delivering suspected war criminals. However, when the Croatian government failed to deliver suspected war criminals to the ICTY, the EU suspended the start of accession talks with Croatia. The most famous of these suspects is General Ante Gotovina, who is charged with war crimes against Serb civilians during a 1995 Croatian offensive.

Among the EU member states, not everyone was pleased with the decision to suspend Croatia's accession talks. Austria, a close ally of Croatia, voiced its concerns and began a quiet diplomacy aimed at bridging the gap between the two sides. The problem did not resolve itself until another accession ran into a serious problem on October 1, 2005. When EU foreign ministers met in Luxembourg to vote on the start of accession talks with Turkey (see the next section), Austria raised objections over the end goal of these talks. Just a few days before, at the EU ambassadors' meeting in Brussels on September 29, 2005, Austria was the only member state that "demanded a clear indication that the talks would be open-ended; an undertaking that membership would depend on the EU's ability to absorb such a large country; and a warning from the outset of talks that Turkey may be offered an 'alternative' to full membership."[27] The Luxembourg summit turned into a marathon session of multilateral diplomacy that saw intervention of U.S. Secretary of State Condoleezza Rice to prevent a train wreck between the EU and Turkey. With mounting pressure from its larger EU partners led by Britain and the United States, Austria lifted its objection, and the foreign ministers approved the start of accession talks with Turkey. However, in an interesting turn of events, the EU also announced the start of accession talks with Croatia—a goal passionately pursued by Austria. Was there a *quid pro quo* between these decisions? It is interesting to note that the EU based its decision on Croatia on a report issued by the UN Chief Crimes Prosecutor Carla del Ponte that Croatia had been working closely with the ICTY to pursue the war criminals. This was a reversal of her statement of disappointment with the Croatian leadership that was issued in 2004.

The Accession Partnership with Croatia covers important priorities and enables this country to benefit from financial assistance (preaccession financial instrument [IPA] for

2007–2013 that replaced Phare, ISPA, and SAPARD programs of 2000–2006). The priorities include:

1. Reforms that cover the Copenhagen political criteria such as democratization and the rule of law (public administration, judicial system, anticorruption policy), human rights, and the protection of minorities;
2. Addressing regional issues and international obligations including return of refugees to their homes, war crimes, and bilateral issues;
3. Economic reform to meet the EU's market realities (competitiveness, budgetary consolidation, and stability policy). These require continuation of structural reforms of public finances, privatization, improving the quality of business environments, land reform, protection of private property rights, and compiling macroeconomic statistics at EU standards;
4. Clear commitment to the *acquis*.[28]

Following the Accession Conference with Croatia on December 19, 2007, this country has made considerable progress toward harmonization and is set to precede Turkey in becoming a member of the EU. So far, Chapters on Science and Research (Chapter 25) and Education and Culture (Chapter 26) are provisionally closed (completed). Negotiations are open on Economic and Monetary Policy (Chapter 17); Enterprise and Industrial Policy (Chapter 20); Customs Union (Chapter 29); Intellectual Property Law (Chapter 7); Right of Establishment and Freedom to Provide Services (Chapter 3); Company Law (Chapter 6); Statistics (Chapter 18); Financial Control (Chapter 32); Information Society and Media (Chapter 10); Financial Services (Chapter 9); Consumer and Health Protection (Chapter 28); External Relations (Chapter 30); Financial and Budgetary Provisions (Chapter 33); and Trans-European Networks (Chapter 21). Chapters on Transport Policy (Chapter 14), Energy (Chapter 15), Freedom of Movement of Workers (Chapter 2), and Taxation (Chapter 16) are under preparation for start in the near future. And, two chapters, on Fisheries (Chapter 13) and Foreign, Security and Defense policy (Chapter 31), remain pending.[29]

Macedonia

Former Yugoslav Republic of Macedonia (FYRM) and the EU first signed a Stabilization and Association Agreement in April 2001, which led to this country's candidacy on December 17, 2005. However, accession talks with this country will not start any time soon for reasons pertaining to national security concerns of some of the current EU member states and the EU's concerns over disturbing political developments in the FYRM that negatively affect ethnic minorities. Greece objects to FYRM referring to itself as the Republic of Macedonia and the Macedonian government's use of the star of Macedonia on its flag and the tower of Salonika on its banknotes.[30] For her part, Bulgaria objects to the FYRM's membership unless "aggression [is stopped] towards the Bulgarian nation or history on behalf of the Macedonian authorities."[31] Positions of these countries on Macedonia pertain to age-old disagreements over who has the legitimate claim over symbols and territory in the Balkans after the decline and fall of the Ottoman Empire in the first two decades of the twentieth century. Despite these issues, the EU has maintained close contact with the government of FYRM, with significant economic assistance that totaled €870 million during 1992–2007.[32] The EU's main institution for managing assistance in the region, the European Agency for Reconstruction (EAR), started overseeing the Macedonia program in 2002. Since then, the EAR distributed €326 million in program assistance for projects covering *democracy and the rule of law, economic and social development, justice and home affairs*, and *the environment*.

Turkey

The case of Turkish membership is a complex one and deserves special attention because of its significance to the EU's other interests—notably, the Cyprus problem and the future of the European Security and Defense Identity (ESDI, discussed in Chapter 12). Whereas accession talks with Turkey began on October 3, 2005, the road leading to this was anything but smooth.

Turkey applied for EU membership in 1987, and on May 18, 1989, the European Commission concluded that the EU was not ready to enter into accession talks with Turkey because the Turkish economy was not as developed as the EU's, the Turkish democracy lacked extensive individual civil and political rights, and unemployment in Turkey posed a serious threat to the EU markets.[33] An additional and very serious problem in Turkey's case was the ongoing Greek–Turkish conflicts over Cyprus, territorial waters, the Aegean airspace, the continental shelf, and the rights of the Greek and Turkish minorities in their respective countries. Given the extent of this conflict, Greece would veto Turkey's membership in the EU even if the latter was to meet all the conditions for membership.

However, all was not lost after this initial European response. Recognizing Turkey's economic and political significance for the EU following the end of the Cold War, European leaders began a series of talks with their Turkish counterparts that eventually resulted in a compromise solution that neither shut the door on future membership nor granted the Turks immediate accession. The outcome was the customs union agreement of 1995, which went into effect on December 31, 1995.[34] This agreement gave the Turks closer economic ties with the EU than any other nonmember country at the time—with the exception of Iceland, Norway, and Switzerland—and opened the Turkish market of 74 million consumers to EU companies. For the Turks, the customs union symbolized their membership in Europe and thus put Turkey on track for membership in the EU. For EU members, however, the customs union was the most Turkey could expect from the EU for the foreseeable future.

The next crucial event in EU–Turkey relations came at the Luxembourg summit of December 1997. At this summit, the EU leaders decided on the list of candidate countries for membership in line with the recommendations of the European Commission outlined earlier in Agenda 2000. The announcement excluded Turkey as a candidate country. The Turkish government reacted harshly on several fronts and threatened to veto the ESDI–North Atlantic Treaty Organization partnership. The Clinton administration intervened, and eventually the EU extended candidacy status to Turkey at the December 1999 Helsinki summit. Despite these developments, EU–Turkish relations once again took a turn for the worse when the Commission did not recommend a timetable for starting accession talks.[35] The Commission's recommendation provided the basis for the 2002 accession assessment of the candidates and served as a guideline for the European Council summit in Copenhagen in December 2002, where the ten CEEC countries received invitations to join the EU on May 1, 2004. As for Turkey, the Council concluded that, "if the European Council in December 2004, on the basis of a report and a recommendation from the Commission, decides that Turkey fulfils the Copenhagen political criteria, the European Union will open accession negotiations with Turkey without delay."[36]

During the next two years, the Turkish government, led by Tayyip Erdogan, pushed ahead with political and economic reforms and made a serious effort to resolve the Cyprus problem before the May 2004 enlargement of the EU. These efforts, despite the Greek Cypriot rejection of the reunification plan in Cyprus, resulted in the opening of a new chapter in EU–Turkey relations at the Brussels summit of December 2004. The decision to start accession talks with Turkey on October 3, 2005, marked a fundamental turning point in the country's long quest for membership in the EU. Yet, Austria, and to a lesser extent France, had second thoughts about this decision when time came to start accession talks. The road ahead is quite challenging. As Martin Wolf of *Financial Times* explains:

> With its decision to open membership negotiations with Turkey, the European Union has taken a heroic gamble. If all were to go well, the EU would absorb a prosperous, democratic, large and overwhelmingly Muslim country. The signal this would send would be beyond price. If the conditions for entry were fudged, the EU's most populous member would be troubled, poor and unstable. Yet if the EU were to reject Turkey unfairly, instead, it would create a dangerously embittered neighbour. The stakes then are huge, so huge that if Turkish membership were being discussed for the first time, the EU would almost certainly reject it. In the eyes of many Europeans, Turkey is too large, too poor and too Muslim to be a successful member. But promises had been made. Rightly, therefore, the EU has proceeded to negotiation. Yet anxiety is not irrational. Fifteen years from now, the EU could well contain 600m people in 33 countries (the existing EU plus Albania, Bosnia, Bulgaria, Croatia, Macedonia, Romania, Serbia and Turkey). With a population of close to 80m by that time, Turkey would be the same size as Germany. An economically stagnant and institutionally paralysed EU might break down altogether. The journey on which the EU and Turkey have embarked will, therefore, demand big changes, on both sides.[37]

This might well be true, but as Omer Taspinar explains, "although Turkey has shown an impressive ability to transform itself, the forthcoming negotiations with the EU will be the real test of Turkey's democratic maturity and political stability. There is no doubt that the slightest sign of political turmoil in Turkey will bolster anti-Turkey skeptics in the EU and derail membership negotiations."[38] These fears became a reality as a result of two significant developments— Cyprus's membership, and veto threats, in the EU and election of Nicolas Sarkozy as the president of France. A staunch opponent of Turkey's membership in the EU, Sarkozy prefers a privileged partnership to the membership and has been lobbying other European leaders to adopt his position. Previously on December 11, 2006, EU–Turkey relations faced another crisis, yet again, over Cyprus when EU ministers agreed to punish Turkey for refusing to open its ports and airports to the EU member Cyprus. At that time, the EU indefinitely froze 8 of 35 accession chapters. Several countries, including Cyprus, Greece, Germany, France, and the Netherlands, had been arguing for stronger punishment. Turkey refuses to open its ports because it wants a de facto embargo lifted on the self-declared Turkish republic of northern Cyprus, which the EU promised to do following Turkish Cypriots' approval of the internationally supported Annan Peace Plan for Cyprus in April 2004. With such dramatic developments, the future of EU–Turkey relations look rather bleak, which is also reflective of public opinion on the subject among citizens of both sides (see below).

PUBLIC OPINION AND EU ENLARGEMENT

Public opinion toward future enlargement has been mixed over the last three years. The Commission's public opinion polls taken by Eurobarometer indicate that about half of the individuals surveyed (in member states and candidate countries) favor future enlargement of the EU (see Figure 6.3).

Most notable shifts in public opinion are seen in Spain, the Netherlands, and UK with 14 percent, 5 percent, and 5 percent increases, respectively, in favor of the enlargement and in Greece and Slovakia with 15 percent and 10 percent decline in support of the enlargement respectively from 2006 to 2007. In the latest survey, support for future EU enlargement also varied according to age group of the individuals. Highest support for enlargement came from

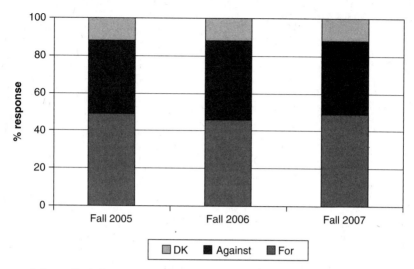

Figure 6.3 ■ Opinion on Future Enlargement of the EU

Source: Eurobarometers 65-67: Public Opinion in the European Union (http:ec.europa.eu/public_opinion/index_En.htm).

individuals aged 15–24 years (60 percent) followed by 25–39 years old (55 percent), whereas only 39 percent of people aged 55 years and above supported enlargement.[39] This is mirrored in responses to questions asked about optimism toward the EU's future. It seems that the younger the age group, the greater is the trust and optimism about the Union's future.[40]

CONCLUSION AND PROSPECTS

The EU has set a course of action for itself that is both ambitious and necessary. Regional developments and global systemic changes have pushed the expansion plans of the EU. The desire of the candidate countries to join the EU helps push completion of the necessary structural (economic and political) reforms in each country. However, there will be a substantial impact of eastern expansion on the EU's internal institutional structure, and the cost associated with enlargement is a major problem as the EU discusses the new 2006–2013 budget. Most of the newcomers fall into the category of the "poor members" of the EU, thus further straining the already tight structural and regional funds. Given the financial impact of enlargement, it is highly unlikely that the EU, despite differences of opinion among member states' governments, would consider the future of Turkey's membership until after the completion of the current budget cycle in 2013.

In terms of global competition and future power transition, the EU's eastern enlargement will add little to its competitiveness against the United States and China because of the small contribution of these new members' economies to the overall EU economy. The EU will not be able to reverse its decline in global competitiveness until two larger Eastern European countries, Turkey and perhaps Ukraine (see Figure 6.2), join its ranks. However, these are unfavorable topics among EU citizens at present.

STUDY QUESTIONS

1. Why is enlargement important for EU integration?

2. What are the Copenhagen criteria for membership?

3. How did eastern enlargement affect the EU?

4. What are the key challenges facing the candidate countries?

5. How does public opinion differ on enlargement and why?

6. Discuss the challenges and benefits of enlargement for deepening of regional integration in the EU in a historical perspective by comparing the eastern enlargement to two previous enlargements of your choice. Make sure you address how the EU confronted challenges and assess its relative success in meeting them.

7. What benefits will the EU get from its most recent and future enlargement(s)?

ENDNOTES

1. EC Economic and Social Council, "Opinion on the Mediterranean Policy of the European Community," *Official Journal of the European Communities*, No. C221/16 (January 25, 1989).

2. Birol A. Yeşilada, "Further Enlargement of the European Community: The Cases of the European Periphery States," *National Forum* (Spring 1992): 21–25.

3. Marc Maresceau, "The European Community, Eastern Europe and the USSR," in John Redmond, ed., *The External Relations of the European Community: The Internal Response to 1992* (New York: St. Martin's Press, 1992), pp. 97–98.

4. Françoise de la Serre, "The EC and Central and Eastern Europe," in Leon Hurwitz and Christian Lequesne, eds., *The State of the European Community: Policies, Institutions, and Debates in the Transition Years* (Boulder, Colo.: Lynne Reinner, 1991), p. 310.

5. Frank McDonald and Keith Penketh, "The European Community and the Rest of Europe," in Frank McDonald and Stephen Dearden, eds., *European Economic Integration* (London: Longman, 1992), p. 193.

6. "Essen Summit Endorses Eastern European Strategy," *Eurecom* 6 (December 1994): 1.

7. European Commission, *Agenda 2000* (Brussels: European Commission, 1997), p. 2.

8. European Commission, *Eurobarometer 56* (Brussels: European Commission, April 2002), p. 71.

9. Ibid., p. 76.

10. "Leaders Agree on Institutional Changes at Nice," *Financial Times*, December 12, 2000, p. 2.

11. Alan Cowell, "Irish Vote for a Wider Union, and Europe Celebrates," *New York Times*, October 21, 2002, http://www.nytimes.com/ads/amexpopup_ftp.html

12. European Commission. http://europa.eu.int/comm/enlargement/enlargement.htm. The ten countries are Cyprus, the Czech Republic, Estonia, Hungary, Latvia, Lithuania, Malta, Poland, the Slovak Republic, and Slovenia.

13. For example, see Desmond Dinan, *Ever Closer Union*, 3rd ed. (Boulder, Colo: Lynne Reinner, 2005); and Brent Nelson and Alexander Stubb, eds., *The European Union: Readings on the Theory and Practice of the European Integration* (Boulder, Colo.: Lynne Reinner, 2003).

14. "Europe's New Protectionism," *The Economist*, June 30, 2005.

15. Birol Yesilada, Brian Efird, and Peter Noordijk "Competition among Giants: A Look at How Future Enlargement of the European Union Could Affect Global Power Transition," *International Studies Review* Vol. 8, no. 4 (December 2006): 607–622.

16. European Commission, "Challenges of Enlargement," http://europa.eu.int/comm/enlargement/docs/index.htm#sec2002-102

17. Ian Traynor, "EU and Russia Clash over Baltic Enclave," *The Guardian* (May 30, 2002), p. 4.

18. BBC, "EU and Russia Reach Kaliningrad Deal," November 11, 2002, http://news.bbc.co.uk/1/hi/world/europe/2440275.stm

19. Radio Free Europe, "Putin Calls for End to Kaliningrad's Isolation from Mainland Russia," November 8, 2005, http://www.rferl.org/newsline/2005/11/1-RUS/rus-081105.asp

20. Republic of Cyprus, *The Treaty of Guarantee*, August 16, 1960, http://www.cypnet.com/ncyprus/cyproblem/ganati.html and http://www.kypros.org/Cyprus_Problem/treaty.html

21. BBC News, "Cyprus 'spurns historic chance,' " April 25, 2004, http://news.bbc.co.uk/1/hi/world/europe/3656753.stm

22. Simon Bahceli, "EU Hopes Rising, but Turkish Cypriots Wary of Broken Promises," *Cyprus Mail*, September 14, 2004.

23. Hugh Pope, "Settling Cyprus," *Wall Street Journal Europe*, February 14, 2008. See http://www.crisisgroup.org/home/index.cfm?id=5294&l=1

24. Ibid.

25. European Commission, "Turkish Cypriot Community," http://ec.europa.eu/enlargement/turkish_cypriot_community/index_en.htm

26. Council of the European Union. *Presidency Conclusions* (Brussels: Council of the European Union, December 17, 2004), p. 3.

27. Nicholas Watts, "EU Warns Austria over Turks," *Guardian*, October 1, 2005.

28. Council of the European Union, *Council Decision of 12 February 2008 on the principles, priorities and conditions contained in the Accession Partnership with Croatia and repealing Decision 2006/145/EC* (Brussels: Official Journal of the European Union), pp. 4–12.

29. European Commission web page for enlargement, see http://ec.europa.eu/enlargement/candidate-countries/croatia/eu_croatia_relations_en.htm

30. Press conference of the Greek Foreign Minister Dora Bakoyannis at the Embassy of Greece in Washington DC on August 29, 2006. Obtained from http://www.greekembassy.org/Embassy/content/en/Article.aspx?office=1&folder=24&article=18371

31. *Southeast European Times*, July 25, 2006, http://www.setimes.com/cocoon/setimes/xhtml/en_GB/features/setimes/newsbriefs/2006/07/25/nb-07

32. European Commission. http://ec.europa.eu/enlargement/candidate-countries/the_former_yugoslav_republic_of_macedonia/eu_the_former_yugoslav_republic_of_macedonia_relations_en.htm

33. European Commission, *Commission Opinion on Turkey's Request for Accession to the Community*, Sec. (89) 2290 final (Brussels: Official Publications of the European Communities, December 18, 1989).

34. Birol Yeşilada, "The Worsening EU-Turkey Relations," *SAIS Review* 19 (Winter–Spring 1999): 144–161.

35. Associated Press, "EU Says Turkey Not Ready for Accession Talks," October 7, 2002.

36. Council of the European Union, *Presidency Conclusions of the Copenhagen European Council* (Brussels: Council of the European Union, January 29, 2003).

37. Martin Wolf, "A Prize for a Divided World," *Financial Times*, October 11, 2005.

38. Omer Taspinar, *Changing Parameters in U.S.-German-Turkish Relations* (Washington, DC: Johns Hopkins University's American Institute for Contemporary German Studies, 2005).

39. *Eurobarometer 67*, p. 33.

40. Ibid., pp. 38–40.

7

Institutional Dynamics in the European Union

This chapter examines the institutions of the European Union (EU) in terms of how they are structured and the processes by which decisions are reached on the ordinary and extraordinary agendas. We have distinguished the two agendas from one another as the plan of action that was set by the Rome Treaty and its informal modifications (the ordinary agenda) and the agenda for the modifications of the treaties themselves (the extraordinary agenda). Most of the formal treaty modifications have been brought together in the four packages of amendments: the Single European Act (SEA), the Maastricht Treaty on European Union (TEU), the Amsterdam Treaty, and the Nice Treaty. Other basic changes have been less formal and have been made on an ad hoc basis, such as the establishment of European Political Cooperation and the European Monetary System in the 1970s. We discussed agenda setting for the main amendment packages in Chapter 4 (SEA and TEU) and Chapter 5 (Amsterdam and Nice Treaties), where we placed emphasis on the role of the heads of state and government in the European Council and the president of the Commission as principal actors in the process of setting the extraordinary agenda. Also in Chapter 5, we saw the breakdown of the attempt to ratify the Constitutional Treaty. In this chapter, we look at the institutions themselves and the functions they perform. The chapter will be based on the distinction between "the governments," organized collectively as the European Council and the Council of Ministers, and the "supranational institutions," namely, the Commission, the European Court of Justice (ECJ), and the European Parliament. Regarding the latter three, we will make the traditional distinctions among executive, judicial, and legislative functions. The chapter concludes with an evaluation of the institutions by democratic standards, along with a demonstration of how democratic treaty ratification processes can assist in the downfall of a treaty that was crafted by a full-scale constitutional convention drawing widely on the political forces of the member countries. Figure 7.1 diagrams the institutions and the functions that link them to one another.

Extraordinary Agenda Setting

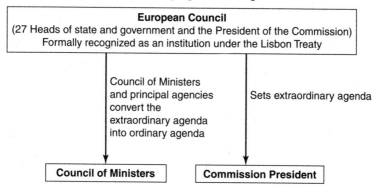

Ordinary Agenda Setting

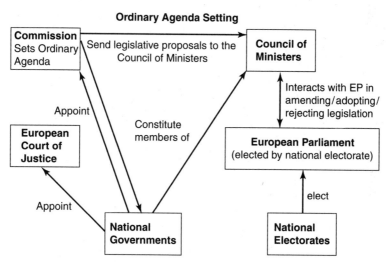

Figure 7.1 ■ Agenda Setting in European Union Institutions

Source: Adapted from BBC, http://news.bbc.co.uk/hi/english/static/in_depth/europe/2001/inside_europe/
eu_institutions/flow_chart.stm.

THE EUROPEAN COUNCIL

The term *council* is often used to refer generally to any of the bodies in which members of the 27 EU governments meet to decide policy issues of common concern. By "members" in this context, we mean heads of state and government and cabinet ministers. There are many more bodies of national civil servants and technical advisers from the 27 governments that meet together for various EU advisory, supervisory, and administrative purposes, but the principal policy decisions that governments make collectively are made by the councils. The most important of these is the European Council—the summit meetings of heads of state and government. The principal focus of the European Council is the extraordinary agenda. Since the Maastricht Treaty, the other councils have collectively been called *the Council of the European Union*, but we will use the older, but still commonly used, term *Council of Ministers* in referring to them. Interpretation of the roles played by the 27 governments and their councils will follow the theoretical perspective we have referred to as intergovernmentalism. (See Chapter 2.)

Because of its unique role and overriding importance, the European Council should be considered separately from the other councils, all the more so because it has become an institution in its own right, and has been ever since the Paris summit of December 1974 determined that the heads of state and government would meet three times a year. Simon Bulmer and Wolfgang Wessels have discussed the reasons why institutionalized summit meetings came into being in the 1970s.[1] The "institutional inertia" of the European Community (EC) itself, especially the deadlocks occurring in the Council of Ministers, made it necessary for the heads to step in with the authority to achieve breakthroughs. Beginning with the Hague summit of December 1969, the heads had been meeting, though not on a regular basis, in part to take pressure off their foreign ministers, who were doing double duty making EC foreign policy, as well as general policy when they met as the General Affairs Council.[2]

The European Council is more than simply the most comprehensive and powerful of the councils established under the Rome Treaty. Initially, the responsibilities of the Council of Ministers were divided between the General Affairs Council and the various functionally specialized councils (e.g., budget, agriculture, and environment) that emerged after 1957. Most of these were already established when the European Council held its first meeting in 1975. By 1989, there were 89 council meetings annually, of which only 3 were meetings of the European Council. An institutional link between the councils is the Council Secretariat, headed by a secretary general, which keeps records of meetings and otherwise works with the Committee of Permanent Representatives (COREPER) and with the Commission in attempting to achieve agreement in council meetings.[3] The General Affairs Council, assisted by the Secretariat, has a role to play in reconciling conflicts between the councils (e.g., between the Finance Council and the Agricultural Council). But since 1975, the leadership role that the foreign ministers attempted to play has been subordinated to that of the heads of state and government in the European Council.[4]

The SEA was the first "constitutional" source of the EC to give any legal recognition to the European Council, which it did in a two-sentence reference to its composition.[5] By that time, the European Council had assumed a leadership role for the EC that exceeded that of the Commission. According to Peter Ludlow:

> The conclusions of European Council meetings are, together with the Treaties, the most authoritative guide to the EC's evolving agenda. They usually include a list of tasks to be carried out by the Commission and/or the Council, as well as a definition of principles in the policy areas discussed at the Council in question.[6]

As a body of such transcendent importance, it should properly be treated separately from the Council of Ministers wearing their various hats.

When originally established, the European Council was to meet three times per year. Usually, two of the three meetings were located in cities of the countries holding the presidency of the Council of Ministers, which rotated every six months in alphabetical order based on the official names of the states in their own languages. The third meeting was usually held in Brussels. The SEA reduced the number of prescribed annual meetings from three to two, one held at the end of each of the year's two six-month presidencies in a city of the country having that status. However, the press of business has been such that in some years third and even fourth European Council meetings have been held. In fact, it has become common for each presidency to schedule a mini-summit to discuss specific problems halfway through its term and an end-of-term summit to deal with the most important issues requiring more formal commitments by the heads of state and government. For example, in the latter half of 2001, the Belgian presidency hosted a mini-summit in Ghent in October to discuss common positions on "post–September 11" terrorism and how to deal with the troubling economic conditions.[7] Then, in December, in Laeken, a suburb of Brussels, the European Council agreed to the holding of a constitutional convention, which produced a draft constitution for the EU. This ill-fated document later gave way to a new draft treaty that came to be known as the Lisbon Treaty. It contained significant reforms to institutional arrangements and governance in the EU (see Chapter 5) and was to be presented to the heads at a meeting of the European Council in late 2003 or in 2004, before being presented, with instructions by the heads, to a 2004 intergovernmental conference (IGC). The IGC would then work on a draft treaty revision for approval by the European Council and ultimate ratification by the member states.

Formal sessions of the European Council are restricted to two representatives from each member state. In most cases, the representatives are the head of state or government and the foreign minister (see Chapter 1). Also attending are the president of the Commission and one other commissioner. Interpreters are, of course, present, as well as a very restricted number of national and European civil servants, the latter from the Council and Commission Secretariats.[8] Overall, the summits have become well-attended events, including the pervasive presence of the media.

At all summit meetings, the heads of state and government discuss the state of the EU economy. This may result in a very general statement of purpose on the part of the member states to work harder to improve economic conditions, and in that sense, it may add some urgency to actions on the separate agendas of the member governments. There may be ordinary agenda matters over which the Council of Ministers is deadlocked, resolution of which requires an appeal to the summit. Nugent gives the examples of budgetary and Common Agricultural Policy (CAP) deadlocks that cropped up frequently in the 1980s and could be resolved only by the heads of the state and government.[9]

When quick action is needed, the heads may instruct their foreign ministers in the General Affairs Council to agree on measures to be taken. In fact, in a newly developing crisis, the foreign ministers may meet one or more times before the heads get together. The heads may also delegate responsibility or signal their general intent to the Commission, thus enabling the latter to take steps on its own, as when responsibility for providing aid to post-Cold War Central European countries was given to the Commission in December 1989. The heads do this simply by virtue of their authority as governmental leaders to act in emergencies without requiring advance approval by their national parliaments and without having to amend the treaties to do so. At the following summit meeting, the heads will then review the action taken and mandate further action by the other bodies as they deem necessary.

There are three institutional sources of summit agenda items that may well become extraordinary agenda items. The most frequent initiator is the Commission, which is represented by its president in European Council meetings and can make recommendations to the heads of state and government regarding matters that it considers to be within its sphere of responsibility. Note that, in cases where the Commission has played an initiating role, the European Council controls its own agenda and will decide what subsequent action will be taken on such items.

Other extraordinary agenda-setting initiatives have come from the country holding the Council presidency; for example, in early 1984, France pushed for the European Council to take concrete steps to advance the goal of European union, which resulted in the decision at the June 1984 Fontainebleau summit to commission an intergovernmental committee (the Dooge committee) to study proposals for political union and make recommendations. And, finally, the European Council itself sets its own extraordinary agenda by creating special intergovernmental bodies to examine issues and report back their recommendations, like the IGC that the December 2001 Laeken summit scheduled for 2004, which produced the failed Constitutional Treaty and the subsequent Lisbon Treaty.

The centrality of the European Council concerning the EU's extraordinary agenda does not rule out the capacity of the normal Rome Treaty institutions to take on new responsibilities in the wake of fast-moving events, such as those that occurred in Europe at the end of the Cold War. These especially required the Commission and the Council of Ministers to take action during the time when the European Council was not in session, dealing initially with the economic problems of the Central and Eastern European states and later with the admission of many of these states to EU membership.[10] It appears that the *existence* of the European Council as a body that will meet later to approve or modify the actions taken by the other bodies in between its meetings lessens the danger of inaction on the part of those bodies in the face of unanticipated situations that demand immediate responses.

From the standpoint of intergovernmentalist theory, the role of the European Council has been to guard elements of national sovereignty, while delegating responsibility to the Council of Ministers and the Commission. This does not preclude the Commission and the other supranational bodies from interpreting the authority granted them in ways that will increase their own powers and responsibilities. The Lisbon Treaty formally recognizes the European Council as an institution and specifies how a president of the EU will be appointed.[11]

THE COUNCIL OF MINISTERS

The Council of Ministers is a body with variable membership and responsibilities. Depending on the subjects of EU policy and administration being discussed, the Council of Ministers has met as any of more than 20 different councils, though efforts have been made to reduce this number.[12] Each one groups a set of ministers from the 27 member countries. The three most important of these, as is clearly measured by the fact that they meet the most often, are the General Affairs Council, the Agricultural Council, and the Economic and Finance Council (ECOFIN). These have met 10–15 times per year. Two of them bring together the ministers who, next to their heads of state and government, are typically the most important members of their governments: the General Affairs Council (foreign ministers) and ECOFIN (finance ministers). The third, the Agricultural Council, groups the ministers concerned with the CAP, which accounts for the largest part of the EU budget. Less important are, for example, the councils of environment ministers and internal market ministers, who meet three or four times per year, and the councils of the education ministers and tourism ministers, who meet once or twice per year. The descending frequency of meetings suggests the descending importance not only of these ministerial posts in national government terms, but also of the policy areas in EU terms.[13]

As discussed above, the European Council and the Council of Ministers are presided over at any given time by the appropriate executive official from the country that holds the EU presidency. Table 7.1 provides the timetable for EU presidency. This responsibility is passed from country to country every six months. The most significant of the various functions of the presidency is the ability of the government that holds it to control the agenda of the Council of Ministers. Insofar as legislative measures are concerned, it is the Commission that puts items on the Council's agenda, but holding the presidency of the Council gives a government that opposes a particular Commission proposal the ability to keep it off the agenda for six months.[14] Until fairly recently, the presidency rotated among the member countries in alphabetical order according to the spelling of the country's name in its own language. The order was altered in 1998 to make it possible for older and newer, as well as larger and smaller, member states to alternate with one another. A "troika" arrangement adds to the effectiveness of the alternation by assuring that the current president will be assisted by those immediately preceding and following him or her.

For most matters that the Council of Ministers deals with, and certainly for all legislative matters, the ministers are dependent on the Commission to initiate the proposals—in other words, to draft the bills. Legislation proposed to the Council of Ministers falls into two categories: (1) regulations and decisions and (2) directives. Regulations and decisions are applicable directly to member states and/or to individuals within them and take effect immediately within member states, obliging governments to enforce them, but without requiring further legislation on their part. Regulations are of general application in all member states, while decisions are

Table 7.1 ■ Rotation of the EU Presidency

Country	Time period	Country	Time period
Germany	January–June 2007	Greece	January–June 2014
Portugal	July–December 2007	Italy	July–December 2014
Slovenia	January–June 2008	Latvia	January–June 2015
France	July–December 2008	Luxembourg	July–December 2015
Czech Republic	January–June 2009	Netherlands	January–June 2016
Sweden	July–December 2009	Slovakia	July–December 2016
Spain	January–June 2010	Malta	January–June 2017
Belgium	July–December 2010	United Kingdom	July–December 2017
Hungary	January–June 2011	Estonia	January–June 2018
Poland	July–December 2011	Bulgaria	July–December 2018
Denmark	January–June 2012	Austria	January–June 2019
Cyprus	July–December 2012	Romania	July–December 2019
Ireland	January–June 2013	Finland	January–June 2020
Lithuania	July–December 2013		

Source: Council of the European Union, http://www.consilium.europa.eu/cms3_fo/showPage.asp?id=242&lang=EN&mode=g

more specific in terms of the member to which they are addressed. Directives are binding on member states in the sense of obliging them to adopt the necessary legal instruments (laws or executive acts) to give the directives force within the member states' boundaries.

According to a study by Thomas Smoot and Piet Verschuren, in 1975 the Council of Ministers considered 329 proposals from the Commission and adopted 75 percent within two years, averaging 150 days from the time they were sent to the Council by the Commission.[15] Smoot and Verschuren showed that the annual volume of Commission proposals rose steadily from 1975, reaching 456 in 1979, with a 77.4 percent success rate, and 522 in 1984, with an 84.3 percent success rate, while the lag time for processing dropped over the decade after 1975 from 150 to 108 days in 1984. Although the SEA, which extended the range of voting by qualified majority, did not go into effect until 1987, in the previous year 617 proposals were made by the Commission with a success rate of 87.4 percent.[16]

Numbers of Commission proposals dropped by more than 50 percent in the mid-1990s, as did their adoption rates. This does not appear to be due to increases in numbers of members,[17] although further decline with the ten-member intake of 2004 may have continued the trend. Many legislative proposals are set aside or returned to the drawing board at early stages, but by the time a measure comes to a vote, the bargaining deals have been firmed up, so that, whether the vote is by qualified majority or unanimity, the requisite number of positive votes will usually be there.[18] Still, the number of positive votes required is of great significance if a bill is to get to the voting stage at all. Enlargement to 27 members has added to the complexities involved.

When qualified majority voting (QMV) applies in the Council of Ministers, France, Germany, Italy, and Britain have 29 votes apiece; Spain and Poland 27; Romania 14; the Netherlands 13; Belgium, the Czech Republic, Greece, Hungary, and Portugal 12; Austria, Bulgaria, and Sweden 10; Denmark, Finland, Ireland, Lithuania, and Slovakia 7; Cyprus, Estonia, Latvia, Luxembourg, and

Slovenia 4; and Malta 3. The qualified majority is at approximately 72 percent. Since November 2004, a qualified majority is reached:

- if a majority of member states (in some cases, a two-thirds majority) approves AND
- if a minimum of votes is cast in favor—which is 72.3 percent of the total (roughly the same share as under the previous system).

In addition, a member state may ask for confirmation that the votes in favor represent at least 62 percent of the total population of the EU. If this is found not to be the case, the decision will not be adopted. The Lisbon Treaty brings a clarification to the QMV system by outlining double majority. Decisions in the Council will need the support of 55 percent of member states (presently 15 out of 27) and should represent a minimum of 65 percent of EU's population. Furthermore, it makes it difficult for a small number of large countries to block a decision since the blocking minority must have at least four member states.[19]

According to Fiona Hayes-Renshaw and Helen Wallace,[20] from December 1993 to December 1994, 64 contested votes were taken in the Council of Ministers out of 261 decisions altogether; that is, 24.5 percent of all decisions were contested. In only five of the contested cases did as many as three or four member states vote negatively. Compromises will normally be reached before a vote is ever taken, failing which the issue will be set aside until such time as a decision by QMV becomes likely. This is all the more true when unanimity must be reached for a measure to pass the Council.[21]

On the grounds of sheer decision-making efficiency, QMV seems necessary. But Nugent observed 30 years ago that unanimity is sought in controversial matters and votes are delayed or not held in order not to isolate a member in disagreement.[22] With further enlargements, and particularly the 2004 enlargement, it is understandable that efforts were made, in the Amsterdam, Nice, and Lisbon, to move categories of legislation from the unanimity requirement to QMV. Although ratification of the Lisbon Treaty is pending, the preceding two treaties considerably expanded the domain of QMV.

Paradoxically, the unanimity principle sometimes makes it *easier* for certain decisions to be reached because when majority voting applies, abstentions count as negative votes. When unanimity is required, abstentions are simply not counted. Ministers may use abstentions when unanimity is required if they wish to permit a positive result, while not having to tell critics at home that they voted for it.[23] But if there is likelihood of a veto when unanimity applies, it may mean that the issue will be set aside for further bargaining or perhaps will be sent to the European Council in the hope that a bargain can be struck that is satisfactory to the government withholding its agreement.

Students of the Council of Ministers who wish to examine the process of voting where QMV applies are hampered by the absence of accurate information on membership preferences and actual votes on the issues. Speculations about "package deals" and "side payments" to enable the requisite number of positive votes to be cast have had to be made on the basis of assumptions about where member governments are placed on pro- or anti-integration spectrums.[24] Once such assumptions are made, it is possible to imagine which countries must join together in order to achieve the qualified majority on issues that can be seen to divide them on these grounds.

Underlying the assumptions and analytical methods is a conflict perspective that draws on rational choice institutionalism (see Chapter 2). Suppose there is a conflict between Euro-skeptics Britain and Denmark, on the one hand, and Italy, the Benelux countries, and several of the 2004 intake, on the other, with France, Germany, and others found somewhere in between. Deadlock can be overcome if the Commission as agenda setter can fashion a proposal that captures the agreement of the pivotal voter whose weighted votes are needed to achieve a qualified majority. Where the unanimity rule applies, coalitions of like-minded members (e.g., Germany and the

Benelux; newer members; Scandinavian countries) are taken as stable building blocks for achieving unanimity behind carefully crafted package deals. Such formulations are useful for making our assumptions clearer, but they may not be very close to reality, which must certainly be that policy making in the EU aligns 27 members in a wide variety of ways depending on the substance of issues and the preferences of parties and leaders in charge of governments.[25] So the composition of winning and blocking coalitions will differ from one issue to another, as studies of bargaining in the IGCs have shown.[26] The assumption of a single ordering or of stable coalitions like the Benelux three may have been less heroic when the EC had only 6 members, but it allows us to make only the most abstract of speculations with 27 members.

A very different approach to the Council of Ministers has been taken by scholars who emphasize the processes by which consensus is fashioned among the individuals who represent their governments in the intergovernmental bodies. In fact, there is a considerable infrastructure of Council civil servants and national civil servants meeting in a variety of committees and working groups. One of the two most important of these bodies is the Council's General Secretariat, which prepares meetings of the Council of Ministers and whose secretary general, a relatively obscure, but powerful official, has had, since the Amsterdam Treaty, an important leadership role in the formulation and execution of Common Foreign and Security Policy (CFSP).[27] The other is the COREPER, consisting of ambassadorial-level officials and a substantial supporting infrastructure. It examines proposals for legislation prior to Council of Ministers' deliberations on them and, together with specialized groups of national civil servants who report to it, actually makes decisions on matters that are the easiest to resolve, which is a high percentage of the total Council decisions.[28]

The more difficult decisions are made by the ministers on the advice of their permanent officials, who have gone over them and identified the points at issue and the positions their fellow ministers are likely to take on them. The COREPER and the specialized committees that deal with the Economic and Monetary Union (EMU), EU commercial policy, CFSP, and Justice and Home Affairs play a very important role in shaping the alternatives between which the ministers will decide.[29] The COREPER, in particular, consists of permanent residents in Brussels who are in constant contact with one another and who have developed a common way of looking at EU issues, which undoubtedly influences the decisions made and often (but certainly not always) enables agreement to be reached in the Council of Ministers itself.

Unlike more restrictive intergovernmental perspectives, including that of rational-choice institutionalism, this is a perspective on EU decision making that stresses consensus-building processes that go on not only under assumptions of confidentiality, but also away from the investigative light of the media. It is more compatible with the neofunctional assumption that pragmatic decisions will be reached leading to greater integration because of an appreciation by experts of what else must be done in order to make already agreed-on tasks more workable.

Member states continue to act on a perception of their own best interests, and negative outcomes do occur. But intergovernmentalist accounts of the work of the councils explain more than vetoes. They explain bargains that are struck and the willingness of member states to delegate authority to supranational bodies. Intergovernmentalist accounts are not confined to accounting for deadlock; they can be reconciled with a "ratcheting" effect, where supranational bodies interpret grants of power to the maximum extent, leaving intergovernmental bodies without the majorities necessary to reverse direction. Both perspectives are needed to fully understand what is decided (or not decided) within the various arenas for making EU policy.[30]

The Treaty of Nice (see Chapter 5) has been analyzed from a rational-choice perspective by George Tsebelis and Xenephon Yatagatos,[31] with very pessimistic conclusions. They point to the complications introduced into the QMV requirement by the additional necessity of gaining support of a majority of member states and, if one member requests, of 62 percent of the total EU population. The first addition strengthens the position of smaller states, while the second advantages larger states, especially Germany, the most populous. Tsebelis and Yatagatos stress the members' veto capacity. But this will not often be expressed in actual votes. It may mean a lengthening of the process of consensus building, but this is happening anyway, given enlargement of the EU from 15 to 27 members.

It must be remembered, however, that past legislation, which had delegated a wide array of responsibilities to the Commission, is regarded as the *acquis communautaire*, a body of laws, regulations, and court decisions that the new members must accept, indeed are already in the process of making part of their own systems of law and administration.

THE SUPRANATIONAL FIRST-PILLAR INSTITUTIONS

In this part of the chapter, we review the supranational EU institutions: the Commission, the European Court of Justice, and the European Parliament.

The Commission

When we examine the decision-making process for legislation authorized by the Rome Treaty, the SEA, and the Maastricht Treaty (first pillar), the strong role of the Commission becomes quite apparent.[32] José Manuel Barroso is the current president of the Commission. The 26 other commissioners—one from each member state—oversee different portfolios and receive assistance from about 24,000 civil servants, most of whom work in Brussels. The Commission is appointed for a period of five years within six months of elections to the European parliament.

The Commission sets the legislative (ordinary) agenda for the Council of Ministers. It generates its own proposals as a result of its interpretation of what has been mandated by the treaties, or it may respond to pressures from interest groups, from the European Parliament, or from member governments speaking individually or collectively in the Council. In preparing a draft legislative measure, the appropriate Directorate General (DG) of the Commission consults with other units of the Commission.[33] In consultation with the COREPER, it takes in the views of governmental and nongovernmental experts, including interest group representatives. Then the DG drafts the proposal. The decision to go ahead is taken by the college of 27 commissioners, usually without dissent, although if a vote is needed, a majority of those present is required for adoption.[34] If approved by the commissioners, the proposal is sent to the European Parliament. This gives the Commission an important role as exclusive legislative agenda setter. Thereafter, the Commission is kept apprised of proposed changes in the legislative measures and, under some procedural circumstances, may reject proposed amendments, suggest alternatives to them, or even withdraw a proposal, so long as the Council has not yet approved it.[35] The legislative process will be examined in greater depth below. The literature on this process has emphasized the interaction between the European Parliament and the Council of Ministers, but it should not be forgotten that the process is not set in motion until the Commission sends a draft proposal to the European Parliament. Moreover, the Commission is in close touch with the other bodies throughout the process.

Most EU legislation is implemented by actions taken at the national level. The Commission oversees this implementation and calls to the attention of the offending government any failure to act or action that is contrary to EU legislative intent. Continued failure of a state to comply with the Commission's wishes may lead the latter to refer the case to the European Court of Justice (ECJ). Several member states show higher rates of noncompliance than do others, Italy being the most notorious footdragger.[36] However, if the ECJ finds that a state has failed to comply with EU law, the failure will usually be rectified. The ECJ has the power, given it by the

Maastricht Treaty on the initiative of the Commission, to levy substantial fines against states that continue to violate its interpretations of their obligations under the treaties.[37]

The Commission also has administrative responsibilities of its own, as in the case of efforts to detect monopolistic and market-sharing violations of EU competition legislation or in the case of agricultural, regional, and social funds, the allocation of which it administers. These supervisory and direct administrative functions of the Commission mostly involve technically complex policy areas, and the phenomena to be dealt with far exceed the capacity of the relatively small Commission bureaucracy. Decisions as to which cases to pursue or which needs to satisfy within the industrialized member countries, each with its own vast bureaucracy, must inevitably be highly selective.[38] This may contribute to a certain negative image of the Commission, which is often accused of bureaucratic interference with national economies, even when it is taking action designed to open the market against state or private-sector interference.

Increasing scholarly attention has focused on the Commission's role in the implementation of EU policy. The assumption is made that the Commission acts as the agent of the member governments in carrying out policies, the choice of which has been largely in their hands. Although this is an oversimplification, given that much of the actual implementation of EU policy is the responsibility of the governments themselves, the Commission oversees their work and will, on occasion, bring a government before the ECJ. Thus, the Commission is in a position to determine in what ways and to what extent EU laws will be enforced. In doing so, according to the analysts,[39] it acts as the agent of a "principal," that is, of the governments. The latter have acted collectively in adopting the legislation, and the Commission acts to see that the governments individually comply with the policies they have collectively chosen.

A public-choice perspective hypothesizes that the Commission will interpret the Council's wishes in such a way as to extend the overall *competence* of the EU as far as possible into policy domains that have previously been under the exclusive individual control of the national governments. In principal/agency theory, as applied to the EU, after the principal (Council of Ministers) has delegated authority to the agent (Commission), it finds that the agent is not easy to control and will be likely to interpret the responsibility placed on it more expansively than the principal intended. Given that the Council is a collective decision-making body, it will be easy for the Commission to satisfy enough of the member governments to make it unlikely that a majority will be found to withdraw the powers that were originally delegated. An example given by Jonas Tallberg[40] is the liberal use of competition policy enforcement powers against multinational corporations, sometimes to the consternation of national governments in the countries where the corporations are based.

The legislative role of the European Parliament is outlined below. But it has another role that has been growing through successive treaty revisions as well. In fact, the Parliament shares with the Council of Ministers the job of overseeing the work of the executive. The Parliament has powers vis-à-vis the Commission akin in some respects to those of national parliaments involved in keeping the executive in check. In Europe's parliamentary and semiparliamentary democracies, parliaments have the power to censure or vote no confidence in the government, which, under a variety of controlled circumstances, can mean the end of the repudiated government's tenure in office. In recent years, the European Parliament has gained a portion of similar powers to hold the Commission accountable. Since the Rome Treaty, it has had the power to censure and thus force the dismissal of the entire Commission by a two-thirds majority. Until 1999, this had never seemed a very realistic possibility, not because two-thirds was an impossibly high bar to clear, but because the Parliament and the Commission were seen as natural allies against the governments and thus unlikely to be seriously at odds with one another on important issues of European integration. But criticism of the Santer Commission's incompetence (which was seen to be undermining the progress of integration) was mounting in the Parliament during the late 1990s. The criticisms were focused on particular commissioners, but the power of censure that the Parliament holds is of the all-or-nothing type. If censured, the whole Commission has to resign, but not if the reprimands are confined to individual commissioners. Yet a reprimanded commissioner is not obliged under the treaties to resign.

In January 1999, a censure vote was taken in the European Parliament against the whole Commission, but the votes necessary for a two-thirds majority were lacking. However, a report by a committee of independent experts confirmed complaints against Santer and other commissioners for avoiding responsibility and, in some cases, for exhibiting favoritism in appointments to responsible positions under their authority. Rather than face another censure vote, the Santer college of commissioners collectively resigned in March 1999.[41]

The European Parliament also has a role to play in the appointment of a new college of commissioners, as in the case of the Romano Prodi Commission, which was approved later in 1999 after its members were individually examined very closely in hearings conducted by the Parliament. The Parliament does not have the power to refuse appointment of individual commissioners, but it can vote down the proposed college of commissioners, including the member of that body whom the governments have designated as president. The Prodi college was accepted, but by its careful scrutiny, the Parliament had served notice that it would be monitoring the commissioners' activities very closely. This is an additional factor that must be taken into account when the Commission decides how energetically it should implement EU policy. But if the Parliament's role as "principal" bears some similarity to that of the Council, its standards for Commission performance are different. The Parliament may even be critical of the Commission for not going far enough in introducing legislation that might exceed the wishes of the member governments.

The Lisbon Treaty replaces the term *European Commission* by the word *Commission* in all treaties.[42] The Treaty also reduces the number of Commissioners starting in 2014, where only two thirds of member countries will have a Commissioner (e.g., with 27 countries, there would be 18 Commissioners), with the posts rotating among the countries.[43] The number of Commissioners can also be changed by the European Council (by unanimous vote).

In another major change, there will be a direct link between the results of the European elections and the choice of candidate for president of the Commission. The president will also be stronger, as he/she will have the power to dismiss fellow Commissioners.[44]

The European Parliament

Today the European Parliament (EP) is a body of 785 members, elected every five years by the voters of the 27 member countries. In the 2004 elections, 732 members were elected to the EP from 25 member states. When Bulgaria and Romania joined EU in January 2007, this number increased to 785, with 35 Romanian and 18 Bulgarian representatives joining the EP. The Lisbon Treaty stipulates that the number of representatives in the EP shall not exceed 751, with the delegate numbers for each country fixed at a maximum of 96 and a minimum of 6 for each member state. With this in mind, the Constitutional Affairs Committee of the parliament approved a proposal for the new allocation of seats starting in 2009, with a further revision of the proposed distribution of seats for the 2014–2019 parliamentary term. Table 7.2 provides a comparison of distribution of seats by member states according to present and proposed rules.

The members are divided into seven parliamentary groups as Christian Democrats, Socialists, Liberals, Greens, and so on, each grouping together members of similar ideological persuasion across the country delegations. The Parliament is also divided into substantively specialized committees, which examine and report their recommendations regarding legislation and conduct fact-finding inquiries. The leaders of the parliamentary groups and committees play important roles in organizing and motivating the Members of the European Parliament (MEPs) in their week-to-week activities.[45]

Table 7.2 ■ New Allocation of Seats in the European Parliament

Member State	Seats Set for 2009 Elections Under Current Rules	Proposed New Distribution 2009–2014
Germany	99	96
France	72	74
United Kingdom	72	73
Italy	72	72
Spain	50	54
Poland	50	51
Romania	33	33
Netherlands	25	26
Greece	22	22
Portugal	22	22
Belgium	22	22
Czech Republic	22	22
Hungary	22	22
Sweden	18	20
Austria	17	19
Bulgaria	17	18
Denmark	13	13
Slovakia	13	13
Finland	13	13
Ireland	12	12
Lithuania	12	12
Latvia	8	9
Slovenia	7	8
Estonia	6	6
Cyprus	6	6
Luxembourg	6	6
Malta	5	6
EU27	**736**	**750**

Source: European Parliament, *Parliament after 2009—How many MEPs?* (http://www.europarl.europa.eu//news/public/story_page/008-10172-253-09-37-901-20070906STO10163-2007-10-09-2007/default_en.htm), and (http://europa.eu/institutions/inst/parliament/index_en.htm)

The role of the Parliament in the legislative process remained quite limited until the SEA extended its legislative powers. Despite the direct elections of MEPs from 1979, before the SEA the Parliament was consulted by the Council of Ministers and the Commission during the legislative process, but neither body had to adhere to its opinions.[46]

In the formulation of the EC annual budget, however, the Parliament gained in power at an early date. A treaty amendment of 1970 gave it the power to propose changes in EC spending of a "noncompulsory" nature. This included the various forms of social and regional assistance that were of considerable interest to MEPs, but did not include the majority of the budget, agricultural spending, which even the Commission and the Council of Ministers could not bring under effective control. Following a treaty amendment of 1975, the Parliament also gained the power to reject the annual budget outright, in which case the three principal Rome Treaty bodies would have to negotiate an agreed budget. This puts the Parliament in a good position to get the Council to approve expenditure increases, at least when the Commission supported the Parliament. The Council votes by QMV on budget issues, which were not subject to the Luxembourg compromise, and it is faced with a timetable of rigid deadlines. These features give the Parliament an opportunity to seek allies among the member states in order to gain concessions from countries such as France and Britain, which are inclined to oppose extensions of the Parliament's powers at the expense of the member states.

Once the SEA went into effect in July 1987, there existed three different procedures for EC legislation: the *assent* procedure; the *consultation* procedure, which is a continuation of the procedure existing before the SEA; and the *cooperation* procedure, which added to the capacity of the Parliament to influence the outcome of legislation. The assent procedure involves an up-or-down vote without amendments and applies today to citizenship, structural funds, and the Cohesion Fund. More importantly, it gives the Parliament a role in the "ratification" of EU-negotiated treaties with third countries, particularly in enlargement and association treaties. But it can neither delay nor amend agreements that have already been reached with non-EU states, so its ability to vote such treaties up or down is not the sharpest of weapons.[47]

Under the Rome Treaty's consultation procedure, the Parliament's role is to give a legislative proposal (henceforth called a *bill*) a *single reading* after it has been received from the Commission. The Parliament may suggest amendments, and if the Commission accepts them, the Council of Ministers must consider them as part of the bill. A Commission-supported measure can be finally adopted by the Council either by unanimity or by qualified majority, depending on treaty specifications. According to a 1980 ruling of the ECJ, the Council must wait until the Parliament has expressed its opinion before acting on the legislation.[48]

The cooperation procedure introduced by the SEA applied to much of the legislation designed to create the single market by the end of 1992. It is more complicated than the consultation procedure, but in essence, it gives the Parliament a *second reading* of a bill after the Council has given it a first reading and adopted a common position (which is the point at which the legislation is adopted in the consultation procedure). The Commission plays a crucial role in being able to accept or reject the Parliament's amendments at the second as well as the first reading. The Parliament may reject the bill outright on second reading if a majority of the MEPs votes against it, in which case the measure can become EC law only if the Council votes unanimously to override the Parliament's veto. The cooperation procedure applied mainly to single-market legislation under the SEA. Today it applies only to aspects of the EMU.[49]

The Maastricht Treaty provided for a fourth procedure, *codecision* (Figure 7.2). This replaced consultation for some, but not all, types of legislation where consultation applied, and it applied in some, but not all, new areas of EU competence under the treaty. Unlike with the cooperation procedure, in codecision, failure of the Parliament and the Council to reach agreement at the second reading touched off a new step, the formation of a conciliation committee, including representatives of both bodies, that would attempt to work out an agreed position. If the committee could not reach agreement on a common version, the proposal would be shelved unless the Council passed its first version (its common position) by QMV. But it was the Commission's job to try to find common ground between the Council and the Parliament. If a commonly agreed version was produced, it could still be defeated when returned to the Council, which needs a QMV to pass it, or to the Parliament, which could defeat the final version in the absence of simple majority. In the first four and a half years that the procedure was in effect, of the 130 completed codecision procedures, "agreement between the Council and the EP was reached in 127 cases, . . . in only three cases did the two institutions fail to agree on a joint text."[50] In essence, with codecision, the

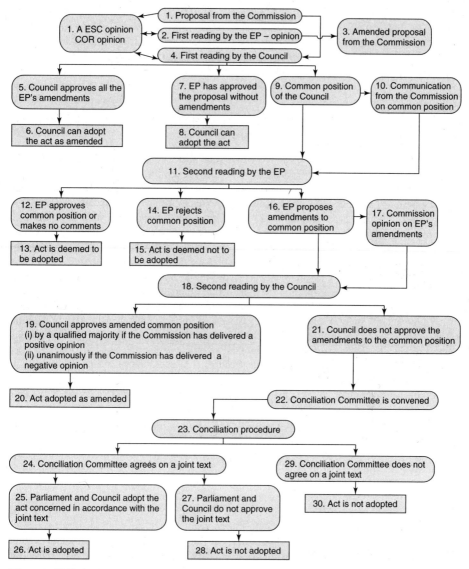

Figure 7.2 ■ Codecision Process in the European Union

Source: European Commission, http://www.europa.eu.int/comm/codecision/images/diagram_en.gif.

Parliament became a coequal legislative body, but only in those domains of policy making where the procedure applied.

Political scientists George Tsebelis and Geoffrey Garrett have questioned whether the codecision procedure of the Maastricht Treaty actually served to increase the powers of the European Parliament vis-à-vis those of the Council of Ministers, although they agree with others that the powers of the Commission were weakened relative to those of both the Parliament and the Council.[51] They first argue that the cooperation procedure established by the SEA puts the Parliament in the position, along with the Commission, of being a "conditional agenda setter."

By this, they mean that the Council of Ministers, after the Parliament's second reading and the Commission's approval of the Parliament's amendments, was faced with the alternatives of voting for the amended measure under the qualified majority rule and of rejecting the Parliament's amendments, which it could do only by a unanimous vote. Basically, although the Council had the final decision, its realistic options were to vote for or vote against a bill that contained the Parliament's amendments. This is because there would be at least a minority of states willing to accept the Parliament's amendments. The rest of the states might be in a position to refuse QMV, but they could not reset the agenda. The measure they voted up or down would contain propositions of EP origin, and the Council might actually have seen some of its original amendments rejected by the Parliament on second reading.

When it comes to the codecision procedure, they argue, the Maastricht Treaty changed the conditional agenda setter from the Parliament (working together with the Commission) to the Council of Ministers. By opposing the Parliament's amendments to the proposed legislation, the Council was in a position, in the conciliation committee deliberations, to hold onto its own version of the proposal essentially as it had been prior to the convening of the Conciliation Committee, after which the Parliament was no longer able to change it and had to vote it either up or down. Tsebelis and Garrett argue that the bill would represent enough of a change in the status quo in the direction the Parliament wanted that members would prefer adoption of a flawed version to none at all. Moreover, the Council might stick to its original version and adopt it by QMV, so the Parliament had a motivation to accede to the Council's wishes in the Conciliation Committee.

It is noteworthy that the Amsterdam Treaty, which was signed in 1997 and went into effect in 1999, gave some support for the Tsebelis–Garrett interpretation by changing the "end game" of the codecision process so that the Council lost its ability to adopt the treaty without the amendments proposed by the Parliament.[52] This put the Parliament in a strong position to move a bill's contents closer to what rational-choice theorists call its median preference, which is further to the supranational side than is the Council's median preference.

However, although the Tsebelis–Garrett argument may be persuasive if one accepts the influence they attribute to conditional agenda setting, other observers have called attention to an informal process of negotiation in the original codecision procedure that the Commission was involved in with the other two bodies before the Conciliation Committee convened. The Commission attempted to broker agreements between the Parliament and the Council during the first reading. According to Michael Shackleton, this made it possible for the Parliament to "win" in the ultimate bargaining more often than the Council of Ministers.[53] At any rate, the Amsterdam Treaty removed cooperation as a process for ordinary legislation, replacing it with the new version of codecision.

It should be acknowledged that both the cooperation and the codecision processes are quite complicated and difficult for all but inside observers to follow very closely. It may well be that to assign "success scores" to the Parliament and the Council is to make these two bodies, and the potential coalitions within both, too concrete to enable us to capture their complex alignments and working procedures. The true coalitions cut across the memberships of the two bodies such that neither one consistently wins or loses; nor does the Commission, which is itself neither a monolith nor a passive bystander.

Amie Kreppel finds the growth of the formal European Parliament's powers in the 1990s to have been accompanied by a considerable concentration of power in the two main Euro-parties that together constitute a majority of the Parliament's membership, the cross-national Party of European Socialists (center-left) and European People's Party (center-right). Together, these two groups have developed a predominance in the Parliament that rivals that of the two major parties in the United States, although in the case of the Parliament's party system, they are not the only two parties to hold seats (see Chapter 8). According to Kreppel, the dominance of these two groups has "led to a highly centralized and largely bipartisan European Parliament that much more closely resembles the U.S. Congress than it does the [British] House of Commons," in the sense that there is a separation of powers, and the Parliament is now in a position vis-à-vis the Commission and the Council of Ministers to give as well as it gets.[54]

The European Court of Justice

The ECJ consists of 27 judges, 1 appointed by each of the member governments. The judges are expected to be appointed on the basis of their stature as jurists, their expertise in jurisprudence, and their independence from political influence. They are appointed for six-year terms, with approximately half of the terms coming to an end every three years. Since the Commission became more active in introducing new legislation in the late 1970s, the ECJ has found itself deciding on many important cases that sort out the respective powers of the member governments and the supranational institutions. Yet already in the 1960s, it had enunciated two doctrines that paved the way for its judicial activism of more recent years. First, treaties have direct effect in the legal systems of the member countries and may be enforced in the courts of the member states. And, second, EC law has supremacy over national law, even if the national laws are adopted after the EC laws.[55] The decisions did not attract a great deal of attention at the time, but they have since formed the basis for extending the court's ability to rule that member governments are in violation of EU law when they implement national laws that violate EU law or fail to implement laws that have been adopted by the EU institutions.

The ECJ has gone further. Article 235 of the Treaty of Rome contains a provision reminiscent of the "necessary and proper" clause of the U.S. Constitution:

> If any action by the Community appears necessary to achieve, in the functioning of the Common Market, one of the aims of the Community in cases where this Treaty has not provided for the requisite powers of action, the Council, acting by means of an unanimous vote on a proposal of the Commission and after the Assembly has been consulted, shall enact the appropriate provision.[56]

This has enabled the Council of Ministers, on the Commission's initiative, and when the Council can attain unanimity, to enter into fields of activity not strictly outlined in the Rome Treaty—in other words, to pursue an extraordinary agenda. Principal examples have been in the domain of environmental policy—for example, a 1980 directive "on the protection of ground water against pollution caused by certain dangerous substances," justified under Article 235 as necessary to improve the "quality of life." This was based on references at the beginning of the treaty to the objective of raising living standards in the member countries.[57] The ECJ has permitted such extensions of the treaty as long as the Council has voted unanimously in favor of them.

Although it operates quietly in the small duchy of Luxembourg, the role of the ECJ in facilitating a looser interpretation of the Rome Treaty should not be underestimated. Anne-Marie Burley and Walter Mattli have persuasively argued that neofunctionalism is alive and well, although it is to be found operating in purer form in Luxembourg than at the Commission headquarters in Brussels.[58] In Luxembourg, "technical-economic" logic is couched in legalistic terms, but the effect is similar to what Ernst Haas had predicted: Community powers have expanded through a gradual process of treaty interpretation by EU institutions under the pressure of economic interests seeking to gain advantages at the EU level that are denied them at the national level. Business and farmers' organizations, as well as national and multinational companies, put pressure on the Commission and the national governments, but they also employ lawyers specializing in EU law. These legal specialists present briefs to the ECJ, offering legal arguments for expanding EU authority.[59]

The judges in Luxembourg have responded by finding authority in the Rome Treaty, as in Article 235, for expanded powers. They have also declared actions—and inactions—by member governments to be treaty violations in that they encroach on or detract from the authority of the original EC institutions as granted by or implied in the Rome Treaty. By its decisions since the 1960s, the ECJ has created an atmosphere that is favorable to the transfer of power from the national to the EU level. The ability of the ECJ to interpret the EU treaties and laws in ways that enhance the freedom of the Commission to make decisions is held by supranational theorists to be the trump card that the Commission holds, enabling it to impose its own interpretations of its powers upon the governments.[60] The principle of judicial independence from political control assists the ECJ in presenting the governments with irreversible supranational interpretations of the treaties.

Since the adoption of the SEA, there have been calls for the ECJ to assume a more juridical, less political stance.[61] Indeed, the Maastricht Treaty clipped the ECJ's wings by preventing its jurisdiction from reaching into new policy domains that the EU enters, most significantly the area of "justice and home affairs."[62] However, subsequently, the Amsterdam Treaty moved visa, asylum, and immigration policy from the third to the first pillar, "thereby bringing these delicate matters almost fully within the normal jurisdiction of the ECJ."[63] The more overtly political organs of the EU have taken greater control of the extraordinary agenda since the mid-1980s, making it less necessary for the ECJ to prod them in the direction of new initiatives. Further, national courts have been emboldened to assert a greater role in examining the validity of national legislation, even in member states where there is no tradition of judicial review.

OTHER INSTITUTIONS

The Economic and Social Committee

The Economic and Social Committee (ESC) was created under the Rome Treaty and now consists of 344 members appointed by the Council of Ministers on the proposal of the national governments. The number of members for each state varies according to their respective populations. Accordingly the distribution is as follows: 24 members each for Germany, France, Italy, and the UK; 21 members each for Poland and Spain; 15 for Romania; 12 each for Belgium, Bulgaria, Greece, the Netherlands, Austria, Portugal, Sweden, Czech Republic, and Hungary; 9 each for Denmark, Finland, Ireland, Lithuania, and Slovakia; 7 each for Estonia, Latvia, and Slovenia; 6 each for Luxembourg and Cyprus; and 5 for Malta.[64] Members are individuals considered representative of important economic interests, especially employers, workers, farmers, and professionals in various categories. In fact, many are leaders of important interest groups at the national level, and as such, their influence on EU legislation comes in at various points in the legislative process, making the collective views of the ESC somewhat redundant. However, when it speaks with one voice on issues, such as social legislation, in which interests might be expected to diverge, it can be influential.

Committee of the Regions

The Committee of the Regions (COR) bears some resemblance to the ESC, outlined immediately above. It was created by the Maastricht Treaty to play an advisory role to subnational autonomous regions such as Scotland and Wales in the United Kingdom, Catalonia in Spain, and the Länder of the German Federal Republic. The European Parliament and the ESC see it as a redundant body that could only compete with their own representative functions, but the COR was established in response to a growing demand for greater regional autonomy and a corresponding belief that, as regions grow in self-governing capacity, they, too, should have a voice in the EU.[65] The COR is located in Brussels and has 344 representatives of regional and local governments of member states based on their population size. The numbers per country are as follows: 24 members each for Germany, UK, France, and Italy; 21 each for Spain and Poland; 15 for Romania; 12 each for the Netherlands, Greece, the Czech Republic, Belgium, Hungary, Portugal, Sweden, Bulgaria, and Austria; 9 each for Slovakia, Denmark, Finland, Ireland, and Lithuania; 7 each for Latvia, Slovenia, and Estonia; 6 each for Cyprus and Luxembourg; and 5 for Malta.[66]

According to Liesbet Hooghe and Gary Marks, the COR is handicapped in its effort to give representation to regions because it must give representation to whatever passes for a region in every country, some of which do not have regions with distinctive traditions and contemporary interests.[67] Regions that are newly empowered in their own countries, such as Scotland and Wales in the United Kingdom, did not benefit from direct COR help as much as they did from their own ability to find leverage within their own national political party system and from the symbolic support that creation of the COR had given member states' regions that were seeking greater autonomy. However, under the proposals of the Lisbon Treaty, increased emphasis on subsidiarity would give regional representatives more power in voicing their citizens' concerns at the EU level.

CONCLUSION

We have discussed in this chapter the structures, powers, and rules of the EU in terms of their bearing on the ways in which the ordinary and extraordinary EU agendas are set and processed. Ordinary agenda setting is primarily the job of the Commission, while processing the agenda involves an interaction between the Council of Ministers and the European Parliament, with the Commission playing a mediating role that often is used in practice to augment the influence of the Parliament. Three different procedures are used, as specified by the Treaty of Rome, the SEA, the Maastricht Treaty, and the Amsterdam Treaty. In order of the ascending importance of the European Parliament, the procedures are (1) consultation, which gives the Parliament a voice; (2) cooperation, which gives it a conditional blocking power; and (3) codecision (Amsterdam Treaty version), which gives it an ultimate veto. The capacity of one member government to block a legislative measure in the Council of Ministers has been diminished further by each treaty, including the more recent Nice Treaty.

The treaties are essentially silent on the question of how democratic the EU institutions ought to be. The burden of making them responsive to voters is in the hands of the directly elected European Parliament. Voters who lose may not be aware of what or how they have lost unless the media or interest groups or political parties focus their attention on the losses. But the issues are often so complicated that only elites can debate them with other elites. In all of the EU countries, elections are held frequently at the national, regional, and local levels, and the EP election every five years is just another of them.

But in the 1990s, EU issues began to appear more frequently on national public agendas. In elections held in the Netherlands, France, and Germany in 2002, immigration was an issue that was linked in the campaigns of extremist parties with the prospect of further EU enlargement, affecting the balance of support for moderate parties committed to enlargement. The 2004 enlargement was a recent event for the voters of France and the Netherlands when they rejected the Constitutional Treaty in 2005. This was taken as a sign that a true "European public opinion" had not yet emerged because it was still fragmented into its 25 different national components, which can produce setbacks for European integration. However, it also demonstrated that a democratic political process is emerging. Voters are exercising their right to be heard. Elite acknowledgment of this development and adjustment to it are the necessary steps toward a democratic EU.

STUDY QUESTIONS

1. Discuss the key institutional reforms that addressed "democratic deficit" in the European Union.
2. Compare and contrast intergovernmentalism and supranationalism as they apply to governance in the European Union. Explain how these two concepts and their presence in EU institutions better or worsen democratic deficit in the Union.

3. How did the TEU, Amsterdam Treaty, and Lisbon Treaty address democratic governance in the EU?
4. Explain the codecision process. How does it address citizens' participation in EU governance?
5. Explain the basic structural characteristics of First-Pillar Institutions.
6. What is the European Council and why is it important for agenda setting?

ENDNOTES

1. Simon Bulmer and Wolfgang Wessels, *The European Council: Decision-Making in European Politics* (Basingstoke, England, and London: Macmillan, 1987), pp. 17–27.

2. Ibid., p. 20.

3. Peter Ludlow, "The European Commission," in Robert O. Keohane and Stanley Hoffmann, eds., *The New European Community: Decision Making and Institutional Change* (Boulder, Colo.: Westview Press, 1991), p. 115.

4. Peter Ludlow, ed., "Introduction: The Politics and Policies of the EC in 1989," in Center for European Studies, *The Annual Review of European Community Affairs: 1990* (London: Brassey's, 1991), pp. xvi–xviii.

5. Neill Nugent, *The Government and Politics of the European Community*, 2nd ed. (Durham, N.C.: Duke University Press, 1991), p. 195.

6. Ludlow, "Introduction," p. xvi.

7. *Financial Times*, October 19, 2001.

8. Nugent, *The Government and Politics of the European Community*, 2nd ed., p. 195.

9. Ibid., pp. 407–408.

10. Anna Murphy and Peter Ludlow, "The Community's External Relations," in Ludlow, ed., *The Annual Review of European Community Affairs: 1990*, pp. 205–217.

11. European Union, *Treaty of Lisbon: Amending the Treaty on European Union and the Treaty Establishing the European Community* (Brussels, December 3, 2007), Article 8A par. 2, p. 19, Art. 9, p. 22, Art. 9B, p. 24.

12. The heads at the Seville summit in 2002 agreed to reduce the number of councils to nine, combining most of the existing councils. "Measures Concerning the Structure and Functioning of the Council," Annex II of European Council, Seville, Conclusion of the Presidency, June 21 and 22, 2002, Bulletin 24.06, 2002, p. 31.

13. Nugent, *The Government and Politics of the European Community*, 2nd ed., Table 7.1, p. 147.

14. Simon Hix, *The Political System of the European Union* (New York: St. Martin's Press, 1999), p. 66.

15. Thomas Smoot and Piet Verschuren, "Decision-Making Speed in the European Community," *Journal of Common Market Studies* 29 (September 1990): 77.

16. Ibid., pp. 77–83.

17. Thomas Konig and Thomas Braunninget, "From an Ever-Growing Towards an Ever-Slower Union?" in Madeline Hosli, Adrian van Deemen, and Mika Widgren, eds., *Institutional Challenges in the European Union* (London and New York: Routledge, 2002), pp. 159–161.

18. Axel Moberg, "The Nice Treaty and the Voting Rules in the Council," *Journal of Common Market Studies* 40 (2002): 259–282.

19. European Union web site on the Lisbon Treaty, http://europa.eu/lisbon_treaty/faq/index en.htm#6

20. Fiona Hayes-Renshaw and Helen Wallace, *The Council of Ministers* (Basingstoke, England, and London: Macmillan, 1977), Table 2.3, p. 55.

21. One study found that the percentage of Council of Minister votes that received unanimous support, with no abstentions, per year from 1994 to 1998, ranged from 75 percent to 86 percent and the percentage of decisions in which at least one negative vote was cast ranged from 12 percent to 19 percent. Mikko Mattila and Jan-Erik Lane, "Why Unanimity in the Council? A Roll Call Analysis of Council Voting," *European Union Politics* 2 (2001): 40.

22. Nugent, *The Government and Politics of the European Community*, 2nd ed., p. 124.

23. Hayes-Renshaw and Wallace, *The Council of Ministers*, p. 148.

24. George Tsebelis, "The Power of the European Parliament as Conditional Agenda-Setter," *American Political Science Review* 88 (1994): 128–142; Geoffrey Garrett, "From the Luxembourg Compromise to Codecision: Decision-Making in

the European Union," *Electoral Studies* 14 (1995): 289–308.

25. Richard Corbett, "Academic Modelling of the Codecision Procedure: A Practitioner's Puzzled Reaction," in Christope Crombez, Bernard Steunenberg, and Richard Corbett, "Forum: Understanding the EU Legislative Process: Political Scientists' and Practitioners' Perspectives," *European Union Politics* 1 (2000): 363–381.

26. E.g., Andrew Moravcsik, *The Choice for Europe: Social Purpose and State Power from Messina to Maastricht* (Ithaca, N.Y.: Cornell University Press, 1998), chap. 6; Andrew Moravcsik and Kalypso Nicolaidis, "Explaining the Treaty of Amsterdam: Interests, Influence, Institutions," *Journal of Common Market Studies* 37 (March 1999): 59–85.

27. For the work of the Secretariat, see Hayes-Renshaw and Wallace, *The Council of Ministers*, chap. 4.

28. Ibid., p. 78.

29. Jeffrey Lewis, "Administrative Rivalry in the Council's Infrastructure: Diagnosing the Methods of Community and EU Decision-Making," paper presented at the Sixth Bicentennial European Community Studies Association Conference, Pittsburgh, Pa., June 2–5, 1999.

30. Peterson and Bomberg argue that several theoretical perspectives are useful, given the complexity of EU decision making. John Peterson and Elizabeth Bomberg, *Decisionmaking in the European Union* (New York: St. Martin's Press, 1999).

31. George Tsebelis and Xenephon Yatagatos, "Veto Players and Decisionmaking in the EU after Nice: Policy Stability and Judicial/Bureaucratic Discretion," *Journal of Common Market Studies* 40(2) (June, 2002): 283–308.

32. Leon N. Lindberg and Stuart A. Scheingold, *Europe's Would–Be Polity: Patterns of Change in the European Community* (Englewood Cliffs, N.J.: Prentice-Hall, 1970), pp. 87–95.

33. The Commission is organized into 28 Directorates General (like the departments of a national government's executive-administrative structure). These are headed by 25 commissioners, some of whom have responsibility for more than one DG or for parts of DGs. Vincent Coen and Riccardo Maestri, "Institutional Actors," in Jorge Juan Fernandez Garcia, Jess E. Clayton, and Christopher Hobley, eds., *The Student's Guide to European Integration* (Cambridge, England: Polity Press, 2004), p. 44.

34. Neill Nugent, *The European Commission* (Basingstoke, England, and New York: Palgrave, 2001), pp. 99–100.

35. Ibid., p. 255.

36. Heather D. Mbaye, "Why National States Comply with Supranational Law: Explaining Implementation Infringements in the European Union, 1972–1993," *European Union Politics* 2 (2001): 269 (Table 2).

37. Anne-Marie Burley and Walter Mattli, "Europe Before the Court: A Political Theory of Legal Integration," *International Organization* 47 (Winter 1993): 67–68.

38. Nugent, *The Government and Politics of the European Community*, 2nd ed., pp. 77–93.

39. Mark A. Pollack, "Delegation, Agency, and Agenda Setting in the European Community," *International Organization* 51 (Winter 1997): 99–134.

40. Jonas Tallberg, "Delegation to Supranational Institutions: Why, How, and with What Consequences?" *West European Politics* 25 (January 2002): 23–46.

41. Neill Nugent, *The Government and Politics of the European Union*, 4th ed. (Durham, N.C.: Duke University Press), pp. 102–103.

42. Lisbon Treaty, p. 17.

43. Ibid., Article 9D, par 5, p. 27.

44. Ibid. par 6, p. 28.

45. Nugent, *The Government and Politics of the European Union*, 4th ed., pp. 223–240.

46. Amie Kreppel, *The European Parliament and Supranational Party System: A Study in Institutional Development* (Cambridge: Cambridge University Press, 2002), p. 70.

47. Desmond Dinan, *Ever Closer Union: An Introduction to European Integration*, 2nd ed. (Boulder, Colo.: Lynne Rienner, 1999), pp. 287–288; Hix, *The Political System of the European Union*, Figure 3.5, p. 86.

48. Dinan, *Ever Closer Union*, 2nd ed., pp. 281–282.

49. Nugent, *The European Commission*, p. 256.

50. Nugent, *The Government and Politics of the European Union*, 4th ed., p. 211.

51. Tsebelis, "The Power of the European Parliament as Conditional Agenda-Setter"; Garrett, "From the Luxembourg Compromise to Codecision."

52. Nugent, *The Government and Politics of the European Union*, 4th ed., p. 208.

53. Michael Shackleton, "The Politics of Codecision," *Journal of Common Market Studies* 38 (June 2000): pp. 325–342; Richard Corbett, "Academic Modelling of the Codecision Procedure," pp. 373–379. Moreover, the European Parliament signaled in the post-Maastricht period that it would vote down the original Council version if the Council held to it. Hix, *The Political System of the European Union*, pp. 93–94.

54. Kreppel, *The European Parliament and Supranational Party System*, p. 10.

55. Alec Stone Sweet and James A. Caporaso, "From Free Trade to Supranational Polity: The European Court and Supranational Governance," in Wayne Sandholtz and Alec Stone Sweet, eds., *European Integration and Supranational Governance* (Oxford and New York: Oxford University Press, 1998), pp. 102–103.

56. "Preamble and Selected Articles of the Treaty Establishing the European Economic Community (March 25, 1957)," in Howard Bliss, ed., *The Political Development of the European Community: A Documentary Collection* (Waltham, Mass.: Blaisdell, 1970), p. 65.

57. J. A. Usher, "The Scope of Community Competence: Its Recognition and Enforcement," *Journal of Common Market Studies* 24 (December 1985): 121.

58. Burley and Mattli, "Europe Before the Court," pp. 41–76.

59. Ibid., pp. 58–59.

60. Tallberg, "Delegation to Supranational Institutions," pp. 33–36; Stone Sweet and Caporaso, "From Free Trade to Supranational Polity," pp. 101–105.

61. Stone Sweet and Caporaso, "From Free Trade to Supranational Polity," p. 71.

62. Ibid., pp. 73–74.

63. Walter van Gerven, *The European Union: A Polity of States and Peoples* (Stanford, Calif.: Stanford University Press, 2005), p. 28.

64. European Economic and Social Committee official Web site, http://eesc.europa.eu/index_en.asp

65. Dinan, *Ever Closer Union*, 2nd ed., pp. 322–323.

66. COR, List of Members, http://cormembers.cor.europa.eu/cormembers.aspx?culture=en

67. Liesbet Hooghe and Gary Marks, *Multi-level Governance and European Integration* (Lanham, Md.: Rowman & Littlefield, 2001), p. 82.

Chapter 8

Electoral Politics and Public Opinion

This chapter examines European citizens' participation in EU governance through elections and assesses the democratic deficit in this regard. It also analyzes public opinion about various institutions, peoples' confidence in the Union, and future expectations from the EU. With the recent enlargement and further expansion on the horizon, there is increased demand by citizens to have their voices heard at EU institutions. The new Lisbon Treaty provides for citizens' participation in governance and addresses the clear role of national parliaments in multilevel governance. However, without increased confidence in EU institutions and participation in European Parliamentary elections by European citizens, it would be difficult to achieve truly democratic governance in the European Union.

THE EU AND DEMOCRATIC GOVERNANCE

Since the 1990s, it has been apparent that the EU is no longer the exclusive property of political elites, to be shaped as they wish whenever there is consensus among them. In the past, the public was consulted from time to time in referenda, usually on the question of whether or not to join the EC after governmental leaders had worked out the terms. The calculations of the elites that the public would support their initiatives proved correct—until the referenda on the Maastricht Treaty.[1] When the treaty was rejected by Danish voters the first time around and almost rejected by French voters, it became apparent that voter approval could be neither taken for granted nor easily manipulated. This demonstrated that putting EU issues into the public domain could be a successful strategy for those who oppose further empowerment of EU institutions.

There is, of course, the European Parliament (EP), the one directly elected body that is part of the institutional arrangements of the EU. However, it has not played a major role in setting EU agendas. Its involvement in processing the ordinary agenda is growing, and it has used its growing capacities effectively, while seeking to gain respect from the Commission and the Council. In fact, the growing concern that the EP, *as the only democratic EU body*, is weaker than the other bodies has come to overshadow the sense of solidarity between the Parliament and the Commission that rested on their common identification as *supranational* bodies, sharing a perspective that challenged the hegemony of the national governments. The fact that the European Parliament is still the least powerful of these three bodies is at the heart of criticisms about a "democratic deficit."[2]

The *democratic deficit* refers to the absence of direct links between the Commission and Council of Ministers and the voters in the 27 member countries. Voters vote for national political leaders in parliamentary elections and, in some countries, in presidential elections as well. However, for the most part, the issues they vote on and the images of the candidates are displayed in terms that bear little direct relationship to Europe. A common European agenda is not put before the voters at national elections to be voted up or down by the public. Instead, voters vote based on *national* issues and the performance of national governing and opposition parties and their leaders. Accordingly, the set of leaders that gets together in the European Council and the Council of Ministers, and which represent a clear stand on issues before the EU, is a coincidental result of 27 separate political processes that have not been coordinated from Brussels or anywhere else. Also coincidental is the set of persons appointed to the Commission as the choices of government leaders in 27 different countries. The commissioners may be able to develop a certain esprit de corps and consensus on EU policy issues through their interaction with one another. However, even then, they are more likely to be influenced by elites in the public and private sectors with whom they interact on a frequent basis than by public opinion in the member countries, which provides weak signals.

European Parliament Elections

The European Parliament is the only directly elected EU body, and it is one that potentially speaks with a consensual voice on EU issues. The question that is relevant to the democratic deficit problem is whether elections to the Parliament are conducted in such a way that voters in the member countries can communicate their wishes to the EU power holders through their representatives in the EP. Elections take place every five years, the last one being held on June 10–13, 2004. Note that it is mandated that the appointment of the new Commission be completed within six months of the election of a new European Parliament.

By its left–right orientation, the party system in the European Parliament reflects the traditional dynamics of party conflict found in national parliaments (Figure 8.1). Most Euro-parties contain members of more than one national delegation to the EP, and most of them can be located in the left–right terms found in member countries' party systems. The two largest multicountry parties, the European People's Party (EPP) and the Party of European Socialists (PES), reflect the center–right Christian Democrats or Conservatives and the center–left Social Democratic parties—both of which are found in all of the countries. However, the two Euro-parties are not far apart in their attitudes toward European integration. Most Members of the European Parliament (MEP) in both parties are strong supporters of further European integration. To find Euro-skeptics in the Parliament, one would have to turn to smaller fringe parties and independent MEP.

There is evidence that parties in power at the national level, especially the center–left PES Euro-party, suffer a substantial withdrawal of voter support in EP elections. This may reflect voter disagreement with these parties more on national-level issues than on EU-related ones, but it suggests a growing disenchantment of European voters with those in power generally in the early years of the twenty-first century.

It should be clear from the foregoing that even in countries where many voters have strong views about EU issues, the opportunities to express them in EP elections are few. In most member countries, most of the parties support the EU as it is today. Wherever a party has taken a stance against a treaty or certain parts of it, many of the voters who agree with the

AFTER AND BEFORE: BREAKDOWN OF SEATS

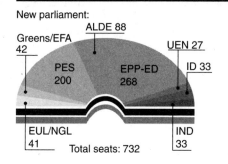

New parliament:

ALDE 88
Greens/EFA 42
UEN 27
PES 200
EPP-ED 268
ID 33
EUL/NGL 41
IND 33

Total seats: 732

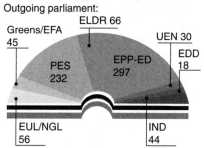

Outgoing parliament:

ELDR 66
Greens/EFA 45
UEN 30
PES 232
EPP-ED 297
EDD 18
EUL/NGL 56
IND 44

The parliament elected in 1999 had 626 seats, but grew to 788 with EU enlargement in 2004

EPP-ED:	European People's Party-European Democrats (Centre–Right)
PES:	Party of European Socialists (Socialists)
ALDE:	Alliance of Liberals and Democrats for Europe (Liberals/Centrists)
EUL/NGL:	European United Left/Nordic Green Left (Far Left)
Greens/EFA:	Greens/European Free Alliance (Greens and regionalists/nationalists)
IND:	Independents, not attached to any group
UEN:	Union for Europe of the Nations (Right wing/Gaullists)
ID:	Independence and Democracy (Eurosceptics)

Groups in old parliament:

ELDR:	European Liberal, Democratic and Reform Party (Liberals)
EDD:	Europe of Diversities and Democracies (Eurosceptics)

Figure 8.1 ■ EP Election Results 2004

Source: The European Parliament, http://www.europarl.eu.int/parliament/archive/staticDisplay.do?id=75& language=en.

party may be supporters of other parties on domestic issues. Many voters who were indifferent to the old EC have become alarmed about where the new EU is headed. There has been uncertainty about the political effects, as well as the social and economic effects, of the massive enlargement of the EU toward the east and the south. Rejection of the Economic and Monetary Union and the euro in 2000 by Danish voters and of the Nice Treaty in 2001 by Irish voters provided further evidence of growing unrest just a few years before the ten new members entered in 2004 and the Constitutional Treaty collapsed with the French and Dutch "no" votes in 2005. (See Chapter 5.) From the standpoint of removing the EU's "democratic deficit," this heightened public concern may not be such a bad sign. Whatever size and shape the EU takes in the future, it cannot even faintly resemble a single democratic polity unless the issues that divide the member governments when they meet in Council are the issues that also divide (or unite) the voters as well as the political parties in each of the member countries.

Ordinary voters in the member countries of the EU have only intermittently been energized by battles over treaty ratification or Euro-elections. Eurobarometer surveys of public attitudes when there were 15 member countries have shown that support for the EU and its institutions declined during the 1990s, but polls also showed that support for member governments and their institutions was on a decline during the same period. The referenda rejections of the Constitutional Treaty in 2005 should not have been a great surprise.

In the 1950s and 1960s, decisions on the part of governments to join together in what was initially called an *Economic Community* had the substantial support of French, German, and Italian citizens, and especially of citizens in the smaller Benelux countries, because it promised economic benefits and a guarantee that the armies of these countries would never again be locked in mortal combat. It was beyond the capabilities of the governments acting alone to guarantee the security of their citizens. By the time additional countries joined in the 1970s, 1980s, and 1990s, the possibility of war between the original members was no longer a realistic concern. Yet the two countries whose voters stopped the Constitutional Treaty in its tracks, France and the Netherlands, were both charter European Economic Community members. They are not the only countries in which the "warfare" of national elections has been extended to EU elections and referenda.

PUBLIC OPINION IN THE EU

In general, EU citizens feel that their voices are not heard at the EU level. Recent Eurobarometer study on the European Parliament clearly demonstrates how widespread this perception is (see Figure 8.2).

As results show, people do not believe that their voices are heard in the EU and that their representation is an indirect one that flows through respective member states. This feeling of distance from the EU is also seen in how people perceive the EP, which is the only supranational institution that directly represents EU citizens. According to results obtained from a special survey of public perception of the EP, one-third of the respondents had nothing positive to identify with the parliament and another one-third had no opinion (Figure 8.3).

This lack of understanding about the EP is general as it applies to the European Union as a whole—both to the "old" and "new" member states. It is also universal to all sociodemographic categories analyzed in the Eurobarometer survey.[3] Yet, it is quite surprising that when

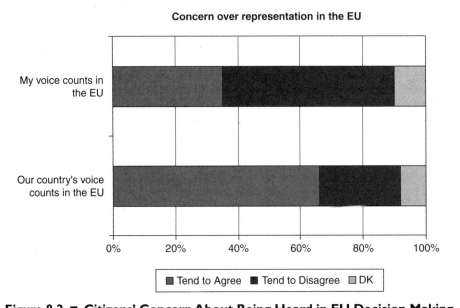

Concern over representation in the EU

Figure 8.2 ■ Citizens' Concern About Being Heard in EU Decision Making

Source: Tabulated from data found in *Eurobarometer 68* (Brussels: Commission of the European Union, December 2007), p. 40.

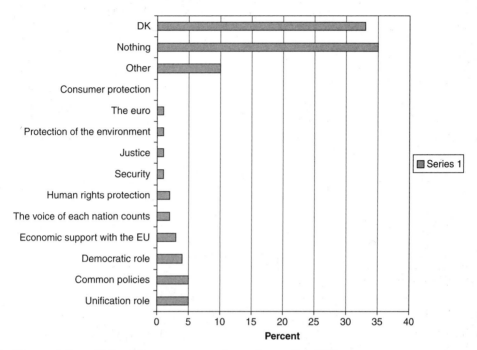

Figure 8.3 ■ What do you appreciate about the EP?

Source: Tabulated from data found in *Special Eurobarometer 288 on the European Parliament* (Brussels: Eurobarometer Surveys, 2008), p. 50.

asked about their level of trust in EU institutions, 55 percent of Europeans said they trust the EP, whereas 27 percent said they did not—despite the observations in Figure 8.3.[4] Over the years, Europeans' trust in this institution ranged from 50 percent in September 1999 to a high of 59 percent in September 2002, and to 55 percent in 2007. In the most recent Eurobarometer survey, trust in the EP ranges from a high of 77 percent in Greece to a low of 25 percent in the UK. Among the candidates, 57 percent of Macedonians trust the EP, whereas the number falls to 40 percent in Croatia and 20 percent in Turkey.

In comparison to the EP, the EU27 average trust in the Commission, the EU organ most distant to citizens in terms of representation, was 50 percent, with a high of 69 percent in Greece and a low of 22 percent in the UK.[5] Over time, EU-wide trust in the Commission improved from a low of 40 percent in September 1999 to 53 percent in September 2002, which was the highest number observed.

Despite their lack of knowledge about EU institutions, people surveyed generally tend to have a positive view of the EU and believe that their country's membership is a "good thing."[6] Highest support is seen in Luxembourg (82 percent), with the lowest observed in the UK (34 percent). Figure 8.4 shows the results in each country—including the candidate states. The EU-wide average on optimism on membership is 58 percent.

While respondents tend to favor membership in the EU, their trust in the Union is another matter. The overall picture shows that, in most countries, EU is more trusted than distrusted (see Figure 8.5). The key exceptions to this rule are the UK (25–53 percent), Germany (39–47 percent), Sweden (40–45 percent), and Finland (43–51 percent). The EU clearly enjoys popularity and trust among the citizens of the newest member states—over 50 percent trust in

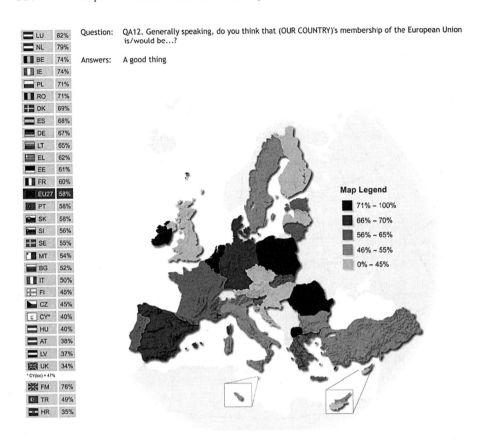

LU	82%
NL	79%
BE	74%
IE	74%
PL	71%
RO	71%
DK	69%
ES	68%
DE	67%
LT	65%
EL	62%
EE	61%
FR	60%
EU27	58%
PT	58%
SK	58%
SI	56%
SE	55%
MT	54%
BG	52%
IT	50%
FI	45%
CZ	45%
CY*	40%
HU	40%
AT	38%
LV	37%
UK	34%

* CY(tcc) = 47%

FM	76%
TR	49%
HR	35%

Question: QA12. Generally speaking, do you think that (OUR COUNTRY)'s membership of the European Union is/would be...?

Answers: A good thing

Map Legend

- 71% – 100%
- 66% – 70%
- 56% – 65%
- 46% – 55%
- 0% – 45%

Figure 8.4 ■ Perceptions on Benefits of Membership in the European Union

Source: Eurobarometer 68 (Brussels: Eurobarometer, December 2007), p. 23. Reproduced with permission.

every state. The only exception to the rule is observed among the Turkish Cypriots, where 56 percent do not trust the EU. This is not surprising in view of the post-referendum developments in Cyprus and the failure of the EU to deliver its promises to the Turkish Cypriots (see Chapter 6). Among the candidate countries, only in Macedonia do we see overwhelming trust in the EU (63–25 percent). In Croatia, 32 percent trust the EU, while in Turkey the number is 25 percent.

Europeans' low level of trust in the EU is not limited to the Union. In fact, when compared to peoples' trust of national governments and national parliaments, the EU comes out looking fairly good. On the average, 34 percent trust national governments and 35 percent trust national parliaments (see Figure 8.6).

The figures for individual countries vary greatly. In Luxembourg, where we observe the highest support for this country's membership in the Union, trust in EU institutions is 54 percent, which is lower than trust in the national government (65 percent) and national parliament (56 percent). In the UK, where we see the lowest trust in the EU (25 percent), citizens also do not trust the national government: 70 percent indicated that they do not trust their government, while 66 percent indicated their distrust of the parliament.[7] It is interesting to note that while trust in the

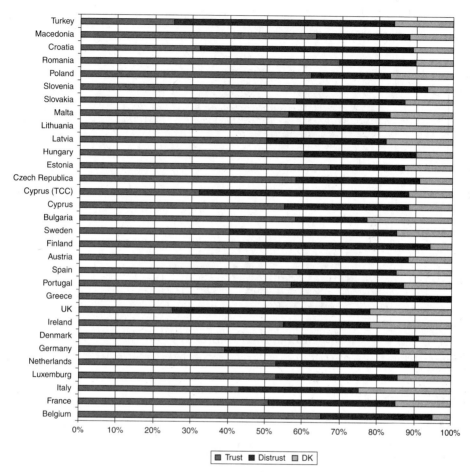

Figure 8.5 ■ Trust in the European Union

Source: Tabulated from data in *Eurobarometer 68* (Brussels: Eurobarometer, December 2007), p. 57.

EU is widespread among the newest members of the Union (with the exception of the Turkish Cypriot community of Cyprus), these countries' citizens have a low opinion of their own national governments and parliaments, as shown in Figure 8.7.

WHAT EUROPEANS EXPECT FROM THE EU

In view of citizens' perceptions of EU institutions, it is also important to address what they expect from the Union. As EU integration deepened over the last two decades, questions arose in academic and policy circles over levels of governance in the Union.[8] Specifically, questions emerged over at what level, national or EU, would it make better sense to address policy challenges facing the Europeans? There is no easy answer to this complicated matter. However, an increasing number of Europeans indicate a preference for cooperation between national governments and the EU in a wide range of policies and also demand their voices be heard in Brussels. Europeans would like to

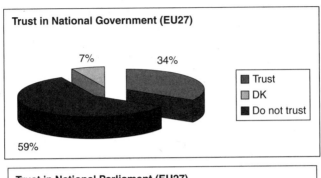

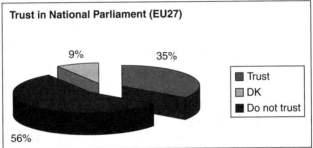

Figure 8.6 ■ Trust in National Institutions

Source: Tabulated from data in *Eurobarometer 68* (Brussels: Eurobarometer, December 2007), pp. 55–56.

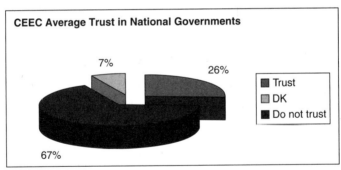

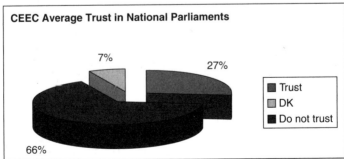

Figure 8.7 ■ Trust in National Governments and Parliaments in Central and Eastern European Members of the EU

Source: Tabulated from data in *Eurobarometer 68* (Brussels: Eurobarometer, December 2007), pp. 55–56.

see more cooperation between national governments and the EU in policies pertaining to fighting terrorism (81 percent), protecting the environment (73 percent), science and technology (71 percent), energy (68 percent), defence and foreign policy (67 percent), immigration (63 percent), fighting crime (61 percent), competition (57 percent), consumer protection (53 percent), and agriculture (53 percent). Policy areas that received a less than 50 percent call for joint approach included transport, fighting inflation, the economy, unemployment, health care, education, taxation, and pension.[9] A recent survey by the German Marshall Fund also showed that in foreign affairs, Europeans favor the EU to take greater responsibility for global threats.[10]

Among topics of concern for the future of Europe, citizens were also asked what issues would strengthen the EU. The three most chosen issues, selected by at least one-third of the respondents, are the fight against crime (36 percent), environmental issues (33 percent), and immigration issues (33 percent). Figure 8.8 shows results from the Eurobarometer study. It should be noted in

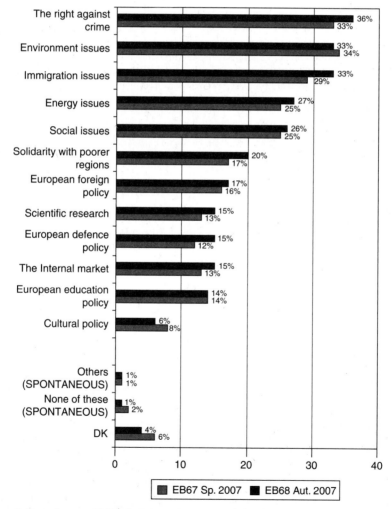

Figure 8.8 ■ Issues Which Stregthen the EU

Source: Eurobarometer 68, p. 38. Reprinted with permission.

this context that these are all areas where at least 6 in 10 respondents consider that decisions should be made jointly at the EU level rather than by national governments alone (see above).

CONCLUSIONS

The future has become a source of apprehension for many Europeans. In medieval Europe, most people felt closer attachment to their immediate locale and often to a local landholder than to a larger entity such as a nation-state.[11] Loyalties to European nation-states developed in the growing and urbanizing populations of the nineteenth and twentieth centuries. Today, the loyalty to the nation-state usually trumps more particularistic loyalties in Western Europe, but attachment to the EU is conditional and is potentially revocable if the economic promise is not realized.

Observations about public opinion in the EU clearly demonstrate the ambivalence of Europeans about multilevel governance and how policies ought to be addressed by different institutions and member sates' governments. Clearly, the desire of the citizens to have their voices heard in the Brussels institutions would go a long way in alleviating the democratic deficit in the EU. The Lisbon Treaty addresses these concerns by providing for official channels for citizens' voices to be heard in supranational institutions. It introduces the European Citizens' Initiative (ECI), where one million citizens coming from a significant number of member states may submit a proposal to the Commission to respond to a proposed change in European law. This would enable European citizens and civil society organizations to directly influence the political agenda of the EU for the first time in history.

STUDY QUESTIONS

1. What are the challenges facing democratic governance in the EU?
2. The relationship between the EU and its citizens seems to be a complicated affair. What are the key elements of this relationship?
3. The Reform Treaty aims to provide more democracy by increasing the powers of both the European Parliament and the national parliaments. However, can this be achieved by reinforcing the communication between the EU and its citizens?
4. What do you make of citizens' trust in EU institutions and their respective national institutions? How do the EU15 compare to new members in this regard?
5. What do people want from the EU?

ENDNOTES

1. The exception before 1992 was the 1972 rejection of membership in the EC by Norwegian voters.

2. Shirley Williams, "Sovereignty and Accountability in the European Community," in Robert O. Keohane and Stanley Hoffmann, eds., *The New European Community: Decision Making and Institutional Change* (Boulder, Colo.: Westview Press, 1991), pp. 155–176; Juliet Lodge, "The European Parliament," in Sven S. Andersen and Kjell A. Eliassen, eds., *The European Union: How Democratic Is It?* (London: Sage, 1996), pp. 187–214.

3. European Commission, *The European Parliament: Special Eurobarometer* (Brussels: Eurobarometer, March 2008), pp. 65–67.

4. European Commission, *Eurobarometer 68* (Brussels: Eurobarometer, December 2007), pp. 33–34.

5. Ibid., p. 31.

6. Ibid., pp. 22–27.

7. Ibid., p. 36.

8. For example, see Mathias Koenig-Archibugi, "Explaining Government Preferences for Institutional Change in EU Foreign and Security Policy," *International Organization* 58(1) (Winter 2004), pp. 137–174; Robert Rohrschneider, "The Democratic Deficit and Mass Support for and EU-Wide Government," *AJPS* 46(2) (April, 2002), pp. 463–475; Neil MacCormick, "Constitutionalism and Democracy in the EU," in Elizabeth Bomberg and Alexander Stubb, eds., *The European Union: How*

Does It Work? (Oxford: Oxford University Press, 2008), pp. 159–176; Liesbet Hooghe and Gary Marks, *Unravelling the Central State, But How? Types of Multi-Level Governance* (Vienna: Institute for Advanced Studies, March 2003); European Commission. 2001. *Enhancing Democracy: A White Paper on Governance in the European Union.* Brussels. Available at http://europa.eu.int/comm/governance/index_en.htm. Accessed on March 31, 2002.

9. Ibid., p. 28.

10. German Marshall, *Fund Transatlantic Trends 2007 Partners* (Washington, DC: German Marshall Fund of the United States, 2007), pp. 12–17.

11. Kees van Kersbergen, *Political Allegiances and European Integration* (Lanham, Md.: Rowman & Littlefield, 2001), p. 82.

Chapter 9

Economic and Monetary Union

The history of the Economic and Monetary Union (EMU) represents a bold adventure that carries with it political and economic risks. With a single monetary authority and a single European currency, the euro (€), replacing the national banknotes and coins of 16 member states, the EMU represents the climax of European economic integration. In this chapter, we will provide an overview of the regional and systemic developments that gave rise to the coordination of exchange rate policy in the European Union (EU) countries, followed by an analysis of the "snake in a tunnel" and the failure of the members to achieve a zone of monetary stability in Europe. We will then examine the European Monetary System (EMS) and the EMU. Finally, we will analyze the economic and political implications of EMU for member states and the global monetary system.

After the creation of the customs union and until the adoption of the EMS in 1978, members of the European Community (EC) experienced serious economic difficulties that threatened the future of economic integration. Whereas many scholars argue that this was a period of disintegration, we believe that this conclusion is misplaced (see Chapter 4). If disintegration was the order of this period, then how can one account for the creation of the EMS, which highlighted a process of trial and learning in exchange rate policy? Moreover, the European Regional Development Fund (ERDF) came into effect in 1975. As we will explain in Chapter 10, this fund was crucial for the development of the underprivileged regions of the EC. Finally, the EC expanded to nine countries when Britain, Denmark, and Ireland became members in 1973.

The economic difficulties experienced by the EC resulted from important changes in the international economic order. The collapse of the Bretton Woods monetary system represented the first serious shock to the EC and tested its seriousness in achieving economic integration. During the 1960s, there were important developments that weakened this monetary system. The weakening of the U.S. dollar strained the stability of European currencies: The West German government revalued the deutsche mark (DM) in 1961 and 1969, and the French government devalued the franc in 1969. These measures were intended to stabilize the U.S. dollar in international markets. However, they failed to eliminate exchange rate instability in the system and persuaded EC leaders that alternative policy options had to be considered for the EC. The policy recommendation came at the Hague summit of 1969, where the EC heads of state and government accepted Willy

Brandt's call for EMU. Subsequently, the Werner plan of 1970 laid down the basic idea for this monetary union.[1] Unfortunately, its introduction coincided with the collapse of Bretton Woods and the rise of the everyone-for-oneself period of the floating exchange rates.

According to Miltiades Chacholiades, "two or more countries form an *economic union* when they form a common market and, in addition, proceed to unify their fiscal, monetary, and socioeconomic policies. An economic union is the most complete form of economic integration."[2] A common market involves establishing a customs union between two or more countries and free movement of all factors of production among the member states. The United States represents the most successful economic and monetary union.

Europeans' interest in EMU stemmed from their fear that continued revaluation of their national currencies vis-à-vis the dollar would threaten the stability of exchange rates, and thus of intra-EC trade, which had existed in the EC since 1957. The customs union and the maintenance of the common agricultural policy required stability; unstable exchange rates threatened the survival of the Community. Therefore, a drastic policy initiative was needed to achieve a zone of monetary stability among the EU member states.

TRIAL AND ERROR IN EXCHANGE RATE POLICIES: THE ROAD TO EMS, 1971–1979

When the Bretton Woods system collapsed, the United States wanted the DM and the Japanese yen to be revalued against the dollar. This would have had the same effect on the U.S. trade deficit as an approximately 10 percent devaluation of the dollar; the difference would be that its impact would have been on those economies that contributed the most to the American trade deficit. The subsequent Smithsonian Agreement of 1971, where the industrialized democracies' leaders attempted to coordinate their monetary policies, failed to bring stability to this situation. More crucial from the European point of view, this agreement and the subsequent reaction of the EC members to the collapse of Bretton Woods demonstrated how uncoordinated the European response was to the apparent crisis.

In accord with the Smithsonian Agreement, the U.S. government devalued the dollar by 10 percent. Intra-EC trade faced immense obstacles from unstable prices due to exchange rate fluctuation. The EC responded to this pressure by establishing the snake in the tunnel and reduced the excursion allowed by the Smithsonian Agreement by half. The limit for fluctuations between EU currencies was to be only 4.5 percent. Before accession to EC membership, Britain, Ireland, and Denmark agreed to join the snake. The par value of each EC currency vis-à-vis the dollar represented the center of the tunnel. According to the agreed formulation, a variation of plus or minus 2.25 percent on either side of the dollar exchange rate determined the walls of the tunnel. Effectively, this arrangement established a joint float (snake) of the EC currencies that stayed within the walls of the tunnel formed by the maximum fluctuations around the dollar.

Despite initial enthusiasm about the snake, this arrangement lasted for only a short period, from April 1972 to March 1973. In June 1972, the British pound left the snake and began to free-float. Ireland and Denmark followed soon after, though Denmark later rejoined the snake. In February 1973, the Italian government took the lira out of the tunnel. Finally, in March 1973, the EC central banks ended their support of the margins vis-à-vis the dollar, and the snake left the tunnel to free-float. To make matters worse, the United States devalued the dollar by another 10 percent in 1973. The subsequent "floating snake" of the EU lasted until 1979, but it included only West Germany and four other members—Belgium, the Netherlands, Luxembourg, and Denmark—which kept their currencies close to the DM.

Problems faced by the Europeans worsened as the U.S. administration continued to pressure its trade partners to undertake enormous economic responsibilities. For example, President

Carter's "locomotive theory" called for West Germany and Japan to assume major responsibilities in reviving the world economy.[3] Furthermore, as the United States continued to experience large balance-of-payments deficits, the dollar crisis of 1978 emerged: The dollar fell by 10 percent between October 1977 and February 1978 and by another 10 percent by the fall of 1978.[4] These were background conditions that influenced the decision to create a European monetary system.

Another dimension of this monetary problem was that the traditional Keynesian macroeconomic policies did not seem to work following the 1973 oil crisis. The countries with the worst inflation, France and Italy, also experienced the highest unemployment rates. In addition, they had the poorest economic growth rates. According to Stephen George, "the tradeoff between inflation and growth did not appear to be working, and accelerating inflation threatened economic collapse."[5] Under these circumstances, it became clear to the EC leaders that they had to protect EC currencies against fluctuations in the value of the U.S. dollar. Furthermore, there was a general dissatisfaction with the floating exchange rates among EC officials because exchange rates had been highly volatile during the mid-1970s due to overspeculation in the currency markets. Lastly, the European leaders believed that fixed rates had a beneficial effect on intra-EC trade.[6]

The answer to these problems seemed to lie in the formulation of a new exchange rate system for the EC currencies. However, the EC leaders had to make sure the mistakes of the snake in the tunnel would not be repeated. They had learned that the previous system failed because of the asymmetry of the exchange rate mechanism and the failure of the exchange market intervention rules to provide the necessary credibility to the margins allowed for currency fluctuations.[7] Under the snake, the central banks had agreed to provide each other unlimited financing for intervention in currency markets. This new facility was the Very Short-Term Financing Facility, administered by the European Monetary Cooperation Fund. Furthermore, the claims and liabilities between the central banks had to be settled within a month. Not only was this period very short, but also there were insufficient funds available under the Very Short Term Financing Facility for intervention by several central banks. As a result, the system did not operate efficiently, and it contributed to the breakup of the snake.[8]

The system that emerged in 1979, the European Monetary System (EMS), was a compromise around a Belgian proposal that combined the German plan with the French, Italian, and British alternative. The West Germans wanted to continue the arrangement of bilateral parities found under the snake, where each currency would be tied to every other currency in the system. Furthermore, in order to ease the pressure on the currencies, the Germans called for wider margins than the old plus or minus 2.25 percent of the snake for exchange rate fluctuations and argued that the central banks should intervene to restore the agreed parities. In the alternative parity grid plan, the French, the British, and the Italians asked that instead of bilateral parities, all currency values be determined in relation to an alternative basket currency system based on the weighted averages of all EC currencies, known as the *European currency unit (ecu)*. They argued that the German proposal was an unfair system because it placed an unnecessary burden on countries with weaker currencies. Finally, a compromise was reached around a Belgian proposal that combined the two systems. It was a substantial improvement over the old snake system. It included four main components: (1) a basket currency, the ecu; (2) the exchange rate mechanism (ERM); (3) credit provisions among the participating central banks; and (4) the pooling of reserve assets among the members.[9]

The ecu was the renamed and restructured European unit of account (EUA, introduced in 1975). It was a basket currency that served four functions: (1) the denominator for the ERM, (2) the basis for a divergence indicator, (3) the denominator for operations in both the intervention and the credit mechanisms, and (4) a reserve instrument and a means of settlement between monetary authorities in the EC.[10] Basket currencies, like the ecu and the International Monetary Fund's special drawing rights (SDR), are stable reserve currencies that counteract exchange rate volatility.

The ERM called for participating countries to maintain their exchange rates within bilateral limits of plus or minus 2.25 percent. More precisely, the upper part of the band was 2.275 percent above the central parity, while the lower part of the band was 2.225 percent below the central parity. Italy negotiated a wider margin of plus or minus 6 percent due to its weak national currency. As Michael Artis and Mark Taylor explain, "According to these provisions, when a currency triggered its divergence indicator threshold (calculated as the ecu value of a 75 percent departure of its bilateral rates against all the other countries), a presumption was created that the country concerned should take corrective action."[11]

To enable member countries to meet this obligation, the EC created a large credit fund, known as the European Monetary Cooperation Fund, and the member states contributed 20 percent of their gold and dollar holdings to this fund in exchange for ecus. The facilities involved in the intervention mechanisms were the Very Short Term Financing Facility, the Short-term Monetary Support, and the Medium-term Financing Assistance. The latter two indicated significant improvements over the system that existed under the snake.

The EMS seemed to work rather well throughout the 1980s, and it looked as though the EC had finally managed to create a zone of monetary stability. During these years, the EC currencies became less variable against one another, as well as against the U.S. dollar and the Japanese yen (Table 9.1). At the same time, the ERM countries experienced a steady decline in inflation.[12] Thus, the European leaders believed that they had found the answer to the currency problems of

Table 9.1 ■ Bilateral Nominal Exchange Rates Against ERM Currencies, 1974–1990*

Currency/ Country	Pre-EMS Period (1974–1978)	Recession Period (1979–1983)	SEA Period (1984–1986)	Post-EMS Period (1987–1990)	Post-SEA Period Average (1979–1990)
Belgium/ Luxembourg franc	1.2	1.3	0.6	0.4	0.9
Danish crown	1.4	1.0	0.5	0.5	0.8
German DM	1.5	1.0	0.5	0.5	0.8
Greek drachma	1.8	2.3	2.5	0.7	2.1
Portuguese escudo	3.0	2.1	0.8	1.1	1.8
French franc	1.9	1.1	0.7	0.5	0.7
Irish punt	2.0	0.7	1.2	0.5	1.0
Italian lira	2.2	1.0	0.9	0.6	0.8
Dutch guilder	1.0	0.8	0.6	0.3	0.5
Spanish peseta	2.8	2.0	1.1	0.5	1.7
UK pound	2.2	2.6	2.4	1.9	2.4
EC mean	1.7	0.7	0.5	0.4	0.4
U.S. dollar	2.2	2.5	2.9	2.7	2.7
Japanese yen	2.3	2.7	2.0	1.9	2.5

Source: International Financial Statistics (Washington, D.C.: International Monetary Fund, quarterly publications)

*Variability is the weighted sum of standard deviations of monthly percent changes.

the EC in the new EMS. With this apparent success, they again moved to consider monetary union among the EC states.

THE EMU AGAIN

The concept of EMU was not new. The Werner plan of 1970 had promoted this idea. Furthermore, while the Single European Act (SEA) did not call for an EMU, it did recall in one of its preambles that in 1972 the European Council "approved the objective of progressively creating an EMU."[13] With the relative success of the EMS in bringing about a zone of monetary stability in Europe during the mid-1980s, the EC moved to reexamine the feasibility of an EMU at the Hanover summit in 1988. At this meeting, the European Council agreed to set up a committee of central bankers and technical experts under the leadership of the European Commission president, Jacques Delors, to prepare a report by the June 1989 Madrid summit on the steps to be taken to achieve EMU. The resulting report, known as the Delors plan, proposed a three-stage plan toward the EMU[14]:

Stage 1

Economic: Completion of the internal market (Project 1992); strengthened competition policy; full implementation of the reform of the structural funds; enhanced coordination and surveillance of economic policies; budgetary adjustments in high-debt/deficit countries

Monetary: Capital market liberalization; enhanced monetary and exchange rate policy coordination; realignments possible, but infrequent; all EC currencies in the narrow bands of the ERM; extended use of the ecu

Stage 2

Economic: Evaluation and adaptation of stage 1 policies; review of national macroeconomic adjustments

Monetary: Establishment of the European System of Central Banks (ESCB) (called a *Eurofed* in the report); a possible narrowing of the EMS exchange rate bands

Stage 3

Economic: Definitive budgetary coordination among the member states; a possible strengthening of the structural and regional policies

Monetary: ESCB or a similar institution in charge of monetary policy; irrevocably fixed exchange rates that would pave the way to replace national currencies with a single currency, the ecu, administered by the European Monetary Cooperation Fund

The Delors plan was much more explicit about the EMU, its institutions, and the necessary deadlines than any previous plan on the subject. Stage 1 was to commence in July 1990 and was linked to the completion of the single market. Stage 2 was to start on January 1, 1994, and stage 3 would be completed by the end of the century.

The European Council accepted the plan at the Madrid summit in June 1989, but the decision was not unanimous. A major objection to the plan came from the British government. Prime Minister Margaret Thatcher made it very clear that she was not pleased with the plan's objective and methods, even though she accepted the general goal of establishing a single market (stage 1). At the following Milan summit, Thatcher outlined the conditions for putting the pound sterling into the ERM: The British inflation rate must be on a falling trend toward convergence with the other member states' rates; there must be tangible progress toward the achievement of the single market; and other members must have dismantled their controls on the movement of capital.[15] Following this move, the British government announced that it would propose its alternative plan to the Delors report. The plan, which the new Chancellor of the Exchequer, John Major, revealed to other members in November 1989, called for a currency parallel to the national currencies. This parallel currency would be used for trade, bank deposits, and the issuance of Eurobonds (which were in substantial use). Against this background, the European Council decided at its Strasbourg summit in December 1989 to set up an intergovernmental conference (IGC) to consider the EMU in Rome in December 1990. The only objection to this conference came from Margaret Thatcher, based on the view that it would undermine British monetary sovereignty. The idea of a parallel currency received little support from the other member countries.

The final agreement on the EMU came during the Maastricht summit in December 1991. The resulting Maastricht Treaty, based on a revised Treaty of Rome, established the European Union, which consisted of the old community (EC), the EMU, and two additions: the Common Foreign and Security Policy (CFSP) and cooperation between the member states' governments in justice and police matters (see Chapter 5). The Maastricht Treaty included several provisions and deadlines that committed the members to implementation of EMU.

First, the treaty specified a timetable that called for stage 2 to start in January 1994. The European Monetary Institute (EMI) would then be in charge of preparing the ground for stage 3. It would coordinate monetary policies, oversee preparations for the transfer to the ecu, and create the right conditions for stage 3. Frankfurt was chosen in 1993 to be the site for the EMI. National governments still retained monetary sovereignty, but their central banks were to be independent by the end of stage 2. The EMI was to become the European Central Bank (ECB) shortly before the final stage of the EMU began.

Second, stage 3 was to begin in 1997 by a decision of the European Council, through a qualified majority vote (QMV), if the majority of EU members met the EMU criteria. Otherwise, the EMU would start in 1999 with as many members as could make the grade.[16]

Third, the treaty specified convergence criteria for qualifying for the EMU: an average inflation rate within 1.5 percent and interest rates within 2 percent of the three best-performing states, a budget deficit of less than 3 percent of gross domestic product (GDP), a ratio of public debt to GDP not to exceed 60 percent, and no devaluation within the ERM for the past two years.

Fourth, the treaty specified how monetary policy and coordination would operate under the EMU. The ECB would have a policy-making council composed of national central bank governors and an executive board. This council would be an independent body similar to the U.S. Federal Reserve Board. The president of the ECB Council would report to the EU finance ministers and the European Parliament. The meeting of the ECB Council president and the Council of Economic and Finance Ministers is referred to as *ECOFIN*. ECOFIN's functions include determining ecu exchange rates in consultation with the ECB and issuing broad guidelines for the EU's economic policy. Moreover, ECOFIN would have the authority to recommend changes to any member states' economic policies if these policies were considered to be inconsistent with the broad goals of the EMU.

As a concession to the United Kingdom, the other members agreed to allow it the right to opt out of the EMU. Moreover, any member that stayed outside the currency union would not be allowed to vote on EU monetary policy. Those inside the EMU would lock their exchange rates irrevocably and later replace their respective national currencies with the ecu. The ECB would determine interest rates in accordance with its commitment to price stability. In determining interest rates, the ECB would also be required to support the EU's economic policies and objectives, such as sustainable economic growth, social welfare, and high employment.

INTERESTS AND MOTIVES FOR AND AGAINST THE EMU

The acceptance of the EMU as part of the Maastricht Treaty by the EC member states owes much to French persistence at the time. The French wanted to have a greater say in monetary policy making than they had under the EMS. This was a calculated move to weaken the Bundesbank's dominant position over monetary policy and to strengthen the EC institutions as a constraint on German power.[17] However, the Germans did not oppose the EMU. On the contrary, the German government was one of the greatest supporters of this idea. So why were the French so eager to push for the EMU at the IGC? One explanation could be that Mitterrand wanted to lock the Germans into the EU before German reunification gave them any idea of opting out of Europe. More generally, as Wayne Sandholtz explains, "many leaders, including key Germans, desired to bind Germany irrevocably to the EU, and monetary union was a crucial means of doing so. In short, foreign policy ideas seem to provide the best explanation for German support for EMU."[18]

Sandholtz also provides other political reasons for the enthusiasm for the EMU. The first is the spillover effect from the single market. The success of the EC in achieving the necessary requirements of Project 1992 persuaded the Commission that there was a functional linkage between the single market and the EMU. The single market was a major step toward a complete economic union where greater economic benefits could be realized.[19] The other explanation relates to the idea of an independent monetary authority, the Eurofed or ECB. This independent institution would provide credibility to monetary policy, guarantee member states low inflation, and assure price stability. As Sandholtz states, "For governments that found it difficult domestically to achieve monetary discipline, EMU offered the chance to have it implemented from without."[20]

The EMU plan also received considerable support from the business sector. In 1992, corporate leaders created an Association for the Monetary Union of Europe. The president of this institution was the president of Philips Corporation and its vice president was the chairman of Fiat of Italy. The main reason for this private-sector support was that big business in Europe had become thoroughly transnationalized. Therefore, complete economic integration with full monetary union promised increased benefits to big business. Even under the single market, the multiplicity of currencies imposes transaction costs and information costs. The transaction costs were estimated to be around 15 billion ecus.

There were other foreseen benefits of the EMU. It would provide macroeconomic stability by sound, coordinated fiscal policies, price stability, and the disappearance of noncooperative exchange rate policies.[21] In terms of its external effects, the EMU, with a common currency, would strengthen the EU's position in the international economic system. It would provide an alternative hard currency to the U.S. dollar, especially in the portfolios market with increases in ecu-denominated assets. Moreover, as the EU's international power increased, it would be able to alter the present balance of power in the international monetary system against the dollar and the yen. The EU would be more likely to absorb rather than set international monetary conditions. Although it is doubtful that the dollar would lose much of its dominance, the EMU could give the EU more influence in the international monetary system.[22]

Critics of the EMU, led by the British government, argued that the costs of monetary union would outweigh its potential benefits. One influential critic, Nobel Prize–winning economist Martin Feldstein, argued that the creation of a single market would not require a single currency and that a single currency would result in the unnecessary loss of monetary autonomy.[23]

It is quite correct that sometimes the effects of exchange rates on trade are exaggerated. Yet events in Europe, especially since the collapse of the ERM in September 1992, suggest that companies and states had sustained considerable costs from volatile exchange rates. This was particularly the case for intra-EU trade-dependent economies. Since all the EU states trade with each other more than they do with non-EU countries, exchange rate stability is an important issue for them.

With regard to the loss of monetary autonomy, the critics are quite correct. The EMU specifically calls for greater monetary union (loss of monetary policy autonomy for the individual states) with exchange rate stability in a highly integrated financial market. The fear was that the weaker economies would lose out when they were tied so closely to the German economy because they would end up following the strict monetary policies of the Bundesbank. Ironically, the Germans, particularly the former president of the Bundesbank, Helmut Schlesinger, worried that Germany would import inflation from its partners. Finally, Margaret Thatcher seemed least willing, among the member state leaders, to share monetary sovereignty with the EU. However, in the present information age, with the internationalization of the financial and money markets and the technological revolution in telecommunications, economic agents are increasingly holding diverse currency portfolios. This means that, even when countries control their money supply, as the UK tried to do in the 1980s, they could not control the domestic inflation rate in the long run because only international monetary policies could ensure any meaningful control of inflation.[24] Thus, monetary autonomy of member states in the EU was already limited.

Although the supporters and critics of the EMU argued over the feasibility of such a union, they were stunned by the collapse of the ERM in September 1992. As speculators continued to test the willingness of the British government to defend the parity of the pound in the ERM, the pound sterling dropped out of its target zone on Black Wednesday, September 16, 1992, and began to free-float. Speculators then began to test one EC currency after another. In the end, the Italian lira also dropped out of the ERM, the other weak currencies (the escudo, peseta, and punt) faced major devaluations, and finally in August 1993, the EC finance ministers revised the target zone of the ERM to plus or minus 15 percent. The causes and effects of the ERM crisis raised serious concerns about the future of the EMU.

Black September: What Went Wrong in the Exchange Rate Mechanism?

During the ERM crisis of September 1992, early explanations of its causes focused too much on German interest rates. However, with 20/20 hindsight, we now realize that there were several factors behind the currency crisis. As David Cameron points out, many factors contributed to the ERM crisis of September 1992:

1. The EMS became a quasi-fixed system that failed to carry out a currency realignment needed since 1987; that is, although the mechanism was supposed to adjust in response to changing pressures from the international currency markets, the EC failed to bring about the necessary realignment of the ERM currencies, with the mechanism behaving as if it were a fixed system.
2. The rapid expansion of the currency markets caused instability.
3. The economic and monetary policies of the German government and the Bundesbank were at fault as they tried to fight inflationary pressures in Germany caused by unification.
4. Political uncertainties resulted from the Danish rejection of the Maastricht Treaty and the possible similar outcome in the French referendum of September 1992.[25]

Two additional factors contributed to the ERM crisis. The first was the British government's failure to control public spending at a time of economic recession in Britain; this increasingly exposed the pound to speculative attacks. The second was the role of the U.S. dollar in international markets. During 1991–1992, the dollar fell and continued to fall. This weakness of the dollar placed the ERM under great pressure as investors and currency speculators switched from dollars to DMs. At the same time, investors and speculators were abandoning the pound sterling in favor of the DM. In view of these developments, we can ascertain whether the EMS was a success in creating a zone of monetary stability.

To appraise the actual performance and soundness of any international monetary system, economists use three tests: adjustment, liquidity, and confidence. *Adjustment* mechanisms involve monetary costs. *Liquidity* means the availability of an adequate supply of reserves in order to make the financing of adjustments possible. And *confidence* means absence of panicky shifts by the monetary authorities from one reserve asset to another. Another element of confidence is the reputation of the monetary system among economic agents.

The founders of the EMS thought that they had eliminated the inherent problems of the snake (insufficient availability of funds for intervention, weak adjustment mechanism, and lack of confidence) from the lessons learned during the 1970s. The economic agents in the financial markets of the late 1980s and early 1990s, on the other hand, discovered that they had the power to crack the system by speculative attacks. In the end, one of the ERM's most important elements, the credibility of the central banks in honoring exchange rate commitments, suffered serious damage. This means that there was very little confidence in the system even though the monetary authorities had announced their willingness to defend any future exchange rate parities.

The fault really lay with the monetary authorities in the EC during the late 1980s and early 1990s. As speculative pressures on the ERM gradually increased, officials refused to acknowledge the seriousness of the problem and realign ERM currencies. One could say that the ERM had become too rigid because the member governments treated it like a fixed exchange rate system. According to *The Economist*, a revaluation of the DM against other ERM currencies was necessary after German reunification in order to offset the inflationary pressures of German budget deficits. Yet the French dismissed this idea, and the Bundesbank was left with no option but to push German interest rates upward.[26] In a similar fashion, the British and French officials publicly asked for a lowering of German interest rates during the spring and summer of 1992, when they knew quite well that the idea was not acceptable to the Germans. They could have instead privately asked for revaluation of the DM against all other ERM currencies, which might have been more acceptable to the Germans.

The failure of EC monetary officials to recognize the urgency of currency realignments was further underscored in a *Financial Times* special report. In their review of the events and actions of finance ministers during the two weeks prior to Black Wednesday, *Financial Times* experts found that, when pressures on currencies mounted and the finance ministers met in Bath on September 4–5, the leaders failed to address the issue of currency realignments largely for political reasons.[27] According to Dutch Prime Minister Ruud Lubbers, "realignment was not possible because England had its pride and France said that it couldn't be done because it was facing a difficult referendum and they couldn't discuss it; and the English said then that the Bundesbank should do something first, and so the discussion went."[28] Basically, the French finance minister, Michel Sapin, and his British counterpart, Chancellor Norman Lamont, succeeded in keeping realignment off the agenda. Lamont repeatedly pressured Helmut Schlesinger to cut German interest rates, which Schlesinger, as "mere *primus inter pares* on the Bundesbank's decision-making council,"[29] could not do on his own even if he wanted to. At the end of the meeting, the ministers decided to defend ERM rates, and the Germans only agreed not to increase interest rates further.[30]

In the days following the Bath meeting, the ERM continued to suffer under speculative attacks that led to its collapse. On September 12, 1992, the Italian government devalued the lira by 7 percent; on September 16, the pound sterling left the ERM, and the lira left the next day; on November 22, 1992, the Portuguese escudo and Spanish peseta were devalued 6 percent each; on January 30, 1993, the Irish punt was devalued 10 percent; and on May 13, 1993, the escudo and peseta faced devaluation once again, by 6.5 percent and 8 percent, respectively. Finally, the French franc, which had been shored up in September 1992, came under speculative attack in

July 1993. Economic recession, high unemployment, and interest rates that remained high to maintain the DM–franc ERM parity convinced the speculators to test France's ability to match the Bundesbank's tight monetary policy.[31] Similar attacks on the Danish crown, the Belgian franc, the peseta, and the escudo followed. The central banks tried to intervene to stabilize the ERM parities, but their efforts failed, and on July 30, 1993, the EC Monetary Committee called an emergency meeting of the finance ministers and central bank governors. At this meeting, following the Bundesbank's decision not to cut its discount rate, EC finance ministers and central bank governors agreed to widen the fluctuation bands between ERM currencies to plus or minus 15 percent of their rates effective August 2, 1993.[32] The only exception to this rule was a voluntary agreement between Germany and the Netherlands to retain the previous plus or minus 2.25 percent between the DM and guilder.

Many factors led to the ERM crisis: Germany's problems in absorbing the East German economy prevented the Bundesbank from lowering its interest rates to help its EC partners, the overvalued DM put immense pressure on other currencies to maintain their par values vis-à-vis the DM within the ERM bands, the budget deficit continued in the UK, speculation arose about the future of the Maastricht Treaty, and the decline of the U.S. dollar had a destabilizing effect on currency markets. What were the lessons learned from this experience and its implications for the future of the EMU?

THE COSTS OF EXCHANGE RATE INSTABILITY: A CRUCIAL REASON FOR EMU

There is no doubt that the collapse of the ERM inflicted political and credibility damage on the EU. But there were some very serious economic costs as well. It is estimated that the Bank of England and other central banks spent £15 to 20 billion to defend the British currency during the days leading to Black Wednesday.[33] When the lira came under attack, the Bundesbank spent DM 90 billion in support of currencies against their ERM margins, and this was on top of some DM 200 billion that were previously expended on currency support.[34] The bulk of these sums went into the hands of the speculators.

The move to more flexible rates did not ease economic recession in the EU. In fact, the 1992–1993 recession in Europe was the deepest since the recession of 1974–1975. Several factors contributed to this problem. During the 15 months following September 1992, the EC currencies fell against the U.S. dollar: DM, 22 percent; franc, 23 percent; guilder, 21 percent; lira, 58 percent; and pound, 34 percent. However, this did not translate into increased overall exports by Germany because the DM also rose sharply against other EU currencies. Because intra-EC trade far outweighs extra-EC trade for the EC members, it was the ERM shifts that had greater consequence for export competitiveness. Unpublished figures from the Organization for Economic Cooperation and Development (OECD) showed that the volume of exports of manufactured goods from Germany fell by 11 percent during the first half of 1993, compared to a 1.9 percent increase during the same period a year before.[35] The French exports also showed a trend similar to that of Germany's. During the same period in 1993, "exports from France declined by 11.3 percent. By contrast, exports of Italy increased by 19 percent and the British trade deficit declined to 7.6 billion pounds from 13.4 billion pounds in the previous year particularly in trade with non-EU countries."[36] By this time, the pound and the lira were both outside the ERM. Exports of EC countries, except Germany and France, showed marked improvement owing to improved exchange rates vis-à-vis the dollar, DM, and franc, but the EC-wide economic recession worsened nevertheless.

The answer was found in the economic problems of Germany and, to a lesser extent, France. Benefits of devalued British, Spanish, and other EC currencies were canceled by the negative economic impact of currency appreciation (with regard to EC currencies) in Germany.

In addition, the costs of German unification contributed to roughly a 1.5 percent contraction of the German economy. Since an average 20 percent of total non-German exports in the EU are destined to Germany's market, this economic contraction contributed to the overall export problems of other member states.

ALL AHEAD WITH THE EMU

Despite these economic difficulties, the EU leaders seemed determined to push ahead with the EMU in order to overcome problems associated with currency alignment. In accordance with a provision in the Maastricht Treaty, Article 109G, the composition of the ecu basket was frozen on November 1, 1993.[37] According to this decision, the ecu basket remained as defined on September 21, 1989, which is the last time it was adjusted. In January 1994, stage 2 started with the establishment of the EMI in Frankfurt. This institution assisted member states in coordination of monetary policies and paved the way for the start of stage 3 on January 1, 1999, when the ECB and the euro (€) entered into effect. At that time, 11 member countries (Austria, Belgium, Finland, France, Germany, Ireland, Italy, Luxembourg, the Netherlands, Portugal, and Spain) joined the new euro zone. With this final stage of the EMU, the participants committed themselves to the timetable in Table 9.2 for the realization of monetary union.

On the day stage 3 came into force, the EMS was replaced by a new exchange rate mechanism (ERM II), which allowed non-euro-zone states of the EU (Denmark, Greece, Sweden, and the UK) to link their currencies to the euro. As in the old ERM, there were two bands, a narrow band of plus or minus 2.25 percent and a wider band of plus or minus 15 percent. Moreover, the Very Short Term Financing Facility provided funds to assist the central banks during interventions. Denmark joined ERM II in the narrow band, while Greece, prior to joining the euro on January 1, 2001, opted for the wider band. The central rate for the Danish crown against the euro was 7.46038, with the upper rate of 7.62824 and the lower rate of 7.29252. The Danish government stayed out of the euro zone by choice, and there are no clear indications from the government about joining in the future. This view is based on the Danish referendum on September 28, 2000, in which the voters rejected the single European currency by a vote of 53 to 47 percent.[38] The significance of the Danish

Table 9.2 ■ Timetable for the EMU

Time Period	Duties to Be Completed	Responsible Parties
January 1, 1999 to January 1, 2002	Change over to the € by the banking and finance industries	Commission and the member states
January 1, 2002	Start circulation of € banknotes and coins; complete changeover to the € in public administration	ESCB and the member states
July 1, 2002	Cancel the legal tender status of national banknotes and coins of countries in the euro zone	ESCB and the member states

Source: "Profile of the EU: Common Policies," outlined by the European Commission delegation in Washington, D.C

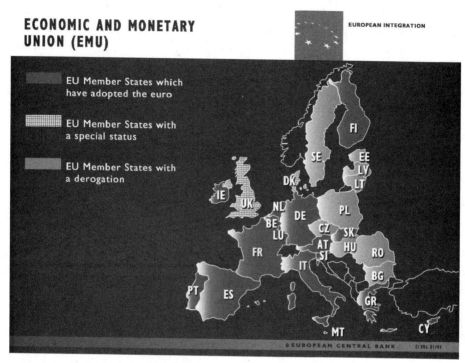

ECONOMIC AND MONETARY UNION (EMU)

EUROPEAN INTEGRATION

EU Member States which have adopted the euro

EU Member States with a special status

EU Member States with a derogation

© EUROPEAN CENTRAL BANK

Map 9.1 ■ Euro-zone Countries

Source: File European Integration from the European Central Bank, http://www.ecb.int/ecb/educational/facts/html/index.en.html

referendum was that it contributed to a "two-speed Europe," allowing some members to go ahead with finalizing the EMU while leaving others behind. The situation is rather complicated because while Denmark is currently outside the euro zone, it is in the ERM II. With Danish currency in the ERM II, only Sweden and the UK were left outside of both the euro zone and ERM II. The British position was discussed earlier under the Maastricht Treaty. Sweden, however, cited technical grounds for its decision to stay out of the euro zone. With eastern enlargement of the EU, the above situation became more complicated. So far, three new countries have joined the euro zone—Cyprus, Malta, Slovenia, and Slovakia. Map 9.1 shows the euro-zone area of the EU. This translates into 328.6 million citizens in 16 countries living in the euro area. More countries are expected to do so in the future. Table 9.3 provides a summary of the next stages of euro adoption in the EU. While some new members of the EU plan to enter the euro zone by 2014, many others have not decided yet, and a two-track monetary union still remains a real possibility for the foreseeable future. Four nonmember states, namely Andorra, Monaco, San Marino, and the Vatican, have also adopted the euro.

THE EUROPEAN SYSTEM OF CENTRAL BANKS

The **European System of Central Banks** (ESCB) defines and implements monetary policy in the euro zone, conducts foreign exchange operations, manages official foreign reserves of euro-area countries, and oversees operation of payments systems. It comprises the central

Table 9.3 ■ Future Enlargement of the Euro Zone

Member State	ERM II Entry Date	Planned Date for Euro Adoption
Bulgaria	Not decided	No target date
Czech Republic	Not decided	No target date
Estonia	June 28, 2004	No target date
Hungary	Not decided	No target date
Latvia	May 2, 2005	No target date
Lithuania	January 24, 2004	No target date
Poland	Not decided	No target date
Romania	Not decided	January 1, 2014

Source: European Commission, "Future Enlargement of the Euro Area," http://ec.europa.eu/economy_finance/
the_euro/joining_euro9413_en.htm

banks of the EU states and the ECB (Figure 9.1). It is important to note that the national central banks (NCBs) are not restricted to those states that have joined the EMU at the present time. The inclusion of the entire membership highlights the end goal of having everyone in the euro zone.

The two major bodies of the ECB are the Executive Board and the Governing Council. The Executive Board has a president, a vice president, and four members, each appointed to eight-year nonrenewable terms. The first president of the ECB was Willem Duisenberg, who served as president of the EMI in 1997–2003. The current president is Jean-Claude Trichet, who was previously the governor of the Bank of France. The Governing Council includes the Executive Board and the governors of the central banks of the euro-zone states. Decisions of

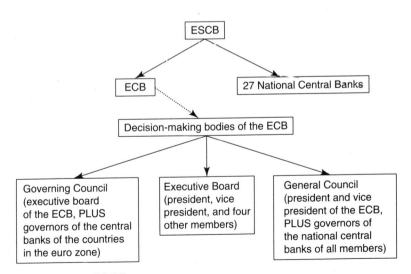

Figure 9.1 ■ The ESCB

Source: "Organization of the ECB," http://www.ecb.int.

the ECB are by simple majority. Once all the member states join the euro zone, the third institution, the General Council, will cease to exist. These are the main responsibilities of the Governing Council:

1. To adopt the guidelines and make the decisions necessary to ensure the performance of the tasks entrusted to the Eurosystem;
2. To formulate the monetary policy of the EC, including, as appropriate, decisions relating to intermediate monetary objectives, key interest rates, and the supply of reserves in the Eurosystem; and
3. To establish the necessary guidelines for their implementation.[39]

The set capital account of the ECB is €5.7 billion. The national central banks of the EU countries are solely responsible for this subscription and are holders of this capital. The respective contribution of each national central bank is based on a key established on the basis of the member's respective share in the GDP and population of the EU (Table 9.4). At present, the 16 euro-zone countries have contributed a total of €4.004 billion, and the EU's 11 non-euro-area NCBs are required to contribute to the operational costs incurred by the ECB in relation to their participation in the ESCB by paying a minimal percentage of their subscribed capital.

The ECB is similar to the German Bundesbank and the U.S. Federal Reserve in its structure, but it is more decentralized. The Bundesbank's council of 17 members includes 9 Landesbank presidents, who have less autonomy than ECB's central bank governors. The U.S. Federal Reserve, on the other hand, has a 12-member open-market committee made up of 7 members of the board of governors and 5 representatives selected from the Federal Reserve Banks.[40]

It is incorrect to assume that the ECB escapes any political oversight. ECOFIN and the Monetary Committee of the European Parliament carefully observe the decisions of the ECB.[41] The president of the ECB presents an annual report to ECOFIN outlining the overall monetary policies and their outcomes, including projections, for the EU. The Parliament, on the other hand, uses the Monetary Committee to request hearings on the activities of the ECB. This committee's operating procedures resemble those the U.S. Senate uses for committee hearings.[42] Finally, while individual member governments cannot influence ECB policies, they can affect future policy orientation of the ECB through the appointment of the bank officials.

THE €

The euro came into existence on January 1, 1999, as the accounting currency of the EU. It replaced the former ecu on a one-to-one basis. From then on, the value of the euro against the U.S. dollar and all other currencies has fluctuated according to market conditions. This new currency became the legal tender in all participating member states on January 1, 2002, by replacing their respective national currencies.

As the new single currency of the EU, the euro has important domestic and international implications. In addition to the domestic implications of a single currency, the new euro zone accounts for 21 percent of the world's GDP. This is much larger than the 4-percent share held by the largest EU member state, Germany. While the combined share of the 15 is less than that of the United States, which is about 36 percent of world GDP, it is more than twice as large as the Japanese share. Internationally, the euro has become one of the key investment currencies, despite the decline in the euro's value against the dollar since 1999. When the euro was first introduced, its exchange rate value against the U.S. dollar was 1.32. Over the last few years, the €-$ exchange rate displayed volatility, with a sharp decline in the value of the euro until July

Table 9.4 ■ **Central Bank's Shares in the ECB (January 2, 2007)**

Central Banks	Key for Subscription to the ECB's capital (%)		Subscribed Share of Capital (EUR)	Paid-up Capital (EUR)
	From 1 May 2004	From 1 January 2007	From 1 January 2007	From 1 January 2007
Nationale Bank van België/Banque Nationale de Belgique	2.5502	2.4708	142,334,199.56	142,334,199.56
Deutsche Bundesbank	21.1364	20.5211	1,182,149,240.19	1,182,149,240.19
Central Bank and Financial Services Authority of Ireland	0.9219	0.8885	51,183,396.60	51,183,396.60
Bank of Greece	1.8974	1.8168	104,659,532.85	104,659,532.85
Banco de España	7.7758	7.5498	434,917,735.09	434,917,735.09
Banque de France	14.8712	14.3875	828,813,864.42	828,813,864.42
Banca d'Italia	13.0516	12.5297	721,792,464.09	721,792,464.09
Banque Centrale du Luxembourg	0.1568	0.1575	9,073,027.53	9,073,027.53
De Nederlandsche Bank	3.9955	3.8937	224,302,522.60	224,302,522.60
Oesterreichische National Bank	2.08	2.0159	116,128,991.78	116,128,991.78
Banco de Portugal	1.7653	1.7137	98,720,300.22	98,720,300.22
Banka Slovenije	–	0.3194	18,399,523.77	18,399,523.77
Suomen Pankki—Finlands Bank	1.2887	1.2448	71,708,601.11	71,708,601.11
Národná Banka Slovenska	0.7147	0.6765	38,970,813.50	38,970,813.50
Subtotal for the Group of Euro Area NCBs	71.4908	69.5092	4,043,154.213.04	4,043,154.213.04
Česká národní Banka	1.4584	1.388	79,957,855.35	5,597,049.87
Danmarks National Bank	1.5663	1.5138	87,204,756.07	6,104,332.92
Eesti Pank	0.1784	0.1703	9,810,391.04	686,727.37
Central Bank of Cyprus	0.13	0.1249	7,195,054.85	503,653.84
Latvijas Banka	0.2978	0.2813	16,204,715.21	1,134,330.06

(Continued)

Table 9.4 ■ (Continued)

Central Banks	Key for Subscription to the ECB's capital (%)		Subscribed Share of Capital (EUR) From 1 January 2007	Paid-up Capital (EUR) From 1 January 2007
	From 1 May 2004	From 1 January 2007		
Lietuvos Bankas	0.4425	0.4178	24,068,005.74	1,684,760.40
Magyar Nemzeti Bank	1.3884	1.3141	75,700,733.22	5,299,051.33
Central Bank of Malta	0.0647	0.0622	3,583,125.79	250,818.81
Narodowy Bank Polski	5.138	4.8748	280,820,283.32	19,657,419.83
Banka Slovenije	0.3345	–	–	–
Sveriges Riksbank	2.4133	2.3313	134,298,089.46	9,400,866.26
Bank of England	14.3822	13.9337	802,672,023.82	56,187,041.67
Subtotal for the Previous Group of Non-euro Area NCBs	28.5092	27.0887	1,560,485,847.38	109,234,009.31
Bulgarian National Bank	–	0.8833	50,883,842.67	3,561,868.99
Banca Naţională a României	–	2.5188	145,099,312.72	10,156,951.89
Subtotal for the New Non-euro Area NCBs	0	3.4021	157,012,341.18	13,718,820.88
Total	100	100	5760652403	4,127,136,230.00

Source: European Central Bank, Directorate Communications Press and Information Division Kaiserstrasse 29, D-60311 Frankfurt am Main, http://www.ecb.europa.eu

2002 and then a steady gain against the dollar. Figure 9.2 shows the €–$ (euro–U.S.dollar) exchange rate during the last two years.

Since its introduction, the euro has become an attractive international currency for financial markets and reserve currency for central banks. The size of the euro-zone economy, its openness to free trade, and ECB's commitment to monetary stability promoted euro's attraction to international financial markets. Today, the euro is used in a variety of financial instruments alongside the U.S. dollar. In international debt markets, the share of euro-denominated debt was 31.4 percent at the end of 2006, compared to 44.1 percent for the U.S. dollar. In the area of international loans and deposit markets, the ratio was 36.3 percent for the euro and 44.8 percent for the dollar. In foreign exchange markets, the euro became the second most actively traded currency in January 2007 and accounted for 37 percent of transactions (both sides of transactions are counted and the total shares add up to 200 percent in FX markets). The U.S. dollar's share was 86.5 percent.[43] A similar attraction for the euro is also found in the reserve currency domain.

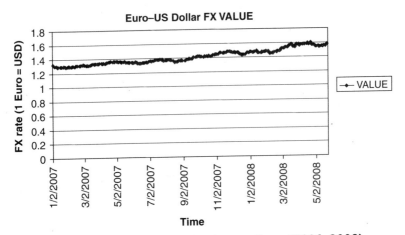

Figure 9.2 ■ The Euro–US Dollar Exchange Rate (2006–2008)

Source: Calculated from FX data from the New York Federal Reserve Bank, http://www.ny.frb.org/markets/fxrates/historical/fx.cfm.

Menzie Chinn and Jeffrey Frankel estimate that the euro and U.S. dollar will reach parity as reserve currency during 2020–2025, with the euro overtaking the dollar thereafter.[44] The euro's share in global foreign exchange reserves was over 25 percent in mid-2007 and close to 29 percent in developing countries.[45]

THE STABILITY AND GROWTH PACT: TOWARD CLOSER ECONOMIC POLICY COORDINATION

With the EMU attained among euro-zone countries, fiscal and monetary policy coordination became essential for stable economic growth in the EU. As the ESCB sets guidelines for monetary policy for the whole of the euro area through interest rates, fiscal policies need to be coordinated among the member states, just as these countries coordinated the EMU target rates during the second and third stages of the Delors Plan. Otherwise, macroeconomic imbalances are likely to emerge between the member economies. This means that with monetary policy surrendered to the ECB, governments have only fiscal policy to rely on when they need to stimulate their economies. Thus, in order to ensure stable economic growth, EU member states signed the Stability and Growth Pact at the Amsterdam European Council in June 1997 as a future commitment to fiscal discipline previously accepted under the EMU convergence criteria.

The Stability and Growth Pact is an agreement among all the member states that requires adherence to specific fiscal and budgetary disciplines as a part of their medium-term economic objectives. The pact has two main rules: (1) a budget in balance or in surplus in the medium term and (2) no budget deficit over 3 percent of GDP.[46] Failure to attain these targets could result in penalties imposed by the Commission equal to 0.5 percent of GDP and/or denied access to the EU's cohesion funds. The fine imposed is in the form of a required non-interest-bearing deposit. This deposit would become a fine after two years, and thus "lost" for that member state, only if the offending member state has not corrected its excessive deficit (a budget deficit of more than 3 percent of GDP) within the two-year period. The architects of the pact, most of them German, argued that the euro's credibility might be tarnished by fiscal negligence among its members. If member states' governments run fiscal deficits resulting in unsustainable borrowing, the NCBs of these countries will be forced to bail them out, thus further inflating the real value of their debts. Such bailouts are not permitted in the euro-zone area, and the pact forces the member governments to adhere to strict fiscal discipline to complement the ECB's position on monetary policy discipline.

Regardless of its merits, the Stability and Growth Pact was bound to run into problems with member states' fiscal challenges. Portugal became the first country to break the rules by running a budget deficit in 2001 of 3.9–4.1 percent of GDP.[47] This was particularly critical for Portugal, since it was one of the four poorer members of the EU that received cohesion funds. If the Commission were to impose the fines of the pact, Portugal stood to lose €6 billion over the next six years, which might have further deepened this country's budget deficit. However, the impact of Portugal's deficit on the euro, in the form of a run on currency, was very slim, given its size as a small partner in the currency zone. The Portuguese problem passed as the government managed to eliminate its fiscal deficit. But soon after, other, more serious challenges emerged on the scene.

France, Germany, Italy, and Portugal (once again) became the next candidates to violate the target set for budget deficit. Among them, France and Germany, being the two largest economies of the euro zone, engineered the suspension of the pact in November 2003, after it became apparent that they would break the rules for a third successive year in 2004. This was not an easy outcome. Initially, the Commission made it clear that member states had to abide by the Stability and Growth Pact and proposed to force France and Germany to make budget cuts in November 2003. The Council of Ministers subsequently overruled it and decided instead to suspend the pact. Member states that had worked hard to remedy their own finances—Austria, the Netherlands, Finland, and Spain—voted against the Council's decision, arguing that letting Berlin and Paris off the hook would be the death warrant of the rules. The Commission responded by saying that the Council had no power to do this and took the matter to the European Court of Justice (ECJ).[48] The ECJ ruled on July 13, 2004, that the Council had no power to suspend the Stability and Growth Pact.

The ECJ's verdict represented a tactical victory for the European Commission, which had feared that its authority would be undermined if the Council of Ministers was allowed to bypass the Commission and set its own agenda without reprimands. The ECJ noted that "responsibility for making the member states observe budgetary discipline lies essentially with the Council of Ministers from the EU governments. But it said once a disciplinary procedure has been implemented and the ministers have adopted recommendations for a country to correct its deficit problem, the ministers cannot modify them without being prompted again by the Commission, which has a right of initiative."[49] With this issue behind them, EU member states met in Brussels in March 2005 to review the pact. They agreed that governments would be able to run a budget deficit at more than 3 percent of GDP only in special circumstances and for a limited period. The ECB has, however, expressed concern that the changes could undermine confidence in European public finances.[50]

CONCLUSIONS

EMU represents the most important aspect of regional integration in Europe. Its growth from a relatively modest EMS to a complete union with a single currency and single system of central bank is a remarkable success story that many around the world thought would not be possible. Even with its 16-member participation, the euro-zone is the largest of its kind. Relative success of the EMU in a short time period is indicative of a promising future for the EU when more member states join the euro -zone. At last, a zone of monetary stability in Europe looks to be a reachable goal. Its future success will depend on member states' commitment to fiscal responsibility and their willingness to proceed ahead with political union of some form to complement EMU. As history shows, monetary unions of large sovereign states that do not have political union carry with them the dangers of failure—even after a long period of time. This is one of the reasons behind *political union* outlined in the Maastricht Treaty, but its specifics have been left for future leaders of the EU to figure out. This explains, in part, the determination of EU leaders to push ahead with further political reform of the Union following the failed constitution. As Commission President Jose Barroso's economic advisor Professor Paul de Grauwe, argues "[w]ithout further political integration one can predict with great confidence that the European Monetary Union will not last."[51]

STUDY QUESTIONS

1. What is EMU?
2. How does EMU work?
3. What are some of the main reasons behind EU's push for an EMU?
4. Provide an assessment of EMU from neofunctionalist and intergovernmentalist perspectives.

5. What are the benefits and challenges of EMU?
6. What major factors led to the crisis of EMS in 1992 and how did EU leaders manage to overcome these problems and achieve the successful formation of the EMU?

ENDNOTES

1. For a detailed discussion of the Werner plan, see John Pinder, *European Community: The Building of a Union* (Oxford: Oxford University Press, 1991), pp. 119–121.

2. Miltiades Chacholiades, *International Economics* (New York: McGraw-Hill, 1989), p. 225.

3. Stephen George, *Politics and Policy in the European Community*, 2nd ed. (London: Oxford University Press, 1991), p. 174; Pinder, *European Community*, pp. 119–124.

4. Pinder, *European Community*, p. 176.

5. George, *Politics and Policy in the European Community*, 2nd ed., p. 176.

6. Dennis Swann, *The Economics of the Common Market* (London: Penguin Books, 1992), pp. 202–203.

7. Neil Thygesen, "The Emerging European Monetary System: A View from Germany," in R. Triffen, ed., *EMS—The Emerging European Monetary System*. Offprint from *Bulletin of the National Bank of Belgium*, 50, no. 1 (1979).

8. Francesco Giavazzi and Alberto Giovannini, *Limiting Exchange Rate Flexibility: The European Monetary System* (Cambridge: MIT Press, 1989), p. 26.

9. For a detailed description of the EMS, see Michele Fratianni and Jürgen von Hagen, *The European Monetary System and European Monetary Union* (Boulder, Colo.: Westview Press, 1992); and Giavazzi and Giovannini, *Limiting Exchange Rate Flexibility*.

10. David M. Wood, Birol A. Yesilada, and Beth Robedeau, "Windows of Opportunity: When EC Agendas Are Set and Why," paper presented at the Third Biennial International Conference of the European Community Studies Association in Washington, D.C., May 27–29, 1993, p. 11. Following three realignments of exchange rates inside the ERM in November 1992, the new ecu central rates (in units of national currencies per ecu) were as follows: Belgian franc, 40.6304; Danish crown, 7.51410; DM 1.96992; Spanish peseta, 143.386; French franc, 6.60683; Irish punt, 0.735334; Luxembourg franc, 40.6304; Dutch guilder, 2.21958; Portuguese escudo, 182.194; Italian lira, 1,690.76; British pound, 0.805748; and Greek drachma, 254.254. These central rates establish a parity grid of bilateral exchange rates between the national currencies.

11. Michael J. Artis and Mark Taylor, "Exchange Rates, Interest Rates, Capital Controls and the European Monetary System: Assessing the Track Record," in Francesco Giavazzi, Stefano Micossi, and Marcus Miller, eds., *The European Monetary System* (Cambridge: Cambridge University Press, 1988), p. 187.

12. For a detailed analysis, see Birol A. Yesilada and David M. Wood, "Learning to Cope with Global Turbulence: The Role of EMS in European Integration," paper presented at the Annual Meeting of the Midwest Political Science Association, Chicago, April 18–20, 1991.

13. Dennis Swann, *Economics of the Common Market*, p. 216.

14. The Delors report as cited in EC Commission, *Report on Economic and Monetary Union in the European Community* (Luxembourg: Office for Official Publications of the European Communities, 1988).

15. According to Stephen George, Sir Geoffrey Howe, then foreign secretary, said that the Madrid

conditions were adopted by the prime minister only after both he and Chancellor of the Exchequer Nigel Lawson threatened to resign unless they were adopted. See George, *Politics and Policy in the European Community*, 2nd ed., p. 183.

16. "Maastricht at a Glance," *The Economist*, October 17, 1992, pp. 60–61.

17. Pinder, *European Community*, p. 139.

18. Wayne Sandholtz, "Choosing Union: Monetary Politics and Maastricht," *International Organization* 47 (Winter 1993): 32–33.

19. Ibid., p. 20.

20. Ibid., p. 38.

21. European Communities, *European Economy: One Market, One Money* (Brussels: Official Publications of the European Communities, 1990), p. 50.

22. Pinder, *European Community*, p. 140.

23. Martin Feldstein, "The Case Against EMU," *The Economist*, June 13, 1992, pp. 19–22.

24. George Zis, "European Monetary Union: The Case for Complete Monetary Integration," in Frank McDonald and Stephen Dearden, eds., *European Economic Integration* (London and New York: Longman, 1992), p. 45.

25. David Cameron, "British Exit, German Voice, French Loyalty: Defection, Domination, and Cooperation in the 1992–93 ERM Crisis," paper presented at the Third International Conference of the European Studies Association, Washington, D.C., May 27–29, 1993, p. 5.

26. "Shooting the Messengers," *The Economist*, August 7, 1993, p. 23.

27. "The Monetary Tragedy of Errors That Led to Currency Chaos," *Financial Times*, December 11, 1993, p. 2.

28. Ibid.

29. Ibid.

30. David Smith, "Ministers Promise to Defend ERM Rates," *Sunday Times* (London), September 6, 1992, Section 3, p. 8.

31. "Currency Crisis Spurs EC to Widen EMS Bands of Fluctuation," *Eurecom* 5.8 (September 1993): 1.

32. Larry Neil, "An American Perspective on the Euro," in Dean J. Kotlowski, ed., *The European Union* (Athens: Ohio University Press, 2000), p. 165.

33. Samuel Brittan, "Black Wednesday's Cost," *Financial Times*, November 30, 1992, p. 18.

34. Ibid.

35. "Fluctuations in the Balance," *Financial Times*, December 15, 1993, p. 13.

36. Ibid.

37. "EMU Moves Forward," *Eurecom* 5 (November 1993): 3.

38. "Denmark Rejects Euro, Holds on to Identity," *The Oregonian*, September 30, 2000, p. D2.

39. "About the ECB," 2000, p. 1, http://www.ecb.int [click on "About ECB"]

40. "Survey: EMU—Nuts and Bolts," *The Economist*, April 11, 1998, pp. 10–14.

41. Simon Hix, *The Political System of the European Union* (New York: St. Martin's Press, 1999), p. 298.

42. Ibid.

43. European Commission, "Economy and Finance: The Euro," http://ec.europa.eu/economy_finance/the_euro/the_euro6484_en.htm. and http://ec.europa.eu/economy_finance/the_euro/euro_in_world9373_en.htm

44. Menzie Chinn and Jeffrey A. Frenkel, "Will the Euro Eventually Surpass the Dollar as Leading International Reserve Currency?" in Richard Clarida, ed., *G7 Current Account Imbalances: Sustainability and Adjustment* (National Bureau of Economic Research Conference Report, 2007), pp. 283–322.

45. http://ec.europa.eu/economy_finance/the_euro/euro_in_world9373_en.htm

46. George Parker, Peter Weis, and Haig Simonian, "Berlin and Paris May Put Stability Pact to Test," *Financial Times*, July 27/28, 2002, p. 4.

47. Ibid. "Too Much Red Ink for the Euro-Zone," *The Economist*, July 6–12, 2002, p. 47.

48. "Government by Judges?" *The Economist*, January 15, 2004.

49. "Court Annuls EU Stability Pact Suspension," *Deutsche Welle*, July 13, 2004.

50. George Parker, "Sweeping Rewrite of EU Stability Pact Agreed," *Financial Times*, March 20, 2005, p. 2.

51. Paul de Grauwe, in an interview with Belgian daily, *De Morgen* (March 18, 2006) reprinted at Free Europe, http://www.free-europe.org/blog/?itemid=316

10

The EU Budget, Common Agricultural Policy, and Cohesion Policies

This chapter will examine the politics of the European Union (EU) budget, its Common Agricultural Policy (CAP), and its cohesion policies—all of which aim to promote economic and social cohesion by reducing disparities between different regions of the EU. These goals are an integral part of Europeans' belief in the social welfare state. The main emphasis is to transfer resources from the more developed regions of the EU to those lagging behind in order to improve the standard of living in those areas and promote economic growth that will make the EU a global competitor, as set out in the Lisbon strategy (see Chapter 6). This strategy seeks to tackle the EU's urgent need for higher economic growth and job creation and greater competitiveness in world markets. Thus, the CAP and cohesion policies are essential for completion of the Lisbon strategy. We will first discuss the budget process and examine the politics involved in "who gets what, when, how?" Discussion of the largest budget item, the CAP, follows. Next, we look at other cohesion policies aimed at reducing economic and social disparities between richer and poorer regions in the EU, including an analysis of industrial and environmental policies that have consequences for and are affected by cohesion policies. Finally, we discuss the future of cohesion policies in the 2007–2013 budget cycle.

THE POLITICS OF THE EU BUDGET

The EU budget funds policies and expenditures of all the EU institutions. The budget covers a seven-year period and cannot be in deficit. Its size is determined by agreement of all the member states. The sources of the budget fall into two categories labeled "own sources" and "other revenue." Own sources include revenue accruing automatically from import duties, agricultural duties, sugar levies, VAT, and gross national income (GNI) contribution based on GNI from the member states. The total amount of own resources cannot exceed 1.24 percent of the GNI of the EU, but can be below this figure, as will be discussed below in the section on the politics of the current budget. Other revenue includes tax and other deductions from staff remunerations, bank interests, and contributions from nonmember countries to certain EU programs. The spending is voted by the European Parliament and the Council, on a Commission proposal. Finally, the European Parliament signs the agreed budget into law.

The procedure for adopting the annual expenditures of the EU also requires codecision among the Commission, the Council, and the Parliament. For each coming year, the European Commission prepares a preliminary draft budget and submits it to the Council in April or early May. The budgetary authority, composed of the Council and the Parliament, amends and adopts the draft budget. First, the Council has the preliminary draft budget examined by the budgetary committee and then by the Committee of Permanent Representatives (COREPER). The draft budget must be adopted by qualified majority in July of every year. The draft budget then goes to the Parliament in October for first reading. If the Parliament decides to amend the draft budget, such amendment requires an absolute majority of votes ($n = 393$). The amended budget goes back to the Council for a review, following a conciliation meeting with a delegation from the Parliament. At this point, the Council can change the draft budget to take account of amendments or proposed modifications voted by the Parliament in its first reading. It may also choose not to accept the amendments proposed by the Parliament. As a rule, the Council has the last word on the budget concerning the original draft, the Council's earlier position, and the proposed amendments of the Parliament. However, the entire budget can be rejected by the Parliament at the end, and if this happens, a temporary budget spending procedure comes into effect until a compromise can be achieved. In case there is disagreement between the two institutions before the end of the year or the Parliament rejects the draft, a system of provisional twelfths (monthly spending) applies until they reach an agreement. When this provision applies, payments may be made monthly up to a limit of one-twelfth of the appropriations entered in the budget of the previous financial year.[1] Once the budget is accepted, it is still possible to amend it in the event of unforeseen circumstances following a Commission proposal for the other two institutions to act upon. Politics of budget has always been a contested and politically highly charged affair. The most recent episode in reaching an agreement over the 2007–2013 budget proved no different.

As explained in Chapter 4, contributions to and receipts from the EU budget almost resulted in another empty-chair crisis, as Britain demanded a more egalitarian burdensharing among the member states. The outcome of these discussions at the Fontainebleau summit in 1984 was the British rebate, which gave back Britain part of her contribution to the EU budget. This was a fair deal because at the time Britain was the third poorest member of the European Community (EC). Basically, the rebate is a two-thirds reduction in Britain's net contribution to the budget, which, in turn, is funded by other member states. Figure 10.1 shows funding of the British rebate in 2004.

During the British presidency of the EU in 2005, this rebate once again became an issue of debate among the member states as Prime Minister Tony Blair proposed a new EU budget for 2007–2013. There has been growing pressure among the member states for the elimination of the British rebate, since Britain could no longer be considered one of the poorest members of the EU. Blair agreed that in principle this was a necessary move, but linked the rebate issue to further farm subsidy reform and member states' higher contributions to help pay for the cost of EU's eastern enlargement.[2]

The British proposal drew criticism from member states, as well as from EU Budget Commissioner Dalia Grybauskaite, who stated, "[The proposal] would lead to a politically short-sighted budget creating a two-speed system, which will divide Europe even more."[3] Hungarian Prime Minister Ferenc Gyurcsany called the proposed cuts to regional funds unacceptable. This sentiment was echoed in the capitals of the Czech Republic, France, Slovakia,

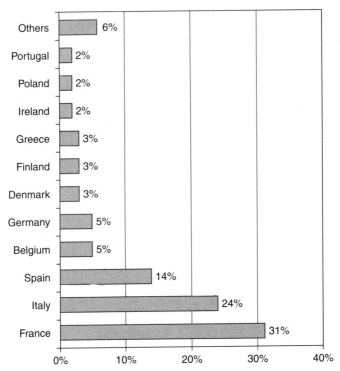

Figure 10.1 ■ Funding for British Rebate, 2004

Source: Based on European Commission data.

and Poland. The French government particularly opposed further cuts in CAP payments that would be part of future farm subsidies. As it seemed likely that the future of the budget would roll over into Austria's presidency during the first half of 2006, a last-minute deal broke the budget deadlock at the Brussels summit on December 17, 2005. The dealmaker at these discussions was the new German Chancellor Angela Merkel, who helped broker a Franco-British agreement over a final €10.5 billion cut in the British rebate. The French had asked for a €14 billion cut and wanted to win an agreement from other EU leaders to reduce VAT in French restaurants from 19.6 percent to 5.5 percent, which President Chirac had promised to French voters in his 2002 election campaign. Merkel persuaded both the British and the French leaders to reach a compromise on Britain's rebate reduction, while maintaining French restaurant VAT at the existing level and securing a modest increase in the overall budget. The compromise can be summarized as follows: The United Kingdom initially proposed 1.03 percent GNI, Luxembourg had earlier proposed 1.06 percent GNI, and the final deal that came from Germany was 1.045 percent GNI. This amounts to €862.36 billion over the next seven years. The UK gave up €10.5 billion of its rebate, which is equivalent to a 20 percent reduction, and, in return, got an agreement from other member states to review EU spending in 2008–2009 in hopes that this would lead to cuts in farm spending.[4] Following this agreement, parties moved ahead and adopted a new budget for the 2007–2013 period. Table 10.1 provides detailed annual line item figures on the EU budget for 2007–2013 and Figure 10.2 shows proportional allocation of funds for the overall budget period.

Table 10.1 ■ Financial Framework for 2007–2013 (billions of €)

Appropriations of Commitments	2007	2008	2009	2010	2011	2012	2013	Total
1. Sustainable Growth	**54,405**	**57,275**	**59,700**	**61,782**	**63,614**	**66,604**	**69,621**	**433,001**
Competitiveness	8,918	10,386	11,272	12,388	12,987	14,203	15,433	85,587
Cohesion	45,487	46,889	48,428	49,394	50,627	52,401	54,188	347,414
2. Preservation and Management of Natural Resources	**58,351**	**58,800**	**59,252**	**59,726**	**60,191**	**60,663**	**61,142**	**418,125**
Market-related expenditure and direct payments	45,759	46,217	46,679	47,146	47,617	48,093	48,574	330,085
3. Citizenship, Freedom, Security, and Justice	**1,273**	**1,362**	**1,523**	**1,693**	**1,889**	**2,105**	**2,376**	**12,221**
Freedom, security, and justice	637	747	872	1,025	1,206	1,406	1,661	7,554
Citizenship	636	615	651	668	683	699	715	4,667
4. EU as a Global Partner	**6,578**	**7,002**	**7,440**	**7,893**	**8,430**	**8,997**	**9,595**	**55,935**
5. Administration	**7,039**	**7,380**	**7,699**	**8,008**	**8,334**	**8,670**	**9,095**	**56,225**
6. Compensation	**445**	**207**	**210**					**862**
Total Commitments Appropriations	**126,491**	**13,2026**	**135,824**	**139,102**	**142,458**	**147,039**	**151,829**	**974,769**
As percent of gross national income	1.06%	1.06%	1.05%	1.03%	1.01%	1.00%	1.00%	1.03%
Total Payments Appropriations	**122,190**	**129,681**	**123,858**	**133,505**	**133,452**	**140,200**	**142,408**	**925,294**
As percent of gross national income	1.02%	1.04%	0.95%	0.99%	0.95%	0.96%	0.94%	0.98%
Margin Available	**0.22%**	**0.20%**	**0.29%**	**0.25%**	**0.29%**	**0.28%**	**0.30%**	**0.26%**
Own resources ceiling as percent of gross national income	1.24%	1.24%	1.24%	1.24%	1.24%	1.24%	1.24%	1.24%

figures in millions of € at current prices

Source: European Commission, *General Budget of the European Union for the Financial Year 2008* (Brussels: Commission of the European Commission Publications, 2008), p. 7.

In 2008, the largest share of the EU budget (45 percent) was allocated to boost economic growth and greater cohesion among the EU27. As a single-area item, agriculture still represents the largest expenditure, as it has been over the last three decades. In 2008, its share of the budget remains over 40 percent.[5]

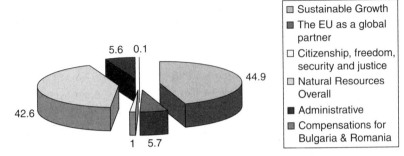

Figure 10.2 ■ The 2007–2013 Budget Key Points

Source: From data in European Commission, *General Budget of the European Union for the Financial Year 2008.* (Brussels: Commission of the European Commission Publications, 2008), p. 7.

THE CAP

Common Agricultural Policy (CAP) is the most controversial of all EU policies. From the signing of the Rome Treaty until the CAP came into effect in 1968, the European Economic Community (EEC) achieved three important objectives. First, it eliminated the national agricultural support systems. Second, it replaced the national systems with a communitywide agricultural support system. And, third, agricultural protection between EEC countries was eliminated and common agricultural prices took effect.[6] The Council of Ministers, following the proposals of the Commission, set annual agricultural support prices. Agricultural policies remain the single most important part of EU's annual budget as this sector represents a crucial dimension of member states' own economies as a support mechanism for farmers (see Map 10.1 for agriculture in EU member states).

Evolution of CAP

The evolution of the CAP was a difficult process. Every year the Council of Ministers held a series of marathon meetings during which package deals were reached on EEC regulations for different products. For example, in December 1961, a marathon meeting resulted in common policies on grains, eggs, poultry and pig products, fruit and vegetables, and wine. In addition, the ministers agreed on general principles regarding the financing of these policies.[7] Other marathon sessions in December 1963 and December 1964 resulted in regulations on milk and dairy products, beef and veal, rice, fats, and grains.[8]

The CAP adopted by the EEC was a unique system known as the variable levy (*prélèvement*). The basic idea was quite simple. The Council of Ministers determined in advance the desired internal price of each agricultural product. This was the support price, known as the target price (*prix indicatif*). It also estimated expected domestic production and consumption of these products. Then the EU imposed a variable levy on non-EU farm products equal to the difference between the lowest world market price and the EU target price. When there was a change in the world market price, the variable levy was adjusted accordingly. In effect, the variable levy shifted the burden of adjustment to variations in EU consumption and production onto third-country providers, thus discouraging the other countries from subsidizing their exports. Other support policies in the CAP include export subsidies, supplementary and fixed-rate aid, and structural aid to farmers. Export subsidies make up the difference between intra-EU prices and world market prices and enable European farmers to compete in international markets. By the early 1980s, export subsidies accounted for about half of all CAP spending. The supplementary and fixed-rate aid, on the other hand, applies to only a handful of commodities for which support

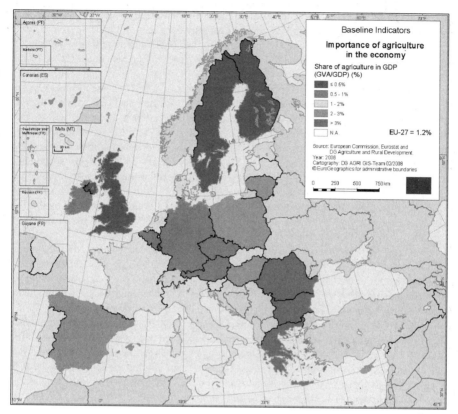

Map 10.1 ■ Agriculture in the EU Member States

Source: European Commission, http://ec.europa.eu/agriculture/agrista/2007/table_en/2012s7M.pdf.

prices remained low (e.g., durum wheat, olive oil, tobacco, and oilseeds). In these cases, the farmers receive direct payments in proportion to their output. Finally, structural aid refers to payments toward farm modernization and improved productivity.

It is important to note that the EEC introduced the CAP payments program during a time of fixed exchange rates. Since the collapse of the fixed exchange rate system in 1972, the CAP financing has faced difficult problems, which forced the use of "green money," a set of special exchange rates that the Commission uses to convert common farm prices into national currencies through a mechanism known as the mandatory compensatory accounts (MCAs).

Following the adoption of the CAP, the Commission introduced a memorandum titled Agriculture 1980, which became known as the Mansholt plan, named after Commissioner Sicco Mansholt, in December 1968.[9] This plan called for restructuring agriculture by encouraging small farmers to leave the land and giving financial assistance for the amalgamation of holdings. The incentives included grants, pensions to farmers over the age of 55, and assistance to younger farmers in finding new careers. However, there was one other point of this plan that created problems with the French and West German farmers. This was the proposal to cut price levels so that inefficient farmers would be forced to leave agriculture.[10] The only supporter of this plan was Britain, which was in the process of applying for a membership in the EC at the time. However, the British government was not eager to make reform of the CAP a condition for the UK's entry into the EC. The result of the growing opposition to this plan in France and West Germany was three years of discussion in the Council of Ministers. When the final decision came in April 1972, the EC revised the Mansholt plan: It provided only for a modest financing of loans to the farmers, early-retirement incentives, and assistance for information and training to increase efficiency. The budget for price support did increase every year, but its component for "guidance" remained rather small.

During the 1980s, additional reform of the CAP occurred. In 1984, the member countries agreed on a system of quotas for dairy products, supports for which had been very costly to the EC budget. During this time, the CAP accounted for about 64 percent of the EC budget. Other reforms included phasing out the MCAs by 1988 and controlling future expenditures on agricultural subsidies and other support mechanisms.[11] The dairy sector reforms were followed by a more serious attack on other sectors. In 1985, the Council of Ministers agreed on a general price package that restricted agricultural price increases to a figure below the EU's inflation rate.

Reform then moved into the beef sector when the EC decided to modify beef support arrangements in 1986. Previously, the EC's intervention price in this sector acted as the floor price. The reforms changed this practice by specifying when support buying would take place. Accordingly, the EU would engage in support buying when (1) the average market price in the EC was 90 percent of the intervention price and (2) the price in the target country was 87 percent of the intervention price.[12] All in all, this meant a 17 percent decline in price. Yet, despite these measures, the cost of the CAP increased by an average of 18 percent per year between 1985 and 1987. One new problem area was cereals, which witnessed a substantial increase in production because of new technological advances, coupled with a decline in world market prices.

The problem proved to be a major cause for concern. In 1986, Jacques Delors announced that the EC was running out of funds and expected an estimated budgetary shortfall of 4–5 billion ecus in 1987. The expansion of the EC to include agricultural countries like Portugal and Spain further complicated this problem. Thus, additional sources of funding seemed to be in order, but not all members agreed to this. The Netherlands and the UK demanded strong limitations on agricultural production. The UK went so far as to indicate that it would not agree to more funds until this issue was seriously addressed. Following intense debates, the European Council accepted a series of measures, known as the Delors package, to reform the CAP:

1. Budgetary discipline was to be realized through an agreed-on resources ceiling of 1.2 percent of EC gross national product (GNP) and an expenditure ceiling of 27.5 billion ecus for the European Agricultural Guidance and Guarantee Fund (EAGGF).[13]
2. The increase in agricultural expenditures was to be equal to or less than 74 percent of the EC's GNP growth rate.[14]
3. It was agreed that from 1988 to 1992 the threshold for cereals was to be 160 million tons. Any production beyond this limit would result in price cuts of 3 percent and continue until production fell within the allowed limit.[15]

During the early 1990s, the EU adopted other policies to reform the CAP. These included the MacSharry II plan, named for the proposals made by the agricultural commissioner in 1991, and provisions covered in Agenda 2000. The former called for a significant reduction in support for cereals and the establishment of much of a two-tier EC farm policy that would favor small and medium-size farms.[16] The MacSharry II reforms represented a major step in achieving what the European leaders envisioned in 1968—namely, the development of a smaller and more productive agricultural sector where the EU could better sustain incomes and levels of production, thus eliminating a major budgetary burden. The reforms introduced in 1992, in the form of direct payments to farmers as compensation for cuts in price supports, made the subsidies more transparent. Furthermore, as we noted earlier, the single market reforms called for elimination of

MCAs by the end of 1992. Yet, with the rapid pace of change in the EU during the 1990s (the completion of the single market, the EMU, and more countries joining the EU), additional reform of the CAP became essential. In 1994, the CAP accounted for half of the EU budget, with a 36.5 billion ecu price tag.

A major push for additional reform of the CAP came from Sir Leon Brittan, the EU trade commissioner, who called for a new debate on the future of the CAP based on four academic reports from Britain, France, Germany, and Italy.[17] These reports examined the CAP in light of the EU's decision to expand its membership to include Eastern European countries in the next decade.[18] The reports indicated that adopting the CAP in its present form would seriously hurt consumers in these countries, although the farmers would benefit. Higher farm prices meant increased output in these countries, and therefore more surplus for the EU. These developments would undermine the EU's commitment to abide by General Agreement on Tariffs and Trade (GATT) agreements on agricultural subsidies. Moreover, the long-term cost of this CAP expansion would be around 23–27 billion ecus, a 70 percent rise in the current farm subsidies. Given the urgency of this picture, in 1997 Agriculture Commissioner Franz Fischler presented a comprehensive reform package for the CAP as part of the EU's Agenda 2000.

When the Commission presented these proposals in March 1998, the idea was to transform the CAP from a policy of price support to one of income support.[19] The main aspects of this package included competition without oversubsidizing agricultural products, commitment to a fair standard of living for the agricultural community, production methods that emphasized consumer demand while being sensitive to the environment, diversity in production methods, a simpler agricultural and rural development policy (known as the "second pillar" of the CAP), and a balance between agricultural expenditures and society's expectations from farmers.[20] In order to achieve these aims, the reforms called for further price cuts in the cereals, beef, and dairy sectors; decentralization of management; rationalization of intervention; and increased indirect aid payments to farmers.[21]

Emphasis on the environment and rural development represents a significant shift in CAP orientation. As a result of the reforms, member states must draft regional and national programs from a comprehensive list of measures in which ecological practices are compulsory. These measures include retraining farmers in new practices and supporting less-developed areas of high ecological value, such as forests. In addition, there is support for funding changes in milk and beef production to make them more environmentally friendly. This last point is especially crucial, given the agreement to cut prices in these sectors. Planned reforms will have varying impact on member states because of their respective shares in EU agriculture.

Another Review of CAP

In accordance with treaty requirements, the Commission carried out a midterm review (MTR) of the CAP in early 2002 and issued far-reaching recommendations for further reforms in light of pending enlargement of the EU.[22] The report stated that public expenditures for the farm sector had to be better justified and yield more in return in such policy areas as food quality, preservation of the environment and animal welfare, environmental landscape, cultural heritage of rural regions, and enhancement of social balance and equity. To achieve these goals, the report proposed

1. Cutting the link between production and farm payments;
2. Making those payments conditional on meeting environmental, food safety, animal welfare, and occupational safety standards;
3. Increasing EU support for rural development;
4. Introducing a new farm audit system; and
5. Introducing rural development measures to increase quality production, food safety, and animal welfare and to cover the cost of farm audits.[23]

The Commission proposed additional measures for specific agricultural commodities in order to strengthen market competitiveness. For example, it called for a final 5 percent cut in the intervention price for cereals, a compensated decrease in the rice intervention price, and further adjustments in the dried fodder, protein crop, and nuts sectors.

Reforms proposed by the Commission were quite modest. They did not eliminate subsidies altogether. Rather, they decoupled subsidies and production and promoted more CAP spending in areas that promote environmentally friendly and rural development projects. Under the new CAP, the rural sector would receive substantial funds to achieve social goals, people working in these areas would be able to stay in the countryside and afford a quality life, and farmers would become greener.

Reforms that the member states agreed to on June 23, 2003, largely followed the guidelines of the Commission's review of the CAP. Under the new CAP, the vast majority of subsidies are paid independently of the volume of production. However, in order to avoid sudden shock to their agriculture sector, member states are permitted to maintain a limited link between subsidy and production under tight oversight of the Commission and linked to the EU's emphasis on respecting environmental, food safety, and animal welfare standards.[24] Key points of the reformed CAP include

1. A single farm payment for EU farmers, independent of production (limited coupled elements may be maintained to avoid abandonment of production);
2. A link between this payment and respect of environmental, food safety, animal and plant health, and animal welfare standards, as well as the requirement to keep all farmland in good agricultural and environmental condition (cross-compliance);
3. A strengthened rural development policy with more EU money, new measures to promote the environment, quality, and animal welfare and to help farmers to meet EU production standards starting in 2005;
4. A reduction in direct payments (modulation) for bigger farms in order to finance the new rural development policy;
5. A mechanism for financial discipline to ensure that the farm budget fixed until 2013 is not overshot; and
6. Revisions to the market policy of the CAP:
   a. Asymmetric price cuts in the milk sector—the intervention price for butter will be reduced by 25 percent over four years, which is an additional price cut of 10 percent compared to Agenda 2000; for skimmed milk powder, a 15 percent reduction over three years, as agreed in Agenda 2000, is retained;
   b. Reduction of the monthly increments in the cereals sector by half; the current intervention price will be maintained;
   c. Reforms in the rice, durum wheat, nuts, starch potatoes, and dried fodder sectors.[25]

The success of these reforms is essential for the Lisbon strategy in a number of ways. First, without a reformed CAP, many rural areas of Europe, which comprise 90 percent of its territory and 50 percent of its population, could face major economic, social, and environmental setbacks. Second, the Lisbon strategy's emphasis on rural development, as part of making the EU the world's most competitive economy, links the CAP's rural development fund (see the following section) with regional and structural funds. In this case, rural development can help, among other things, with improvement in education and training, research and development, and the promotion of innovation and sustainability. And, third, these reforms are exactly in line with what EU citizens would like to see in modern agricultural development. According to a recent survey by the Commission, 66 percent of EU citizens consider the adjustment of the CAP from a system based on production-linked subsidies to one that funds the protection and development of the overall rural economy (as well as providing direct support to farmers) to be a good thing.[26]

Agricultural Spending: Who Gets What?

As of January 2007, the EU started to use a single legal framework for financing CAP spending by creating two new funds under the general EU budget: the European Agricultural Guarantee Fund (EAGF) and the European Agricultural Fund for Rural Development (EAFRD). The EAGF finances refunds for exporting farm produce to non-EU countries, intervention measures to regulate agricultural markets, direct payments to farmers under the CAP, certain informational and promotional measures for farm produce implemented by member states both on the internal EU market and outside it. And, with regard to expenditure managed centrally by the Commission, EAGF financing will cover the Community's financial contribution for specific veterinary measures, veterinary inspections and inspections of foodstuffs and animal feed, animal disease eradication and control programs and plant health measures, promotion of farm produce, either directly by the Commission or via international organizations, measures required by Community legislation to conserve, characterize, collect, and use genetic resources in farming, setting up and running farm accounting information systems, and farm survey systems.[27]

In the second category, the EAFRD generally finances only expenditure managed jointly by the member states and the Commission. These include rural development programs implemented in accordance with the legislation proposed by the Council Regulation (EC) No 1698/2005.[28] The budget commitments for this purpose come in the form of prefinancing, interim payments, and payment of the final balance.

CAP spending by product category in 2004 is shown in Figure 10.3, reflecting priorities that favor traditional products of the original six members of the EEC. Cereals, beef/veal, and dairy products still account for the bulk of CAP funding. However, with the southern enlargements of the 1980s and the recent addition of Central and Eastern European countries, new crops (e.g., cotton, tobacco, olives) are starting to alter the pecking order. France is the largest recipient of CAP payments at 22 percent of the total payment, followed by Spain, Germany and Italy, each receiving between 12 and 15 percent (Figure 10.4). Their subsidies roughly equal their shares of the EU's agricultural output. These countries are followed by the UK (9 percent), Greece (6 percent), and Ireland (4 percent). The new member states began receiving CAP subsidies in 2004, but at only 25 percent of the rate paid to the older member states. Under the new budget, this will change, and Poland, with over 2 million farmers, will become a major contender

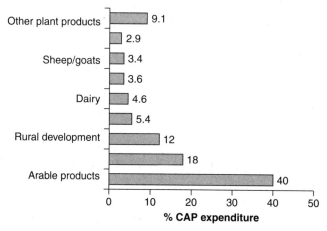

Figure 10.3 ■ CAP Spending by Product Category, 2004 (Before Enlargement)

Source: European Commission data sources.

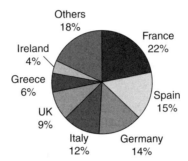

Figure 10.4 ■ CAP Payments as a Percentage of the Total, 2004 (Before Enlargement)

Source: Agricultural commissioner data sources.

for CAP payments. The future of CAP payments is likely to reflect changing agricultural demographics of the EU following the recent enlargement. Figure 10.5 shows the percentages of EU agricultural land accounted for by both older and newer member states. These figures show the significance of Poland in changing the landscape of the EU.

Recent Internal Market Crises in Agriculture

Two very expensive crises—mad cow disease (bovine spongiform encephalopathy) and foot-and-mouth disease—put severe strain on the EU's internal agricultural and trade policies. In each case, the country of origin (Britain) had to kill thousands of farm animals and was prohibited from exporting meat products to other EU countries. While the worst seems to be over, some areas of Britain are still under quarantine by the Commission in order to eradicate the problem.

Mad Cow Disease

Bovine spongiform encephalopathy (BSE) is a disease of the brain in cattle. It first appeared in the UK in 1986. The disease reached epidemic proportions because meat and bone meal produced

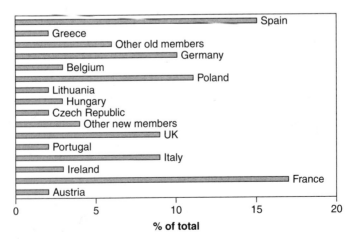

Figure 10.5 ■ Percentage of EU Agricultural Land by Member State

Source: Agricultural commissioner data sources.

from animal carcasses were included in cattle feed. The Commission introduced a worldwide ban on export of British beef in March 1996 amid fears over the threat of BSE. By February 28, 2001, there had been 180,903 cases in the UK and 1,924 cases elsewhere in the EU. If transferred to humans, the disease can be lethal. In response to the outbreak of the disease, the European Commission put in place a comprehensive set of measures to fight BSE:

- A ban on the feeding of mammalian meat and bone meal to cattle, sheep, and goats.
- Higher processing standards for the treatment of animal waste in order to reduce infectivity to a minimum.
- Surveillance measures for the detection, control, and eradication of BSE.
- A requirement to remove specified risk materials (e.g., spinal cord, brain, eyes, tonsils, parts of the intestines) from cattle, sheep, and goats throughout the EU as of October 1, 2000, from the human and animal food chains (also mandatory for imports of meat and meat products from third countries into the EU, except Argentina, Australia, Botswana, Brazil, Chile, Namibia, New Zealand, Nicaragua, Norway, Paraguay, Singapore, Swaziland, and Uruguay).
- The introduction of targeted testing for BSE, with a focus on high-risk animal categories.
- A prohibition on the use of dead animals not fit for human consumption in feed production as of March 1, 2001.[29]

Moreover, in response to the crisis in consumer confidence that followed, the Commission introduced a series of additional measures to combat mad cow disease:

- A ban on the use of ruminant meat and bone meal and certain other animal proteins in feedstuffs for all farm animals, to avoid risks of cross-contamination, at least until the end of June 2001.
- The testing of all cattle over 30 months of age destined for human consumption.
- The extension of the list of specified risk materials to include the entire intestine of bovines and the vertebral column.
- A ban on the use of mechanically recovered meat derived from the bones of cattle, sheep, and goats in feed and food.[30]

To ensure transparency of the implementation of these measures, the Commission's Food and Veterinary Office carries out inspections to verify correct enforcement of Community legislation by member states' relevant authorities and publishes its findings on the Commission's Web site.[31] On May 3, 2006, the European Commission's ban on export of British beef officially ended, meaning that live cattle born after August 1, 1996, can be exported as cab beef from cattle slaughtered after June 15, 2005. This decision brought the UK back into line with other EU countries on beef export.

Foot-and-Mouth Disease

Foot-and-mouth disease is economically the most significant infectious livestock disease. While it is usually a disease of low mortality in animals and has no public health relevance, it has important consequences for animal welfare and production. Clinically diseased animals normally suffer quite seriously, especially animals of highly productive breeds, and there are serious losses of growth and milk production.[32]

Foot-and-mouth disease hit Britain in February 2001 for the first time since 1967. The British government and the Commission immediately took steps to prevent the spread of the disease in the EU. Exports of milk, meat, and livestock products were banned; movement in the countryside was restricted; and farm animals across Europe were burned. However, these measures had limited effect. As new cases were discovered in Britain in March 2001 and subsequent outbreaks occurred in Ireland, France, and the Netherlands, the Commission and the respective national governments decided to widen the application of the measures. Other EU member states took sanitary measures at ports of entry to make sure those who had traveled to Britain had their shoes disinfected prior to entering the respective country. In all, the eradication program has been successful, as well as costly. Over 4 million animals were killed and destroyed.[33]

As for financial assistance to farmers affected by this disease, the Commission provides compensation, up to 60 percent, toward the costs of animals destroyed, disinfection, and so on, under an Emergency Veterinary Fund. An advance of €400 million was provided from the 2001 budget, with €355 million foreseen for the UK, €39 million for the Netherlands, €2 million for Ireland, and €3 million for France. A further €400 million was earmarked for 2002.[34] The total amount paid depends on the receipt and acknowledgment of all requests for compensation and may take years until final settlement.

COHESION POLICIES

Cohesion policies comprise regional policy, some aspects of social policy, and part of the CAP. Regional policy seeks to reduce the gap between the developed and the less-developed regions of the EU. The parts of the social policy relevant for cohesion pertain to combating long-term unemployment and providing vocational education and training. As the most crucial part of cohesion policy, regional policy relies on structural funds to achieve its objectives. The EU's enlargement exacerbated economic disparities across regions of the EU and resulted in reshuffling of distribution between the "old" and "new" *poorer* regions. Under the new budget, member states like Ireland and Spain are called to contribute to the development of poorer regions of central and eastern European states. Before enlargement, the main beneficiaries of Structural Funds were Greece (42.6 percent), Portugal (35.2 percent), Ireland (26.7 percent), east German states (18.9 percent), Mezzogiorno Italy (17.4 percent), and Spain (14.7 percent).[35] In the 2007–2013 budget cycle, cohesion policy accounts for 37.5 percent (€347.4 billion) of the total budget. In the 2007–2013 period, the Cohesion Fund concerns Bulgaria, Cyprus, the Czech Republic, Estonia, Greece, Hungary, Latvia, Lithuania, Malta, Poland, Portugal, Romania, Slovakia, and Slovenia. Spain is eligible for a phase-out fund.

Evolution of the Structural Funds and Regional Objectives

One major accomplishment of the EU during the difficult times of the 1970s was the establishment of the European Regional Development Fund (ERDF) in 1975. This fund originally provided compensation to the UK for the budgetary loss it suffered from participating in the CAP.[36] However, from the day the EEC was established, the Commission worked hard to develop a system by which it could tackle the challenges of the regional problems in the EEC. The Action Program of 1962, the Memorandum on Regional Problems in 1965,[37] and the Memorandum on Regional Policy in 1969 addressed the problems in detail. These proposals recommended the coordination of national policies and EEC policies to overcome regional imbalances and the creation of the ERDF. Of the original members, only Italy, which had its own regional development problem, viewed these proposals favorably. The other two larger members of the EEC, France and West Germany, did not want to provide more funds for the EC budget or surrender more national regional policies to the Commission. The sovereignty issue particularly disturbed the French, and the Germans were feeling the pressures of making large contributions to the CAP.[38] Nevertheless, the UK application for membership in the EU changed the views of these countries about the ERDF. At the Paris summit of the European Council in 1972, the EC leaders announced that a high priority should be given to correcting regional imbalances in the EC, which could otherwise hinder the future development of the Economic and Monetary Union (EMU). Therefore, they agreed to establish the ERDF by the end of 1973. However, internal disagreements delayed the outcome until the Paris summit of December 1974, when the leaders announced the launching of the ERDF with a small budget of 1,300 million European units of account (EUA), which was considerably lower than the Commission's proposal of 2,500 million EUAs.

Since its establishment, the ERDF has operated under five separate sets of rules: 1975–1979, 1980–1984, 1985–1988, rules that became effective after 1989 as a result of the Single European Act (SEA), and changes recommended by Agenda 2000. Initially, the allocation of funds was based on the quotas of the member states, subject to approval by the Council of Ministers. In 1979, the Council amended the structure of the ERDF to allow for a proportion of the fund to be disbursed on a strictly regional basis, separate from the national allocations. This was an important development because it allowed the consideration of region-specific problems without having to deal with national politics.[39] It is important to note that the net impact of the ERDF was greatly hampered by other EC policies, notably the CAP. The CAP was not based on regional needs. Rather, it provided assistance based on productivity and type of product and did not take into account the regional distribution. In this way, the CAP, which had a much bigger budgetary allocation, often worked in the opposite direction of the ERDF, allocating funds to regions less in need of them than others. Nevertheless, significant developments over time resulted in a much-improved ERDF. The first was the expansion of EC membership to include Greece (1981) and Portugal and Spain (1986). And the second was the adoption of the SEA in 1986. Addition of the three Mediterranean countries increased the pool of the countries with large underdeveloped regions: Greece, Ireland, southern Italy, Portugal, Spain, and the northern UK. Finally, it became essential to review cohesion policy and recommend necessary reforms as the EU prepared for expansion eastward (see Agenda 2000 in Chapter 6).

The EU's structural funds initially had five objectives. Following the membership of Austria, Finland, and Sweden, objective 6 was added to the list. However, with the adoption of recommendations made in Agenda 2000, the EU reconfigured these objectives to three.[40] In addition to these objectives, the EU set up separate Community initiatives funded by the structural funds. Between 1994 and 1999, the EU set aside €14 billion to finance such programs as planning and cooperation between border regions; support to labor in job transition and employment opportunities for women; structural changes in regions that traditionally relied on the steel, defense, and coal-mining industries; rural development; small and medium-sized enterprise development; urban renewal; integration of peripheral regions; and promotion of peace in Northern Ireland. Finally, the Cohesion Fund was established in 1994 for purposes of implementing the Maastricht Treaty by assisting poorer members (Greece, Ireland, Portugal, and Spain) in meeting the EMU criteria. In total, this fund had €15 billion available to support projects related to environmental protection and infrastructure.

With the Berlin decision of March 1999 on Agenda 2000, three new objectives replaced the previously mentioned programs under new headings and with an expanded budget. The structural funds had a budget of €213 billion for the period 2000–2006. They targeted financial assistance under three objectives (93 percent of the budget) and four Community initiatives (5.35 percent of the budget).[41] Objective 1, with a budget of €135.9 billion, focused on the development and structural adjustment of regions whose development was lagging behind. The financial assistance for it came from the ERDF, the European Social Fund (ESF), the EAGGF, and the Financial Instrument for Fisheries Guidance. The regions concerned had 22 percent of the total population of the EU living where per capita gross domestic product (GDP) was below 75 percent of the EU average, the Finnish and Swedish regions of the former objective 6, and the most remote areas like the French overseas departments, the Canary Islands, the Azores, and Madeira. Under the new regulations, regions that were eligible for objective 1 during

1994–1999, but lost this entitlement, received transitional assistance. In addition, objective 1 supported two special programs: the Peace Program in Northern Ireland (2000–2004) and an assistance program for certain Swedish regions that met the low population density defined in objective 6 and the Swedish Act of Accession (2000–2006).[42]

Under objective 2, the EU addressed regions that faced structural difficulties in industries, rural areas, urban areas, and areas dependent on fisheries. The funds available in this objective totaled €22.5 billion for the period 2000–2006 and came from the ERDF and the ESF. Industrial areas had to meet three conditions: an unemployment rate above the EU average, a higher percentage of jobs in the industrial sector than the EU average, and a decline in industrial employment. Rural areas had to have a population density of less than 100 individuals per square kilometer or have workers in the agricultural sector at a ratio higher than twice the EU average. A decline in population or an overall unemployment rate higher than the EU average also made rural regions eligible for objective 2 funds. For urban areas, the EU emphasized poverty, unemployment, damaged environment, high crime rate, and low education level.[43] The fisheries' dependence was measured by the percentage of labor employed in this industry and the degree of reduction in its employment.

The main goal of objective 3 was the development of human resources. Its funds totaled €24.05 billion for 2000–2006, allocated from the ESF. Areas of support included policies to combat unemployment, improve access to jobs for those facing social exclusion, establish education and training programs to improve people's chances in getting jobs, and promote equal opportunities for men and women.[44]

THE NEW COHESION POLICY FOR 2007–2013

On July 14, 2004, the Commission adopted a new legislative proposal on how to reform the cohesion policy and its objectives in response to the challenges presented by eastern enlargement. With one-third of the budget earmarked for cohesion policies, the proposal aims to link regional objectives to the EU's Lisbon strategy, target more funds for least-favored regions of the EU (regions where the per capita GDP is less than 75 percent of the average for the enlarged EU), and develop less complicated administrative procedures.[45] Funding of cohesion policies comes from ERDF, ESF, and the Cohesion Fund. During 2007–2013, ERDF will cofinance investments that would lead to the creation or maintenance of jobs, infrastructure, and local development initiatives of small- and medium-sized industries. All development areas are covered under ERDF and it represents the largest structural funds of the Union. The ESF is one of the EU's structural funds and is set up to reduce differences in prosperity and living standards across EU member states and regions, thereby promoting economic and social cohesion. The ESF is devoted to promoting employment in the EU. It helps member states make Europe's workforce and companies better equipped to face new, global challenges. During the current budget cycle, ESF has allocated €75 billion for distributing to the EU member states and regions. Cohesion Funds during 2007–2013 aim to help member states reduce economic and social disparities and stabilize their economies; it has a budget of €62.99 billion.

The Structural Funds and Cohesion Policy

The new cohesion policy has three objectives (Table 10.2). The whole of EU is covered by one or more objectives of the cohesion policies determined by statistical data tabulated by the Commission using the common Nomenclature of Territorial Units for Statistics (NUTS). Accordingly, each member state is divided into NUTS I–III classifications. Small countries like Cyprus and Malta are NUTS I only, whereas larger states like Germany are divided into regions I–III.

Table 10.2 ■ Cohesion Policy, 2007–2013 (All Monetary Figures Are Proposals and Are Subject to Final Decision by the Council and the European Parliament)

Convergence objective 78.5% (€264 billion)

Regional and national programs (ERDF and ESF)	Regions with a GDP/head <75% of EU25 average Statistical effect: Regions with a GDP/head	• Innovation; • Environment/risk prevention; • Accessibility; • Infrastructure; • Human resources; • Administrative capacity	*67.34%* ` *= €177.8 billion* *8.38%* *= €22.14 billion*
Cohesion fund	Member states with a GNI/head 90% of EU 25 average	• Transport (TENs); • Sustainable transport; • Environment	*23.86%* *= €62.99 billion*

Regional competitiveness and employment objective 17.2% (€57.9 billion)

Regional programs (ERDF) and national programs (ESF)	Member states suggest a list of regions (NUTS I or II) "Phasing-in" Regions covered by objective 1 in 2000–2006 period and not covered by the convergence objective	• Innovation; • Environment/risk prevention; • Accessibility; • European employment strategy	*83.44%* *= €48.31 billion* *16.56%* *= €9.58 billion*

European territorial cooperation objective 3.94% (€13.2 billion)

Cross-border and transnational programs and networking (ERDF)	Border regions and greater regions of transnational cooperation	• Innovation; • Environment/risk prevention; • Accessibility	*35.61%* *cross-border* *12.12% ENI* *47.73%* *transnational* *4.54% f.* *networks*

Source: European Commission, *Cohesion Policy: The 2007 Watershed* (Brussels: Directorate General for Regional Policy, 2005), p. 4.

The convergence objective (formerly objective 1), funded by the ERDF, the ESF, and the Cohesion Fund, aims to speed up economic convergence among the regions of the EU. Investment in human and physical capital, developmental technology and innovation, environmental awareness, and economic sustainability receives priority in this objective. About 67 percent of funding will be allocated to regions whose per capita GDP falls below 75 percent of the EU15 average. Regions that qualify under objective 1 are as follows: **Bulgaria**: the whole territory; **Czech Republic**: Střední Čechy, Jihozápad, Severozápad, Severovýchod, Jihovýchod, Střední Morava, and Moravskoslezsko; **Germany**: Brandenburg-Nordost, Mecklenburg-Vorpommern, Chemnitz, Dresden, Dessau, Magdeburg, and Thüringen; **Estonia**: the whole territory; **Greece**: Anatoliki Makedonia, Thraki, Thessalia, Ipeiros, Ionia Nisia, Dytiki Ellada, Peloponnisos, Voreio Aigaio, and Kriti; **Spain**: Andalucía, Castilla-La Mancha, Extremadura, and Galicia; **France**: Guadeloupe, Guyane, Martinique, and Réunion; **Hungary**: Közép-Dunántúl, Nyugat-Dunántúl, Dél-Dunántúl, Észak-Magyarország, Észak-Alföld, and Dél-Alföld; **Italy**: Calabria, Campania, Puglia, and Sicilia; **Latvia**: the whole territory; **Lithuania**: the whole territory; **Malta**: the whole island; **Poland**: the whole territory; **Portugal**: Norte, Centro, Alentejo, and Região Autónoma dos Açores; **Romania**: the whole territory; **Slovenia**: the whole territory; **Slovakia**: Západné Slovensko, Stredné Slovensko, and Východné Slovensko; and **United Kingdom**: Cornwall and Isles of Scilly, West Wales, and the Valleys.[46]

A phasing-out system is granted to those regions that would have been eligible for funding under the convergence objective if the threshold of 75 percent of GDP had been calculated for the EU **at 15** and not **at 25**. These territories are **Belgium**: Province du Hainaut; **Germany**: Brandenburg-Südwest, Lüneburg, Leipzig, and Halle; **Greece**: Kentriki Makedonia, Dytiki Makedonia, and Attiki; **Spain**: Ciudad Autónoma de Ceuta, Ciudad Autónoma de Melilla, Principado de Asturias, and Región de Murcia; **Austria**: Burgenland; **Portugal**: Algarve; **Italy**: Basilicata; and **United Kingdom**: Highlands and Islands.[47]

The regional competitiveness and employment objective (formerly objective 2), funded by ERDF and ESF, is for the rest of the EU and comprises a twofold strategy. First, through regional programs financed by the ERDF, cohesion policy will help regions and the regional authorities to anticipate and promote economic change in industrial, urban, and rural areas by strengthening their competitiveness and attractiveness. In planning these programs, regional authorities will take into account existing economic, social, and territorial disparities and address strategic planning for future development. Second, through programs financed by the ESF, cohesion policy will help people to anticipate and adapt to economic change by supporting policies aiming at full employment, quality and productivity at work, and social inclusion in accordance with EU's social policy.[48]

One major difference between the new cohesion policy and the previous ones is the absence of rural development, which will be under the new CAP budget. The Commission proposed to simplify the different financial instruments that support rural development and the fisheries sector by grouping them in one single source under the CAP. This simplifies funding for rural development, and the funds will be allocated for projects that will increase agricultural competitiveness and enhance the environment and countryside through support for land management and quality of life. Parallel to this financial instrument, the cohesion policy will support diversification of the rural economy (areas dependent on traditional farming and fisheries) by providing funding for economic structural reforms. All regions that are not covered by the convergence objective or by the transitional assistance (NUTS I or NUTS II regions, depending on the member states) are eligible for funding under the competitiveness and employment objective.

A phasing-in system is granted until 2013 to NUTS II regions that were covered by the former Objective 1 but whose GDP exceeds 75 percent of the average GDP of the EU15. Regions eligible for transitional assistance under the Competitiveness and Employment Objective are as follows: **Éire-Ireland**: Border, Midland, and Western; **Greece**: Sterea Ellada and Notio Aigaio;

Spain: Canarias, Castilla y León, and Comunidad Valenciana; **Italy**: Sardegna; **Cyprus**: tout le territoire; **Hungary**: Közép-Magyarország; **Portugal**: Região Autónoma da Madeira; **Finland**: Itä-Suomi; and **United Kingdom**: Merseyside and South Yorkshire.[49]

The Territorial Cooperation Objective (formerly objective 3) emphasizes closer cooperation among member states, especially where there exist wide cross-border disparities, and it is aimed at economic and social integration, improving existing transport and communication systems, and creating jobs. The main parts of objective 3 are as follows:

1. **Cross-border cooperation:** It addresses NUTS level III regions along all internal land borders and certain external land borders and all NUTS level III regions along maritime borders separated by a maximum distance of 150 km.
2. **Transnational cooperation:** The list of regions covered was adopted by the Commission in its decision of October 31, 2006.
3. **Interregional cooperation:** All regions in Europe are eligible.[50]

The Social Policy

Social policy in the EU evolved over two phases. The first phase began with the Treaty of Paris and continued until the SEA. During this period, the Treaty of Paris included provision for the Coal and Steel Community's High Authority (the forerunner of the Commission) to address occupational safety in the coal and steel industries and to sponsor research that would achieve better safety standards in these areas. The EEC treaty also addressed the need to achieve economic and social cohesion in the EC. The second phase began with the SEA and continues through the present, during which time social policy has received more attention on the EU agenda.

During the first phase, there was general concern about the need to improve "health and safety at work, to facilitate free movement of labor, to improve the equality of men and women in the work place, to harmonize social security provisions, and to promote a social dialogue between management and workers at the Community level."[51] Articles 117–122 of the Rome Treaty addressed these needs, and Articles 3 and 123–128 focused on the European Social Fund, which was essential to the retraining and resettlement of unemployed workers and to the maintenance of occupations while enterprises changed their activities due to economic difficulties. However, the role and functioning of the ESF underwent significant revision. The financing of the ESF changed from reliance on levies of member states to an allocation in the EC budget. In addition, two sets of broad objectives were identified: (1) to facilitate employment adjustment resulting from EU policies and (2) to overcome structural problems experienced by regions or economic sectors.[52] These goals required reallocation of some 90 percent of the fund's resources to vocational training. During the 1970s, as unemployment became a serious problem for the EC, the fund's resources increased fourfold.

The Paris summit of 1972 was very crucial for the social image of the EC. At this meeting, the leaders called for a proposal from the Commission on social policy. The Commission produced a Social Action Program in 1973 that was accepted by the Council of Ministers in January 1974 for implementation from 1974 to 1976. The policy goals covered three areas: attainment of full and better employment, improvement and harmonization of living conditions, and involvement of management and labor in the economic and social decisions of the EC and of workers in the operations of their companies.[53] However, due to the economic recession, little progress was made on these fronts until the mid-1980s, when the SEA was adopted.[54]

The second phase of the social policy began with the French idea of the "social area" in 1981, which Commission President Jacques Delors endorsed in 1985. This idea argued for greater equality in EC-wide social standards, because in an increasingly competitive environment, caused by the creation of the single market, countries with lower standards of social protection would undercut other members, a process known as "social dumping."

The SEA revised the section of the Rome Treaty concerned with social policy. Article 118A required member countries to encourage improvements in the health and safety of workers by continuing the harmonization of policies. A second amendment, Article 118B, emphasized the need to promote a social dialogue at the EC level. Furthermore, the SEA placed important proposals that had significant social policy implications (e.g., measures relating to free movement of labor and professionals) on the EC agenda. What eventually came out of these various efforts toward social policy was a document of wide-ranging social commitments known as the Proposal for a Community Charter for Fundamental Social Rights, or Social Charter. It did not receive the unanimous support of the EC members at the Strasbourg summit in December 1989. The strongest opposition came from the United Kingdom and was sustained at Maastricht in 1991. Because of the British opposition, the other 11 members signed a separate social protocol as a move to renew their commitment to EC-wide social policy.[55] The Social Charter specified the following commitments:

1. *The right to freedom of movement.*
2. *The right to employment and remuneration.*
3. *The right to improved living and working conditions.*
4. *The right to social protection.*
5. *The right to freedom of association and collective bargaining.*
6. *The right to vocational training.*
7. *The right of men and women to equal treatment.*
8. *The right to worker information, consultation, and participation.*
9. *The right to health and safety protection at the workplace.*
10. *The right to protection of children and adolescents.*
11. *The right of elderly people to receive an income that guarantees a decent standard of living.*
12. *The rights of disabled persons.*[56]

Social Policy After Maastricht

The social policy of the EU continues to cause divisions within the EU because of labor–management relations in each member state. There is no question that the Maastricht Treaty significantly expands the scope of social policy. The allocation of the ESF now requires the consideration of the goal of "economic and social cohesion." Initially, the UK chose to opt out of the Social Charter that was agreed to by the other 11 states in the Maastricht Treaty. The compromise agreement between the UK and the EC 11 in 1992 was called the Social Protocol, but the UK did not adhere to it. This protocol kept unanimity voting in sensitive policy areas like social security. At the Amsterdam Treaty negotiations, the UK agreed to incorporate the protocol into the Social Charter, and in 1997, the Blair government opted in.

The decision of the British government to opt out of the Social Charter created additional concern for other members of the EU; they felt that the UK might be trying to gain unfair advantage over its EU partners by becoming a very attractive site for European investors because businesses would not have to pay the full price for labor costs.[57] These concerns were all the more relevant to the EU leaders as they faced the task of reducing the ranks of the unemployed from 20 million workers.[58]

The Amsterdam Treaty incorporated the Social Protocol into the Social Charter, with Britain going along with the other members (see Chapter 5).[59] This treaty added provisions for cooperation in fighting unemployment and outlined decision-making procedures for Council voting and the role of the European Parliament in different policy issues: Council voting is based on qualified majority vote (QMV), with the Parliament having a codecision role in the policy areas of health and safety at work, working conditions, information and consultation of workers, social inclusion, equal opportunities and treatment of the sexes, and equal pay for both sexes. Unanimity in the Council and a consultative role for the European Parliament are specified for social security. No role is given to the Parliament in the area of contractual agreement between management and labor.[60] The Nice Treaty expanded on these rights by incorporating the Charter of Fundamental Rights of the Council of Europe into EU law. The Lisbon Treaty attempts to bring clarity to citizens' fundamental rights as far as the Charter is concerned. It refers to the Charter of Fundamental Rights as a list of rights that citizens of the EU should enjoy. Six chapters of the Charter that cover individual rights related to integrity, freedoms, equality, solidarity, and rights linked to justice, and citizenship status complement the ideals of the Social Charter. The institutions of the EU and member states' governments must respect the rights written in the Charter, and the ECJ has the power to oversee that the Charter is implemented correctly. As noted previously, Poland and the UK have reserved their position on the Charter specifically; the Protocol for these two countries on the application of the Charter specifies that "the Charter does not extend the ability of the Court of Justice of the European Union, or any court or tribunal of Poland or of the UK, to find that the laws, regulations or administrative provisions, practices or actions of Poland or the UK are inconsistent with the fundamental rights, freedoms and principles that it reaffirms."[61] As the members of the British Law Society correctly conclude, the position of Poland and the UK appears to suggest that the British and Polish governments have interpreted it as introducing new rights into EU law.[62] However, this is incorrect as the Charter does not create new general rights under national law, and only applies when national governments are implementing EU law.

Other Cohesion Policies

Education and Training Policies

Education and training policies represent major challenges for the EU. Although both topics affect the lives of all EU citizens, EU-wide policies in these areas were introduced only recently, in conjunction with the single market, and have faced serious financing problems and political obstacles on the grounds of national sovereignty.[63] Prior to the SEA, the EC initiated a limited training program to tackle unemployment problems in the 1970s. The European Center for the Development of Vocational Training (CEDEFOP) administered this program and had only limited support from some of the EC countries. However, the challenges of the single market, and post-Maastricht Europe, required a more comprehensive policy package. As an essential part of the Lisbon strategy of 2000 aims to make the EU the world's leader in the quality of its education and training systems, associated policies hold the key to success or failure in these areas. Following are the EU's new education and training programs:

- **The Lifelong Learning Program.** This is the flagship education and training program of the EU. It covers learning opportunities from childhood to old age and is the first such comprehensive program of its kind in EU's education programs. For the period of 2007–2013, a budget of €7 billion has been allocated to promote projects and exchanges between educational systems of the member and candidate states. This program is the successor of the Socrates, Leonardo da Vinci, and eLearning programs of the 2000–2006 budget cycle.[64]
- **Erasmus Mundus.** This higher education program promotes the EU as a center of excellence in learning. The program is aimed at attracting third-country nationals for higher education partnerships with EU universities. It supports European top-quality Masters Courses and enhances the visibility and attractiveness of European higher education in third countries. It also provides EU-funded scholarships for third-country

nationals participating in these Masters Courses, as well as scholarships for EU nationals studying in third countries. Erasmus Mundus will support about 100 Erasmus Mundus Masters Courses of outstanding academic quality. It will provide funding for some 5,000 graduate students from third countries to follow these Masters Courses and for more than 4,000 EU graduate students involved in these courses to study in third countries. The program will also offer teaching or research scholarships in Europe for over 1,000 incoming third-country academics and for a similar number of outgoing EU scholars. Finally, Erasmus Mundus will support about 100 partnerships between Erasmus Mundus Masters Courses and higher education institutions in third countries.[65]

- **Tempus.** This program is a trans-European cooperation scheme for higher education as adopted by the Council on May 7, 1990. It recently concluded its Phase III (2000–2006) and was part of the EU's overall program for the economic and social restructuring of the Central and Eastern European countries, including Technical Assistance for Central and Eastern Europe (PHARE program), and for the economic recovery of the former Soviet Union countries and Mongolia, including Technical Assistance in the Confederation of Independent States (TACIS program). At present, a new Tempus Phase IV program is developed for further cooperation between the EU and Albania, Bosnia-Herzegovina, Croatia, FYRM, Montenegro, Kosovo, Serbia, Kazakhstan, Kyrgystan, Tajikistan, Turkmenistan, and Uzbekistan.

Industrial Policy and Research and Development

Unlike regional policy, industrial policy provides assistance to sectors of the economy, regardless of geographical location, at least in initial policy choices. The Treaty of Rome made no specific reference to an EC-wide industrial policy. This is not surprising, since industrial policies of the member states vary greatly: In France and Germany, the state intervenes to shape industrial policy, whereas in the UK there is a relatively hands-off approach. However, with the launching of Project 1992, the Commission argued that in order to have a viable EU-wide industrial base, with a strong competition policy, coordinated policies were essential.[66] According to John Kemp, the Commission supported the idea of subsidiarity where "the EC would only become involved when national policies of the member states were ineffective, or harmful to other member states."[67] The Commission further argued that policy coordination was necessary between industrial policy and other policy areas (common external policy, social and environmental policies, research and development [R&D] policy) and that greater coordination of the member states' national industrial policies was needed.

The EC adopted two main programs to support R&D at the European level. The first set of programs, known as the framework programs, started in 1985 and are run by the Commission. The second set, known as EUREKA, consisted of much less coordinated R&D programs involving 18 European countries and the EU.[68] The framework programs started in 1985 with the introduction of the European Strategic Program for Research and Development in Information Technologies (ESPRIT). The second framework program went into effect in 1987 and lasted through 1991; it was followed by the third phase (1990–1994). The other R&D framework programs that were introduced under the second and third phases include the following:

- RACE, Research in Advanced Communications in Europe
- BRITE, Basic Research in Industrial Technologies for Europe
- EURAM, European Research in Advanced Materials
- SCIENCE, Plan to Stimulate the International Cooperation and Interchange Needed by European Research Scientists
- SPES, European Stimulation Plan for Economic Sciences
- STEP, Science and Technology for Environmental Protection
- DELTA, Development of European Learning Through Technological Advance[69]

Following Maastricht, the EU accepted the Commission's proposal for the size and funding of the fourth phase of the framework programs to cover the period between 1994 and 1998. The Commission's proposal called for a budget of 13.1 billion ecus as compared to the 6.6 billion ecus for the third phase. Nevertheless, in real terms, the budget remained at about 4 percent of the overall EC budget.[70]

The Commission's push for R&D was also a critical part of the Delors 1993 White Paper. The paper stressed that one of the main reasons for Europe's decline in competitiveness was the slowdown in infrastructure investment during the 1980s. In order to meet the challenges of the twenty-first century, the White Paper called for new investments in information highways, pan-European transport, energy, and environmental infrastructure.[71] The development of new information technologies and highways would be financed by private capital, and a mixture of public and private sources would cover transport and energy networks. The paper also argued that the new information highways and technologies could not reach their potential advances unless the current industries were decentralized. Decentralization represented a major problem for several EU countries where information and telecommunication industries were state monopolies. For the information industries, the Commission estimates a cost of 150 billion ecus over a period of ten years.[72] In addition, a task force would be needed to start the drive with a mandate from the EU countries. The transport and energy infrastructure, on the other hand, would require an estimated 250 billion ecus to establish better road, rail, airport, and gas pipeline infrastructures between the EU and its neighbors in Eastern and Southern Europe.[73] On March 25, 1996, the Council and the European Parliament modified the budget to account for the new members of the EU. This decision added 800 million ecus to the programs and 100 million ecus to the EURATOM program.

Next, the EU revised the R&D policies and adopted the fifth framework program for 1998–2002.[74] This package identified priorities for EU research, technology, and development strategies and differed from previous programs in that its subprograms were aimed at solving problems and socioeconomic challenges facing EU citizens. Its two main parts were the EC framework program covering research and technological development and the EURATOM program for research and development in nuclear industries. The budget for the EC part was €13.9 billion; for EURATOM, it was €979 million.[75]

The sixth phase of industrial policy followed the general goals and guidelines of the Lisbon strategy and integrated with other cohesion policies that emphasize job creation and economic structural adjustment of the regions.[76] The EU economy has been experiencing a decline in the industrial sector over the last two decades. In a report from the Commission on industrial growth and economic structural problems, we learn that the industrial share of the EU15 GDP from 1979 to 2001 was 11.8–8.8 percent.[77] The report also explains decline in labor productivity in the core economies of the EU. These findings closely follow those of Yeşilada, Efird, and Noordijk, discussed in Chapter 6. Unless concrete steps are taken to reverse these trends, the EU is highly unlikely to meet its Lisbon goals. It should be noted, however, that in its reports on the state of industrial competitiveness and labor productivity, the Commission identified the United States as its major rival and failed to recognize the rising challenge of China.

The most recent version of EU industrial policy addresses challenges faced by enlargement of the Union and globalization. It calls for innovative approaches in R&D for sustainable growth, competitiveness, and job creation within the context of the Lisbon Strategy.[78] The Commission proposal in 2005 called for a €4 billion funding during 2007–2013 to boost competitiveness and productivity through three interrelated programs:

1. The **Entrepreneurship and Innovation Program**, which brings together activities in the areas of entrepreneurship, small and medium enterprises, industrial competitiveness, and innovation;

2. The **ICT Policy Support Program**, which will promote the speedy adoption of information and communication technologies (ICTs) and comprises existing measures such as eTEN, eContent, or Modinis; and

3. The **Intelligent Energy-Europe Program**, which brings together actions to accelerate the uptake and promotion of energy efficiency and to increase investments in and awareness-raising of renewable energy sources. Existing measures such as "SAVE," "ALTENER," and "STEER" are part of this subprogram.

The EU faces enormous challenges in achieving these goals of the Lisbon strategy. With vast differences in industrial bases of member states, further complicated by eastern enlargement, it is a daunting task to try to harmonize industrial growth and R&D across the Union that meet EU's sustainability objectives. The EU's goal for R&D expenditure is to reach 3 percent of EU's GDP by 2010 and to have at least two-thirds of this expenditure to come from the business sector. Member states show mixed results in this area. Data from Eurostat shows that R&D expenditure across the EU's 25 countries was between 1.8 and 1.9 percent of GDP during 2001–2005 and it increased by 3.9 percent per year at constant prices (in real terms) between 1998 and 2005.[79] However, more than 70 percent of all R&D expenditure is contributed by the top three countries—UK, France, and Germany—and, in these markets, growth in R&D expenditure was well below the EU average. In the UK, average annual growth was 3.52 percent, but in France and Germany, it was only 2.36 percent and 2.70 percent respectively. Double-digit growth in expenditure came in smaller markets led by Estonia, Cyprus, and Hungary, while there were decreases in R&D spending in Poland and Slovakia. Only Sweden and Finland have passed the "research intensity" target (research intensity is the share of GDP taken by R&D expenditure). In Sweden, R&D expenditure accounts for 4.27 percent of GDP, and in Finland, it represents 3.5 percent.[80]

Environmental Policy

The Rome Treaty did not refer to environmental policy, and the topic did not enter the EC agenda until 1971, when the Commission gave its first detailed report on the environment to the European Council. At the subsequent 1972 Paris summit, the Council agreed to adopt an EC environmental policy and establish the Environmental Protection Service.[81] Since then, the environmental policy goals have been defined in four different environmental action programs (EAPs). Unfortunately, these programs did not represent a definitive commitment from the member states to implementation because each country has maintained its own set of environmental regulations. Nevertheless, the EAPs represent a growing emphasis in the EU on better coordinating its industrial policy with protecting the environment. It has become clear that most environmental problems transcend national boundaries and cannot be dealt with at the national level alone. Furthermore, with the Maastricht Treaty, the Commission attained more influence over EU environmental policy. "Towards Sustainability," the fifth Community Action Program (renamed from EAP) on the environment, established a strategy for voluntary action in 1992–2000 and marked the beginning of a cross-EC approach to all causes of environmental pollution. The Amsterdam Treaty further emphasized sustainable growth as one of the main goals of the EU.

The first EAP (1973–1977) set the main principles of the EC's environmental policy: the "polluter pays" principle, an emphasis on preventive measures, and the need to consider the environmental impact of the EC's socioeconomic decisions. These principles were endorsed in the second EAP (1977–1981). The third EAP (1982–1986) placed stronger emphasis on environmental protection. It stated, "[A]n overall strategy has to be formulated in which prevention, rather than cure, should be the rule."[82] Later, the principle of prevention was included in the SEA and became a central issue in the fourth EAP.

The developments under the SEA are important for the future implementation of environmental policies. Even though Article 130 of the SEA, which deals with environmental policies, still required unanimity among the Council of Ministers, Article 100A permitted directives approved by a qualified majority. As David Vogel explains, this provided an alternative means of "enacting environmental legislation, one which deprived any single member state of the power to block approval."[83] The SEA also expanded the role of the European Parliament in shaping EU legislation. This is significant because the Parliament has been stricter on environmental regulations than the Council of Ministers.[84] Finally, after the Chernobyl disaster in the former Soviet Union and a massive spill of toxins into the Rhine River in 1986, citizens concerned about the environment placed ever-increasing pressure on EU leaders to respond to these challenges.

The fourth EAP (1987–1992) reflected these concerns; it was a more comprehensive proposal with a greater emphasis on environmental management. This program emphasized urgent action in the use of agricultural chemicals, treatment of agricultural wastes, protection of animal species, and general guidelines for product standards throughout the EU.[85] In order to stimulate action around these policy concerns, the European Environment Agency (EEA) was established in 1990. The original task of the EEA was to collect data and publish reports on environmental issues and to publish a report on the state of the environment every three years.

The EU measures on environmental management became far more explicit in the fifth Community Action Program (1992–2000). The program specified a holistic approach to sustainability and development and included the following components:[86]

- **Instruments.** This section outlined funding and guidelines for implementation of the various parts of the program. It included technical aspects such as ecolabeling, the EC system of environmental management, and auditing. The EEA served as an advisory body on these matters, as, for example, when the EU was considering the introduction of environmental taxes based on the "polluter pays" principle.
- **Waste Management.** This included eliminating waste at the source by improving product design, encouraging the recycling and reuse of waste, and reducing pollution caused by waste management.[87] The EU's approach has been to assign more responsibility to the producer. For instance, the 1997 draft directive on end-of-life vehicles provided for the introduction of a system for collecting such vehicles at the manufacturer's expense. At the international level, this approach was also adopted at the first Conference of the Parties to the OSPAR Convention for the Protection of the Marine Environment of the North-East Atlantic. One of the tasks of this conference was to negotiate the dismantling and disposal of offshore oilrigs and natural gas platforms. The Parties to the Convention adopted the position supported by the European Commission: that the dumping of such installations at sea should be banned and that the costs of dismantling and disposing of such installations should be borne by their owners. The EU is also a Party to the Convention on the Control of Transboundary Movements of Hazardous Wastes and Their Disposal (the Basle Convention), which has been signed by more than 100 countries. The EU has already ratified the amendment to this convention, banning exports of hazardous wastes from the Organization for Economic Cooperation and Development (OECD) countries, the EU, and Lichtenstein to non-OECD countries regardless of whether such waste is for disposal, recycling, or use.[88]
- **Noise Pollution.** Noise has been a long-term concern of the Commission. The goal was to reduce noise emissions at the source, develop exchanges of information, and give greater force and consistency to EU programs to combat noise. Thus, in its 1996 Green Paper,[89] the Commission proposed extending this strategy by reducing noise emissions at the source, developing exchanges of information, and giving greater force and consistency to EU programs to combat noise.

- **Water Pollution.** Since 1976, several directives had set common standards for surface and underground water, drinking water, and the discharge of toxic substances. The current proposals for directives were aimed at further improving the ecology of surface waters, introducing EU action on fresh waters and surface waters, and protecting estuaries, coastal waters, and groundwater. The EU is a party to various international conventions aimed at protecting the marine environment (the OSPAR Convention, the Barcelona Convention for the Protection of the Mediterranean Sea Against Pollution).
- **Air Pollution.** The EU had been adopting stricter directives on air pollution by cars, large combustion plants, power stations, and machines since 1970. The EU signed the Kyoto agreement, calling for reducing greenhouse gas emissions by at least 5 percent of their 1990 levels between 2008 and 2012. In November 1998, the EU also participated in the Buenos Aires conference on implementing the Kyoto accords and became a strong supporter of the action plan adopted under this agreement.
- **Nature Conservation.** Since 1982, the EC had introduced a number of measures to conserve wildlife (protection of certain species, such as birds and seals) and natural habitats (protection of woodlands and watercourses). Moreover, the EU signed a number of international conventions—for instance, the Bern Convention on the Conservation of European Wildlife and Natural Habitats and the Bonn Convention on the Conservation of Migratory Species.

Successful implementation of the fifth program required extension of these policies to candidate countries, as well as for development of the next plan to tackle growing problems in the enlarged EU. Eastern enlargement involved serious environmental difficulties, as the candidate countries' Cold War–era industrialization policies paid little or no attention to the environment. Before accession, these countries had to incorporate into their national legislation all existing EC environmental law as part of the *acquis*. In its work program for 1999 [OJ C 366, 26.11.1998], the Commission identified environmental protection as one of the fundamental challenges facing the EU. It stated that growing industrialization, food hazards, and the rapid degradation of the natural environment require a strategy of sustainable development, involving balanced resource management. As stressed by the European Council in Vienna, the only way that such a strategy could succeed was to make protection of environment and sustainable development an integral part of all EC policies, as provided for by the Amsterdam Treaty. Thus, the European Council called on its members to finalize strategies to take fuller account of the environment in transport, energy, and agriculture policy; to focus on this side of its development, industrial, and internal market policies; and to put emphasis on cross-sectoral issues such as climate change and the environmental dimension of employment and enlargement.

The Sixth Action Program, adopted in 2002, identifies sustainable development as the top priority for the EU.[90] It proposes five priority avenues of strategic action: improving the implementation of existing legislation, integrating environmental concerns into other policies, working more closely with the market, empowering people as private citizens and helping them to change behavior, and taking account of the environment in land-use planning and management decisions.[91] Furthermore, the Sixth Environment Action Program focuses on four priority areas for action: climate change, biodiversity, environment and health, and sustainable management of resources and wastes.[92] In climate change in the short term, the EU's aim is to achieve the objectives of the Kyoto Protocol—that is, to reduce greenhouse gas emissions by 8 percent compared to 1990 levels by 2008–2012. In the longer term, by 2020, it will be necessary to reduce these emissions by 20–40 percent by means of an effective international accord. The objective in biodiversity is to protect and restore the structure and functioning of natural systems and stop the loss of biodiversity both in the EU and on a global scale. The remaining action areas emphasize the need for protecting the environment, educating the citizens about sustainable economic growth, and pressing ahead with zero-waste environmental policies where recycling of all waste products becomes a long-term goal.[93] The Sixth Program also addresses external implications of the EU's environmental policies. With regard to eastern enlargement, the program suggests that there should be an extended dialogue with the administrations in the candidate countries on sustainable development and that the Commission should establish close cooperation with the nongovernmental organizations and businesses in the candidate countries. In addition, the program strongly encourages application of international agreements on the environment to EU and candidate country policies.

The current environmental policy of the Union is incorporated in the Renewed EU Sustainable Development Strategy that was adopted by the European Council in June 2006. It is an overarching strategy for all EU policies and sets out how we can meet the needs of present generations without compromising the ability of future generations to meet their needs. The Sustainable Development Strategy deals in an integrated way with economic, environmental, and social issues and lists the following seven key challenges: (1) climate change and clean energy; (2) sustainable transport; (3) sustainable consumption and production; (4) conservation and management of natural resources; (5) public health; (6) social inclusion, demography, and migration; and (7) global poverty.[94] Among these policy items, the EU's goal in meeting global warming challenges is one of the most ambitious in the world. As noted before, it calls for cuts of up to 20–40 percent in CO_2 emissions by 2020. Under Kyoto, the EU15 committed themselves to making an 8 percent reduction in emissions by 2008–2012 from their 1990 levels. Yet, they are far from reaching this goal because as of the end of 2004, the EU15 was 2.3 percent away from the target set by the Commission for 1990–2010.[95] Figure 10.6 shows the total greenhouse gas emissions in EU15 against Kyoto target.

Some countries are doing better than others in meeting their target. Spain still has a long way to go to reach its target, whereas the UK and Sweden appear to be on track to meet their commitment with room to spare. A number of other countries, including Austria, Belgium, Denmark, Ireland, Italy, and Portugal, do not think they will be able to meet their targets. In contrast, the newer member states of the EU25—which constituted the EU from May 2004 to January 2007, that is, until Bulgaria and Romania joined—generally have a better per capita record on emissions than the EU15 powers.

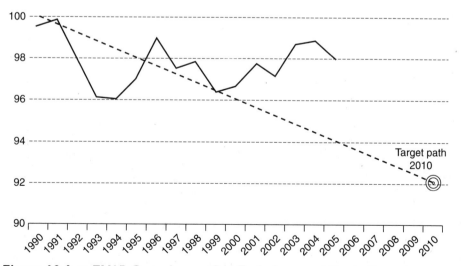

Figure 10.6 ■ EU15 Greenhouse Gas Emissions and Kyoto Target

Source: European Commission, *Measuring Progress Towards a More Sustainable Europe: 2007 Monitoring Report of the EU Sustainable Development Strategy* (Brussels: Eurostat Statistical Books, 2007), p. 43.

STUDY QUESTIONS

1. What is new in the EU budget for 2007–2013?

2. What are the main effects of eastern enlargement on distribution of cohesion funds?

3. Explain the main reforms of CAP since the early 1960s.

4. What is the EU's social charter, and how does it fit the Union's goal of achieving unity in diversity?

5. Discuss the politics of the EU budget process. Is it a good example of liberal intergovernmentalism or historical institutionalism?

6. What are the EU's policy priorities for the decades ahead?

7. How should policy goals be reflected in spending?

8. Discuss the relations between citizens and the distribution of EU budget?

ENDNOTES

1. European Commission, "Deciding the Budget," http://europa.eu.int/comm/budget/budget_detail/deciding_en.htm

2. *BBC News*, December 2, 2005, 16:41 GMT.

3. Ibid.

4. *BBC News*, December 17, 2005, 17:53 GMT.

5. European Commission, *General Budget of the European Union for the Financial Year 2008.* (Brussels: Commission of the European Commission Publications, 2008), p. 9.

6. Dennis Swann, *The Economics of the Common Market* (London: Penguin Books, 1991), p. 229.

7. Ibid.

8. Ibid.

9. Commission of the European Communities, "Memorandum on the Reform of Agriculture in the European Economic Community," in *Bulletin of the European Communities: Supplement 1/69 Z* (Brussels: European Communities, 1969).

10. John Pinder, *European Community: The Building of a Union* (London: Oxford University Press, 1991), pp. 84–85.

11. Stephen George, *Politics and Policy in the European Community*, 2nd ed. (Oxford: Oxford University Press, 1991), p. 148.

12. Swann, *The Economics of the Common Market*, p. 247.

13. Fiona Butler, "The EC's Common Agricultural Policy (CAP)," in Juliet Lodge, ed., *The European Community and the Challenge of the Future*, 2nd ed. (New York: St. Martin's Press, 1993), p. 116.

14. Ibid.

15. Swann, *The Economics of the Common Market*, p. 248.

16. John Gibbons, "The Common Agricultural Policy," in Frank McDonald and Stephen Dearden, eds., *European Economic Integration* (London: Longman, 1992), p. 139.

17. Caroline Southey, "Britain Seeks CAP Debate After Critical Reports," *Financial Times*, January 16, 1995, pp. 1–2.

18. The reports are by Allan Buckwell of Wye College, University of London, England; Stefan Tangermann, University of Göttinger, Germany; Secondo Tarditi, University of Siena, Italy; and Louis Mahe, University of Rennes, France.

19. Simon Hix, *The Political System of the European Union* (New York: St. Martin's Press, 1999), pp. 252–253.

20. European Commission, *Agenda 2000: Setting the Scene for Reform* (Brussels: European Commission Publications, 1998), p. 8.

21. Ibid., pp. 8–9.

22. EC Commission, *Communication from the Commission to the Council and the European Parliament: Mid-Term Review of Common Agricultural Policy* (Brussels: European Commission Publications, 2002).

23. Ibid., pp. 18–26.

24. EU Commission, *CAP Reform* (Brussels: Agriculture Directorate Publications, 2005), pp. 3–5.

25. Ibid.

26. European Commission, *Europeans and the Common Agricultural Policy*, Special Eurobarometer 221 (Brussels: Eurobarometer, 2005), p. 43.

27. European Commission, "Structure of Rural Development Policy," Council Regulation (EC) No. 1698/2005 from the Web site http://ec.europa.eu/agriculture/rurdev/index_en.htm

28. Ibid.

29. European Commission, Directorate General for Health and Consumer Protection, *BSE Frequently Asked Questions* (Brussels: Agriculture Directorate Publications, April 9, 2001), pp. 2–4.

30. Ibid.

31. See http://europa.eu.int/comm/food/fs/inspections/vi/reports/index_en.html for current and past reports.

32. European Commission, Agriculture Directorate, *Questions and Answers on Foot-and-Mouth Disease* (Brussels: Agriculture Directorate Publications, December 12, 2001), pp. 1–2.

33. Ibid., p. 1.

34. Ibid., p. 6.

35. EurActiv.com, "The New EU Cohesion Policy," http://www.euractiv.com/en/future-eu/new-eu-cohesion-policy-2007-2013/article-131988

36. Loukas Tsoukalis, *The New European Economy: The Politics and Economics of Integration* (New York and London: Oxford University Press, 1991), p. 41.

37. Swann, *The Economics of the Common Market*, p. 289.

38. George, *Politics and Policy in the European Community*, 2nd ed., pp. 192–193.

39. Judith Tomkins and Jim Twomey, "Regional Policy," in McDonald and Dearden, eds., *European Economic Integration*, p. 105. The original objective 1 referred to the development of structurally backward regions and received funds through the ERDF, the ESF, and the EAGGF. In these regions, the per capita GNP was less than 75 percent of the EC average. Objective 2 pertained to restoring regions facing industrial decline with funding through the ERDF and ESF. The UK was the chief beneficiary under this program. Objectives 3 and 4 received funding through the ESF and addressed the need to combat long-term unemployment and youth unemployment. Objective 5 had two parts. The first referred to adjustment of agricultural structures (related to reform of the CAP) and was funded under the EAGGF. The second part addressed development of rural areas and was funded by the ERDF, the ESF, and the EAGGF. Between 1989 and 1993, a sum of 2.64 billion ecus reached member states under this objective. Objective 6 (1995–1999) comprised the northernmost parts of Finland and Sweden with a low GDP per capita that faced depopulation due to high unemployment. The population density was only 2.1 per square kilometer. Funds targeted job training for 110,000 individuals and totaled €991 million for Finland and €156.7 million for Sweden.

40. See the European Commission DG Regional Policy Web site, located at http://www.inforegio.org/wbpro/prord/prords/history_en.html

41. See the European Union Web site, located at http://europa.eu.int/comm/regional_policy/activity/erdf/erd1b_en.htm

42. Ibid.

43. Ibid.

44. Ibid.

45. European Commission, *Cohesion Policy: The 2007 Watershed* (Brussels: Directorate-General for Regional Policy, 2005), pp. 1–4.

46. European Commission, "Which regions are Affected?," http://ec.europa.eu/regional_policy/policy/region/ index_en.htm

47. Ibid.

48. European Commission, *Proposal for a COUNCIL REGULATION Laying Down General Provisions on the European Regional Development Fund, the European Social Fund and the Cohesion Fund* (Brussels: Commission of the European Communities, 2004), p. 5.

49. Ibid.

50. Ibid.

51. George, *Politics and Policy in the European Community*, 2nd ed., p. 203.

52. Stephen Dearden, "Social Policy," in McDonald and Dearden, eds., *European Economic Integration*, p. 85.

53. Swann, *The Economics of the Common Market*, p. 299.

54. For a detailed discussion of these years, see Michael Shanks, *European Social Policy Today and Tomorrow* (Oxford, England: Pergamon Press, 1977).

55. Beverly Springer, *The Social Dimension of 1992* (Westport, Conn.: Praeger, 1992), pp. 39–41.

56. European Community, *1992: The Social Dimension* (Luxembourg: Office for Official Publications of the European Communities, 1990), pp. 83–85.

57. Ibid., p. 156.

58. "EU Urged to Catch Up with the World," *Financial Times*, December 8, 1993, p. 2.

59. European Commission, *Intergovernmental Conference 1996–1997: Commission Opinion— Reinforcing Political Union and Preparing for Enlargement* (Luxembourg: Office for Official Publications of the European Communities, 1998).

60. Hix, *The Political System*, p. 229.

61. The Law Society, *A Guide to the Treaty of Lisbon: European Union Insight* (London: The Law Society, January 2008), p. 10.

62. Ibid.

63. Glenda Rosenthal, "Educational and Training Policy," in Leon Hurwitz and Christian Lequesne, eds., *The State of the European Community: Policies, Institutions, and Debates in the Transition Years* (Boulder, Colo., and London: Lynne Reinner/Longman, 1991), p. 273.

64. Socrates program focused on educational cooperation aimed at a wide range of people and

institutions at all levels of education. It involved around 31 European countries including Turkey. Its main objective was to build up a Europe of knowledge and thus provide a better response to the major challenges of the new century: to promote lifelong learning, encourage access to education for everybody, and help people acquire recognized qualifications and skills. In more specific terms, Socrates sought to promote language learning and to encourage mobility and innovation. There were seven categories for cooperation: Comenius for school education, Erasmus for higher education, Grundtvig for adult education, Lingua for language teaching and learning, Minerva for information and communication technologies in education, Observation and Innovation in educational systems and policies, and Joint Actions with other EU programs. Leonardo da Vinci was a community vocational training and action program. It had two planned phases: 1995–1999 and 2000–2006. During the first phase, the program's key objective was to support the development of cross-EC projects. With a budget of €620 million, it provided coverage not only to member states, but also to the three countries of European Free Trade Association (EFTA) and the European Economic Area—Iceland, Liechtenstein, and Norway—and to the candidate countries of Central and Eastern Europe. The eLearning program aimed to effectively integrate Information and Communication Technologies (ICT) into education and training systems in Europe.

65. See the European Commission Web site, located at http://europa.eu.int/comm/education/programmes/mundus/index_en.html

66. John Kemp, "Competition Policy," in McDonald and Dearden, eds., *European Economic Integration*, p. 78.

67. Ibid.

68. The members of EUREKA were Austria, Belgium, Denmark, Finland, France, Germany, Greece, Iceland, Ireland, Italy, Luxembourg, the Netherlands, Norway, Portugal, Spain, Sweden, Switzerland, Turkey, UK, and the EC, represented by the Commission.

69. EC Delegation to the United States, *The European Community in the Nineties* (Washington, D.C.: EC Office, 1992), p. 15.

70. "R&D in a Tussle over EC Funding," *Financial Times*, October 26, 1993, p. 9.

71. "EU Urged to Catch Up with the World," *Financial Times*, December 8, 1993, p. 2.

72. Ibid.

73. Ibid.

74. European Commission, *Fifth Framework Programme, 1998–2002*, http://europa.eu.int/scadplus/leg/en/lvb/i23001.htm

75. Ibid.

76. European Commission, *Implementing the Community Lisbon Programme: A Policy Framework to Strengthen EU Manufacturing—Towards a More Integrated Approach for Industrial Policy* (Brussels: Communication from the Commission, 2005).

77. European Commission, *Fostering Structural Change: An Industrial Policy for an Enlarged Europe* (Brussels: Commission of the European Communities, 2004), p. 6.

78. European Commission, *Miditerm Review of Industrial Policy* (Brussels: European Commission, July 2007), pp. 3–8.

79. Estimated from economic data available at European Commission, Statistics, Eurostat, http://ec.europa.eu/growthandjobs/key-statistics/index_en.htm

80. David Mort, "Good For Research? Good for Publishers?," *Research Information* (May/June 2005), http://www.researchinformation.info/features/feature.php?feature_id=80.

81. John Hassan, "Environment Policy," in McDonald and Dearden, eds., *European Economic Integration*, p. 122.

82. Angela Liberatore, "Problems of Transnational Policymaking: Environmental Policy in the European Community," *European Journal of Political Research* 19 (1991): 292.

83. David Vogel, "Environmental Protection and the Creation of a Single European Market," paper presented at the Annual Meeting of the American Political Science Association, Chicago, September 3–6, 1992, p. 11.

84. Ibid., p. 12.

85. Hassan, "Environment Policy," p. 124.

86. See the European Communities Web site, located at http://www.eurunion.org/legislat/agd2000/index.htm.

87. European Commission, *Commission Report COM(98)711 Final* (Brussels: European Commission Publications, 1998).

88. Ibid.

89. European Commission, *Action Against Noise: Green Paper* (Brussels: European Commission Publications, November 4, 1996).

90. European Commission, *Sixth Environmental Action Programme 2010: Our Future, Our Choice* (Brussels: European Commission Publications, January 24, 2001).

91. Ibid.

92. Environment DG, *Information Brochure: An Introduction to the Directorate-General for the Environment of the European Commission and to Sources of Information on EU Environmental Policy* (Brussels: European Commision, 2002), p. 6.

93. EuroActive Web site, "6th Environment Action Programme," http://www.euractiv.com/en//environment/article-117438

94. European Commission, *Sustainable Development Strategy*, http://ec.europa.eu/sustainable/welcome/index_en.htm

95. European Commission, *Measuring Progress Towards a More Sustainable Europe: 2007 Monitoring Report of the EU Sustainable Development Strategy* (Brussels: Eurostat Statistical Books, 2007), p. 43.

11

Chapter

External Economic Relations of the European Union

In this chapter, we will look at the external economic relations of the European Union (EU) with special emphasis on the United States, the Mediterranean Basin and the Lomé (African, Caribbean, and Pacific, or ACP) states, and other major trade partners of the EU. We maintain that the policy packages adopted toward these states are crucial to understanding the EU's competition with the United States and other major economies as an emerging world economic power.

MULTILATERAL TRADE POLICY

The EU's common trade policy is known as the Common Commercial Policy (CCP) and is an integral part of pillar I. This means that in foreign trade, the EU acts as one single actor. The Commission negotiates its trade agreements and the current trade commissioner, Peter Mandelson, represents the EU27's interests. Article 133 of the Treaty of Rome provides the legal basis of the external trade policy of the EU. This article, as amended in the Nice Treaty, calls for the establishment of a special committee, known as the Article 133 Committee, composed of representatives of the member states to consult with the trade commissioner in matters pertaining to trade.[1] The committee meets in Brussels on a weekly basis and considers trade issues affecting the EU. The trade commissioner sets the agenda for discussions and, if some formal policy decision is to be made (e.g., agreement to conclude formal trade negotiations), secures a recommendation from the committee for consideration by the Council of Ministers. The final decision on such matters rests with the Council. While the Council has a direct decision-making role in trade policy, the European Parliament has a far less limited role. While the Commission regularly obtains the opinion of the Parliament, the treaty only calls for the "assent of the [Parliament] for major treaty ratifications when covering more than trade."

The EU is one of the key players in multilateral trade negotiations in the world and the world's largest trading bloc, accounting for about 30 percent of global merchandise exports (including intra-EU trade) in 2006. Excluding intra-EU trade, the share of EU25 in total world exports was 16.2 percent of total world exports.[2] As the EU becomes a stronger economic union, its voice in multilateral trade negotiations carries more weight. Simon Hix explains that the EU has been a strong advocate of the World Trade Organization (WTO) even when this organization has ruled against the EU.[3] In these instances, the Commission pressed the Council of Ministers to reform the internal market and the CCP to adhere to WTO principles. With this in mind, the EU approach to the WTO Millennium Round trade negotiations is based on the following policy aspirations:

1. To create substantial benefits for the world economy through trade liberalization of goods and services and better rules in a number of policy areas (in particular, competition, investment, intellectual property, trade facilitation, and government procurement).
2. To contribute to harnessing globalization.
3. To better integrate developing countries into the world economy by working for a more equitable distribution of the benefits of trade liberalization.
4. To further strengthen the WTO multilateral system so that it can become a truly universal, fair, and transparent instrument for the management of international trade relations in support of sustainable development.
5. To ensure that the Millennium Round benefits the environment.[4]

The WTO launched the Doha Round Trade Talks (2001–2005), in order to open world markets to agricultural and manufactured goods. The participants agreed to link trade and the environmental issues in an attempt to boost sustainable economic growth. Although not every participant has the same views on these topics, the decision to launch a new round of trade negotiations was a significant step forward in settling disputes between members of the WTO. Under the WTO plan, developing countries have the right to produce drugs cheaply in case of a medical emergency; the EU agreed to reduce some agricultural subsidies; the other WTO members accepted the EU's demand that investment, competition, and environmental rules be placed on the agenda; India retained an effective veto (if it gained enough support from other countries) to push EU items off the agenda; and the United States agreed to relax some import curbs. All of these items present formidable challenges to WTO countries as they discuss, negotiate, and reach a final agreement. At the time of writing, WTO negotiations in Hong Kong, aimed at finding a compromise between the developed and the developing countries on a variety of topics, resulted in some agreement on the issues, and negotiations were extended into 2006. On agriculture, they reached a modest deal, with the EU promising to end agricultural subsidies by 2013.[5] However, developing countries failed to secure more access to rich countries' agricultural markets (as there was no agreement on reduction of tariffs), the services sector got pushed into further talks, and the EU has introduced a fourth element into the trade talks, a development package, with the explicit aim of gaining some tangible benefits for developing countries. In practical terms, this new EU proposal makes it clear that:

> the EU wants other countries to adopt its plan for duty-free, tariff-free access to its markets for the world's poorest countries, the 50 least developed countries (LDCs) which together account for less than 1 percent of world trade. The package also includes increased "Trade for Aid" which aims to give money to the LDCs to help them improve their trade infrastructure and compensate them for losses as a result of free trade. The US has problems with some elements of this package, since it would mean that some big textile importers like Bangladesh would enjoy duty-free access to the US market. But the US has signaled in principle that it is prepared to accept it, and announced an increase in its own Trade for Aid package.[6]

Is this a true proposal or an empty gesture? This discussion continues in the capitals of developing countries. At the time of writing, no tangible breakthrough has been reached in these talks.

Impact of the CAP on External Trade

In EU's multilateral trade relations, the Common Agricultural Policy (CAP) remains a major issue that presents problems for the EU in international trade talks. It is true that other countries like the United States also have agricultural subsidy issues that further complicated successful completion of the Doha Round. It is often noted that the CAP has had a negative effect on world market prices by subsidizing exports and by contributing to instability in the market. However, it is unfair to single out the EU as the only guilty party. The debate over agricultural policy dates back to steps taken during the previous international trade negotiations, known as the Uruguay Round.

The Uruguay Round trade talks, started in September 1986 in Punta del Este, Uruguay, were by far the most complex and ambitious talks on free trade since the founding of the General Agreement on Tariffs and Trade (GATT) in 1947. This was the first time that members addressed trade rules for agriculture, textiles, services, intellectual property rights, and foreign investment. The negotiators did not have an easy time getting the parties to sign a trade agreement, and the continued existence of the GATT was thrown into question. The breakthrough came in November 1992, with the Blair House agreement between the U.S. and EU negotiators.[7]

Initially, the French government reacted angrily to the agreement and stated that the deal did not jibe with the EU's reform of the CAP, which France supported. It then called for reopening the agreement for more negotiations. The French position created a division within the EU and prompted John Major to threaten to block French initiatives on Europe. After long arguments between the different parties, the United States decided to make some concessions in order to secure French acceptance of the GATT accords:

1. Exempt the EU's existing 25-million-ton cereal stockpile from the Blair House agreement.
2. Switch the base year from which subsidized exports must be reined in from the 1986–1989 average to 1992. Since the EU's subsidized cereal exports rose from 17 million tons to over 20 million tons in 1992, the change significantly reduced the impact of the Blair House accord and, over the six-year life of the implementation of the agreement, allowed the EU (primarily France) to export an additional 8 million tons of cereal.
3. Extend from six to eight years the "peace clause" under which the United States would not challenge the EU's export subsidy regime.[8]

In response to the U.S. concessions, the Europeans agreed to improve market access for American pork, grains, dairy products, and specialty goods (nuts, vegetables, almonds, and processed turkey). These allowances, however, did not mean much. They were not expected to significantly increase the sale of American goods in the EU markets because the demand was not expected to increase significantly. The EU also agreed to other concessions for the United States: Tariffs on steel, wood, pulp, and paper would be cut to zero; semiconductor equipment would also see tariff reduction to zero, but the semiconductors themselves would retain protection averaging 3 percent; and tariffs on nonferrous metals would also be reduced.[9]

The signing of the Uruguay Round, however, did not mean that the EU–U.S. trade relations were without future problems. Soon after, more issues surfaced that required mediation by the newly established WTO. At the Doha Round (2001–2005) of international trade negotiations, agricultural subsidies and their impact on free trade continued to be an area of dispute between the EU and the United States. Both sides maintain expensive policies. The cost per capita to U.S. citizens (total support estimate, TSE) of U.S. farm policy is $338/capita/year, while the cost per capita of the EU farm policy is $276/capita/year. This translates to $20,000/farmer in the United

States and $14,000/farmer in the EU.[10] Today trade policies on agricultural products continue to cause major disagreement among the EU, the United States, and the rest of the world. Midterm review of the CAP and subsequent reforms adopted by the EU should help alleviate some of the dispute. The EU's agreement to phase out agricultural subsidies by 2013 is also a positive step toward meeting the demands of the developing countries. However, challenges facing agriculture have also increased during the last years. Nontrade concerns, such as food safety and environmental protection, have become increasingly important and attracted growing public interest. As a result of public pressure on governments as well as international organizations, this debate has been extended to the WTO talks.

THE EU AS A GLOBAL ECONOMIC ACTOR

The EU is the world's largest trade bloc. Table 11.1 shows data on EU trade with its major trading partners. The figures show how intra-EU trade increased with the deepening of integration and the expansion of membership. Furthermore, the EU continues to be the main trade partner of countries on its periphery. This is especially the case for candidate countries like Turkey and those that are members of the European Economic Area (EEA), like Norway and Switzerland. Another significant development is seen in the rise of China's imports from and exports to the EU. Finally, the United States continues to be the single-largest trade partner of the EU.

EU–U.S. Economic Relations

The EU and the United States have been each other's most important trade partner. They are the world's two largest economies, accounting for 57 percent of global gross domestic product. Over the years, several trade disputes threatened to disrupt relations between the two allies, but they have maintained close ties and looked for ways to resolve their differences without damaging greater transatlantic security relations. The New Transatlantic Agenda (NTA) and the subsequent declaration of the Joint EU–U.S. Action Plan that was adopted at the EU Madrid Summit meeting of December 3, 1995, provide a clear joint-action program that commits the EU and the United States to collaboration in foreign policy, national security, drug trafficking, migration, environment, health, international crime, and concrete steps toward "building bridges across the Atlantic."[11]

Transatlantic Trade

The EU and the United States are the two largest economies and markets in the world. Taken together, they constitute half the world economy. The EU and the United States both account for around one-fifth of each other's bilateral trade, a matter of €1.7 billion a day. In 2006, exports of EU goods to the United States amounted to €268 billion (23 percent of total EU exports), while imports from the United States amounted to €176 billion (13 percent of total EU imports), as shown in Table 11.1. Moreover, the combined foreign trade figures of the two partners equal 40 percent of world trade. Furthermore, the total amount of two-way investment amounts to over €1.7 trillion, with each partner employing directly and indirectly about 6 million people in the other. The share of EU investment in the United States amounted to more than 52 percent of EU foreign direct investment (FDI) over the period 1998–2001 (€162.663 billion a year on average). The U.S. investment in the EU amounted to more than 61 percent of the EU's FDI inflows over 1998–2001 (€72.041 billion a year on average).[12]

As these figures show, EU–U.S. economic ties represent a very important component of transatlantic relations. At the last EU–U.S. Summit on April 30, 2007, Commission President Barroso, German Chancellor Merkel, and U.S. President Bush signed the "Framework for Advancing Transatlantic Economic Integration between the USA and the EU." Main points of

Table 11.1 ■ EU25 Trade by Main Trading Partners (1,000 million ecu/euro)

Leading Client and Supplier Countries of the EU25 in Merchandise Trade (value %)

2006 Excluding intra-EU trade

	The Major EU Import Partners*				The Major EU Export Partners				The Major EU Trader Partners		
Rank.	EU Imports from	Mio euro	% world	Rank.	EU Exports to	Mio euro	% world	Rank.	Imports +Exports	Mio euro	% world
	World	1,350,494	100.0		World	1,166,109	100.0		World	2,516,604	100.0
1	China	191,342	14.2	1	USA	267,672	23.0	1	USA	443,486	17.6
2	USA	175,813	13.0	2	Switzerland	86,392	7.4	2	China	254,590	10.1
3	Russia	136,847	10.1	3	Russia	71,791	6.2	3	Russia	208,638	8.3
4	Norway	79,019	5.9	4	China	63,248	5.4	4	Switzerland	157,214	6.2
5	Japan	75,631	5.6	5	Turkey	46,350	4.0	5	Japan	120,219	4.8
6	Switzerland	70,822	5.2	6	Japan	44,588	3.8	6	Norway	117,075	4.7
7	Turkey	38,488	2.8	7	Norway	38,056	3.3	7	Turkey	84,838	3.4
8	Korea	38,064	2.8	8	Romania	27,193	2.3	8	Korea	60,874	2.4
9	Brazil	26,175	1.9	9	Canada	26,473	2.3	9	India	46,355	1.8
10	Taiwan	26,139	1.9	10	United Arab Emir.	24,654	2.1	10	Canada	45,991	1.8
11	Libya	25,736	1.9	11	India	24,030	2.1	11	Romania	44,796	1.8
12	Algeria	24,125	1.8	12	Korea	22,809	2.0	12	Brazil	43,829	1.7
13	Saudi Arabia	23,440	1.7	13	Hong Kong	21,589	1.9	13	Saudi Arabia	40,839	1.6
14	India	22,326	1.7	14	Australia	21,274	1.8	14	Taiwan	39,364	1.6

(Continued)

Source: Eurostat (Statistical regime 4).

Table 11.1 ■ (Continued)

Leading Supplier Countries of the EU25 in Merchandise Trade (Imports)

EU Imports	2006		2005		2004		2003		2002	
				Excluding intra-EU trade						
				The Major EU Import Partners						
	Rank.	Mio euro	Rank.	Mio euro	Rank.	Mio euro	Rank.	Mio euro	Rank.	Mio euro
World		**1,350,494**		**1,182,476**		**1,032,206**		**940,347**		**941,885**
China	1	191,342	2	158,481	2	127,463	2	105,389	2	89,610
USA	2	175,813	1	162,545	1	158,364	1	157,385	1	181,867
Russia	3	136,847	3	109,612	3	80,722	4	67,777	4	61,999
Norway	4	79,019	5	67,083	6	55,219	6	50,964	6	47,962
Japan	5	75,631	4	73,417	4	74,204	3	72,005	3	73,328
Switzerland	6	70,822	6	66,133	5	61,605	5	58,790	5	61,417
Turkey	7	38,488	8	33,617	7	30,946	7	25,854	8	23,584
Korea	8	38,064	7	33,879	8	30,295	8	25,718	7	24,276
Brazil	9	26,175	10	23,449	10	21,208	10	18,781	10	18,081
Taiwan	10	26,139	9	23,834	9	23,598	9	22,367	9	23,226
Libya	11	25,736	13	19,814	19	13,673	20	10,995	22	9,519
Algeria	12	24,125	12	20,879	17	15,252	15	14,594	14	14,378
Saudi Arabia	13	23,440	11	22,574	13	16,266	17	12,991	17	12,352
India	14	22,326	14	18,915	14	16,234	16	13,975	16	13,608
Canada	15	19,518	16	17,170	12	16,267	11	15,836	11	16,625

(Continued)

Table 11.1 ■ (Continued)

Leading Client Countries of the EU25 in Merchandise Trade

Excluding intra-EU trade

The Major EU Export Partners

EU Exports	2006 Rank	2006 Mio euro	2005 Rank	2005 Mio euro	2004 Rank	2004 Mio euro	2003 Rank	2003 Mio euro	2002 Rank	2002 Mio euro
World		1,166,109		1,062,638		964,650		878,483		900,424
USA	1	267,672	1	251,813	1	234,615	1	226,432	1	247,022
Switzerland	2	86,392	2	82,436	2	75,053	2	71,243	2	72,647
Russia	3	71,791	3	56,572	4	45,832	5	37,066	5	34,279
China	4	63,248	4	51,646	3	48,189	3	41,170	4	34,869
Turkey	5	46,350	6	41,883	6	38,009	6	29,444	7	25,448
Japan	6	44,588	5	43,641	5	43,343	4	40,948	3	43,432
Norway	7	38,056	7	33,768	7	30,693	7	27,557	6	28,029
Romania	8	27,193	10	21,849	12	18,039	13	14,777	19	13,137
Canada	9	26,473	9	23,768	8	22,015	8	21,513	8	22,830
United Arab Emir.	10	24,654	8	25,341	11	18,728	11	16,467	15	14,679
India	11	24,030	11	21,092	14	17,031	14	14,517	16	14,271
Korea	12	22,809	14	20,156	13	17,843	12	16,370	10	17,594
Hong Kong	13	21,589	13	20,434	10	19,165	9	18,297	9	20,238
Australia	14	21,274	12	20,714	9	19,885	10	17,515	11	16,864

Source: EU Trade Commissioner, http://epp.eurostat.cec.eu.int/portal.

this agreement include a work program for cooperation and the creation of the Transatlantic Economic Council (TEC) to oversee implementation of the work program. The TEC is chaired by Commission Vice President Günter Verheugen and the Assistant to the U.S. President for Economic Policy and Director of the National Economic Council Al Hubbard.

However, trade between the two allies has not been smooth or free of disputes over the years. At the heart of most of these disagreements, among other issues, are U.S. complaints over EU subsidies for production and exports in such sensitive areas as agriculture, steel, and aircraft. The EU complains about unilateral U.S. measures such as Section 301 of the 1974 U.S. Trade Act and the Super 301 provision of the 1988 Omnibus Trade Act, which allow the U.S. government to impose unilateral punitive sanctions on goods from U.S. trade partners without consultation with the GATT (now the WTO), and the U.S. policy on steel, which resulted in the largest transatlantic dispute in history.

The Super 301 provision requires the United States to list publicly the countries that trade unfairly with it, to negotiate removal of such practices, and to take retaliatory action if negotiations with those countries fail. The United States' trade partners have been highly critical of this policy, and their concerns were echoed in a GATT report in December 1988. They fear that different U.S. administrations could resort to the political use of Super 301 to gain an advantageous position in their bilateral trade relations with other countries.[13]

Agricultural products

Other important issues have continued to present problems in EU–U.S. trade in the post–Uruguay Round years. Some of the key areas of contention are the banana import decision of the EU, the EU's ban on the use of growth hormones in livestock and the subsequent ban on importing meat from the United States, the U.S. farm subsidies versus the EU subsidies, the steel industry, the Foreign Sales Corporation (FSC) subsidies, and the U.S. Helms-Burton Act.

The banana trade dispute did not directly affect U.S. exports to the EU, but it does affect U.S. companies that grow bananas in Lomé countries (former European colonies in Africa, the Caribbean, and the Pacific). In 1993, the EC adopted a common market organization (CMO) for bananas that was designed to give preferential treatment to banana imports from the Lomé countries.[14]

The United States objected to this decision and threatened to impose punitive tariffs against selected imports from the EU. The case eventually ended up in the WTO when the EU complained about U.S. threats. In 1997, the WTO ruled that the EU banana CMO was illegal. This decision prompted the EU to revise its scheme in January 1999. However, the WTO also found the revised scheme illegal. The United States continued to press for EU reversal of the CMO. When the Commission failed to satisfy the U.S. demand, the Clinton administration imposed trade sanctions with an annual value of $191 million on imports from the EU. This was carried out in the form of punitive tariffs (100 percent customs duties) on an equivalent amount of trade (measured by the loss of export income to EU markets by U.S. banana growers in non-ACP countries). Furthermore, the United States chose to carry out these sanctions on a rotating basis by identifying which imports to target every six months. The banana dispute entered a new phase during the Bush administration, when the EU agreed with Ecuador and the United States in 2001 to move from a complex import system based on a combination of tariffs and quotas for bananas to a regime based solely on a tariff by January 1, 2006, and obtained two waivers from its WTO obligations for the preference granted to bananas from the African, Caribbean, and Pacific countries (ACP) countries under the terms of the ACP–EC Partnership Agreement (the Cotonou Agreement). The Commission proposed a single tariff of €187 per ton for bananas imported from countries—mainly in Latin America—enjoying most-favored-nation status and a duty-free quota of 775,000 tons for ACP bananas to be effective as of January 1, 2006. However, the WTO arbitrators rejected this proposal on October 27, 2005.[15] Finally on May 19, 2008, the

WTO panel issued a report in favor of the United States, but the matter is not quite closed as the EU has the option of appealing the report to the WTO Appellate Body.

The EU's decision to ban beef and other livestock products that have been produced with growth hormones produced another serious trade dispute. The disagreement between Brussels and Washington has been ongoing for several years, with no end in sight. The United States initially claimed losses of $202 million annually, but the WTO arbitrator estimated the level at $116.8 million.[16] The reluctance of the EU to lift the ban resulted in U.S. retaliation through a 100 percent ad valorem duty rate on mainly agricultural products. The problem is not likely to disappear any time soon, since the EU's Scientific Committee of Veterinary Measures Relating to Public Health (SCVPH) reported on the risk to human health of six growth hormones in livestock.

Dispute over agricultural support levels resurfaced in 2002 following the adoption of the Farm Security and Rural Investment Act of 2002 by the U.S. Congress.[17] This new U.S. program sets out various agricultural support schemes under ten titles, notably the commodity (farm subsidy) program, conservation, and trade, and will last for six years. The estimated spending on the programs is between $15 billion and $20 billion and represents a 70 percent increase in the amount previously set at the end of the FAIR Act. The EU argues that the new support level of the United States most likely violates the aggregate measure of support (AMS) agreed on at Doha.[18] The United States counters EU criticism by explaining that the American AMS level is far below the overall European figures, and that corrective measures will be taken to assure U.S. compliance with the AMS target of $19.1 billion. In response, the EU accuses U.S. officials of engaging in creative bookkeeping and excluding certain figures, like $4 billion–$5 billion in price supports for sugar and dairy industries, from the overall statistics.

Steel Industry

Another crucial trade dispute between the EU and the United States concerns the steel industry, with each side accusing the other of unfair trade practices. Both sides heavily subsidize their steel industries, the United States by import quotas and the EU by various policies implemented under the European Coal and Steel Community (ECSC). One episode in this dispute involved the U.S. Department of Commerce's announcement of preliminary countervailing duties on flat-rolled steel imports from six EU countries in 1992 and again in 1994.[19]

The EU–U.S. trade war in this sector took a turn for the worse in 2002, when the Bush administration decided to impose duties on steel imports to protect domestic industries. The United States unilaterally imposed tariffs up to 30 percent on imported steel for three years, claiming that other countries are dumping steel at below the cost of production and damaging its domestic industry. The U.S. claim is bitterly disputed by the EU, Japan, and other major steel producers, which argue that the measure is designed to protect inefficient American industry. The EU took its complaint to the WTO and threatened to impose its own countersanctions against a range of U.S. products worth $350 million. When the EU complaint was followed by similar complaints from Brazil, China, Japan, Korea, New Zealand, Norway, and Switzerland, the WTO reviewed the case and issued a ruling that the U.S. measures violated the WTO Safeguard Agreement and the GATT 1994.[20] Soon after, the EU followed this decision with a threat of retaliation. Faced with this mounting pressure, the Bush administration terminated U.S. steel safeguard measures on December 4, 2003, some 16 months before its scheduled ending. In return, the EU terminated its countermeasures on December 12, 2003.[21]

The FSC Issue

This topic pertains to substantial U.S. tax breaks, through exemption from the general tax rules, for American companies exporting through FSCs. The scheme was introduced in 1984 as a replacement for the earlier U.S. policy that GATT had found in violation of free-trade agreements. Once again, the EU complained to the U.S. administration to reverse this policy. When consultations failed, the EU took the case to the WTO. Acting on EU complaints of violation of free and fair trade, the WTO concluded that the U.S. tax breaks for exporters contravened international trade rules and cost European companies billions of U.S. dollars a year in lost trade.[22] The level of permitted retaliation was up to $4 billion. The U.S. Congress responded by partially repealing the FSC policy, but, according to Fritz Breuss, this decision fell short of EU expectations and guarantees future dispute in this policy area.

The Helms–Burton Act

The EU also opposes the extraterritorial provisions in the Helms–Burton Act. Helms–Burton was created in retaliation against Cuba, which downed two unarmed U.S. civilian airplanes flying just outside Cuba's territorial waters. The act authorizes U.S. citizens to sue investors who trade with or invest in Cuba. Furthermore, those who do business with Cuba can be denied visas to the United States. The EU, other countries such as Canada, and the WTO contend that the United States has no right to dictate which countries can and cannot trade with Cuba.

Airbus Versus Boeing

While U.S. defense industries dominate the high-end market of military aircraft, the same cannot be said about commercial aviation. In this sector, the competition between EU's Airbus Industries and the U.S.-based Boeing Corporation provides a textbook case of struggle for market domination, coupled with various government subsidies aimed at achieving that goal. Airbus was created in 1970 as a European consortium and has been the pride and joy of the EU since. During the 1990s, Airbus slowly gained market share against Boeing and eventually surpassed the latter in aircraft sales in 2004 with delivery of 315 jets compared to Boeing's 285.[23] The United States maintains that Airbus has an unfair market advantage because it received up to $17 billion in "launch subsidies for its planes" over the last 35 years, while the EU argues that Boeing received R&D subsidies of $23 billion during the last 13 years.[24] The issue of "launch subsidies" refers to what political economists call strategic trade policy under which governments tend to provide subsidies to strategic industries (strategic in terms of market rather than defense) to provide added incentive for these companies to launch new products in a market where demand does not support production by more than one manufacturer. Thus, strategic trade policies aim to promote exports or discourage imports in particular sectors in order to increase a nation's welfare. While some policy makers advocate the policy, many economists have raised questions over its justification and validity. Among many strategic trade policies, this section analyzes "industrial subsidy" using game theory.

The economics of the game in this industry is perhaps best described by the following summary provided by *The Economist* magazine:

> The origins of this long-running dispute lie in the economics of the development and manufacture of large commercial aircraft. Modern planes sell for between $50m and $250m, depending on whether they are 120-seaters or jumbos. Each new model contains huge technical risks. Will it fly as safely and efficiently as the engineers calculate? Can it be built to the required price? A new plane also requires huge upfront R&D spending before the first test flight. The latest Airbus, the A380 double-decker to carry 555 passengers, had cost around $12 billion even before its first test flight a couple of months ago. The new Boeing 787 will probably cost at least $10 billion to develop.
>
> Once production starts, the learning curve is steep and difficult. Each doubling of production generally yields a cut of one-fifth in unit cost per plane. Consequently, it takes production of about 500–600 aircraft before a model starts to earn a profit. That would typically amount to around ten years of production. Total industry demand in good years runs around 700–800 planes but is spread across a wide range from short-haul, single-aisle models to long-range and jumbo aircraft. The combination of these factors

explains why the industry has a tendency towards natural monopoly. It also explains why a company such as Boeing, which has enjoyed over two-thirds of the market since the launch of the 747 over 30 years ago, does not rush to bring new models to market—it wants to milk its incumbent dominance.[25]

Here is a game theoretic description of this strategic game. Boeing and Airbus are competing in a world market. They can choose to produce (P) a new aircraft or not (N), as displayed in Figure 11.1a. The market situation is such that

- If they both produce, competition will drive down the price and they will both lose—payoff (−5, −5).
- If neither produces, neither gains—payoff (0, 0).
- If one produces and the other doesn't, the producing company takes the entire market share and the other company gets nothing—payoff (100, 0) or (0, 100), depending on who produces and who does not.
- Here we find two Nash equilibria (P, N) and (N, P). In a Nash equilibrium, no player has an incentive to deviate from the strategy chosen, since no player can choose a better strategy, given the choices of the other players.
- The logical outcome of this scenario is for both companies not to produce.

Now suppose that the European government regards the aircraft industry as very important. To encourage Airbus to enter the market, the EU decides to give Airbus a "launch subsidy" of $10 billion. This changes some payoffs and changes the game's structure (Figure 11.1b):

- If Boeing chooses P, Airbus will choose P because the latter cannot lose—payoff (−5, −5).
- If Boeing chooses N, Airbus will still choose P—payoff (0, 110).
- Now Airbus has a dominant strategy, P. Then, theoretically, Boeing calculates its payoff again and finds that N is its best strategy.

Although this looks attractive for Airbus, there are other factors to consider. The United States can retaliate by subsidizing Boeing with its own launch subsidy and create a subsidy war that could get out of control. Then Boeing will keep producing (strategy P), which will incur losses to both producers. The net losers in this case will be the consumers and taxpayers.

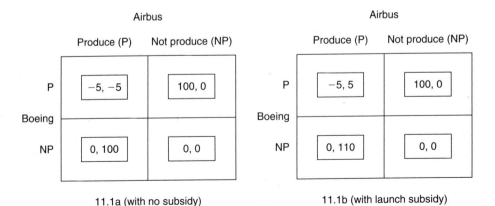

Figure 11.1 ■ Strategic Payoff Matrix of the Airbus Versus Boeing Game

At present, both companies are busy developing new and better versions of older aircraft to capture significant markets. Airbus will modify its A340 with a new A340–600 to compete with Boeing's newest version of 777, which broke the longest flight record without fueling. Airbus's double-decker A380, capable of carrying 555 passengers, entered the market in 2006. Boeing recently announced that it will modify the jumbo jet, resulting in the 747–748, to increase passenger capacity from 416 to 450 and reduce operating cost by 20 percent compared to the A380.[26] Finally, Boeing has been very successful in developing a midrange aircraft, known as the dreamliner, and expects to complete orders for 112 of the aircraft during 2008–2009. Not surprisingly, Airbus announced that it intends to develop a new plane, the A350, to compete with Boeing's dreamliner.

The tit-for-tat accusations of unfair subsidies by the EU and United States finally ended up at the WTO in July 2005, following the U.S. decision to go to the arbitrating body in October 2004 over the case of the A350 and A380 versus Boeing. The WTO set up panels to investigate these accusations, which promises to be the costliest and most complicated case in the organization's history.

The most recent dispute in the Airbus–Boeing rivalry emerged over the U.S. Air Force's (USAF) decision to choose the European aircraft maker for supplying a new generation of air refueling tankers worth $35 billion. The USAF decision to choose the modified version of A330 that will be a joint product of the EADS and American Northrop Grumman angered Boeing executives as well as key politicians in the House Appropriations Defense Subcommittee of the Congress. Representative Norm Dicks, whose district is home to many Boeing workers in the state of Washington, said that Airbus had an unfair advantage due to large subsidies it receives from European governments.[27] Other politicians echoed this point of view. The USAF acquisition chief Sue Payton disputed these claims and noted that the Buy America Act allows the Department of Defense to treat companies in several countries including France and Germany as U.S.-based ones.[28] However, domestic political pressure resulted in cancellation of the USAF decision and reopening of the bid in July 2008, following a report by the US Government Accounting Office that faulted the USAF's estimation of costs associated with each proposal.[29]

Trade Row Over Information Technology Products

Following the EU's decision to impose tariff duties on certain high-tech goods that included flat-screen televisions and multifunctional printers, the United States filed a formal complaint with the WTO requesting dispute settlement. It is estimated that the tariffs imposed by the EU affect a market worth more than €450 billion.[30] The United States is joined by Japan in this complaint. They claim that the EU decision violates the Information Technology Agreement (ITA) of 1996, which aimed at expanding trade in IT and telecommunication products by eliminating tariffs on a wide range of goods. Today 71 countries are signatories to this agreement. What angered the United States and Japan is the EU's policy not to consider new products developed from goods already in the ITA, as covered by the agreement. As such, traditional printers are duty-free in the EU, while more recently evolved versions, which are also capable of scanning or faxing, are not. The United States maintains that such technological developments were foreseeable and that new machines should benefit from similar tariff reductions as those already developed ten years ago. The European officials' response is that the 1996 Agreement was explicit regarding which products it covered and that a new negotiation is needed to review the list of new products.

Microsoft Versus The EU

The dispute between Microsoft and the EU dates back to 1998, when the European Commission began investigating this company's business practices, based on a complaint from Sun Microsystems. It is a classic case of anti-monopoly in international commerce. The original claim against Microsoft stated that the company had failed to provide technical information necessary for servers running Sun's Solaris operating system to fully interoperate with personal computers running Windows. In August 2000 and August 2001, the Commission issued two statements criticizing Microsoft's business practices. It also alleged that Microsoft engaged in unfair competition with Real Networks and other vendors of media players by tying Windows Media Player with the Windows operating system. These statements led to discussion between Microsoft and the Commission that lasted two years. On March 24, 2004, the Commission issued its final decision that found Microsoft in breach of European competition law through "abuse of a dominant market position" and fined the company €497 million. It called Microsoft to create a version of Windows without its Media Player and to license Windows server communications protocols.[31] Microsoft responded by introducing a draft of the licensing program for its server communications protocols and released a version of Windows in Europe that did not include its media program. However, in November 2004, the Commission found the draft unsatisfactory and threatened to impose €2 million a day penalty if the company did not comply with the earlier decision by December 15. When Microsoft dragged its feet on the matter, the Commission slapped a fine of €280.5 million in July 2006 and announced that any further delay on compliance would result in additional fines of up to €3 million per day. Microsoft's response on November 23, 2006, that included its final revised package announcing the availability of documentation to potential licensees did not satisfy the Commission and resulted in the fifth EU statement that concluded this company's incompliance with the March 2004 decision. The outcome of all this was the Commission's announcement in February 2008 that it was fining Microsoft a record €899 million for charging "unreasonable" prices to rivals for access to its software.

EU–China Economic Relations

There is no doubt that China has become a major economic power in the world. As discussed in Chapter 6, China, as the rising challenger in global power transition, has received the attention of the United States in the last decade and of the EU in recent years. In 2006, China (excluding Hong Kong) became the EU's second-largest trade partner (Table 11.1). The EU25, on the other hand, became China's largest trade partner as of 2004. In 2006, the EU's trade with China was worth €255 billion and reflected a growing trade deficit for the Europeans—€128 billion in 2006.

The EU was China's biggest supporter for the latter's WTO membership. There is no surprise then in the EU's recent focus on China's growing importance in global affairs. Current EU policy toward China is based on a policy paper of the Commission that the Council endorsed on October 13, 2003.[32] The strategy calls for enhanced political cooperation and dialogue on illegal immigration and in the economic and trade field, placing priority on cooperating on the Doha development agenda in the WTO and monitoring China's compliance with its WTO commitments. During the last three years, EU–China cooperation in science and technology also increased: In 2002, a mutual agreement was signed on maritime transport; on October 30, 2003, they signed a new agreement on cooperation under the EU's Galileo satellite navigation program; the science and technology agreement was renewed at the seventh EU–China Summit at the Hague on December 8, 2004; and they signed an agreement covering cooperation in nuclear energy research (linked to the Euratom agreement). In addition, Airbus and China's airlines signed substantial agreements for the purchase of European passenger aircraft. Finally, in June 2007 at a joint trade ministerial meeting in Brussels, the EU and China initiated a new dialogue in the fields of intellectual property rights, competition policy, enterprise policy, textiles, and environment and identified new initiatives on macroeconomic and financial issues, sanitary standards, and human resources development. All of these initiatives show the growing importance of EU–China relations.

However, as trade between the EU and China grows, so do areas of dispute. As Iana Dreyer and Fredrik Erixon explain, economic relations between the two partners took a downward turn during autumn 2007, when EU officials frustrated over the growing trade deficit and alleged Chinese currency manipulation called for corrective measures that included antidumping tariffs.[33] EU Trade Commissioner Peter Mandelson also indicated that litigations against China in the WTO would likely increase. At the heart of the problem are access to Chinese markets by European businesses and EU-based foreign direct investment (FDI) in China. Currently, EU represents 8 percent of FDI in China and views this figure to be extremely low. EU identifies China's investment regulations, especially in financial services, ineffective enforcement of key intellectual property rights, and technology transfer requirements as key obstacles facing European businesses.

EU–India Economic Relations

As noted in Chapter 6, India is the second rising economic giant of the twenty-first century. Moreover, if one considers the EU as an international organization that has statelike aspirations, the EU and India represent the world's two largest democracies. The EU–India foreign trade relations go back to 1994, when the two sides signed a cooperation agreement to promote a wide range of economic areas.[34] Earlier, India was among the first group of countries that established diplomatic relations with the EEC in the early 1960s and proceeded to sign bilateral agreements with the EC in 1973 and 1981 for trade promotion. Over the last two decades, trade between the EU and India grew to reach €46.4 billion in 2006 (Table 11.1), making this country EU's 17th-largest trade partner. In comparison, the EU is India's largest trading partner and main source of FDI. In 2005, EU investment outflows to India amounted to €2.2 billion and represented 1.3 percent of EU's total FDI outflows. EU investment has mainly taken place in the power/energy, telecommunications, and transport sectors. During 2007, the two sides adopted a Joint Action Plan to further improve bilateral trade, which was followed by an Indian proposal on May 20, 2008, to sign a free-trade agreement between the two sides.[35]

EU–Japan Economic Relations

Japan has been an important economic partner of the EU. As figures in Table 11.1 show, trade between the two has been significant. The EU's imports from Japan fell from a high of €91.8 billion in 2000 to €75.7 billion in 2006, while EU exports to Japan averaged €40 billion to €44 billion during the same time period. Yet, as any European business would remind us, Japan is a closed market for imports. At the same time, the EU is an important market for Japanese companies. This relationship has not been free of difficulties. The EU's relations with Japan suffer from the quantitative trade restrictions and voluntary export restraints (VERs) that the EU took over from its members as a result of the single market. Articles 113 and 115 of the Rome Treaty have played an important role in this area.

According to the Rome Treaty's Article 113, there was to be a common external tariff schedule for the EU member states by 1969. This was achieved in 1968 as part of the customs union. However, Article 115 provided an escape clause in permitting individual national trade policies as long as relevant parts of the common policy remained on the EU agenda as unsettled.

Protectionist trade policies continue to trouble EU–Japan relations, but the creation of the single market presented an important opportunity for the EU to abolish VERs and other quantitative restrictions on imports from Japan. VERs always cost the consumer, not the domestic producer and foreign exporters of the same products. In an attempt to reduce serious trade friction between the EU and Japan, the two sides reached an agreement on a post-1992 policy in July 1992. This agreement stated:

1. Intra-EC trade will be liberalized by the adoption of an EU-type approval scheme by January 1, 1993, and all national import restrictions will be abolished by the same date.
2. Imports of cars from Japan will be unrestricted after December 31, 1999, and in the intervening period will be limited to the level of 1.23 million (approximately the 1991 level of imports).
3. Cars produced in Japanese-owned plants in the EU will have unrestricted access to the EU markets.
4. There is an understanding about the levels of Japanese imports to France, Italy, Spain, Portugal, and the UK: a deliberate attempt will be made by Japanese firms to reduce adjustment pressures in the markets from which national import restrictions have been removed.[36]

This agreement seemed to allow for better relations in the future, but some outstanding issues remained in EU–Japan trade relations. The first was the continuous Japanese balance-of-payments surplus with the EU. Second, Japan's legal barriers limit EU exports to that country. Third, it is difficult for EU firms to sell consumer goods in Japan unless they have Japanese subsidiaries. The Japanese marketing and distribution system requires close collaboration among the producers, wholesalers, and retailers, which makes marketing and distribution costs higher for EU firms in Japanese markets than they are for Japanese companies in EU markets. Japanese companies maintain close collaboration with each other under the auspices of the Japanese Ministry of International Trade and Industry (MITI). Such collaboration inherently damages non-Japanese firms' access to fair competition. This sort of activity would be illegal in the EU market.[37] In an effort to overcome such problems, the two parties held a summit on July 19, 2000, to discuss avenues of cooperation. The final document covered all areas of international relations important to both parties.[38]

While the Japanese are not as well positioned as the Americans in the EU market, they are rapidly expanding their investments in such areas as banking, cars, electronics, computers, and the information industry. According to data provided by the EC, the trend in flows of FDI had been quite dynamic over the past decade, with a substantial increase of two-way investment flows in the period 1999–2000 and a moderate decrease in the following years: "Japan is a major investor in the EU. In 2003, 4.1 percent of EU inflows came from Japan. At the end of 2003, 5.03 percent of the stock of EU inward FDI came from Japan, while 0.6 percent of the EU outflow went to Japan. Over the past five years, the EU has become an important investor in Japan. At the end of 2003, 1.82 percent of the stock of EU outward FDI was in Japan, with a negative inflow (0.58 percent) in 2003. Japan's inward FDI has soared since the mid-1990s."[39]

At the last EU–Japan Summit in Tokyo, on June 22, 2004, Japan and the EU reconfirmed the importance of forging a strong strategic partnership.[40] They agreed to strengthen trade and bilateral investment links and endorsed a Cooperation Framework aimed at promoting two-way investment via concrete actions in areas such as the establishment of new regulations, regulatory transparency, standards and conformity assessment, and facilitation of conditions for foreign residents. Furthermore, the agreement called for continuation of the current intellectual property rights dialogue between the two sides, including the area of geographical indications, and presented a joint initiative to promote protection and encourage enforcement of intellectual property rights in Asia. This point is of particular importance for current WTO negotiations. Whether these agreements will reduce tension between the two parties over trade and investment imbalance or not remains to be seen.

European Economic Area

The EEA extends the freedoms of the single market (free movement of goods, services, capital, and people) to European Free Trade Association (EFTA) countries (Iceland, Liechtenstein, and Norway), but excludes Switzerland. In turn, these countries have adopted relevant parts of the *acquis communautaire* and case law associated with the first pillar of the EU. The EEA Agreement is concerned principally with the four fundamental pillars of the internal market, "the four freedoms": that is, freedom of movement of (1) goods (excluding agriculture and fisheries, which are included in the agreement to only a very limited extent), (2) persons, (3) services, and (4) capital. Horizontal provisions relevant to these four freedoms in the areas of social policy, consumer protection, environment, company law, and statistics complete the extended internal market. It is in these areas that the EEA–EFTA states take on Community legislation.

With the collapse of communism in Europe, concerns about neutral countries' impact on EU security policies largely disappeared. After 16 months of negotiations, the two communities (the EC and EFTA) agreed to create the world's largest trading area, the EEA. The original agreement, initially encompassing 19 European states[41] and 380 million citizens, called for the free flow of capital, services, workers, and most goods throughout the EEA as of January 1, 1994. This new trade area accounted for 46 percent of total world trade. At the same time, both the EU and individual EFTA countries maintained their individual tariff schedules for imports from third parties. Furthermore, the EFTA countries remained outside of the CAP and maintained their own, even more protectionist, agricultural policies.[42]

Despite initial enthusiasm about the EEA, the agreement suffered some setbacks. First, negotiations broke down because of a reservation registered by the European Court of Justice (ECJ). The ECJ's main concern was the proposed joint EU–EFTA tribunal, which would include 5 of the 13 judges of the ECJ, to resolve EEA-related disagreements. This raised a question: Would these EU judges still be allowed to rule on an EU case if a similar case had already been decided by the other body? The problem ended when the EU foreign ministers agreed to give the Commission more negotiating flexibility with EFTA by dropping the demand that EFTA countries apply EU laws uniformly under the EEA. The EU decided to drop the idea of the joint court envisaged under the EEA accord and proposed an arbitration procedure to settle any future disputes between the two communities. In return, EFTA members agreed to adopt future EU single-market legislation.

The second problem with the EEA was the Swiss rejection of the accord. This rejection came after Austria, Finland, Norway, and Sweden ratified the EEA and the ratification process was fully under way in EU member states. Furthermore, the European Parliament had approved the agreement. The Swiss rejection destroyed the chances of the EEA's starting on the same day as the single market and required renegotiation of the original accord to exclude Switzerland from the document.

Following these developments, four EFTA countries entered into membership talks with the EU and completed the terms for accession on March 1, 1994 (Austria, Finland, and Sweden) and March 15, 1994 (Norway). The delay with Norway involved fishing rights. On June 12, 1994, the Austrians voted by a 2-to-1 margin in favor of joining the EU. This vote provided a boost to the pro-EU position in other candidate countries. Finnish and Swedish voters adopted the referenda in the fall; however, Norwegian voters rejected membership by a majority of 52.2 percent to 47.8 percent.[43] As a result of these referenda, the EU membership expanded by three on January 1, 1995.

Most recently, a major challenge in 2003–2004 was to ensure that the EEA was enlarged at the same time as the EU, so as not to disturb the good functioning of the internal market. Therefore, the EU member states, the candidate acceding countries of the eastern enlargement, and the three EFTA countries signed an EEA Enlargement Agreement. The EEA Enlargement Agreement came into force on May 1, 2004, simultaneously with the enlargement of the EU.

Most of the elements of the EEA Enlargement Agreement are technical adaptations, but one of the major substantial results of the enlargement negotiations was a tenfold increase in the financial contribution of the EEA–EFTA states—in particular, Norway—to social and economic cohesion in the internal market (€1.167 billion over five years, €600 million from all three EEA–EFTA states, and an additional €567 million from Norway as a bilateral Norwegian contribution). Another element of the EEA Enlargement Agreement was that the Community would open additional quotas for certain marine and agricultural products from the EEA–EFTA states.[44]

The EU's Mediterranean Policy

The Mediterranean countries are collectively the EU's third-largest customer and its fourth-largest supplier of imports, including roughly 20 percent of its energy needs. The Global Mediterranean Policy (GMP), adopted at the 1972 Paris Summit, has been the blueprint for the EU's relations with the nonmember Mediterranean Basin countries (NMBCs). This policy aims to promote closer trade and financial relations between the EU and the NMBCs. It represents a crucial shift from the EC's bilateral relations with each country in the region to a multilateral approach in which the Mediterranean Basin is treated as a single region. The final agreement between the EU and its Mediterranean partners is the 1995 Barcelona Declaration, which represents the most comprehensive approach the EU has taken toward this region. Table 11.2 provides a summary of various association agreements signed between the EU and its Mediterranean neighbors.

There were political as well as economic motives for the EC's approach to the Mediterranean Basin. The strategy called for using economic power to promote regional stability, improve trade relations between the Community and the Mediterranean states, and check Soviet expansionism in the region.[45] However, despite such ambitions, several problems stood in the way of the GMP. First, the economies of the EC and the NMBCs were not sufficiently compatible to promote the desired level of trade. Second, while the industrial products of the NMBCs received easy access to EC markets, agricultural goods were not included in the GMP because of

Table 11.2 ■ Progress of Negotiation on Euro-Mediterranean Association Agreements

Partner	Conclusion of Negotiations	Signature of Agreement	Entry into Force
Tunisia	June 1995	July 1995	March 1998
Israel	September 1995	November 1995	June 2000
Morocco	November 1995	February 1996	March 2000
Palestinian Authority	December 1996	February 1997	July 1997
Jordan	April 1997	November 1997	May 2002
Egypt	June 1999	June 2001	June 2004
Lebanon	2002	June 2002	March 2003
Algeria	2002	April 2002	—
Syria	October 2004	—	—

Source: European Commission, *The Barcelona Process, Five Years On: 1995–2000* (Brussels: European Commission, 2000), p. 37 and update from EC Web site, http://europa.eu.int/comm/external_relations/euromed/med_ass_agreements.htm.

the CAP. Third, even in industrial products, key exports of the NMBCs—textiles and clothing, ships, steel, synthetic fibers, paper and paper products, machine tools, and cars—faced quota restrictions because the EC labeled these as "sensitive industries" that required Community protection. And, finally, there was the question of migrant workers from the NMBCs.[46]

One other issue creates friction between the EU and its Mediterranean neighbors: migrant workers. When the flow of workers reached its peak in 1980, there were over 6 million guest workers and their families in the EC.[47] The largest number came from Turkey: 714,000 workers and their dependents, of whom 591,000 were located in Germany. At one time, the guest workers were welcomed in the EC states because they were willing to work in manual-labor jobs that the citizens did not want. However, after three serious economic recessions in the EC, in 1974–1975, 1980–1983, and 1991–1993, the governments of the member states adopted strict controls on the influx of guest workers and refugees (particularly asylum seekers in Germany). Militant right-wing extremists in the recipient countries began to attack these foreigners, causing many deaths and serious injuries.

To address these policy concerns, the Council called for a four-stage program—a blueprint for the construction of the new Mediterranean policy. The first stage called for adoption of an EU position paper setting out general guidelines for revitalizing the Mediterranean policy. During the second stage, a "Mediterranean Forum," consisting of EC and NMBC representatives, would be established. Its purpose would be to prepare specific guidelines for sectoral policies, launch major pilot development agreements, and coordinate and support member states' policies toward the region. The third stage would involve the establishment of a center or agency that would provide technical support for the development agreements. And, finally, an EU–NMBC joint development convention would convene to establish specific institutions for the previously mentioned purposes.[48]

In accordance with the guidelines, the Commission, upon the request of the Council of Ministers, proposed a policy package for the GMP that called for providing economic and technical assistance to the NMBCs, improving nonmembers' access to EC markets, and promoting direct foreign investment in the Mediterranean Basin.[49]

In September 1990, the Mediterranean members of the EC, led by the Italian foreign minister, Gianni De Michelis, called for the establishment of a Conference on Security and Cooperation in the Mediterranean.[50] This idea was modeled after the Conference on Security and Cooperation in Europe. The Italian and Spanish officials feared that the growing economic and demographic disparities between the EC members and the NMBCs would be damaging to the long-term interests of the EC. While they argued that such a conference should include all of the eastern Mediterranean states, even extending to the Persian Gulf and Iran, the French maintained that cooperation ought to start with a more narrow focus—namely, the Maghreb (Morocco, Algeria, and Tunisia). Despite the appearance of some differences in approach to the GMP, it was clear that the Mediterranean Basin had once again become one of the important issues on the EU agenda.

The EU leaders provided some answers at the June 1994 Summit meeting in Corfu, Greece. At this meeting, they invited the Commission to draft a new southern strategy for the Mediterranean Basin.[51] The Commission responded by proposing the biggest free-trade zone in the world, to include the EU and its North African and Middle Eastern neighbors. According to Manuel Marin, EU Commissioner for Mediterranean Affairs: "In broad terms, what we would be offering is something like the EEA. The main difference would be that whereas four of the seven members of EFTA—Austria, Finland, Sweden, and Norway—are poised to enter the EU next year, membership would not be on offer to Euro-Med partners [except Cyprus, Malta, and Turkey]."[52]

The Commission's proposal received support from the EU leaders at the December 1994 Essen Summit. At this meeting, the EU reiterated its support for a Euro-Mediterranean partnership with a long-term goal of free trade. The final result came in the form of a bold agreement between the EU and 12 Mediterranean countries (plus the Palestinian Authority), known as the Barcelona Declaration, signed in November 1995. This agreement commits the two sides to creating an area of peace and prosperity, improving mutual understanding between the peoples of the region within a free and flourishing civil society, engaging in political cooperation to promote democracy and human rights and fight international crime, and establishing a free-trade zone in the Mediterranean Basin by 2010.[53] In addition to these priority areas, the work program covers social reforms, environment, migration, weapons of mass destruction, and counterterrorism (see Table 11.3). The financial assistance program of the EU for Mediterranean partnership is the MEDA program. MEDA 1, which lasted from 1995 to 1999, had a budget of €3,435 million, plus another €425 million for the peace process (aid to the Palestinians).[54] During this period, the European Investment Bank also made loans of €4,808 million to the Mediterranean region. Furthermore, the new Mediterranean partnership helped increase trade between the EU and the Mediterranean countries. EU's imports from Mediterranean countries amounted to €98.6 billion

Table 11.3 ■ New Initiative of the Commission for Euro-Med Policy

2005	• The Euro-Med partners should launch regional negotiations, on a voluntary basis, on the liberalization of services and establishment. The Commission will submit negotiating guidelines for approval by the Council to this effect.
	• Euro-Mediterranean partners should agree on a road map for agricultural liberalization, including processed agricultural products and fisheries. The Commission will submit negotiating guidelines for approval by the Council to start negotiations with partner countries.
	• The Pan-Euro-Med Protocol of Origin will be progressively implemented throughout the Euromed, from 2005.
	• Organize a workshop on Weapons of Mass Destruction 2005.
	• A Euro-Mediterranean Transport Ministerial should take place before the end of the year with the participation of the European Investment Bank (EIB), to endorse a regional transport infrastructure network interconnected to the Trans-European Transport Network, and agree on the priorities of the Euro-Mediterranean Transport cooperation for the next few years.
	• A Ministerial Conference on economic and financial affairs will take place in Rabat.
2006	• A Euro-Mediterranean Conference will be held, prepared at the sub-regional level, on human rights and democratization.
	• Approximation work in the field of technical legislation, standards and certification procedures should have intensified so as to pave the way for negotiations on conformity assessment agreements (ACAAs). The Conference should concentrate on the comparison of best practices within the region to raise the role of women in society and their contribution to human development.
	• Adoption of a timetable with concrete measures with the objective of a thorough de-pollution of the Mediterranean by 2020.
	• In the light of the FEMIP experience, and following consultations with partner countries, the Commission will assess before the end of the year the possibility of establishing a Euro-Mediterranean Development Bank.
	• The Commission will launch a Scholarship scheme for university students either within the existing Erasmus Mundus program or by reinforcing mobility activities inside the Tempus scheme.
	• A Euro-Mediterranean Energy Ministerial should take place in view of progressing sub-regional energy integration markets and infrastructures.

2007
- Euro-Mediterranean Partners should reach agreement before the end of the year on a code of conduct on measures to fight terrorism.
- A Euro-Mediterranean conference of Justice and Home Affairs Ministers, with the participation of local authorities, should be held to discuss management of migratory flows and social integration.
- A regional program on rural development and optimization of quality production should be identified for implementation.
- After consultation with partner countries, the percentage devoted to bilateral cooperation in the education sector should be increased by 50 percent of the national and regional indicative program.
- The Democracy Facility will enter into force.

2010
- All South-South free-trade agreements should be concluded and implemented by the end of the year, including for services and establishment as well as agriculture.
- Completion of Euro-Mediterranean electricity and gas markets and infrastructure interconnections.

Source: European Commission, *Commission Launches 5-Year Work Programme to Reinforce Euro-Mediterranean Partnership*, IP/05/419, Brussels, 12 April 2005, http://europa.eu.int/comm/external_relations/euromed/barcelona_10/docs/10th_comm_en.pdf.

in 2006, while its exports to these countries totaled €106.3 billion.[55] Finally, the two parties began collaboration on initiatives to protect cultural heritage, youth projects, and civil society.

Once again, these are ambitious proposals that are aimed at promoting development in these countries and reducing problems EU countries face with illegal immigration and security vulnerabilities on their southern borders (discussed in Chapter 12). Yet, despite the soundness of these proposals, much depends on stability in the region.

The ACP Countries

The centerpiece of EU–ACP relations is the Lomé IV Convention, signed on December 15, 1989, in the capital of Togo by the EC and 68 African, Caribbean, and Pacific states, most of which were former European colonial territories. The number of ACP countries increased to 77 in 2000. The Lomé IV Convention is in the tradition of the earlier agreements between the two sides: Yaoundé I (1963), Yaoundé II (1969), Lomé I (1975), Lomé II (1979), and Lomé III (1984). According to Catherine Flaesch-Mougin and Jean Raux, the Lomé IV Convention was "a symbol of continuity, renovation, and innovation."[56] The history of the Lomé conventions resembles that of the GMP in that the initial enthusiasm quickly gave way to cynicism. The conventions neither changed the basic structures of North–South relations nor improved the economic conditions of the ACP countries. From the ACP point of view, the erosion of trade preferences through the EU's General System of Preferences (GSP) and GATT, combined with the refusal of the EU to open its markets to more imports from ACP countries, seriously damaged the trade and industrial cooperation agreements of these conventions. Furthermore, according to John Ravenhill, the aid aspect gradually replaced commercial cooperation as the cornerstone of the Lomé agreements, since aid is far cheaper for the EC.[57] This development is clearly different from the experiences of the GMP countries, where commercial relations dominate the agenda.

Problems with the Earlier Agreements

Trade had been a major disappointment in the former conventions. For ACP countries, trade was of crucial importance, since the EC was the principal trading partner for most of them. The Lomé conventions granted unilateral free access for ACP products to the EC markets without being subject to tariffs, quotas, or other restrictive regulations. However, there was a serious restriction concerning agricultural products that fall under the CAP. Furthermore, the EC reserved the right to change trade policies in case of serious economic or trade imbalances of the EC members. Such regulations proved to be detrimental for products like textiles and clothing, when the EC decided to label these industries sensitive industries, subject to special protection. The ACP countries viewed these special clauses as indications of growing protectionism in the EU.

Lomé I–III provided multilateral funds, mainly through the European Development Fund (EDF) and the EIB, for financial and technical assistance to ACP countries. Lomé I specified 3.5 billion ecus for this purpose. Lomé II raised this figure to 5.6 billion ecus, and Lomé III further increased it to 8.5 billion ecus. Yet these increases are in reality decreases over time due to the high population growth rates and inflation in ACP countries and the increase in the number of countries signing on to the Lomé conventions. Thus, there was a decline in financial assistance in real and per capita terms from Lomé I to Lomé II and from Lomé II to Lomé III.[58] The convention's duration is ten years.

Lomé IV trade provisions remained unchanged from the previous conventions—that is, ACP countries continued to have free access to EU markets without reciprocity. The trade arrangements, however, were adjusted to provide better conditions for some ACP products.[59]

In addition, STABEX and SYSMIN were overhauled and redefined. The EU added cocoa derivatives, essential oil products, and squid to the program and lowered the threshold limit for its implementation. It was also agreed that in the future, the system would cover commodities that make up 5 percent of an ACP country's total exports to EU and other ACP states. This figure would be 1 percent for the less-developed countries. These figures were 6 percent and 1.5 percent, respectively, under the previous Lomé agreement.[60] Furthermore, under Lomé IV, the STABEX allocation increased by 66 percent from Lomé III figures to 1.4 billion ecus. SYSMIN, on the other hand, extended product coverage to include uranium and gold.

The financial protocol of Lomé IV provided for 12 billion ecus (10.8 billion from the EDF and 1.2 billion from the EIB) for aid to ACP states. Even though this is a substantial increase from the 8.5 billion ecus provided under Lomé III, it is considerably less than the amount requested by ACP countries (15.5 billion ecus). This protocol also included structural adjustment support for ACP countries in the amount of 1.15 billion ecus. While this figure is rather small, the decision of the EU to include such financing, along with international debt rescheduling, showed that the EU was prepared to assert itself as a principal financial actor in international economic restructuring alongside the World Bank and the International Monetary Fund.[61]

After the expiration of Lomé IV, the EU and ACP successfully negotiated a new ACP–EC Partnership Agreement (ACP–EC PA) that entered into effect on March 1, 2000, for a period of eight years. This period is shorter than the earlier trade regime, which lasted ten years. It is a regulatory regime that is designed to help the ACP countries integrate into the world economy through multilateral trade. The banana protocol of the previous agreement is excluded from the ACP–EC PA due to pressures from the WTO and the United States.

New ACP–EU Agreement

Today's relations with the ACP are governed by the ACP–EU PA, signed in Cotonou, Benin, on June 23, 2000, and concluded for a period of 20 years. At the same time, the remaining overseas countries and territories (OCTs) continue to be associated to the Community through successive association decisions of the Council. In 2004, trade with the ACP members totaled €55 billion and imports from these countries amounted to €28.4 billion. For most of the ACP countries, the EU remains their key trade partner. The new agreement is similar to the Euromed agreement in both scope and ambition and covers five main pillars of cooperation: comprehensive political cooperation, participatory approaches, strengthened focus on poverty reduction, a new framework for economic and trade cooperation, and a reform of financial cooperation.[62] For this purpose, the EU commits to a €13.5 billion European Development Fund (EDF) covering the agreement's first five years and support for the ACP governments in their attempts to create a balanced macroeconomic picture with expansion of the private sector and improvement of both the quality and the coverage of social services. A sum of €10 billion is allotted for long-term allowance, €1.3 billion is for regional allowance, and €2.2 billion is for investment facility. In addition, €9 billion remains from the previous EDF and another €1.7 billion is available at the EIB.

Political cooperation emphasizes democratic institution building, dialogue, respect for human rights, and peaceful resolution of conflicts. The participatory approaches refer to the inclusion of nongovernmental organizations and interest groups in decision-making processes and the creation of participation channels for them. Economic development is the most comprehensive aspect of the new agreement, with the EU committing itself to develop ACP economies, include women in mainstream economic sectors, eliminate poverty, and reduce unemployment. With trade and financial issues, the EU provides preferential trade to imports from ACP countries and liberalizes trade regimes and introduces financial instruments to support development projects (see the preceding discussion).

Despite significant improvements in cooperation agreements, ACP countries face an uncertain future in their relations with the EU. As the EU places greater emphasis on the "deepening of integration" and enlargement, the ACP countries' preferential position is likely to be undermined in a way similar to the problem faced by the GMP countries. Furthermore, there are external pressures on the EU from the WTO and the United States to make substantial reforms to the preferential trade provisions of the Lomé agreements (e.g., the banana crisis), discussed previously in this chapter.

STUDY QUESTIONS

1. Explain the nature of the EU–U.S. trade conflict within the context of the WTO negotiations. How does the EU trade policy relate to the Union's internal policies of redistribution after Eastern enlargement? What is the nature of this connection in terms of EU politics?
2. Discuss the evolution of EU's Mediterranean policy using the neoliberal intergovernmentalism model.
3. Discuss EU as a global actor in the context of its evolving foreign trade policies.
4. What are the key components of the European Economic Area?
5. Explain the key aspects of EU's trade policy towards China, Japan, and India.
6. What are the Lomé Agreements, and how do they affect EU's trade relations with third-party countries?

ENDNOTES

1. *Treaty of Nice: Amending the Treaty of the European Union, the Treaties Establishing the European Communities and Certain Related Acts.* (2001/C80/01). Art 2, par. 8.
2. Data obtained from Eurostat trade statistics, http://ec.europa.eu/trade/issues/bilateral/data.htm
3. Simon Hix, *The Political System of the European Union* (New York: St. Martin's Press, 1999), p. 338.

4. European Commission, *The EU and the Millennium Round: More Trade Based on Better Rules*, http://europa.eu.int/comm/trade/2000
5. *BBC World News*, December 18, 2005, 18:13 GMT.
6. Ibid.
7. David Gardner, "Hopes Rising That Deal Can Be Saved," *Financial Times*, September 20, 1993, p. 3.

8. David Dodwell, "Concessions by U.S. Sweeten GATT Pill," *Financial Times*, December 6, 1993, p. 3.

9. Ibid.

10. Presentation by Commissioner Franz Fischler at Commission Seminar on MTR, April 17, 2002, at http://www.europa.eu.int/comm/agriculture/mtr/mtr_en.pdf, accessed 09/23/2002.

11. European Commission, *Report on United States Barriers to Trade and Investment, 2000* (Brussels: European Commission, July 2000), p. 1.

12. See the European Commission External Trade Web site, located at http://europa.eu.int/comm/trade/issues/bilateral/countries/usa/index_en.htm

13. For a complete list of EU–U.S. trade disputes and the final settlement clause and/or current status of each case, see the Commission Web site on external trade pertaining to dispute settlement by trade partner and commodity trade, located at http://mkaccdb.eu.int/miti/dsu

14. See European Commission Web site, located at http://europa.eu.int/comm/trade

15. European Commission, "European Commission Disappointed with WTO Arbitrators' Ruling Against Proposed Banana Import Tariff," http://europa.eu.int/comm/trade/issues/respectrules/dispute/pr281005_en.htm

16. Ibid.

17. See the European Commission Web site, located at http://www.europa.eu.int/comm/trade/pdf/farmbill_qa.pdf

18. For a more detailed discussion of the issues involved in this dispute, see the European Commission Web site located at http://europa.eu.int/comm/trade/goods/agri/pr110702.htm

19. "EC and US Reach Farm Trade Agreement," p. 2.

20. Fritz Breuss, "Economic Integration, EU–US Trade Conflicts and WTO Dispute Settlement," in *European Integration Online Papers* 9, no. 12 (2005), http://eiop.or.at/eiop/texte/2001-006a.htm

21. Ibid.

22. Ibid., pp. 12–15.

23. Robert Samuelson, "The Airbus Showdown," *Washington Post*, December 8, 2004, p. A31.

24. "Nose to Nose: Why Has the Trade Dispute Between the World's Two Big Aircraft-Makers Suddenly Become So Bitter," *The Economist,* June 23, 2005, http://www.economist.com/displaystory.cfm?story_id=4102185

25. Ibid.

26. *BBC World News*, November 15, 2005, 13:19 GMT.

27. Gayle S. Putrich and John T. Bennett, "Opposition Musters for USAF Tanker Deal," *This Week in Defense News* March 10, 2008, http://www.defensenews.com/story.php?i=3413037&c=FEA&s=CVS

28. Ibid.

29. http://news.bbc.co.uk/2/hi/business/7498546.stm

30. EurActive, "EU-US Trade Row Erupts over IT Products," Friday 30 May 2008, http://www.euractiv.com/en/infosociety/eu-us-trade-row-erupts-products/article-172835?Ref=RSS

31. Euroepan Commission, "EU Commission Concludes Microsoft Investigation," News Release No. 45/04, March 24, 2004 (Brussels: European Commission).

32. European Commission, *A Maturing Partnership: Shared Interests and Challenges in EU-China Relations* (Brussels: Commission of the European Communities, 2003).

33. Iana Dreyer and Fredrik Erixon, "An EU-China trade dialogue: A new policy framework to contain deteriorating trade relations," *Policy Briefs* No. 03/2008 (Brussels: European Center for International Political Economy), pp. 1–16.

34. European Commission, *Cooperation Agreement between the European Community and the Republic of India on partnership and development* (Brussels: Official Journal of the European Communities, 1994).

35. EU Business, "EU gives cautious welcome to India's free trade proposal," May 20, 2008, http://www.eubusiness.com/news-eu/1211287624.09

36. Peter Holmes and Alasdair Smith, "The EC, the USA, and Japan: The Trilateral Relationship in World Context," in David Dyker, ed., *The European Economy* (New York and London: Longman, 1992), pp. 201–202.

37. Frank McDonald, "The European Community and the USA and Japan," in Frank McDonald and Stephen Dearden, eds., *European Economic Integration* (London and New York: Longman, 1992), p. 207.

38. European Commission, *Joint Conclusions—EU-Japan Summit* (Brussels: Commission of the European Communities, July 19, 2000), p. 2.

39. European Commission, "Bilateral Relations with Japan," http://europa.eu.int/comm/trade/issues/bilateral/countries/japan/index_en.htm

40. Ibid.

41. These countries were the EC12 and Austria, Finland, Iceland, Liechtenstein, Norway, Sweden, and Switzerland. Switzerland, however, later chose to withdraw from the EEA as a result of a national referendum on the subject on December 6, 1992. Austria, Finland, and Sweden later joined the EU on January 1, 1995.

42. "EC, EFTA Create a Larger Common Market," *Eurecom* 3 (November 1991): 1; "Lest a Fortress Arise," *The Economist*, October 26, 1991, pp. 61 and 81–82.

43. Hugh Carnegy and Ian Rodger, "Outsiders Hit by a Strain of Euro-Fever," *Financial Times*, June 3, 1994, p. 2; "Norwegian PM Warns of Tough Times Ahead as Voters Spurn EU," *Financial Times*, November 30, 1994, p. 1.

44. European Commission, "External Relations: EEA," http://europa.eu.int/comm/external_relations/eea/index.htm

45. Roy Ginsberg, "The European Community and the Mediterranean," in Juliet Lodge, ed., *Institutions and Policies of the European Community* (New York: St. Martin's Press, 1983), pp. 161–162.

46. Birol A. Yesilada, "The EC's Mediterranean Policy," in Leon Hurwitz and Christian Lequesne, eds., *The State of the European Community: Policies, Institutions, and Debates in the Transition Years* (Boulder, Colo. and London: Lynne Rienner/Longman, 1991), p. 361.

47. European Communities, *The European Community and the Mediterranean* (Luxembourg: Office for Official Publications of the Communities, 1984), p. 100.

48. Birol Yesilada, "Further Enlargement of the European Community: The Cases of the European Periphery States," *National Forum* (Spring 1992): 21–25.

49. European Commission, "EEC/Mediterranean Countries: Refurbishing the Mediterranean Policy," *External Relations*, no. 1544 (November 29, 1989), as cited in Yesilada, "The EC's Mediterranean Policy," p. 369.

50. "The Second Trojan's Empire," *The Economist*, September 29, 1990, p. 57.

51. "Brussels Urges Wider Trade Zone," *Financial Times*, October 20, 1994, p. 2.

52. Ibid.

53. Birol Yesilada, "Mediterranean Policy," in Desmond Dinan, ed., *Encyclopedia of the European Union* (Boulder, Colo.: Lynne Reinner, 1997), pp. 337–339.

54. European Commission, *The Barcelona Process, Five Years on 1995–2000* (Brussels: European Commission, 2000), p. 22.

55. European Commission, *Euro-Mediterranean Statistics: 2007 edition* (Brussels: Eurostat Publications, 2007), p. 65.

56. Ellen Frey-Wouters, *The European Community and the Third World: The Lomé Convention and Its Impact* (New York: Praeger, 1980), p. 37.

57. John Ravenhill, "Collective Clientelism: The Lomé Conventions and North-South Relations," in Hurwitz and Lequesne, eds., *The State of the European Community*, p. 9.

58. Ibid.

59. Catherine Flaesch-Mougin and Jean Raux "From Lomé III to Lomé IV: EC-ACP Relations," in Hurwitz and Lequesne, eds., *The State of the European Community*, p. 351.

60. Ibid., pp. 352–353.

61. Christopher Piening, *Global Europe: The European Union in World Affairs* (Boulder, Colo.: Lynne Rienner, 1997), pp. 181–188.

62. European Commission, *The Cotonou Agreement: The New ACP-EC Agreement*, http://europa.eu.int/comm/development/cotonou/overview_en.htm

12

Pillar II: Common Foreign and Security Policy

Today in international relations, the EU's powers stem from a transfer of power from member states to the EU. In power relations, the members also know this is a limited surrender of sovereignty to the EU.[1] As a collective body, the EU maintains diplomatic relations with sovereign states and has observer status in the United Nations (UN) and in the various UN agencies. At present, some 150 countries have diplomatic missions in Brussels, and the EU maintains, in the name of the Commission rather than the EU per se, over 130 diplomatic offices around the world. In these offices, EU representatives enjoy the same diplomatic rights as regular diplomats of sovereign countries and cooperate closely with the EU states' local diplomatic missions, thus serving the purpose of cooperation in maintaining a common foreign policy position among the member countries.

HISTORICAL BACKGROUND

According to Peter Ludlow, three major forces contributed to the foreign policy profile of the EU during the postwar era: "the external implications of the EU's internal objectives and achievements; the voluntary agreement of its member states to enlarge their power and influence in the world through common action; and, by no means least, the gravitational pulls of its regional and global environment."[2] The road to a common foreign and security policy has been rather rough.

During the 1950s, the experiment with the European Defense Community (EDC) ended in a disaster, but because this experiment demonstrated how the EU members have viewed collective foreign and security policies, a brief review of the EDC is in order. After the outbreak of the Korean War in June 1950, Jean Monnet argued that the answer to the increasing Soviet threat in Europe could be found in pooling the military resources of the European democracies. The six members of the European Coal and Steel Community (ECSC) decided to set up a parallel body, the EDC, complete with a parliament, joint-defense commission, council of ministers, and court of justice. The EDC Treaty was signed in 1952.

"Now, the federation of Europe would have to become an immediate objective," Monnet had argued.[3] It was clear that this proposed pooling of defense capabilities would inevitably restrict the independent foreign policies of the member countries. Therefore, integration in defense also necessitated some level of political integration. Italian federalist Altiero Spinelli convinced the Italian government that the only way to control a European army was to have federal European institutions. He then persuaded the other five partners. As a result, the six members of the ECSC asked the Consultative Assembly of the Council of Europe, in conjunction with the "co-opted members of the Assembly,"[4] to draft a treaty for a European political community. The outcome was a quasi-federal constitution, drafted in 1953, which would complement the EDC Treaty. According to this plan, there would be one European executive responsible to a European parliament (composed of a people's chamber elected by the citizens and a senate elected by the national parliaments), a council of ministers, and a single European court of justice that would replace the parallel institutions found under the ECSC and EDC Treaties.

This development was to be a remarkable deepening of integration among the six members soon after the horrors of World War II. The parliaments of the Benelux countries, West Germany, and Italy ratified the EDC Treaty, but the idea came to an abrupt halt in the French Assembly on August 30, 1954. Several factors contributed to the French rejection. First was a general opposition to a supranational political community. Second was the French left's opposition to the rearming of Germany. And third was the French right's opposition to placing French troops under foreign command.[5]

Troubles with developing a CFSP followed in the ensuing years. After Charles de Gaulle became president of France, he tried to promote cooperation in foreign policy in the Community on an intergovernmental basis. France proposed the Fouchet plan, which called for coordination of foreign and defense policies outside the framework of the Community.[6] The European Community (EC) continued to discuss the plan until de Gaulle vetoed the British application for membership in the Community, after which the Benelux countries refused to discuss the Fouchet plan any further (see Chapter 3).

A decade later the EC moved to create a mechanism for political cooperation, known as the Davignon machinery, based on a plan proposed by the Belgian foreign ministry. This mechanism consisted of biannual meetings of the foreign ministers, though in practice the meetings have occurred more often. Also, until the 1973 oil crisis, the matters pertaining to the European Political Cooperation (EPC) and the EC were kept separate. As Stephen George relates: "This reached the heights of absurdity in November 1973, when the Foreign Ministers of the then nine member states met in Copenhagen one morning under the heading of EPC, and then flew to Brussels to meet in the afternoon of the same day as the EC Council of Ministers."[7]

When the EC decided to enter into talks with the Arab world in 1974, the matters pertaining to the separation of EPC and EC finally ended. These talks demonstrated that it was no longer possible to separate political matters from commerce. Soon after, the Commission, which had been excluded from the EPC, became involved in coordinating links between the EPC and the Council of Ministers.

The merging of the EPC political and EC economic interests proved to be helpful in promoting the Community's status in the international system and provided a more viable mechanism for dealing with complex foreign policy issues. In 1980, the European–Arab dialogue resulted in the Venice Declaration, by which the European Council made it clear that it recognized the right of the Palestinians to a homeland.[8] Other achievements included aspects given below:

1. Common EC stances in the Conference on Security and Cooperation in Europe (CSCE) in Helsinki in 1975, in Belgrade in 1977, and in Madrid in 1982;
2. A common foreign policy toward South Africa; and
3. A more harmonious position in UN voting, both in the General Assembly and in the Security Council.

The Single European Act (SEA) further emphasized the necessity to coordinate the EPC. It stated "that the EPC could include the 'political and economic aspects of security,' and that the European Parliament should be closely associated with the EPC."[9] Finally, with the end of the Cold War, a more multilateral approach to security and foreign policy in the EU gained momentum.

MAASTRICHT AND THE COMMON FOREIGN AND SECURITY POLICY

The Treaty on European Union (TEU) established the CFSP as the second main pillar of the EU and made the Western European Union (WEU; discussed subsequently) an integral part of the development of the EU, while maintaining its autonomy and giving it the task of defining and implementing defense and security issues. When considering the nature and purpose of the CFSP, it is crucial to note that this effort is an expansion of the EU's earlier attempts during the 1970s and 1980s to coordinate external policies of the member countries. The specific objectives of the CFSP are provided in Article J-1 (2) of the TEU:

- To safeguard the common values, fundamental interests, and independence of the EU;
- To strengthen the security of the EU and its member states in all ways;
- To preserve peace and strengthen international security, in accordance with the principles of the UN Charter, as well as the principles of the Helsinki Final Act and the objectives of the Paris Charter;
- To promote international cooperation; and
- To develop and consolidate democracy and the rule of law, as well as respect for human rights and fundamental freedoms.[10]

Furthermore, paragraph 3 of the same article states that the EU, in pursuing these objectives, needs to establish systematic cooperation among its members "by gradually implementing, in accordance with Article J-3, joint action in the areas in which the Member States have important interests in common."[11]

Responsibility for defining and managing the CFSP lies with the Council and the presidency, respectively.[12] According to Article J-3(1):

> The Council shall decide, on the basis of general guidelines from the European Council, that a matter should be subject of joint action. Whenever the Council decides on the principles of joint action, it shall lay down the specific scope, the EU's general and specific objectives in carrying out such action, if necessary its duration, and the means, procedures and conditions of its implementation.[13]

Moreover, Article J-8(2) states that "the Council shall act unanimously, except for procedural questions and in the case referred to in Article J-3(2)."[14] Article J-3(2) specifies that, "when adopting the joint action and at any stage during its development, [the Council shall] define those matters on which decisions are to be taken by a qualified majority."[15] Thus, the Council of Ministers clearly has a major role in defining the scope, the principles, and the objectives of the CFSP. However, the European Council has a decisive contribution to make to this process by providing the general guidelines of the CFSP. All of these policy-making steps require agreement among the member states. When the EU lacks such agreement, the members can follow their own policy preferences, and the only restraint on their actions would be the threat of unilateralism (acting in the interest of a single member country, rather than the common interest of all members) to the well-being of the EU.

The implementation of the CFSP is entrusted for six-month periods to the presidency of the Council, as stated in Article J-5(2). In this capacity, the presidency is assisted, if necessary, by the previous and next member states that hold the presidency.[16] Furthermore, the Commission is to be fully associated in such tasks.[17]

It should be noted that there is virtually no democratic control over the CFSP, even though the presidency is required "to consult the European Parliament on the main aspects and the basic choices of the common foreign and security policy and ensure that views of the European Parliament are duly taken into account."[18] This does not mean that the European Parliament plays a major role in formulating CFSP. At times of emergency, there would not be time for the presidency to have prior consultation with the EP. According to Lodge: "The Presidency will act on its own initiative, or at the request of the Commission or a member state, to convene an extraordinary Council meeting within forty-eight hours or, in an emergency, within an even shorter time."[19]

Thus, consultation with the European Parliament would likely be after the fact and of limited assistance. This is not different from the dilemma faced in democratic countries. Furthermore, it is quite possible for the member states not to honor their commitment to consult each other prior to taking unilateral action. As we will show later, Germany's behavior prior to the Yugoslav crisis serves as an example of this problem. In addition to the previously mentioned clauses, Article J-4(1) calls for closer cooperation between the EU and the WEU and among the EU countries of the North Atlantic Treaty Organization (NATO). The same is also expected in the CSCE activities.[20] Nevertheless, such cooperation among the EU countries requires imaginative policy coordination because not all members of the EU are members of the WEU and NATO (see the discussion of the European Security and Defense Policy [ESDP] in the section "From the WEU to the ESDP/ESDI").

THE EMERGENCE OF THE ESDP/ESDI

There are three areas of developments that demonstrate evolution of EU's ESDI. These are EU–WEU, EU–NATO, and intra-EU decisions that created the military and other defense structures of pillar II. With gradual inclusion of the WEU tasks within the EU, the signing of the ESDI–NATO partnership, and the willingness of the EU to undertake military peacekeeping operations beyond its borders, pillar II objectives of the TEU have come into reality during the last decade and a half.

Improvements after the Amsterdam and Nice Treaties

The Amsterdam Treaty enhanced provisions of CFSP under Title V of the TEU in order to pave the way for a common defense policy through significant changes. The treaty distinguishes between "common strategies" and more sharply defined "joint actions." Decisions can be taken without strict unanimity if a member who does not wish to participate in the implementation of a decision is willing to see other members implement it. Thus, the European Council may agree on common defense policies, while some member countries retain the right to remain neutral.[21] These developments proved useful during subsequent years as the EU moved to replace the WEU with an integrated part of the EU for creating a European Security and Defense Identity (ESDI) framework within the EU.

The Treaty of Nice contained new CFSP provisions that increased the areas that fall under qualified majority voting and enhanced the role of the Political and Security Committee in crisis management operations in the following areas:

1. Enhanced cooperation will be possible for the implementation of a joint action or common position if it relates to issues that do not have any military or defense implications. If no member states object or call for a unanimous decision in the European Council (the "emergency brake"), enhanced cooperation is adopted in the Council by a qualified majority, with a threshold of only eight member states.[22]
2. The Political and Security Committee will be authorized by the European Council to make appropriate decisions to exercise political control and strategic direction of a crisis management operation. This gives it an even more prominent role in the ESDP.[23]

The Nice Treaty also approved the establishment of three new permanent political and military bodies that will oversee the EU's ESDP. These are the Political and Security Committee (PSC),[24] the European Union Military Committee (EUMC),[25] and the European Union Military Staff (EUMS).[26] With these developments, the EU member states proceeded to bring necessary institutional capabilities into force to meet treaty obligations.

THE LISBON TREATY AND ESDP

The Lisbon Treaty brings substantial revisions to existing Pillar II institutions and foreign policy goals of the EU. It sets out common principles and objectives for the Union's external action: democracy, the rule of law, the universality and indivisibility of human rights and fundamental freedoms, respect for human dignity, and the principles of equality and solidarity.[27] It combines the functions of the High Representative for CFSP with those of a Vice President of the Commission and establishes a new institutional office known as the High Representative for Foreign Affairs and Security Policy/Vice President of the Commission. This person will be supported by the creation of a European External Action Service (EEAS), made up of EU officials and national civil servants and designed to coordinate with the diplomatic services of the EU countries. Under the new arrangement, the EU countries or the High Representative, rather than the Commission, will propose common foreign and security initiatives, with the European Council deciding by unanimity whether or not to implement the proposals. According to Antonio Missiroli, the new treaty has many things in common with the rejected Constitutional Treaty, when it comes to ESDP.

> - the end of the rotational presidency in foreign relations, with a role for the President of the European Council (appointed for two and half years, renewable once) not only in protocol matters but also in crisis situations (new art.13);
> - the creation of the double-hatted High Representative, also appointed by the European Council (with the agreement of the President of the Commission) acting, if necessary, by qualified majority, and also subject to a vote of consent by the European Parliament;
> - the separation of such a role and function from that of Secretary-General of the Council;
> - the establishment of the new Foreign Affairs Council, separate from the General Affairs Council;
> - the establishment of the European External Action Service (EEAS), set "to work in cooperation with the diplomatic services of the member states", and comprising "officials from relevant departments of the General Secretariat of the Council and of the Commission as well as staff seconded from national diplomatic services of the member states" (Declaration 22, attached to the Treaty, reiterates also that "preparatory work" to this end should begin as soon as the new Treaty is "signed");

- the adoption of a single "legislative" procedure, the Council's "European decision" (thus overcoming the distinction between common positions, joint actions, and common strategies), but with virtually no change to the existing consensual rule;
    - the expansion of the scope of ESDP, now called *Common Security and Defence Policy* (CSDP), and of its missions (new art.27 and 28), including: 1) a "solidarity clause" and a "mutual defence" commitment, both with substantial qualifications and provisos; 2) the possibility for the Council "to entrust the implementation of a task to a group of member states which are willing and have the necessary capability" (new art.29); and 3) the possible establishment of "permanent structured cooperation" in the field of defence (new art.31 + relevant Protocol);
    - the creation of a new "start up" fund for ESDP operations (art.28);
    - last but certainly not least, the establishment of a single legal personality for the Union.[28]

These proposals confirm and strengthen the intergovernmental character of CFSP and especially ESDP. At the same time, the European Commission and the European Parliament retain their administrative and budgetary roles.

The EU–WEU Relations and the EU Institutions of Pillar II

The WEU was set up by the Treaty of Economic, Social, and Cultural Collaboration and Collective Self-Defense, which was signed in Paris on October 23, 1954, and came into effect on May 6, 1955. The Paris agreement was a modification of an earlier agreement, the Brussels Treaty, which was signed by Belgium, Luxembourg, the Netherlands, France, and the UK, and laid the foundations of the EDC. The Paris agreement also permitted Italy and West Germany to join the organization, a recognition that World War II was behind them. The preamble of the Paris agreement displays the purposes of the signatories:

> to reaffirm their faith in fundamental human rights . . . and in the other ideals proclaimed in the Charter of the United Nations . . . to preserve the principles of democracy . . . to strengthen . . . the economic, social and cultural ties by which they are already united [by cooperating] to create in Western Europe a firm basis for European economic recovery . . . to afford assistance to each other . . . in resisting any policy of aggression . . . to promote the unity and to encourage the progressive integration of Europe.[29]

The subsequent protocols, II to IV, contained further provisions relating to the levels of armed forces and armaments of member countries and established the Agency for the Control of Armaments. The Brussels Treaty was also very specific about the commitment to collective security of the member states. Article 5 specified as follows: "If any of the high contracting parties should be the object of an armed attack in Europe, the other high contracting parties will, in accordance with the provisions of Article 51 of the Charter of the United Nations, afford the party so attacked all the military and other aid and assistance in their power."[30]

The WEU consists of a council, a consultative assembly, a secretariat, the Standing Armaments Committee, and the Agency for the Control of Armaments. Between 1955 and 1984, the political achievements of the WEU were facilitating the integration of West Germany into NATO and serving as a link between the EU and the UK until the latter became a member of the Community. Otherwise, the WEU was not a major player in the Community's subsequent foreign policy making, and the organization remained inactive until 1984.

Frustrated with the U.S. nuclear missile and Strategic Defense Initiative policies, France started a campaign to reactivate the WEU in the 1980s. Another important reason for the French initiative was that at the time EPC excluded matters relating to defense and security. On October 26–27, 1984, in Rome, the foreign and defense ministers of the member countries agreed to reactivate the WEU.[31]

Following the signing of the Maastricht Treaty, the WEU Council of Ministers for Foreign Affairs and Defense held a meeting in Bonn on June 19, 1992, and issued the Petersberg Declaration regarding their views on European defense and security matters.[32] This declaration emphasized the importance of the CSCE in promoting peace and stability in Europe and called for strengthening the CSCE's capabilities in conflict prevention, crisis management, and peaceful settlement of international disputes. It specified that the WEU would support implementation of conflict prevention and crisis management measures, including peacekeeping operations of the CSCE or the UN Security Council. Furthermore, the declaration reaffirmed the members' commitment to strengthen the European leg of the Atlantic Alliance and to invite other EU members and European members of NATO to join the WEU.

In accordance with these developments, nine WEU members held a meeting with six candidates for WEU membership (Denmark, Greece, Iceland, Ireland, Norway, and Turkey) in Rome on July 16, 1992. After a series of negotiations, the WEU decided on November 20, 1992, to admit Greece into its ranks. At the same time, Iceland, Norway, and Turkey were given associate membership in the WEU, and EU members Denmark and Ireland were admitted as observers to the WEU.[33] Further developments followed soon after the expansion of membership. During the meeting of the 13 countries' defense ministers in the Independent European Program Group (IEPG) in Bonn on December 4, 1992, the participants agreed to transfer the IEPG's function to the WEU. The WEU's Council of Ministers approved the transfer at its Rome meeting on May 19, 1993, and established a new structure within the WEU, the Western European Armaments Group (WEAG), which inherited the work previously done by the IEPG.[34] A follow-up agreement allowed Denmark, Norway, and Turkey to participate in the new institution even though they were not full members of the WEU. The significance of this development was that the new institution and its operating agreements with the nonmembers helped promote "the objective of WEU's 1984 Rome Declaration—to provide political impetus for European cooperation in the field of armaments."[35] Finally, during the Council of Ministers meeting in Luxembourg on May 9, 1994, the WEU issued the Kirchberg Declaration, which gave Bulgaria, the Czech Republic, Estonia, Hungary, Latvia, Lithuania, Poland, Romania, and Slovakia associate partnership in the WEU.[36] While this move was aimed at improving ties with the former Eastern Bloc countries, the particular association status granted to these states was not as comprehensive as that granted to Iceland, Norway, and Turkey. According to the Kirchberg Declaration, the previously mentioned Central and Eastern European countries (CEECs) might participate in the meetings of the Council and "associate themselves with decisions taken by the member states concerning humanitarian and rescue tasks, peacekeeping tasks, tasks of combat forces in crisis management, including peacekeeping."[37] Iceland, Norway, and Turkey, on the other hand, could nominate officers to the Planning Cell in order to "increase WEU's planning capabilities and to enable WEU to draw more easily on the Associate Members' expertise and resources."[38] The present categories of WEU members and associates are shown in Table 12.1.

With the Amsterdam Treaty, the WEU drew closer to the EU. In this regard, the role of the WEU in providing the EU with access to an operational capability was confirmed, the Petersberg tasks were incorporated into the EU treaty, and the possibility of the integration of the WEU into the EU, should the European Council so decide, was mentioned. In 1998, the EU launched a new debate on European defense and security. At Saint-Malo, in December 1998, France and the UK adopted a joint declaration:

> The European Union needs to be in a position to play its full role on the international stage. . . . To this end, the EU must have the capacity for autonomous action, backed up by credible military forces, the means to decide to use them and a readiness to do so, in order to respond to international crises. . . . In this regard, the European Union will also need to have recourse to suitable military means (European capabilities pre-designated within NATO's European pillar or national or multinational European means outside the NATO framework).[39]

Table 12.1 ■ The WEU Membership

Members (Modified Brussels Treaty 1954)	Associate Members* (Rome 1992)	Observers** (Rome 1992)	Associate Partners† (Kirchberg 1994)
Belgium	Czech Republic (1999)	Austria (1995)	Bulgaria
France	Hungary (1999)	Denmark*	Estonia
Germany	Iceland	Finland	Latvia
Greece (1995)	Norway	Ireland	Lithuania
Italy	Poland (1999)	Sweden (1995)	Romania
Luxembourg	Turkey		Slovakia
Netherlands			Slovenia (1996)
Portugal (1990)			
Spain (1990)			
United Kingdom			

Source: WEU, http://www.weu.int

*Also members of NATO.

**Also members of the EU.

†All signatories of a European Agreement with the EU. Following a decision made on June 14, 2001, the secretary general stated during the 1352nd meeting of the Council of Western European Union on June 28, 2001, that, with regard to the period from January 1, 2002, the member states deemed it unnecessary, in present and foreseeable circumstances, to make any formal change to the status of non–full members.

Later, at the Washington summit in April 1999, when NATO allies met to celebrate the 50th anniversary of the founding of NATO and to recognize formally its most recent expansion, the leaders acknowledged the resolve of the EU to have the capacity for autonomous action, confirmed their willingness to build on existing WEU–NATO mechanisms in the creation of a direct NATO–EU relationship, and declared their readiness to "define and adopt the necessary arrangements for ready access by the European Union to the collective assets and capabilities of the Alliance, for operations in which the Alliance as a whole is not engaged militarily as an Alliance."[40] Furthermore, the European Council decided to commit itself to establish the necessary capabilities to meet a full range of conflict prevention and crisis management tasks in Europe at its Cologne meeting in June 1999. In this context, the WEU Luxembourg ministerial meeting in November 1999 reaffirmed its readiness to allow EU Council bodies direct access to the expertise of the WEU's operational structures. This marked a significant movement for closer ties, if not full integration, between the WEU and the EU in formulating ESDI. Finally, at the Helsinki European Council in December 1999, the EU agreed on the specifics of the political and military bodies necessary for ESDI:

1. By 2003, member states would be able to deploy within 60 days and then sustain, for at least one year, forces capable of the full range of Petersberg tasks, including the most demanding, in operations up to corps level (50,000–60,000 persons).
2. New political and military bodies would be established within the Council: a Political and Security Committee, a Military Committee, and a Military Staff would be established within the Council.
3. Modalities would be developed for full consultation, cooperation, and transparency between the EU and NATO, taking into account the needs of all EU member states.

4. Appropriate arrangements would be defined that, while respecting the EU's decision-making autonomy, would allow non-EU European NATO members and other interested states to contribute to EU military crisis management.

5. A nonmilitary crisis management mechanism would be established to coordinate and make more effective the various civilian means and resources, in parallel with the military ones, at the disposal of the EU and the member states.[41]

The inclusion of WEU functions necessary for the EU concerning the Petersberg missions signifies the accomplishment of the EU's pillar II mission, but this decision in itself does not signify the end of the WEU. It simply continues operating in a more integrated framework with the EU. The various institutions established to further ESDP tasks play important roles in the EU–WEU partnership.

The PSC (more often referred to by the French abbreviation COPS) consists of ambassadors of each member state and meets twice a week in Brussels. This committee deals with all aspects of the CFSP and ESDP. Its function is to manage developing crises, organize evaluation and planning, and give political advice to the European Council. When the EU decides to deploy military units abroad, the COPS controls day-to-day direction of such military operations.

The EUMC is officially made up of the chiefs of the defense staffs of member countries. However, in practice, the EUMC is attended by military delegates of the chiefs. This committee is responsible for giving advice and recommendations to the COPS and the European Council and for issuing military directives to the European Military Staff. Its chairman, General Gustav Hägglund, attends sessions of the Council when it is making decisions having defense implications. The European Military Committee is the EU's most senior military body and an effective forum for consultation and cooperation between member states.

The third institution created is the EUMS, which provides expertise for the ESDP, especially with respect to the military crisis management operations. The EUMS is directed by General Rainer Schuwirth. It is responsible for early warning, situation evaluations and strategic planning for Petersberg missions that include the earmarking of national and international European forces. It also acts as an interface between political and military authorities of the EU. It gives military support to the European Military Committee during the strategic planning phase of crisis management situations for the complete range of Petersberg missions and develops working methods and operational concepts based on or compatible with those of NATO.[42]

The final development in pillar II is the establishment of European Defense Agency (EDA), which the EU authorized under a joint action of the Council of Ministers on July 12, 2004. The purpose is "to support the Member States and the Council in their effort to improve European defence capabilities in the field of crisis management and to sustain the European Security and Defence Policy as it stands now and develops in the future."[43] The EDA has various functions in areas pertaining to research and technology, defense capabilities development, cooperation in armaments production, and development of the integrated industrial base for defense industries. The EDA is headed by EU High Representative Javier Solana, who is also the chairman of the EDA's Steering Board. This board is the decision-making body, composed of the defense ministers of the 26 participating member states (except Denmark) and the Commission. The Steering Board acts under the Council's authority and within the framework of guidelines issued by the Council.[44]

The EU–NATO Partnership

In parallel with the above developments, the EU and NATO have been trying to work out the details of how ESDI could be established as a partner of NATO and have access to the latter's intelligence, planning, and transport capabilities. At the December 2000 Nice summit of the

European Council, the members agreed to establish a rapid-reaction force by 2003 to meet this goal. However, the members had differing views on the nature of this force and its relationship to NATO. France wanted the force to be independent of NATO's integrated military command. The UK, being the key U.S. ally in NATO, insisted on close ties to NATO, while maintaining autonomy. The United States warned, "NATO would become a 'relic' unless the European Union's plans for an autonomous military capability were closely linked with the 19-member transatlantic alliance."[45] In reality, however, there was no threat to NATO, at least in the short run, from the establishment of the ESDI: The new European defense force would have had to rely on NATO's heavy-lift equipment and intelligence capabilities to function. Given this fact, it would not have been possible for the European force to act independent of NATO's integrated military structure. The EU's response to these developments required careful balancing of the member states' and the EU's roles in the ESDI, renamed the ESDP, and in NATO. Table 12.2 provides the membership status of the EU states in these institutions.

The EU recommendation, known as the "Berlin Plus" arrangements, which received support from the United States, called for NATO to provide equipment and intelligence for the European-only missions as long as the former did not undermine the Atlantic alliance by creating its own bureaucracy and independent capabilities.[46] However, Turkey, which felt left out of the accession talks at the Nice summit, feared that anything short of being included in the ESDI

Table 12.2 ■ Overlapping Memberships

NATO	NATO and EU	EU
Canada	Belgium	Austria
Iceland	Bulgaria	Cyprus
Norway	Czech Republic	Finland
Turkey*	Denmark	Ireland
USA	Estonia	Malta
	France	Sweden
	Germany	
	Greece	
	Hungary	
	Italy	
	Latvia	
	Lithuania	
	Luxemburg	
	Netherlands	
	Poland	
	Portugal	
	Romania	
	Slovakia	
	Slovenia	
	Spain	
	UK	

Source: "The Many Tricky Ways of Widening Europe," *The Economist,* December 9, 2000, p. 55 and updated information.
*Indicates candidate status with ongoing accession talks.

decision-making mechanism (even when NATO troops are not needed) would simply result in Turkey becoming further distanced from Europe. At the NATO foreign ministers' meeting in Brussels on December 14, 2000, Turkey refused to give the EU, which it is trying to join, assured access to NATO's planning skills for missions in which NATO as a whole is not involved.

The solution to the Turkish veto emerged, known as the Ankara Agreement, after an extensive British campaign, in which Turkey received assurances from NATO that the new EU force would not be used against Turkey's geographic and security interests. The new agreement required EU approval, but ran into a Greek objection at the Seville summit in June 2002.[47] The matter was settled at the December 2002 summit in Copenhagen where the EU and NATO agreed to "effective mutual consultation, equality and due regard for the decision-making autonomy of the EU and NATO, respect for the interests of the EU and NATO members states, respect for the principles of the Charter of the United Nations, coherent, transparent and mutually reinforcing development of the military capability requirements common to the two organizations."[48] Following this political decision of the leaders, the two sides adopted the "Berlin Plus" arrangements of March 17, 2003, which provide the basis for NATO–EU cooperation in crisis management by allowing EU access to NATO's collective assets and capabilities for EU-led operations. These arrangements allow NATO to support EU-led operations in which the alliance as a whole might not be involved. The specifics of the Berlin Plus arrangements include the following:

1. NATO–EU Security Agreement (covers the exchange of classified information under reciprocal security protection rules);
2. Assured EU access to NATO's planning capabilities for actual use in the military planning of EU–led crisis management operations;
3. Presumed availability of NATO capabilities and common assets, such as communication units and headquarters for EU-led crisis management operations;
4. Procedures for release, monitoring, return, and recall of NATO assets and capabilities;
5. Terms of reference for NATO's Deputy SACEUR—who in principle will be the operation commander of an EU-led operation under the "Berlin Plus" arrangements (and who is always a European)—and European command options for NATO;
6. NATO–EU consultation arrangements in the context of an EU-led crisis management operation making use of NATO assets and capabilities;
7. Incorporation within NATO's long-established defense planning system, of the military needs and capabilities that may be required for EU-led military operations, thereby ensuring the availability of well-equipped forces trained for either NATO-led or EU-led operations.[49]

With the above agreements, the EU–NATO partnership entered a new chapter of full cooperation that can address security challenges on the EU's periphery. However, as soon as this agreement was reached, new challenges emerged that would test the partnership. France tried to negate Berlin Plus in a couple of ways. First, the French tried to create a separate military headquarters even though the agreement allowed access to NATO's command structure. Second, France initiated an ESDP mission in Congo that included Canada but did not seek U.S. or NATO approval. Through this action, the French sought to negate any notion of NATO's right of first refusal to such operations.[50] This was followed by a decision between Belgium, France, Germany, and Luxembourg (known as the Tervuren Four) to seek the creation of a new EU defense headquarters near Brussels. Initially, the UK distanced itself from this idea but soon decided to join in arguing that a growing EU needed such an institution for coordination purposes.

Other problems in the ESDI–NATO partnership revolve around duplication of Rapid Deployment Forces (RDF) and Turkey's refusal to permit participation of Cyprus and Malta in

NATO–ESDP meetings and operations. The latter is a product of the ongoing dispute over the Cyprus problem discussed in Chapter 6. At the September 2002 NATO summit in Prague, U.S. secretary of defense Donald Rumsfeld proposed creation of a NATO RDF composed of 21,000 troops coming mostly from European members of the organization to defend against nuclear, biological, and chemical weapons.[51] France insisted on the establishment of a separate European RDF for two reasons. First was the French determination to establish a European force that was separate from participating countries' NATO commitments. Second, the European RDF was necessary if it were to involve participation of non-NATO EU states like Cyprus and Malta, which are kept out of NATO–ESDI operations by Turkey. This position of the Turks angers the French, who insist that EU means the presence of all member states.

Testing CFSP

In recent years, important international crises have put to test the EU's efforts to promote a common foreign and security policy. At present, EU operations under the European Security Strategy are as follows:

EUFOR Althea—EU military operations in Bosnia and Herzegovina, launched on December 2, 2004.

EUFOR Tchad/RCA—EU military operations in Eastern Chad and North Eastern Central African Republic, launched on March 15, 2008.

EUPM/BiH—European Union Police Mission in Bosnia and Herzegovina, started on January 1, 2003.

EULEX KOSOVO—A European Union Rule of Law Mission in Kosovo, launched on February 16, 2008.

EUPOL COPPS/Palestinian Territories—An EU Police Mission in the Palestinian territories, established on November 15, 2005.

EUBAM Rafah/Palestinian Territories—An EU Border Assistance Mission at Rafah crossing point, started on November 21, 2005.

EUJUST LEX Iraq—A civilian crisis management operation in Iraq started on July 1, 2005.

EUPOL Afghanistan—A police mission in Afghanistan, launched in mid-June 2007.

EUPOL RD Congo—An EU police force in RD Congo that replaced the previous mission EUPOL-Kinshasa.

EUSEC RD Congo—EU military operation in support of the UN.

EU SSR Guinea-Bissau—A mission to provide assistance and advice on security sector reform in Guinea Bissau.

Moldova and Ukraine Border Mission—A mission to improve the capacity of the Moldovan–Ukrainian border and customs services order to prevent and detect smuggling, trafficking of goods and human beings, and customs fraud by training local officers, established on November 30, 2005.[52]

In this section, we examine the EU's response to some of these challenges and their implications for transatlantic relations.

The Gulf War

After Iraq invaded Kuwait on August 2, 1990, the president of the WEU Assembly issued a communiqué condemning the Iraqi aggression and demanding prompt withdrawal of Iraqi troops from Kuwait. He also called on the WEU countries to respond to the crisis and asked the UN to take all necessary steps to defend the sovereignty of Kuwait. Yet, despite the urgency of the situation, it took the WEU countries 19 days to meet to discuss the situation. By that time, the United States had initiated its own diplomatic and military efforts to remove Iraq from Kuwait and asserted American leadership within the UN and NATO.[53]

The WEU Council of Ministers agreed to take all necessary steps to comply with the embargo on Iraq in accordance with UN Security Council Resolution (UNSCR) 661. On the basis of experiences in the Persian Gulf during the 1987–1989 operations, the WEU established an ad hoc group of foreign and defense ministry representatives to provide cooperation between the member states' capitals and the forces in the Gulf.

The WEU also coordinated its members' response to the second operation in this crisis. On September 18, 1990, another meeting of the Council of Ministers decided to "strengthen the WEU coordination and to extend the coordination at present operating in the maritime field to ground and air forces and, within this framework, to identify the forms that these new deployments will take, to seek to ensure that they are complementary, to harmonize the missions of the member states' forces and to pool their logistic support capabilities as required."[54] When Desert Storm began on January 16, 1991, WEU members France, Italy, and the UK participated with aircraft. The next day the WEU Council of Ministers held an extraordinary meeting and decided to provide full support for the operation. Parallel to the operations in the air and sea, ground forces from the WEU participated in the massive UN buildup in Saudi Arabia. Following the successful operations in Kuwait, the WEU decided to continue to play an active role in the implementation of the UNSCRs pertaining to the protection of the Kurds in northern Iraq and the Shiite Arabs of Basra.

The Yugoslav Crisis

The breakup of Yugoslavia and the subsequent civil war in Bosnia-Herzegovina and Croatia represented potentially a very divisive issue for the WEU members. This crisis shows that the WEU and the EU were not prepared to deal with a problem of this magnitude, and the subsequent disagreements among the Community's members over how to respond to the problem highlight the member countries' inability to coordinate their national foreign policy priorities.

During these crises, the main international security organizations—the UN, NATO, and the WEU—attempted to bring about an end to hostilities by coordinating their political and military efforts. While they were partially successful in Croatia, the civil war in Bosnia-Herzegovina proved too difficult for the allies to reach a common position. Several factors contributed to this failure. First, the EU and the UN, and later NATO, failed to provide a common and effective position on the crisis. Time after time, these organizations failed to respond to Serbian actions in Bosnia even when they followed strong ultimatums from the West. Second, the EU sponsored the London peace process in the fall of 1992, which included the participation of the UN. In this setting, conflict management became an issue that required cooperation between the EU and the UN.

As the war worsened, it became quite apparent that the WEU lacked the necessary military structure to intervene effectively to stop the bloodshed. When human suffering reached new heights, the UN agreed to send peacekeepers, mostly from the WEU countries, to provide humanitarian assistance to the civilians. However, the only organization that had the military power to stop the war was NATO. No other organization had the integrated military structure, hardware, and logistical planning and operational capabilities to deal with a crisis like Bosnia. NATO's intervention, directly or indirectly, meant involvement of the United States. Under normal circumstances, this would not be a problem for NATO. However, at the time, the Clinton administration's inconsistencies over its Bosnian policy worried the allies. When the UN decided to impose an embargo on Yugoslavia and the former Yugoslav states of Croatia and Bosnia-Herzegovina and to sponsor Operation Sharp Guard and Operation Deny Flight, NATO was asked to oversee these military operations. Once again, the success of the operations depended on cooperation among the UN, NATO, and the WEU.

Operation Sharp Guard's mission was to monitor and enforce compliance with UN sanctions, particularly against Serbia, in accordance with UNSCRs 713, 757, 787, and 820. A combined task force was given the responsibility of preventing unauthorized shipping from entering the territorial waters of the Yugoslav Federal Republic. The operation was equipped with surface warships from Canada, France, Germany, Greece, Italy, the Netherlands, Norway, Portugal, Spain, Turkey, the UK, and the United States. In addition, eight fighter aircraft from Italy and maritime patrol aircraft from Canada, France, Germany, Italy, the Netherlands, Portugal, Spain, the UK, and the United States, supported by NATO Airborne Warning and Control (AWAC) systems, provided air support for this operation. By the end of March 1994, this operation had challenged 17,000 merchant vessels in the Adriatic Sea and on the Danube, halting 1,700.[55]

Operation Deny Flight, on the other hand, had a fourfold mission:

1. To conduct aerial monitoring and enforce compliance with UNSCR 816, which bans flights by fixed-wing and rotary-wing aircraft in the airspace of Bosnia-Herzegovina.
2. To provide air cover (close air support) at the request and under the control of the UN Peacekeeping Forces in the Former Yugoslavia (UNPROFOR) under the supervision of UNSCR 836.
3. To be ready to carry out, in coordination with the UN, air strikes on heavy weapons if they fire from outside (or inside) the 20-kilometer exclusion zone into Sarajevo or if they return to the exclusion zone.
4. To be ready to carry out air strikes at other locations to aid UNPROFOR in humanitarian relief operations as authorized by the North Atlantic Council and in coordination with the UN.[56]

The Serbian testing of NATO and UN resolve continued during the autumn of 1994. The Serbs launched a massive attack on the Muslim enclave of Bihac after the latter had a brief military success that resulted from a surprise offensive against Serbian positions. The Serbian counteroffensive also included attacks on Bihac from Serb-controlled areas of Croatia. When the subsequent UN and NATO threats against the Serbs failed to stop the Serbian attacks, the international media and influential political figures began to question the role of the UN peacekeepers and NATO air power in Bosnia.

The inability of the WEU, NATO, and the UN to coordinate an effective policy over Bosnia also affected the European Council summit in Essen. At this meeting, the British and French leaders stated that there was a good chance of withdrawing UN peacekeeping forces from Bosnia within weeks unless the Serbs agreed to the UN–EU peace plan.[57] The host of the summit, Helmut Kohl, on the other hand, expressed a strong interest in maintaining a consensus within the EU in favor of a diplomatic solution.

These developments showed that the WEU and the UN lacked the necessary integrated military command structure and the logistical means to cope with the crisis in Bosnia. The job had to be carried out by NATO. Whereas such close consultation among NATO, the WEU, and the UN meant slow reaction to Serbian actions in Bosnia, the military undertakings of the allies were not without some limited success. First in Sarajevo, and later in Gorazde, NATO ultimatums, followed by close air support, resulted in lifting the Serbs' siege around these cities. Yet, in Bihac, the UN and NATO failed to stop the Bosnian Serbs.

Under these circumstances, the United States decided to take a decisive action to end the crisis and coordinated its efforts with Britain, France, Germany, and Russia. Together these countries became known as the Contact Group and facilitated the signing of the Dayton Agreement on November 21, 1995, thus ending the war in Bosnia-Herzegovina. The Dayton Agreement called for a peacekeeping mission under the command of NATO. The terms of the mission specified that a multinational military implementation force (IFOR), composed of troops from NATO and Russia, under the command of NATO and with authority granted by the UN, would have the right to monitor and help ensure compliance with the agreement.[58] In addition to the military agreement, the Dayton accords called for an economic restructuring of Bosnia-Herzegovina that relied heavily on the EU.

The EU's assistance to Bosnia-Herzegovina has been extensive. It covers a wide range of activities: assistance with ethnic reconciliation, the establishment of functioning institutions to promote democracy, economic aid, training for the local police force, peacekeeping by EUFOR (EU Forces), and efforts to bring the country closer to EU standards and principles. Since 1992, EU's assistance has amounted to over €2 billion. Some of the large projects include integrated reconstruction involving buildings, houses, the water supply, energy distribution networks, and transportation. Also, the Sarajevo and Mostar airports have been completely rebuilt with EU funds and assistance.[59]

EUFOR is the realization of the EU's rapid deployment force. It is the international military force of 7,000 from 33 countries (mostly from the EU) that took over operations from NATO's SFOR on December 2, 2004, to ensure continued implementation of the Dayton Agreement. It is coordinated under the offices of the High Representative for the CFSP and Secretary General of the Council Javier Solana. This operation is a great example of how the new ESDI–NATO partnership functions. A strategic-level headquarters of EUFOR is created by NATO's Allied Command Operations.

Kosovo

The Kosovo crisis in Yugoslavia involved the demand of ethnic Albanians, about 90 percent of the province's population, for autonomy, and the brutal response of the Slobodan Milosovic government in Belgrade. By 1998, the Serbian riot police and military units carried out attacks against Albanian civilians and a small, armed resistance group known as the Kosovo Liberation Army (KLA). As Serbian atrocities against civilians mounted, more and more young Albanian men joined the ranks of the KLA to fight the Serbs. This resulted in an all-out Serbian attack on Kosovo to drive the Albanians out of the province. As tens of thousands of refugees fled into neighboring countries, Western powers, led by the United States, warned the Milosovic government to stop its military campaign or face NATO retaliation. When Milosovic refused, NATO warplanes began massive air attacks against Serbian military and strategic industrial sites. NATO's strikes lasted for 78 days and caused severe economic damage in Serbia. The Milosovic government agreed to pull its troops from the province and accepted a NATO-led international security force in Kosovo.

The response of the Western allies and Russia to the Kosovo crisis is an example of cooperation among NATO, the WEU, and the Organization for Security and Cooperation in Europe (OSCE). On June 10, 1999, Kosovo came under UN administration, and the UN mission in Kosovo—known as UNMIK—was set up under UNSCR 1244. In addition, the allies imposed extensive sanctions on Yugoslavia to force the Milosovic regime into resignation. This goal, however, was not realized until he lost the presidential election in 2000.

The EU has been present since the very beginning of the international effort to build a new future for Kosovo. As the single largest donor, the EU is currently playing a prominent role in the reconstruction of Kosovo. In 1999, the European Commission provided €378 million in emergency humanitarian assistance for the victims of the Kosovo crisis and a further €127 million for reconstruction programs. In 2000, the EU continued to support Kosovo with funds totaling €400 million.[60] The funds went to finance infrastructure development, housing, institution building, environmental cleanup, education, and other human development programs. In addition to providing development assistance, the EU is a key participant in the peacekeeping operations in Kosovo. Some 36,000 soldiers from EU nations are currently serving as members of the Kosovo Force (KFOR). This is about 80 percent of the total force. Furthermore, 800 civilian police from EU member states serve in Kosovo. On a related matter, the WEU began a security surveillance mission in the region following a request from the EU. The initial focus of the general security surveillance mission was to gather information for the EU as well as the NATO and OSCE missions on the implementation of the Belgrade agreements and on the situation of refugees and displaced persons. With KFOR troops and other international representatives in the region, the mission of the Satellite Center has concentrated on creating a digital map of Kosovo for use in reconstruction and removal of land mines.[61]

Following the democratic transition in Serbia on October 5, 2000, EU foreign ministers announced the lifting of sanctions and the immediate repeal of the oil embargo and the flight ban. They declared the extension of the European Reconstruction Agency to Serbia and Montenegro and promised to help with the clearing of the Danube. Following these decisions, member states of the EU began to normalize their relations with Serbia. Finally, at the October 2000 Biarritz European Council meeting, Commission President Romano Prodi announced an emergency package totaling €200 million.

The Macedonia Question

The division among the EU countries over foreign policy coordination toward the former Yugoslav republics was also evident in Macedonia. Following Macedonia's declaration of independence from Yugoslavia, Greece blocked the EU's recognition because Macedonia is the name of one of its provinces. Greece maintained that Macedonia had territorial ambitions on the Greek province, by virtue of its name, its constitution, its bank notes—which have a picture of the tower of Selonika—and its national flag, which bears the ancient Macedonian dynastic emblem discovered in northern Greece in 1975. Despite Greek opposition, six members of the EU (Denmark, France, Germany, Italy, the Netherlands, and the UK) established full diplomatic relations with Macedonia in December 1993, just before Greece took over the presidency of the Council in January 1994.[62] Belgium followed suit in early 1994. The crisis over Macedonia worsened in February 1994, when Greece moved unilaterally to impose a trade embargo against the former Yugoslav republic. The worsening of this crisis was prevented when Macedonia agreed to be known as the Former Yugoslav Republic of Macedonia, thus ending Greece's opposition to this state.

The EU mission in Macedonia, code-named EUPOL PROXIMA, was launched on December 15, 2003.[63] It initially covered a period of one year. The EU experts trained local police and monitored efforts against organized crime in the country. The EU mission in Macedonia also supported a variety of other efforts aimed at preparing the country for eventual membership in the EU. The efforts are as follows:

1. The consolidation of law and order, including the fight against organized crime, focusing on the sensitive areas;
2. The practical implementation of the comprehensive reform of the Ministry of the Interior, including the police;
3. The operational transition toward creation of a border police as a part of the wider EU effort to promote integrated border management;
4. The local police training and confidence building within the population; and
5. Enhanced cooperation with neighboring states in the field of policing.[64]

The Israeli–Palestinian Problem

The conflict between the Israelis and Palestinians continues to divide the transatlantic alliance. At the heart of the current U.S.–EU divide is the unconditional support the Bush administration has given to Israel. According to William Wallace, the transatlantic divide reflects a "broad difference of understanding about western interests in the region and about relations between the industrialized democracies and the Arab and Muslim world. The immediate focus is on Israel and occupied Palestine; but the broader differences extend across Iraq through Saudi Arabia to Iran."[65] Wallace argues that for the past 20 years, the EU and the United States collaborated well in the region, with the Americans defining the Western priorities toward the Middle East and the Europeans providing economic assistance. However, in recent years, the dominance of the U.S. military power, coupled with close ties between Washington and the Israeli government, has left the Europeans with little influence in the peace process.[66] The revitalized Euro-Med policy aims to increase the EU's influence in the region (see Chapter 11). At present, the EU maintains two operations in the region: the EU Police Mission in the Palestinian Territories and the EU Border Assistance Mission at Rafah crossing point. The EUPOL COPPS is a three-year project that supports the Palestinian Authority in establishing effective and sustainable police operation. The Rafah crossing is a third-party assistance and observation mission to assist Palestinian Authority in border and customs management.

The War on Terror and Iraq

Following the terrorist attacks on the Pentagon and the World Trade Center on September 11, 2001, the EU leaders rushed to align themselves with the United States. The NATO members of the EU, led by Britain and acting on the alliance's collective security charter, provided military assistance to the U.S. war effort in Afghanistan. During the first six months of 2002, Britain led the international peacekeeping mission in Kabul. Furthermore, the intelligence agencies of the transatlantic allies closely monitor suspicious activities and assist each other in tracking suspected terrorists. To that effect, the U.S. Justice Department issued a long list of organizations with ties to terrorism and requested assistance in shutting down their operations and freezing their financial assets.[67] The EU's response to American requests was positive, and the two transatlantic allies have been collaborating in the war against terrorism ever since. This cooperation gained more momentum following terrorist attacks in Madrid and London in which many EU citizens lost their lives.

However, since the Bush administration's policy toward Iraq over Saddam Hussein's violation of UNSCRs on Iraqi disarmament and subsequent invasion of Iraq by American forces, relations between the United States and some of its EU allies have soured. Initially, many EU members, with the exception of Britain and Spain, opposed unilateral American military action in Iraq unless it was backed by a UN resolution on weapons inspection. Even in Britain, the public opinion (52 percent opposed to 34 percent in favor) was against a military campaign in Iraq.[68]

Among the European critics of U.S. policy, France was the most outspoken. When President Bush spoke of the "Axis of Evil" in the world, referring to Iraq, Iran, and North Korea, the French foreign minister quickly called this simplistic and dangerous. The French worried that an American military campaign in Iraq would engulf the region in a larger war, drawing in both Iran and Turkey, with wider implications for NATO.[69]

Germany was both uncomfortable with U.S. policy toward Iraq and eager to improve its relations with the Bush administration following Chancellor Schröder's statement during the September 2002 German election campaign that "he has categorically rejected any German support for an American-led attack on Iraq, even if backed by a United Nations mandate."[70] Despite such reservations, even the French admitted that the EU was incapable of stopping a U.S. military action in Iraq. The crisis took a new turn following the UN Security Council's unanimous adoption of a new resolution on Iraqi weapons inspection on November 8, 2002. The U.S-sponsored new UNSCR gave inspectors sweeping new rights and Iraq 30 days to submit a detailed list of its weapons. It also gave the Security Council a key role before any possible attack, but did not force

Washington to seek authorization for war. Under the terms, Iraq had until November 15 to respond to the UN, and inspectors traveled to Baghdad on November 18 to set up communications, transport, and laboratories.[71]

Following these developments, the Iraqi government permitted the UN inspectors to begin their inspections for weapons of mass destructions (WMD) in Iraq. However, the slow pace of these inspections, coupled with the repeated delaying tactics of the Iraqi government, caused serious discomfort in Washington and London. The Bush administration, supported by the Blair government in the UK, continued to mass troops in the Persian Gulf and asked Turkey to permit placement of American troops in southeastern provinces of that country for a possible northern front in the pending war in Iraq. This request was later rejected by the Turkish Parliament. The problem within the EU worsened as it spilled over into the intra-EU domain when 10 ex-communist countries forming the so-called Vilnius group awaiting EU membership signed a letter supporting the U.S.–UK position on Iraq.[72] Relations between the U.S.–UK and France–Germany–Belgium were further strained when the former abandoned all diplomatic efforts to resolve the Iraqi standoff and launched a military campaign to topple the Saddam regime on March 20, 2003. The war started after the United States, Britain, and Spain abandoned their quest for explicit authorization to go to war from the UN Security Council.[73] Subsequently, several EU members and accession countries at the time decided to support the U.S. invasion of Iraq. These countries were what the U.S. administration called the "coalition of the willing": Bulgaria, Czech Republic, Denmark, Estonia, Hungary, Italy, Latvia, Lithuania, the Netherlands, Poland, Slovakia, Spain, and the UK.

ESDP After the Iraq crisis

Despite the Iraq war and all the problems it created for EU solidarity and the future of pillar II, ESDP remains stable and viable. First, despite the fact that this war created the most severe crisis in transatlantic relations, the EU–NATO cooperation remained intact and continues to function. Second, as described in the previous section on ESDP, the EU has made major breakthroughs in operationalization of its ESDI policies despite the internal disagreements over the war. It adopted a common action plan in June 2003 to fight against the proliferation of WMD. It also, for the first time in its history, framed a common strategic concept titled *A Secure Europe in a Better World*. It outlines three pillars for the EU's strategic position:

1. Extending the security zone around Europe by developing the instruments for stabilization used in the Balkans to the benefit of eastern neighbors such as Ukraine and Moldova, but also in the Mediterranean, which involves resolving the Israeli–Palestinian conflict;
2. Establishing effective multilateralism based on the UN, the fundamental framework of international relations, while reaffirming the need to become involved in a preventive way and act when the rules are infringed; and
3. Responding to the global threats of terrorism and the proliferation of weapons of mass destruction and organized crime by recognizing that the traditional form of defense is a thing of the past since the fall of the Berlin Wall and that the first line of defense now lies abroad.[74]

This strategy further outlines differences in the EU's approach to security challenges and policy responses from those held by the United States. It emphasizes that, first of all, Europe is at peace and not at war. With this premise, it goes on to explain that, even if the European analysis of the threats of terrorism and proliferation of WMD is similar to that of the United States, the ways in which Europe addresses them are and ought to be different. That is, the fight against these threats cannot be limited to military force alone and must include a broader approach, combining the political and the economic methods.[75]

Successful evolution of the ESDP is further exemplified by the EU's response to crisis beyond the European theater. When UN Secretary General Kofi Annan called for an immediate intervention in Ituri Congo following a series of massacres and the withdrawal of Ugandan troops in the spring of 2003, the EU (led by France) responded with a military intervention of 1,800 troops. This operation took place in a very short time and displayed the ability of the EU to initiate its rapid response force. The EU further provided economic and political assistance to Congo to assist in establishing stability in the country. For sure, ESDP has evolved to be a more comprehensive policy that has a European identity (see list of operations above). As Kouris Kalligas explains, the EU is proceeding to transform its Pillar II institutions into something that would enable the EU to become a military giant in the future.[76] The road after the Iraq war suggests that there might be no turning back from this ambitious goal.

CONCLUSIONS

The EU's foreign and security policies are probably the least integrated of all of the EU's policy dimensions. Despite efforts at transforming the WEU, the EU's response to foreign policy challenges in Bosnia and Kosovo clearly demonstrated that it lacks the necessary military structure to be an effective alternative to NATO. EU members also have different commitments under NATO, the WEU, and the new ESDI/ESDP. Also, some members remain neutral in foreign and security affairs. In terms of military capabilities required for meeting ESDP goals, NATO still remains the only security organization that has the unified command and military structure to respond to threats to European security. On the positive side, the ESDP has come a long way since the inception of the WEU. In recent years, the organization presented a united EU policy in the Gulf crisis, Congo, Kosovo, Macedonia, and the war on terror. The future of ESDP depends on the solid partnership of ESDI–NATO, as shown in EU operations in the Balkans. Furthermore, one thing is quite clear: Transatlantic cooperation is needed as much today as it was during the days following World War II.

STUDY QUESTIONS

1. Write an analysis of EU's common security and defense policy from a constructivist perspective.
2. Compare and contrast the neoliberal intergovernmentalist and historical institutionalist explanations of the causal factors behind ESDP.
3. Present a critical assessment of the evolution of the ESDP/ESDII since the early days of the EU and the WEU, with reference to critical events that affected this process. What are some of the key issues facing the transatlantic allies in this process? Explain in detail.
4. What is the Berlin Plus agreement?
5. How does the Lisbon Treaty affect Pillar II of the EU?

ENDNOTES

1. Juliet Lodge, "From Civilian Power to Speaking with a Common Voice: The Transition to a CFSP," in Juliet Lodge, ed., *The European Community and the Challenge of the Future*, 2nd ed. (New York: St. Martin's Press, 1993), p. 227.

2. Peter Ludlow, "The Foreign Policy of the EU," in Peter Ludlow, ed., *Setting European Community Priorities, 1991–92* (London: Brassey's for CEPS, 1991), p. 102.

3. Jean Monnet, *Memoirs*, trans. Richard Mayne, as cited in John Pinder, *European Community: The Building of a Union* (London: Oxford University Press, 1991), p. 7.

4. Dennis Swann, *The Economics of the Common Market* (London: Penguin Books, 1992), p. 8.

5. Henri Brugmans, "The Defeat of the European Army," in F. Roy Willis, ed., *European Integration* (New York: New Viewpoints, 1975), pp. 38–49.

6. Stephen George, *Politics and Policy in the European Community*, 2nd ed. (London: Oxford University Press, 1991), p. 32.

7. Ibid., p. 219.

8. Ibid., p. 221.

9. John Pinder, *European Community*, p. 193.

10. Council and Commission of the European Communities, *Treaty on European Union* (Luxembourg: Office for Official Publications of the European Communities, 1992), title V, art. J-1(2), pp. 123–124.

11. Ibid., p. 124.

12. Lodge, "From Civilian Power," in Lodge, ed., *The European Community*, pp. 244–245.

13. Council and Commission of the European Communities, *Treaty on European Union*, pp. 124–125.

14. Ibid., p. 128.

15. Ibid., p. 125.

16. Ibid., p. 127.

17. Council and Commission of the European Communities, *Treaty on European Union*, art. J-5(3).

18. Council and Commission of the European Communities, *Treaty on European Union*, art. J-7, par. 1.

19. Lodge, "From Civilian Power," in Lodge, ed., *The European Community*, p. 246.

20. Ibid.

21. Simon Hix, *The Political System of the European Union* (New York: St. Martin's Press, 1999), pp. 344–345.

22. Treaty of Nice, pt. 1, Substantive Amendments, art. 1.2.1 (pertaining to art. 17 of the TEU).

23. Ibid., art. 1.5 (pertaining to art. 25 of the TEU).

24. European Council, *Council Decision of 22.1.2001*, OJ L 27 of 30.1.2001, p. 1.

25. Ibid., p. 4.

26. Ibid., p. 7.

27. European Commission, *Treaty of Lisbon Q&A*, http://europa.eu/lisbon_treaty/faq/index_en.htm#15.

28. Antonio Missiroli, *The Impact of Lisbon Treaty on ESDP* (Brussels: European Parliament, 2008), p. 7.

29. WEU, "Preamble," *Paris Agreement*, October 23, 1954.

30. WEU, *Paris Agreement*, October 23, 1954, art. V.

31. WEU, Committee for Parliamentary and Public Relations, *Western European Union* (Brussels: WEU, 1993).

32. John McCormick, *The European Union: Politics and Policies*, 2nd ed. (Boulder, Colo.: Westview Press, 1999), p. 270.

33. Peter van Ham, "Western European Union," in Desmond Dinan, ed., *Encyclopedia of the European Union* (Boulder, Colo.: Lynne Reinner, 1998), p. 486.

34. Willem van Eekelen, "WEU Prepares the Way for New Missions," *NATO Review* 41, no. 5 (October 1993): 19–23.

35. Ibid.

36. WEU, *Kirchberg Declaration* (Brussels: WEU, May 9, 1994).

37. Ibid., pt. II.

38. Ibid., pt. III.

39. WEU, "A New European Impetus," http://www.weu.int/eng/index.html

40. Ibid.

41. Ibid.

42. For an excellent overview of EU–NATO and transatlantic relations, see Stanley Sloan, *NATO, the European Union, and the Atlantic Community* (New York: Rowman & Littlefield, 2003).

43. See the European Defence Agency Web site, located at http://www.eda.eu.int/background.htm.

44. Ibid.

45. Alexander Nicoll, "US Warns EU of Need for Close Link with NATO," *Financial Times*, December 6, 2000.

46. "The Many Tricky Ways of Widening Europe," *The Economist*, December 9, 2000, p. 56.

47. Judy Dempsey and Kerin Hope, "Diplomats Press Greece on Deal for EU Force," *Financial Times*, November 21, 2002, p. 4.

48. NATO, "The NATO–EU Declaration on ESDP," http://www.nato.int/issues/nato-eu/policy.html

49. Ibid.

50. Stephanie B. Anderson, *Crafting EU Security Policy: In Pursuit of a European Identity* (Boulder: Lynne reinner, 2008), pp. 98–99.

51. Ibid., pp. 101–102.

52. Council of the European Union, homepage of Javier Solana http://www.consilium.europa.eu/cms3_applications applications/solana/index.asp?lang=EN&cmsid=246

53. David Garnham, "European Defense Cooperation," in Dale L. Smith and James Lee Ray, eds., *The 1991 Project and the Future of Integration in Europe* (New York: Sharpe, 1993), p. 210.

54. WEU, "Western European Union," http://www.weu.int/eng/weu.html

55. NATO/WEU, "Operation Sharp Guard Fact Sheet."

56. NATO, "Operation Deny Flight Fact Sheet."

57. "Britain and France Firm on Bosnia," *Financial Times*, December 10–11, 1994, p. 2.

58. European Commission, "Fact Sheet Released by the Bureau of Public Affairs," December 11, 1995.

59. European Commission, *Facts and Figures: 1991–99 Assistance to Bosnia-Herzegovina*, http://europa.eu.int/comm/external_relations/see/bosnie_herze/index.htm

60. European Commission, *Facts and Figures: 1991–99 Assistance to Bosnia-Herzegovina*, http://europa.eu.int/comm/external_relations/see/kosovo/assistance.html

61. WEU, "General Security Surveillance Mission in Kosovo," http://www.weu./int/eng/index.html

62. "Macedonia Backed by Half of EU," *Financial Times*, December 17, 1993, p. 3.

63. Council of the European Union, *Council Joint Action 2003/681/CFSP.*

64. Council of the European Union, "European Union Police Mission in the former Yugoslav Republic of Macedonia (EUPOL PROXIMA)," http://ue.eu.int/cms3_fo/showPage.asp?id=584&lang=EN

65. William Wallace, "The Old Argument," *Financial Times*, June 27, 2002, p. 15.

66. Ibid.

67. U.S. Department of the Treasury, Office of Foreign Assets Control, *Terrorism: What You Need to Know About U.S. Sanctions* (Washington, D.C.: U.S. Department of the Treasury, 2001).

68. "You Can Be Warriors or Wimps; or So Say the Americans," *The Economist*, August 10, 2002, pp. 43–44.

69. "Allies at Odds—All Around," *The Economist*, April 13, 2002, p. 49.

70. "Why Gerhard Schroder Has Gone Out on a Limb," *Financial Times*, September 14, 2002, p. 51.

71. "Reuters, "Arab Ministers Welcome U.N. Resolution on Iraq," November 8, 2002.

72. "Chirac Vents over Behaviour of EU Candidates," *Financial Times*, February 18, 2003.

73. "A Fight to the Finish," *The Economist*, March 22, 2003, p. 20.

74. Javier Solana, *A Secure Europe in a Better World: European Security Strategy* (Brussels: December 12, 2003).

75. Ibid., p. 8.

76. Kouris Kalligas, *A Historical Institutionalist Analysis of the Security and Defence Policy of the European Union,* MA Thesis in Politics and International Studies, University of Warwick, Summer 2006, pp. 50–51.

Chapter 13

Justice and Home Affairs

The third pillar of the Maastricht Treaty (Title VI, Article K) contains provisions on cooperation in justice and home affairs (JHA). According to these provisions, member states' interior ministers are required to work together on asylum, immigration, frontier rules, crime, customs, and police cooperation regarding terrorism and drug control.[1] Four areas of citizens' rights and internal security fall under the third pillar, the EU law and the individual rights of citizens: free movement of persons between member states; citizenship rights (such as equal opportunities, individual political and civil rights) across the European Union (EU); immigration policy; and judicial and police cooperation. The Schengen Treaty had anticipated the subsequent Amsterdam Treaty, which brought two changes to freedom of movement of individuals. The Lisbon Treaty aims to further clarify the policies pertaining to Pillar III. Even if Pillar II (see Chapter 12) remains intergovernmental for the foreseeable future, almost all policy areas of Pillar III will come under the "Community method," establishing a single area of freedom, security, and justice, where QMV and codecision will become the general rule of decision making.

EU LAW

Implementing pillar III policies requires adherence to EU law, which member states must incorporate into their national legal systems. The final decision-making body on interpretation of EU law is the ECJ. The interaction between Community law and national law covers those areas where the two systems complement each other. Article 10 of the EC Treaty is very clear on this matter. It states, "Member States shall take all appropriate measures, whether general or particular, to ensure fulfillment of the obligations arising out of this Treaty or resulting from action taken by the institutions of the Community. They shall facilitate the achievement of the Community's tasks. They shall abstain from any measure which could jeopardize the attainment of the objectives of this Treaty."[2]

The primary (or fundamental) law consists of the treaties establishing EU institutions, which fundamentally shape the EU. These include the four main treaties and accession treaties of the EU with various annexes and protocols attached to them, as well as later additions and amendments. They thus set the constitutional framework for the life of the EC, which is then fleshed out in the Community interest by legislative and administrative action by the Community

215

institutions. The treaties that make up the primary law include the following: The ECSC Treaty (1951); Treaty of Rome (1957); the EURATOM Treaty (1957); Merger Treaty (1965); the Acts of Accession of the UK, Ireland, and Denmark (1972); the Budgetary Treaty (1970); the Budgetary Treaty (1975); the Act of Accession of Greece (1979); the Act of Accession of Spain and Portugal (1985); the SEA (1986); the Maastricht Treaty (1992); the Act of Accession of Austria, Finland, and Sweden (1994); the Treaty of Amsterdam (1997); the Treaty of Nice (2001); the Treaty of Accession (2003); the Treaty of Accession (2005); and *if ratified by member states,* the Treaty of Lisbon (2007). All relevant protocols and annexes found in the accession treaties are also part of primary law.

The secondary (or ordinary) law is the law created by EU institutions and includes legislation and decisions of the ECJ. Legislation included in the secondary law falls into four categories: regulations, directives, decisions, and recommendations and opinions. Other sources of the EU law include the EU's international agreements (including association agreements with nonmember countries), general principles of administrative law, and conventions between the member states. It has been ruled many times by the EJC that EC-Pillar I law is superior to national law. When there is a conflict between EU law and national laws, the latter must be revised to comply with the former. In EU law, the *Four Freedoms* is a common term for a set of treaty provisions, secondary legislation, and court decisions that protect the ability of goods, services, capital, and labor to move freely within the internal market of the EU. As such, they are part of the primary law of the EU. These freedoms are as follows:

1. The free movement of goods;
2. The free movement of persons (and citizenship), including free movement of workers, and freedom of establishment;
3. The free movement of services; and
4. The free movement of capital.

Among these, the free movement of labor enables citizens of one member state to travel to work in another member state without facing discrimination. It touches the very fiber of the fundamental rights of EU citizens discussed in Chapter 10 under the Social Charter.

FUNDAMENTAL RIGHTS OF EU CITIZENS

The Maastricht Treaty outlines the principles of fundamental rights of EU citizens. The treaty states:

1. The Union is founded on the principles of liberty, democracy, respect for human rights and fundamental freedoms and the rule of law, principles which are common to the Member States.
2. The Union shall respect fundamental rights, as guaranteed by the European Convention for the Protection of Human Rights and Fundamental Freedoms signed in Rome on 4 November 1950 and as they result from the constitutional traditions common to the Member States, as general principles of Community law.
3. The Union shall respect the national identities of its Member States.
4. The Union shall provide itself the means necessary to attain its objectives and carry through its policies.[3]

In the subsequent article (Article 7), the treaty continues to introduce a political mechanism in order to prevent violations of the principles mentioned in Article 6 by the member states.

This is a clear commitment to harmonization of fundamental rights in the EU; as internal borders disappeared, it became quite evident that the EU needed a genuine Union-wide area of freedom, security, and justice for its citizens and residents. That was why EU leaders, in Tampere in October 1999, approved a set of concrete measures for achieving such an ambitious goal. The key product of this is the Charter of Fundamental Rights of the European Union, which brings together all the personal, civic, political, economic, and social rights enjoyed by the citizens and residents of the EU.[4] This is the first document of its kind that collects the texts of all other relevant documents into a single document and takes the EU to a higher level of conformity in terms of individual rights than that found in previous documents like the Social Charter. As discussed in Chapter 10, the draft constitution attempted to incorporate the Charter of Fundamental Rights into EU law but failed. Now the Lisbon Treaty attempts to accomplish this goal. For the first time in EU history, this Charter outlines the whole range of civil, political, economic, and social rights of European citizens and everyone residing in the EU. These rights are divided into six sections: Dignity, Freedoms, Equality, Solidarity, Citizens' rights, and Justice.[5] They are based, in particular, on the fundamental rights and freedoms recognized by the European Convention on Human Rights, the constitutional traditions of the EU member states, the Council of Europe's Social Charter, the Community Charter of Fundamental Social Rights of Workers, and other international conventions to which the European Union or its member states are parties.

Freedom of Movement

The Schengen Treaty, signed in June 1990, began as a Franco-German plan in 1985 to abolish all frontier controls on the movement of people and of goods and services between the two countries.[6] The Benelux countries joined France and Germany in 1985. The provisions relating to the free movement of goods and services became effective with the Single European Act, and the group then focused its attention on issues relevant to the free movement of people. However, the signing of the Schengen Treaty was delayed until June 1990 because of the insecure borders of the former East Germany. The treaty listed 45 countries whose nationals would be subject to border controls in an effort to curb immigration and to deal with refugee and asylum problems.[7] The Schengen group expanded when Italy signed on in November 1990, followed by Spain and Portugal in June 1991, and Greece in 1992. Denmark, Sweden, Finland, and Norway acceded in 1995. It is clear that the issues covered by the Schengen Treaty are addressed in the Treaty on European Union (TEU). However, it was not clear when all of the EU countries would harmonize their immigration, refugee, and asylum policies. This was one of the main reasons behind the intergovernmental conference (IGC) in 1996 that resulted in the Amsterdam Treaty.

The Amsterdam Treaty states that all EU member states will remove controls on persons, be they citizens of the EU or nationals of third countries, crossing their borders within five years of the signing of the new treaty.[8] The procedure outlined for this goal is a consultative one vis-à-vis the European Parliament, with unanimity required in the Council of Ministers. Second, the treaty formally incorporated the Schengen Treaty into the legal framework of the EU. The Cologne and Tampere summit meetings in June and October 1999, respectively, called for the establishment of a charter of fundamental rights of the EU. A convention comprising personal representatives of the 15 national governments, 30 member state parliamentarians, 16 members of the EP, and the Commission drafted a charter and presented it to the European Commission prior to the Nice summit. The European Court of Justice (ECJ) and the Council of Europe had observer status at the convention. The European Council welcomed the draft charter as the first text that combined civil, political, social, societal, and economic rights of citizens in a single document.[9] It called for the Commission to disseminate the charter to the member states and EU citizens and deferred decision on the charter's enforcement to the future.

Further developments in this field include the Hague Program, which the European Council adopted on November 4, 2004, and which set the objectives to be implemented in the area of freedom, security, and justice in the period 2005–2010.[10] This new program takes into account the final evaluation made by the Commission on the Tampere Program and comments received from the citizens through the online consultation held in July–August 2004. Subsequently, the Commission presented an action plan in May 2005 that detailed measures and a calendar to implement the provisions of the Hague Program. The Council approved this plan in June 2005 and put it into force as the framework of reference for the Commission for the period of 2005–2010.

One of the main objectives of the Amsterdam Treaty and the subsequent actions is to maintain and develop the EU as an area of freedom, security, and justice, in which there is free movement for persons combined with suitable measures pertaining to the control of external borders, asylum, and immigration, as well as the prevention and combating of crime. That would ensure smooth completion and maturing of regional integration in the EU. The Schengen Treaty was extended over time to all 15 old member states, but it has special arrangements for Denmark and is only partially applicable in Ireland and the UK. Ireland and Britain do not take part in the Schengen rules on the free movement of persons, external border controls, and visa policy, and representatives of these member states do not vote on these matters in the Council of Ministers' meetings. Among the 12 new member states, 9 have joined the Schengen area. They are the Czech Republic, Estonia, Hungary, Latvia, Lithuania, Malta, Poland, Slovakia, and Slovenia. Two nonmember European countries, Iceland and Switzerland, also participate in Schengen in differing levels. Iceland is a full participant, whereas partial coverage is extended to Switzerland. Map 13.1 shows the current Schengen arrangement in the EU.

The Schengen agreement stipulates uniform rules of entry for all the member states. In order to enter the Schengen area, the nationals of the European Economic Area (EEA) must present a valid identity card or a valid—or expired—passport less than five years old. For non-EEA nationals, the requirement for entry includes documents justifying the purpose and the conditions of their visit and the availability of sufficient funds for both the duration of their stay and their return to their home country. Non-EEA nationals who are exempted from the visa requirement, that is, U.S. citizens, enjoy free movement in the Schengen area for a maximum period of three months (90 days) per half-year from the date of first entry. Residence beyond this limit requires a Schengen residence visa. For non-EEA nationals who are subject to the visa requirement according to their nationality, the visa they obtain from a Schengen country they intend to make their entry into specifies the duration of the authorized stay, with the limit of 90 days in any half-year.

Immigration and Asylum Policies

The TEU, as amended by the Amsterdam Treaty, defines the objectives of the EU in the following fields:

1. Removal of any controls on persons—citizens of the EU or nationals of third countries—when they cross internal borders from any EU member state to another.
2. Standards and methods of control and rules concerning visas when individuals cross the external borders of member states—that is, when they come into the EU.
3. The conditions under which the nationals of third countries can circulate freely within the EU for a maximum period of three months.
4. Requests for asylum (criteria and mechanisms for determining which member state is responsible for considering an application for asylum, minimum standards on the reception

Map 13.1 ■ The Schengen Area

Source: http://www.mediavisa.net/shengen-area.php

of asylum seekers, minimum standards for the conditions to be fulfilled to obtain refugee status, and procedures for granting or withdrawing refugee status).

5. Refugees and displaced persons from third countries (minimum standards for giving temporary protection and ensuring a balance among the efforts made by the member states in receiving and bearing the consequences of receiving refugees and displaced persons).

6. Measures against illegal immigration of nationals of third countries, including repatriation of such persons illegally resident in a member state.

7. Definition of rights and conditions under which nationals of third countries who are legally resident in a member state may reside in another member state.

8. Immigration measures concerning conditions of entry and stay of third-country nationals and procedures on the issuance of long-term visas, including those for family reunification purposes.[11]

The Amsterdam Treaty mandates that all these measures be adopted within five years of the entry into force of the treaty, with the exception of measures listed under points 7 and 8. There are, however, exceptions to the rule. Title VI of the EC Treaty is not applicable to the UK, Ireland, and Denmark.

At a special European Council summit at Tampere, Finland, in October 1999, the EU agreed to establish a European "area of freedom, security, and justice" and further refined the political guidelines in the field of asylum and immigration.[12] The leaders agreed that the EU needed a comprehensive approach to migration that addressed political rights, human rights, and development issues in countries and regions of origin and transit. Obviously, this necessitated cooperation with the third countries concerned. Therefore, the European Council called for more efficient management of migration flows, in close cooperation with countries of origin and transit; information campaigns on the actual possibilities for legal immigration; and campaigns to prevent all forms of human trafficking. This last issue is very important because of the loss of life resulting from the underground traffic of nationals from the former Soviet Union, the Middle East, North Africa, and Turkey.

Immigration was one of the heated topics at the Seville 2002 summit. Most member states—led by Spain, Britain, and Italy—favored imposing sanctions on countries that failed to control the flow of illegal immigrants to the EU. Such sanctions covered trade and economic cooperation agreements, suspension or limitation of which would have serious consequences for the economies of these countries. France opposed this idea and, with the support of Sweden, blocked its adoption at the summit. The sanction plan, though supported by British Prime Minister Tony Blair, was opposed by UK Development Secretary Clare Short, who argued that, if the sanctions were to pass, her aid programs would have been used as a form of blackmail to try to prevent the flow of unwanted immigrants from developing countries.[13]

The dilemma facing the Europeans over illegal immigration is best stated by Ruud Lubbers, the UN High Commissioner for Refugees: "it is irrational for governments to spend millions of euros on reinforcing borders, various deterrence measures, custody and detention centers . . . without simultaneously investing in solutions at the source of the problem."[14] Yet, at this time of economic downturn in EU countries, coupled with the rise of antiforeign right-wing political forces, it is far too optimistic to assume increased European economic assistance to nonmember countries in Asia, the Middle East, and North Africa. But there are policy complications in this matter stemming from the intergovernmental and supranational characteristics of the EU.

When one examines the EU's policy making in everything from asylum and immigration to drug trafficking to cross-border crime, it becomes clear that we are dealing with two "aspects" of the EU decision-making processes. Police and judicial cooperation on crime is entirely intergovernmental. On the other hand, EU institutions partly decide asylum and immigration policy. In this second policy area, the Commission and member state governments share the right of initiative for new measures. While they share competences, the member states retain their national right of oversight in issues pertaining to asylum and immigration. They need only consult the European Parliament in these matters. As long as this division of authority remains, problems in EU-wide asylum and immigration policy will continue to be divisive policy issues. This is a serious problem in view of the half-million illegal immigrants entering the EU every year.

In an attempt to better coordinate these policies in the EU, the Hague Program addressed problems faced and prompted the Council of Ministers to ask the Commission to develop EU-wide initiatives for member states to adopt and implement. Recent achievements in this regard include four main legal instruments on asylum: the Reception Conditions Directive, the Asylum Procedures Directive, the Qualification Directive, and the Dublin Regulation.

The Reception Conditions Directive guarantees minimum standards for the reception of asylum seekers, including housing, education, and health. The Asylum Procedures Directive ensures that all procedures at first instance are subject to the same minimum standards throughout the EU. The Qualification Directive contains a clear set of criteria for qualifying either for refugee or for subsidiary protection status and sets out what rights are attached to each status. It also introduces a harmonized regime for subsidiary protection in the EU for those persons who fall outside the scope of the Geneva Convention, but who still need international protection, such as victims of generalized violence or civil war. This is of increasing importance as the number of persons in need of this type of protection is growing both in member states and on a worldwide scale in light of the recent scandal involving secret CIA operations against suspected terrorists that included secret prisons in some EU and accession countries.[15] Finally, the Dublin Regulation contains clear rules about the member state responsible for assessing asylum applications. This regulation is an important instrument for the prevention of multiple asylum demands (people seeking asylum in more than one EU member state) in member states.[16]

In dealing with immigration policy, the Commission proposed two sets of policy packages that follow the guidelines of the Amsterdam and Nice Treaties. In the case of legal immigration, the policy package addresses family reunification, an EU long-term resident status definition, students, workers, and integration and employment. For illegal immigration, the proposals include an action plan to combat illegal immigration of and trafficking in human beings, to return such individuals to their countries of origin, and to assist third countries in combating these problems at home.

The obvious area of necessary cooperation for implementing immigration and asylum policies is border control. As discussed earlier, an important part of the Schengen accord was the reinforcement of external border controls. The Schengen Treaty, now incorporated into EU law, provided for cross-border police cooperation, information exchange, surveillance, and cross-border pursuit. In addition, the EU set up the Schengen Information System (SIS) to record refusals of entry for asylum seekers, arrest warrants, missing persons, and stolen objects. Now, a new system that extends the database (SIS II) became operational in 2007. SIS II includes more information on individuals like biometric data on travel documents. Furthermore, in response to possible problems associated with the borders of Eastern European members, the EU established in May 2005 a European Agency for the Management of Operational Co-operation at the External Borders (also known as the European Border Control Agency). This is a coordinating body that monitors land, air, and sea borders between member states and supports national authorities with training and risk assessment. Despite efforts aimed at establishing harmonized policies among EU countries, not everyone participates in EU-wide immigration policies. Denmark opted out of Title IV of the Treaty establishing the European Community, and Britain and Ireland decide on their involvement on a case-by-case basis (see Schengen Treaty discussed earlier).

Riots by Muslim immigrants in France in late 2005 highlight the growing importance of an EU-wide policy on immigration and asylum, as well as pointing to internal problems associated with inclusion of immigrants into member states' mainstream economies. The riots began when two boys of North and West African origin were electrocuted in a Paris suburb after running from police, who they believed were chasing them. Residents of the country's poor, largely immigrant suburbs, where most of the unrest took place, complained of racism and heavy-handed policing. During the ensuing 20 nights of riots that spread throughout France, rioters burned almost 9,000 cars and destroyed shops, while the police made 2,888 arrests. The French government responded by activating an emergency law, initially used during the French Algeria riots, that allows local authorities to impose a state of emergency in cities and towns.[17] The riots highlighted how little EU states have worked to integrate immigrant populations into their mainstream economies. Statements made by French officials further highlighted how removed they are from the plight of the immigrant populations. For example, French Employment Minister Gérard Larcher blamed multiple marriages among immigrants as being one reason for the racial discrimination that ethnic minorities faced in the job market. He further stated that overly large polygamous families sometimes led to antisocial behavior among youths who lacked a father figure, making employers wary of hiring ethnic minorities.[18] He did, however, acknowledge that the unemployment rate among young people in France was twice the national average, but said other European countries faced similar problems. He also pointed a finger at the United States, where he said the unemployment rate among blacks aged 16–19 was twice that of their white counterparts. Such statements show how detached the officials have been from the immigrant population and demonstrate their unwillingness to accept the blame and instead point the finger at others.

The EU is aware of the shortcomings in minority issues and took a bold initiative and declared year 2007 as the European Year of Equal Opportunities for All. The goal is to raise public awareness of the substantial Community *acquis* in the field of equality and nondiscrimination and to mobilize everyone concerned to drive forward the European Union's new framework strategy on nondiscrimination and equal opportunities. The objectives include the following: (a) raising public awareness of the right to equality and nondiscrimination, (b) encouraging a debate on ways of strengthening participation in society, (c) celebrating and welcoming diversity, and (d) working toward a more solidarity-based society.[19] The goal is to increase awareness on equality of everyone regardless of their ethnic, religious, linguistic, and cultural backgrounds. Moreover, the EU will provide modest sum of funds to promote events, information campaigns, and surveys at the community and national level. Given this emphasis on harmonious relations, respect for all, diversity, and tolerance, how does the EU presently look in terms of religion and secular politics? Is clash of civilizations a valid argument and concern for future of the Union? Or is the EU immune to religious biases due to its successful secular politics of half a century? The EU's success in these areas depends on coordinated efforts of its surpanational institutions, member states, and ultimately its citizens.

COOPERATION OF POLICE AND CUSTOMS MATTERS

The Amsterdam Treaty outlines the goals and procedures for cooperation between the police forces and the customs authorities of EU member states (Title VI, Articles 29–42). The goal is to provide EU citizens and others with a high level of safety within an area of freedom, security, and justice because international crime, cross-border smuggling, and trafficking in drugs, arms, and people recognize no national frontiers. In the post–Cold War era, these issues became more urgent as illegal activities, coupled with growing cross-border crime, increased across Eurasia.

The main tool for dealing with multinational and cross-border crime is closer cooperation between the EU's national and local police forces and between customs authorities on either side of national borders. Additional support for this cooperation comes from Europol, which is the European law enforcement organization that was set up under the Maastricht Treaty. Its purpose is to facilitate cooperation between member law enforcement institutions in combating organized crime, drug trafficking, and terrorism. The Commission works closely with EU member states and the other EU institutions in promoting this cooperation in accordance with the decisions reached at the Vienna summit of December 3, 1998, and the Tampere summit in 1999. The main activities in this field are

1. Setting up a European police college to train the next generation of police officers and other law enforcement personnel to work and operate in a European context;
2. Establishing a task force of European police chiefs, which had its first meeting in Lisbon in April 2000;
3. Setting up civil-crisis management machinery in the EU; a European rapid reaction force (ERRF) is being set up so it can be sent to hot spots, like Kosovo, to reintroduce civil peacekeeping, law enforcement, and internal security after the military has left;

4. Enhancing customs cooperation in the fight against crime by improving customs authorities' mutual information systems and implementing the Naples II Convention of 1997 on cooperation between customs authorities; and
5. Setting up joint police and customs command centers in border regions to ensure that all interested law enforcement forces can work together on either side of national borders.[20]

Much has been achieved in this area since the Tampere summit. EU law, primary and secondary, coupled with the growing importance of the ECJ, highlights significant movement in the supranational aspects of EU governance. It also appears that the member states are working together more closely to establish common EU policies on political asylum, immigration, border controls, and cooperation in police matters. However, continued separation of justice, freedom, and security policies translates into difficulties in coordination of policies pertaining to police and judicial cooperation in criminal matters.

CONCLUSION

During the last several years, significant progress has been made in Pillar III policies to meet challenges encountered with eastern enlargement. Significant progress is apparent in First-Pillar areas such as fundamental rights, citizenship, civil justice, the European strategy on drugs, asylum, and migration, and visa and border policies, as well as in the fight against global terrorism. However, there are recurrent difficulties in the implementation of previously agreed initiatives at the national level. The Lisbon Treaty reinforces the commitment to offer citizens an area of freedom, security, and justice. It facilitates decision making, increases the powers of the European Parliament, and extends the competences of the European Court of Justice with regard to certain domains.

STUDY QUESTIONS

1. Why is the deepening of integration necessary in Pillar III for Pillar I policies to be effective?
2. What kinds of reforms have brought further integration in Pillar III?
3. Write your opinion about the following statement: "The rule of law is one of the most important sovereign rights of a nation and the EU should not have jurisdiction over it."
4. Some would argue that national police forces best know their own countries and cultures, and, therefore, external interference and centralized bodies could hinder effective criminal investigations. What do you think about this?

ENDNOTES

1. Council and Commission of the European Communities, *Treaty on European Union* (Luxembourg: Office for Official Publication on the European Communities, 1992), title VI, art. K. 1–3, pp. 131–133.
2. *Treaty Establishing the European Community*, art. 10.
3. Council and Commission of the European Communities, *Treaty on the European Union*, art. 6.
4. For the complete text, go to EU Web site, located at http://europa.eu.int/comm/justice_home/unit/charte/index_en.html

5. European Commission, *Charter of Fundamental Rights of the European Union* (Brussels: Commission of the European Communities, 2000), pp. 3–22.
6. Dennis Swann, *The Economics of the Common Market* (London: Penguin Books, 1992), p. 170.
7. Juliet Lodge, "Internal Security and Judicial Cooperation," in Juliet Lodge, ed., *The European Community and the Challenge of the Future*, 2nd ed. (New York: St. Martin's Press, 1993), p. 321.

8. Simon Hix, *The Political System of the European Union* (New York: St. Martin's Press, 1999), p. 311.

9. European Commission, *Nice Summit: Presidency Conclusions* (Brussels: European Commission, 2000), p. 2.

10. Council of the European Union, *The Hague Programme: Strengthening Freedom, Security, and Justice in the European Union* (Brussels: December 13, 2004).

11. European Commission, Justice and Home Affairs, *Immigration and Asylum: Community Responsibility*, http://europa.eu.int/comm/justice_home/unit/immigration_en.htm

12. European Commission, *Tampere European Council Conclusions* (Brussels: Commission of the European Communities, 1999).

13. Quentin Peel, "Europe's Immigration Muddle," *Financial Times*, June 24, 2002, p. 15.

14. Ibid.

15. Reuters, "CIA Secret Prisons Reports Credible," December 13, 2005, 12:35 PM ET.

16. European Commission, "The European Union Policy towards a Common European Asylum Policy," http://europa.eu.int/comm/justice_home/fsj/asylum/fsj_asylum_intro_en.htm

17. Martin Arnold, "*Liberté, égalité et fraternité*—but Only for Some," *Financial Times*, November 7, 2005, p. 1.

18. Martin Arnold, "French Minister Says Polygamy to Blame for Riots," *Financial Times*, November 15, 2005, p. 1.

19. European Commission, http://europa.eu/scadplus/leg/en/cha/c10314.htm

20. European Commission, Justice and Home Affairs, *Immigration and Asylum.*

Chapter 14

Conclusion

Throughout this text, we have shown that the European Union (EU) has followed a continuing, though irregular, course of integration. It has been a course that has always found a middle way between integration that is strictly economic in nature and integration that is strongly political, and it has, with each integrative step, brought institutional changes representing compromises between the principles of intergovernmentalism and supranationalism. In the 1950s, the effort to achieve a strongly political and supranational form of integration, a European Defense Community, was rejected and ultimately replaced by an important step toward economic integration, the European Economic Community (EEC), which assumed a more intergovernmental form. When the principal supranational agency of the EEC, the Commission, took steps in the mid-1960s to increase its own power, it was thwarted by the French president, who had a contrasting intergovernmentalist conception of political integration and who preferred not to move beyond the extent of economic integration envisaged in the Rome Treaty.

By the 1970s, the Commission had retreated to a more passive role, while the governments of the member countries, including the new entrants, Britain, Denmark, and Ireland, settled into a more intergovernmentalist mode of agenda setting and decision making, which featured the regularization of summit meetings of the heads of state and government in the European Council, institutionalized in 1974–1975. This was a period of learning and experimentation in the realm of economic integration, especially in the tentative steps taken toward the elusive goal of Economic and Monetary Union (EMU). Finally, in the mid-1980s, with another new member, Greece, in place and two new members, Portugal and Spain, about to join, the governments concurred on a package that advanced the original Rome Treaty idea of a common market beyond the customs union achieved two decades earlier. It also took some modest steps in the direction of greater political union, particularly with the extension of qualified majority voting in the Council of Ministers, in order to facilitate the implementation of further economic integration.

The supranational institutions of the European Community (EC), especially the Commission, kicked back into gear from January 1985 under the dynamic leadership of Jacques Delors. It was Delors who spearheaded the public relations campaign in favor of the Single European Act (SEA) and who, in the late 1980s, pushed budget reform, regional and social policy advances, and, ultimately, EMU onto the extraordinary agenda, gaining the support of the European Council. Delors, with the support of François Mitterrand of France and Helmut Kohl of Germany, was able to overcome the opposition of British Prime Minister Margaret Thatcher and her successor, John Major, to greater political and economic integration. They could not stop the latest thrust of economic integration; Major succeeded only in getting the acceptance of Britain's right to "opt out" of the Social Charter and the EMU.

More quietly, the European Court of Justice (ECJ), by successfully asserting its authority to interpret the treaties, had strengthened the likelihood that national governments and courts would implement the single-market legislation. And the European Parliament had been gaining power by pressure on the governments to support formal accretions in the SEA and the Treaty on European Union (TEU or Maastricht Treaty). The EU came into being with the Maastricht Treaty, which made the European Parliament a coequal of the Council of Ministers in many legislative areas and extended EU competence in already existing areas of legislation, as well as in some new ones. Most notable of the expanded powers under Maastricht were the planned stages for attaining EMU and the new Common Foreign and Security Policy and the Justice and Home Affairs pillars.

But after the TEU was signed, further political integration came under a cloud when the Danish referendum failed in June 1992 and the French referendum commissioned by President Mitterrand nearly failed in September 1992. The British Parliament also refused ratification unless the Danes reversed their vote, which they did in 1993. But by this time, Britain had pulled out of the exchange rate mechanism in the crisis of September 1992, and Major was facing fierce opposition to ratification in his own party. Although the treaty was eventually ratified by all 12 countries and the EU moved ahead with the entry of three new members, Austria, Finland, and Sweden, there was general dissatisfaction with its outcome, especially in light of the expected enlargement that would take place when ten or more Central and Eastern European countries (CEECs) became eligible for membership. In order to make the EU ready for such a large influx, another treaty revision was undertaken in 1996–1997, culminating in the approval of the Treaty of Amsterdam. This extended the capacity of the EU to act in foreign and defense policy and internal security matters. The Lisbon Treaty, which is undergoing ratification by member states, further deepens integration in Pillar II and establishes the office of the High Representative for Foreign Affairs and Security Policy/Vice President of the Commission.

The Maastricht Treaty had been significant for the impetus it gave to economic as well as to political integration. EMU, with its prospect of a single currency for EU member countries and a single central bank, became a firm EU commitment because of the agreement between Chancellor Kohl and President Mitterrand in 1990: France wanted the commitment and made a concession to Germany in the matter of reunification. Britain's opt-out at the Maastricht summit indicated that only a portion of the EU members would go ahead with EMU when the third stage began in January 1, 1999. Eventually, 11 members did so on that date, and Greece adhered two years later, leaving Britain, Denmark, and Sweden outside because of decisions reached through their domestic political processes.

Early in the twenty-first century, the EU has faced another of its critical crossroads at which it can choose to move ahead toward "a more perfect union," to remain at essentially the point where it was as the old century ended, or to reinforce the dominant features of the late-twentieth-century EU. Those dominant features allowed the governmental heads of the member states not only to control the pace of European political integration, but also to set its outer limits, as they continuously do in pulling up short of decisive steps toward a federal European state. The pressure to change the EU in more fundamental ways produced a constitutional convention, whose work began at the end of 1992. However, the constitution that emerged was rejected in 2005 by French and Dutch voters, keeping the balance between intergovernmentalism and supranationalism where it was before the convention began its work.

While this reexamination of the EU's structure and purposes was proceeding, the final steps took place to increase the number of members from 15 to 27. Already, the Nice Treaty,

agreed to in 2000 and fully ratified in 2002, had made adjustments, most notably in the composition of the Commission and the voting weights in the Council, to accommodate a large influx of
members. These efforts reflected a concern that the substantially enlarged EU would be incapable of acting coherently in areas of vulnerability where failure to act as a unitary body could
have severely damaging socioeconomic and possibly political consequences for the EU members
in their relations with one another and with the rest of the world. Further reforms brought about
by the Lisbon Treaty clearly demonstrate determination to streamline decision making with
particular attention to democratic deficit. The European Council agreed that the new system will
take effect in 2014. In the first three years, until 2017, a member state may request that an act be
adopted in accordance with the qualified majority as defined in the current Treaty of Nice.

In international economic relations, the EU has become a major actor alongside the United
States, China, India, and Japan. On the one hand, competition with Japan and the United States
has intensified on several grounds, as shown by trade in "sensitive industries" and the race for
economic dominance in Eastern Europe and the Mediterranean Basin. However, despite intense
competition, the single market and EMU are likely to promote better commercial and financial
relations among the three economic giants. The fear of Fortress Europe does not seem to be
founded on rational economic grounds. The extent of direct foreign investment and trade flows
supports the argument that protectionism is not likely to be the rule in future economic relations
among the three giants. Conflicts in the political realm have been more in evidence, most notably
in the reaction to the U.S. invasion of Iraq, as Britain and Poland, among the larger EU members,
joined the U.S. effort, while France and Germany opposed it.

The ten-member EU enlargement of 2004, followed by accession of Bulgaria and Romania,
while it visibly slowed the integration process, was in the strategic and economic interests of EU
members to maintain good relations with the new democracies of Central and Eastern Europe.
The EU needed to expand its economic base by absorbing new areas into its framework in order to
compete with the United States and Japan—not only in regional terms, but also on a global scale.
Moreover, because the periphery states seek the economic benefits of membership in the EU, it
promises to reduce the danger of their experiencing political instability and a return to authoritarian
regimes. Nonmember Mediterranean Basin countries (NMBCs) and African, Caribbean, and
Pacific (ACP) countries stand to lose in the single market as the EU shifts its attention to its near
neighbors. Both groups continue to receive preferential trade and financial assistance from the EU,
but the magnitude of these aid packages is not expected to increase substantially. An added problem
for the ACP countries is the adverse ruling of the World Trade Organization (WTO) on the EU's
preferential trade agreements with them. In addition, as the EU looks to the southeast, there are
major difficulties along the way there as well: (1) the Cyprus problem, (2) territorial and other
issues between Greece and Turkey, (3) Turkey's slow progress in meeting the Copenhagen criteria,
(4) accession challenges facing Croatia, (5) issues of Former Yugoslav Republic of Macedonia, and
(6) future of Western Balkans (Albania, Kosovo, Montenegro, and Serbia).

In external security matters, the provisions stated in the Maastricht and Amsterdam
Treaties suggest that the EU remains a weak security community that requires intergovernmental
coordination of common policies. In this regard, the member states are less willing to surrender
additional sovereignty to the EU. The various provisions of the treaty do not prevent members
from following their own foreign policy preferences. Furthermore, while the members have
strengthened the ties between the EU and the Western European Union (WEU), it is not clear
how the North Atlantic Treaty Organization (NATO) obligations of some EU member countries
will be reconciled. Thus, potential problems exist in formulating common external security policies. The dispute in late 2000 over access to NATO intelligence and transport capabilities and
Turkey's veto of an EU–NATO agreement, when added to earlier experiences in the Persian Gulf
and in the former Yugoslavia, support an attitude of skepticism. During the Gulf War, after the
United States had asserted leadership, the EU countries managed to coordinate their policies

within the EU and between the WEU and NATO. However, inconsistencies during the Balkans crisis, separate stances regarding American actions in Iraq, and dispute over rapid deployment forces and an integrated command headquarters of EU and NATO demonstrate the serious challenges member states face in further integration of Pillar II policies and in the attainment of an independent European defense structure.

In domestic security matters, the provisions of the Maastricht and Amsterdam Treaties clearly call for cooperation among the member states in the policy areas of political asylum, immigration, border controls, customs, and police cooperation in combating crime. The Commission and the Council have taken steps to improve performance in these areas. The Treaty of Lisbon will facilitate more future action at the European level through the use of the "Community method," that is, qualified majority decision making based on proposals from the Commission. This will also involve increased role of the European Parliament, increased democratic control from national parliaments, and a scrutiny role for the Court of Justice. It should be noted, however, that special arrangements will be extended to Denmark, Ireland, and the United Kingdom until these countries fully accept provisions of the treaty.

As the successor to the EC, the EU of the twenty-first century has not yet assumed a shape distinct from that of its predecessor, but it is moving more and more toward achieving that goal. The primacy of the intergovernmental bodies, especially the heads of state and government meeting as the European Council, will continue to be true of the EU for the near future. This is because in today's interdependent world, domestic and foreign policy cannot be separated easily; nor can economics and politics. With the expansion of the EU's functions into areas of once exclusive domestic policy competence and with increasing involvement of the EU in the political changes going on in Eastern and Southern Europe, the highest political leaders of the member countries have compelling reasons to meet frequently and to coordinate their policies. The media and ever-larger segments of the citizenry in the member countries closely watch the deliberations and joint decisions of the EU leaders. This is an inevitable outcome, since the public increasingly goes to the ballot box to help settle EU matters, while their verdicts have become increasingly unpredictable.

In the commitments made in successive treaty revisions and subsequent steps toward EMU and political union, we can observe that the EU is an emerging political community, but a community unlike the familiar nation-states that have preceded and helped to build it. In the first decade of the twenty-first century, it remains a mix of separately identifiable intergovernmental and supranational features. Cutting across this division are democratic features that are far more important today as popular consultation has become more the norm and less the carefully chosen and carefully staged exception.

Given how far the EU has come in its five-decade history, it begs the question, what does it all mean for European citizens? We might also add, what does it mean for Europe and the world? Discussions in this volume suggest that the EU is evolving into something similar to a statelike organization that has made significant progress on its economic integration but lags far behind essential political union to attain rational balance of the two realms. Without further progress on political union of some sort, fulfillment of EMU, including all financial services, will continue to face significant obstacles. Historical experiments like those in the early years of the United States suggest that it is not possible to attain a fully functioning economic union without a political union. These problems are further compounded by democratic deficit in the EU. The EU needs to have a constitution, but short of this, it will have to move ahead with the Reform Treaty (Lisbon Treaty) in order to make progress on the political union front. Despite various difficulties faced, the EU has emerged as a global power and looks for further Europeanization of its Pillar II policies to complement its economic influence in the international system.

As for what the EU means for its citizens, results obtained from the Eurobarometer surveys cited throughout this volume are quite telling. Citizens of the EU member states generally trust the EU institutions more than they trust their national governments. They also want more cooperation in policy making between the EU and the member states and insist on these institutions to hear peoples' voices. A recent survey by Armando Garcia-Schmidt and Dominik Hierlemann on *EU 2020* gives important insight into peoples' preferences.[1] An overwhelming majority of the respondents believed that deepening of integration and enlargement of the EU would continue, although they were skeptical of the future membership of Turkey and Ukraine. Furthermore, they believed that institutional reform would follow the kind of integration that the EU experienced and will eventually lead to an EU constitution by 2020.

ENDNOTE

1. Armando Garcia-Schmidt and Dominik Hierlemann, *EU 2020—the View of the Europeans* (Gutersloh: Bertelsmann Stiftung, 2006).

Index